MW01100720

the

BOY
FROM
MEADOW
LAKE

J. Elmer Benoit

◆ FriesenPress

Suite 300 - 990 Fort St
Victoria, BC, Canada, V8V 3K2
www.friesenpress.com

Front Cover: Elmer, Age 3 – Riding Ned
Back Cover: Elmer, Fellow of The Society of Management Accountants of Canada – 2007

ISBN
978-1-4602-8218-2 (Hardcover)
978-1-4602-8219-9 (Paperback)
978-1-4602-8220-5 (eBook)

1. Biography & Autobiography, Personal Memoirs

Distributed to the trade by The Ingram Book Company

Foreward

This book is intended to tell my story, and of the people who touched my life in various ways to make me the person I am, not necessarily the person I would be like to be. I have tried to omit material that might be hurtful either directly or indirectly to people that I love, while maintaining the integrity of my story. A few items have been omitted at the request of the people involved.

First of all, I would like to explain that through my childhood, I had no dreams of what I would like to do after I grew up. When you're a kid on the farm in the 1930s, growing up with no telephone, television or internet, and the family had only recently got its first radio, you don't learn much about what is going on in the outside world, or what other people do with their lives.

My father had gone to school for about six months in total, but learned to read and his handwriting was laborious. He was proud to be able to give three of his six children a grade twelve education, and felt that we were now equipped to do anything. The other three siblings simply had to quit school after about grade eight or ten and work at home.

When I was in about grade two or three, a family with a son of my age, came from Poland and homesteaded nearby. The son, Eddy, told us at school of all the different cities he had been to, or knew of, and the countries and rivers and even the oceans and seas. He described the big ships, bridges and buildings that he had seen, and I wondered if I would ever be so fortunate to see those things. I forgot them for the most part, but I was always very impressed when I actually came in contact with anything new.

When my dear wife, Phyllis, and I were traveling, particularly in scenic spots of other countries, I remarked most days, as we sat eating pate and crackers and sipping on cold drinks or good wine, "I wonder what the folks are doing in Meadow Lake", not in a superior way, but as a recognition that in spite of my humble childhood, I was able to now enjoy the many pleasures that so many people take for granted.

Phyllis, was the most positive influence in my life and gave me such happiness that I still believe that she came into my life as a gift from God to fill a specific need in the lives of me and my children. If she wasn't perfect, she was certainly more than adequate, and certainly more than I deserved. She was a wonderful wife and mother for my children, as well as a perfect travel companion.

My parents had a deep faith in God, and did their best to pass it on to us. My sister, Mirelda, and brother, Lawrence, were the only siblings that maintained that faith through their lives. I lapsed for several years, before returning to it in my retirement years. In 1985, I was partially paralyzed and near death, when I silently cried out to my Lord, and I was returned to my family. Soon after, I joined the Presbyterian Church and later got involved in studying the bible as part of a group that gave Phyllis and me support, and helped us to reach the point where we were ready to face our final judgment. On several occasions I have had my prayers answered when it made a real difference. When people question the existence of God, I think, "I'd rather live my life as though there is a God, and find when I die that there isn't a God, than live my life as though there is no God and when I die, find that there is a God."

The failure of my first two marriages caused me to consider if I was destined to live with no true, or lasting love, and I would then just bounce along from one relationship to another. In fact, I almost felt a real hatred for my first wife when I ran away due to the mental abuse I suffered, and only in later years I realized that she really was sick, and then I was able to forgive her. My second wife was not really ready for marriage and, certainly, not for adopting three children within about four years. The reason for the compressed time frame to complete the adoption of our children was that I would not be able to adopt after I turned forty, and I was now thirty nine when Holly came into our family. I bear no ill will to Pat for running away from me and the kids, as she was definitely not equipped to cope with all of the stress at that time. Both of those marriages were difficult to recover from, but they did make me stronger, and able to be a better husband to Phyllis. We learn from our mistakes and as you will learn from this book, I made many but only a few are mentioned.

My children have given me great joy and I am proud of them. My step-children were pretty well grown when I appeared in their lives, and didn't need a second father. All of my grandchildren and great grandchildren from both families have shown me love and I am proud of all of them too. On average, my marriages were a great success, because Phyllis tipped the scales far more towards my happiness than the negatives of the first two.

Before telling my story, I would like to express my gratitude to my parents, brothers and sisters and their children and grandchildren for their everlasting love and kindness; my parents also for always providing for my needs, and my siblings for never showing regret for another mouth to feed when times were tough. In fact, I received encouragement at every step of the way.

I wish to say that Meadow Lake, Saskatchewan, and the people that I knew there, for the most part, were an industrious lot, caring for each other, as everyone struggled just to get by. I am proud to say that I am "The Boy From Meadow Lake".

I hope you enjoy reading this book about my life, because I certainly enjoyed living it.

J. Elmer Benoit

Chapter 1

PARENTS AND GRANDPARENTS

The original member of the Benoit's who emigrated from France was named Claude, and he settled near Les Trois Rivieres, on the north side of the St. Lawrence River.

My grandfather, Eugene Benoit, born on February 29, 1849, lived at Nicolet, Quebec, and the family owned land near the St. Francis River. My father, Joseph, was born on May 25, 1883, in Kingsey, Quebec. Grandfather Eugene then left Quebec for Oak Lake, Manitoba, with his wife, Odelie, and eight children. Three more children were born in Manitoba. Grandfather Eugene died at age 48, in a traffic accident in 1897 when his team of horses ran away. Grandmother Odelie remarried but died soon after. A brother of Grandmother Odelie Benoit came and took some of the children to Manchester, in the U.S.A. Others returned to Quebec to live with relatives.

My father, Joseph, and his brother, Uncle Ovila, who was a year younger than Dad, stayed in Manitoba and went to work at a farm. Dad was fourteen years old. When Dad was about fifteen years old, he lied about his age and joined the army, cavalry brigade, to fight for the British during the Boer War in South Africa. However, the war ended just before his unit was scheduled to ship out. He and Uncle Ovila later moved to Marcelin, Saskatchewan, where Dad met my mother and they were married on January 9, 1911.

My maternal grandfather, Louis Blair, was born January 9, 1850, in Lotbiniere, Quebec. He later moved to the U.S.A. where he married Matilda Semion, who was five years younger than him. They lived in Chippewa Falls and then in Tilden, Wisconsin, where my mother, Adele, was born on March 25, 1891. There were ten beautiful daughters and one son. Grandpa Blair worked as a timber cruiser. He moved Grandma and five daughters to Leask, Saskatchewan, a few miles from Marcelin. Although he lived with us for a time in Meadow Lake, I don't remember him at all, and he died in 1935 in Prince Albert.

My parents, Joseph and Adele Benoit, moved from Shell River, near Prince Albert, Sask., to the Meadow Lake area in 1917 to start a new life. The family consisted at that time of my Mom and Dad, my brother Emile, aged 5 1/2, my sister Mirelda, not quite 2, and my brother Lawrence, 2 months.

They were part of a group of settlers travelling to a newly opened area of farms and ranches; there were several horse-drawn wagons, one McLachlin touring car, accompanying cattle, dogs, chicken, ducks, geese, etc.

The trip via North Battleford, took three days, on a dirt road which was, for the last hundred miles, a dim trail that was suffering the effects of a windstorm, and blown down trees had to be cleared from the road every few hundred yards.

The family finally arrived at their destination, about 15 miles north of what is now Meadow Lake, in an area called Crowesford, but which I remember was always referred to as "The Big Swamp". My brother, Louis, was born there in 1921.

The family ranched until 1920 when the price of cattle dropped badly, and in 1922 the family moved into town which now had three general stores and a school that the two older children could attend. Supplies for the stores were obtained from the nearest rail point, a seven day round-trip, by horse and wagon.

My folks had brought some cows from the ranch and they started selling surplus milk to their neighbors in town. There were no bottles at the time, so they used jam tins - 10 cents for a jam tin of milk. Their first customer was the local doctor.

By 1923, the town had grown considerably and now included such amenities as a barber shop, beer parlour, telegraph office, hotel, blacksmith shop, post office and dance hall. In that year, the town held its first stampede. The year also marked the start of construction of Highway 4, actually just a dirt road that became a quagmire whenever it rained. I recall when I just a boy of six or seven, travelling all day plus most of the night during a storm on our way home from visiting Mirelda and her family in Prince Albert, some 150 miles and we got stuck in the mud several times. The long drive was partly due to Dad's reluctance to go more than 15-mph even on good roads. He enjoyed alternately praising or criticising the crops in the various fields as we slowly passed. If Dad had driven at even forty miles per hour, we would have reached home before the rain started.

About 1925, Dad got a homestead south of town, which he began to clear for farming. At about that time, he received a contract from the highways department to maintain about 17 miles of the "highway". He set up two camps, one on the homestead and the other at the far end of his line. The grader was towed by horses. I don't believe there was ever a directive as to the correct way to grade the road; so in one section, the road would be graded flat in which case your car would bog down in its tracks, whereas in the next section, the road would be graded to have a crown, so the rain would run off on the slope, and cars would then slide off into the ditch. It made for many interesting discussions.

My sister, Yvette, was born in late 1925. In that year, Dad bought a Model "A" Ford sedan. I remember that it had a canvas roof, no windows, started by use of a crank, and the controls consisted of levers mounted on the steering column - a choke, a spark, and the accelerator. Besides the brake and clutch was a parking brake lever on the floor. Emile always boasted that he could steer the car with his knees while holding his girlfriend, Julia, in both arms. Maximum speed of the car was probably about 30-mph.

Until 1930 the main source of income in the area was still ranching. But with the extension of the railway from Prince Albert to Meadow Lake in the fall of 1931, farming became more popular and brought many more settlers to the area. A branch line was later built to North Battleford.

Nevertheless, 1931 went down in history most notably as the year in which I made my appearance on the family tree. When I was born, Dad was 48 years old and Mom was 40. So ended the "Benoit Begetting" phase of their lives.

J. Elmer Benoit

Grandma & Grandpa Blair

Dad, Emile, 2yrs, Mom, Grandma & Grandpa Blair – 1913

Chapter 2

THE DAIRY FARM

About the time of my birth, the family moved to a dairy farm just north of town in order to accommodate the expanded Benoit Dairy. The dairy now featured such modern equipment as a cream separator, various sizes of glass bottles, and a horse-drawn milk-cart. The manual drudgery, however, still continued – hand milking, hand turning the milk separator and butter churn, working the butter and forming it into one pound bricks, and hand washing everything. This was prior to the process of pasteurizing milk had begun, but most milk drinkers survived.

Also, this was the time of the Great Depression, so times were tight for most people, including the Benoit family. Few people could pay for the milk that they needed for their children, so we sold it on credit. Some paid their bills or part of them, but many didn't. No families were denied. Years later, Dad and Mom occasionally received money to pay off the old bills.

When I was just a few months old, Mom developed pleurisy and had to be hospitalized in the sanatorium at Prince Albert to recover, a process that involved complete bed rest for about a year.

Because of the depression, there was no money to hire someone to help with the cooking, cleaning, etc., so the kids had to carry the load. Emile was 21, Mirelda was 15 or 16, Lawrence was 14, Louis 11, and Yvette was 6.

Lawrence and Lou cleaned the barn, brought in the cows from the pasture, fed and milked them, and, with Mirelda, ran the milk through the separator, bottled it, loaded it onto the cart, hitched up the horse, Ned, and then woke Emile to deliver it. Emile had married Julia in 1933, so he really needed all the rest he could get, or maybe he was motivated to a lesser degree.

Mirelda had to quit school, and she did most of the house work and cooking and, oh yes, got to look after me. It must have been a real pleasure because I was so darned cute.

I'm told that when I needed new clothes, which we couldn't really afford to buy, she decided to have some new rompers made for me by a neighbor in return for milk. She knew that flannelette would be nice and warm, so she bought some material at the store - a bright check pattern. When the rompers were delivered, she took a photo of me in my new outfit and proudly sent it to Mom in the sanatorium. When Mom saw the picture of me all dressed up like a little clown, she burst into tears.

Our family wasn't as hard up as some others - we had a phonograph which played music recorded on wax rolls. I was able to change rolls for any particular song requested just by identifying the patterns of fly specks and stains on the labels. About 1933, the family upgraded to a new phonograph which played the new flat records. It was a cabinet model that had a crank on the side to wind it up, and used a steel needle that fit in the groove on the surface of the record and provided much superior sound.

Whenever Mirelda had a boy come calling, I was right there, stuck to her. One evening she put me to bed and when I finally fell asleep, she went to the dance in town with a boyfriend. About an hour later I awoke and, not finding Mirelda there, I screamed until Dad couldn't stand it any longer and had to send one of the boys to the dance to bring her home.

Whenever she went out with a boyfriend, I went with them, usually just for a walk. Then when we came home, my brothers would ask what the couple had been doing. I always showed them, making kissing sounds. I don't know if they actually were kissing but we did enjoy teasing Sis.

When Mom finally came home I didn't recognize her and screamed bloody murder every time she tried to hold me. I guess that's why Mirelda and I always had a special feeling for each other.

All four of my oldest siblings claimed to have to have raised me. I guess it was because each one could recognize their own best qualities in me. Seriously, I do have some good qualities; you just have to look deep enough.

One other incident that I still recall from our time on the dairy occurred when one of my brothers returned from delivering the milk. After unhitching Ned from the cart near the house, he put me on the back of the horse and gave it an open-handed slap on the rump. The horse automatically headed for the barn. I was quite happily having a ride, holding onto the harness hames as Ned trotted along, leaving my brother to follow on foot. I remember that I spotted the open barn door fast approaching and that the top of the opening provided about 12 inches of clearance. I started screaming too late, and only saved myself by lying backwards on the horse as it trotted through the door and into his stall. My brother explained that he assumed the barn door would be closed and Ned would stop outside. I was about three years old at the time and I had a lot of nightmares reliving that.

Mirelda, Lawrence and Lou went to school in town and the boys had some very traumatic experiences in those years.

For several years my two brothers ran a gauntlet getting to school. Several First Nations and Metis boys would wait for them on the road and my brothers would have to fight them to get to school. Their teacher, named Mr. Carpenter, would see them fighting and would give Lawrence a strapping. After school, it was the same on their way home. On top of it, Mirelda would run ahead and tell Dad that Lawrence had got a strapping from the teacher, so when they got home, Lawrence would get another licking from Dad. Because Lawrence was small for his age, he was picked on by other kids and naturally he naturally developed a persecution complex and a kept a chip on his shoulder.

Mr. Carpenter was a brutal disciplinarian. He seemed to enjoy throwing erasers or chalk at kids who caused any noise or disruption. One First Nations kid was thought to have become deaf, but when the nurse examined him, it was found that his ears were full of dried blood caused by injury in the classroom – blows to the head.

The boys told of one occasion when a little First Nations kid in school who was wearing socks and rubbers (the usual foot wear during the winter), put on two more, larger, pairs of rubbers on top of his own, and then, suddenly during class, stood up in the aisle, and, grinning, he danced a little jig, then sat down. Mr. Carpenter brought out the strap, and strapped the boy about ten times on each hand. A few minutes later, the boy stood up and, grinning again, did his little jig and sat down. Again he received the same punishment. The little kid did his little jig once more and finally gave up because his hands had become quite raw. It certainly was an amusing and impressive show that he put on, and was greatly enjoyed by all the class. Heroes are made, not born, and in unusual circumstances.

Mom always knitted woolen sweaters, mittens, toques and stockings for all the family. One winter, the boys' sweaters became worn out at the elbows, and their stockings wore out at the toes and heels. So Mom had a brain wave that would save her a pile of knitting. She cut the worn sleeves off the sweaters at the elbows, and the worn feet off the socks, and then sewed the stocking legs onto the sweaters and presto, reconditioned sweaters, almost as good as new. When the boys were presented with the sweaters, they didn't want to wear them. But Mom insisted.

The next day at school the kids laughed at them, so they came home and refused to ever wear them again. A few weeks later, there was a knock on the door, and standing there were two of the Ross children (a really poor family), "Please Mrs. Benoit, do you have any spare clothes. It don't care if they're a little bit broke." Mom had the exact donation: two perfectly good, warm, reconditioned sweaters. The funny part is that the next day at school the Ross kids were bragging and proudly showing off their "new" sweaters. All the other kids were very impressed, while the Benoit boys were pissed.

We had a bull on the dairy that was just plain mean. It didn't like anybody or anything except the cows and even with them he showed very little love or respect.

Apparently, when I was just a baby, my sister, Yvette, who was about six years old decided that she should take me for a ride in her doll carriage. Not content with the idea of pushing me just around the yard, she pushed me under the fence of a small hay field to a spot that was probably about fifty yards inside the fence.

That was when she noticed that the bull, which was grazing at the far end of the field, was on his way over to investigate and to guard his territory. Yvette was looking after her own skin first, so she raced for the fence and crawled under to safety, leaving me to the mercy of the bull. The bull was more interested in Yvette and ignored me, thankfully, and I was rescued by one of my brothers.

That same bull scared the dickens out of me a few years later. The family was preparing to move to the farm. Dad had a buyer for the bull and the two men were examining the bull. The bull had a ring in its nose which was tied to a post in the middle of the corral, with about six feet of slack in the rope.

Mom had asked me to gather up all the chicken eggs wherever there might be a nest. I was wearing my new parka that Mom had just made for me. Of course it was much too big for me, because it would be my only winter coat until I grew out of it in a few years. I recall that it was really warm and had fur around the hood.

I remember I was doing a good job of finding lots of eggs in nests in the hay stacks abutting the corral and putting them in my pockets carefully so they wouldn't break. I even, unknowingly, picked up several eggs that had been there for weeks and were quite rotten. I remember I was in the corral searching for eggs in an adjacent hay stack when I got too close to the bull and he lunged at me. He only got as far as the end of the tether but I had already taken to my heels across the corral and dove between the rails of the corral.

Naturally, the eggs in my pockets were all smashed and my parka reeked of rotten eggs. No matter how often my mother washed it, the stink lingered. I guess the reason why I recall the event, is that I had to wear that parka for about four more winters.

Aunt Edme, Mom, Elmer

Elmer 18 months, on our first cart – 1932

Elmer – Age 3

Mirelda, 16 & Elmer, 1

Chapter 3

THE FARM

In this chapter I will try to give a picture of life on the farm during the following eleven years until we moved to the city, noting that I was away at school for most of the final three years.

In 1935, my Dad traded the homestead south of town for another about seven miles north of town, in the Meadow River district. The rationale was that, although he had cleared about fifty acres on the first one, the soil was sandy and not very productive, while the land he was getting was black loam and the increased yield would more than compensate for the fact that it was only fifteen acres cleared. Also, he now had two strong sons, Lawrence and Louis, to clear the land. He was right on all counts, as he was able to retire after only farming for thirteen blessed years.

I remember moving to the farm in 1935 when I had just turned four. It was quite a production because it involved moving three granaries which, combined, would comprise our home. It was winter with snow-covered roads, so the buildings were transported on horse-drawn sleighs. Fortunately, there were no hills along the road - just flat prairie, except for a small dip at the bridge crossing the creek.

Two buildings were placed side by side and the third was placed perpendicular to them, with about five feet of space between each juncture. One building was partitioned to form the kitchen and mom and dad's bedroom, the second was the dining-living room, and the third was divided into two bedrooms - boys and girls. Mirelda and Yvette shared one while Lou and I shared the other. One space between the first two buildings was filled in to form a double pantry, and the space between the second and third buildings was filled in to provide for an indoor toilet for use in the winter. During the rest of the year we used an outdoor latrine. Toilet paper consisted mainly of the Eaton's catalogue which was pretty harsh on the bum, and Christmas was looked forward to partly because then we had softer mandarin orange wrappers to use. Yvette used to disappear right after meal time and would spend a half-hour reading the catalogue and would return when she was sure the dish washing was done.

Dad built a large enclosed veranda off the kitchen for storage and, later, it housed the washing machine. During the first years, Mom had to use a wash tub and scrubbing board. The washing machine, when it arrived, was the "latest" - a noisy gas motor (sounded like a power mower), and it had a powered wringer. Hanging the sheets out on the line to freeze-dry in the winter seemed to make them whiter and smell even fresher.

In the pantry was a trapdoor with a ladder leading down to the cellar where we stored the potatoes, plus shelves for storing most of the jars of canning that mom prepared with the produce from the garden, wild fruit that we picked, and meat from the steers and pigs that we butchered. The cellar was about eight feet deep and ten feet square, with only a dirt floor and walls; food was kept at a fairly constant cool temperature. I recall that when spring came, the potatoes started to sprout, and we used some of the last ones for seed.

During the first year, the house exterior was covered with tar paper, while alterations were being made. The next year we had the outside stuccoed and painted and the interior was wall-papered and painted and linoleum covered the floors. The wall paper was a plain, heavy texture and was painted pale green. Mom and my sisters painted a narrow border around the room near the ceiling and the space within the border was covered in a green leafy design with little red berries, copied from a picture in a magazine, and was painstakingly done by hand.

In the kitchen there was a large wood box that had a small counter mid-way from the floor for the wash basin and soap dish, and another shelf on the top to support the water bucket. Heating during the winter was provided by a large wood fired range in the kitchen and a 45-gallon drum heater in the living room. The bedrooms were warmed by leaving the connecting doors open. Starting the fire in the kitchen range in the morning could be exciting at times. Normally, somebody would take a couple pieces of kindling and shave the edges with a butcher knife before bedtime so it would be ready for lighting in the morning with just a match. But occasionally it was forgotten, so in the cold morning, the quickest way to get a fire going was to pour a bit of coal oil (kerosene) on the fire wood and toss a match in. If too much coal oil was used, the resulting flare would be a minor explosion which would lift the lids off the stove and shake the stove pipe. My first attempt, after the older boys left home, to use the fast method did not go well, and I was instructed to only use kindling after that. My burnt eyebrows grew back over the next few months, as well as my hair above my forehead.

A funny story involved the wood box. The kitchen table was in front of the windows with a chair between the table and the wood box. We had a hired man, an old Frenchman named Arthur Emot, who needed a place to live, and Mom took pity on him and hired him to do some light chores in return for board and room for several years. One afternoon just after Mom and old Arthur had finished their lunch and were enjoying their coffee, he reached into his pants pocket for some loose coarse tobacco to fill his crooked pipe. Unfortunately, there was also a 22-calibre rifle shell in his pocket which unknowingly ended up in his pipe. I should now mention that Arthur was easily startled and any sudden noise would cause him to jump violently and stutter. You guessed it. Arthur was contentedly puffing on his pipe when suddenly there was a bang, Arthur's pipe disintegrated, and the bullet ended up in the wood box. Arthur started yelling, waving his arms about, and stuttering incoherently. It was quite a while before he was able to talk rationally again. It was lucky that no one was injured. Anyways, the family had a good laugh later, when they pictured Arthur's reactions.

Another Arthur Emot story: There was a movie theater in town that the family attended to see silent films. Seating was on rough benches. My brothers once took Arthur to see his first movie and when he saw the characters walking around and talking, with the words appearing at the bottom of the screen, he started to laugh and eventually became so hysterical that the manager asked my brothers to take him outside and not come back. Later, the talkies came along and we were able to see more modern films. Western movies were most common but we did get to see some good dramas and musicals. Mr. Emot was not invited to see the talkies.

Our bedroom had a tin roof, so whenever there was a storm with thunder, rain, lightning and hail, I hurried into the bedroom and enjoyed the show. The sound of hail on the roof was deafening and exciting. Afterwards, the air smelled so clean and fresh. Later, I learned that Mom was terrified of the thunder and lightning and would go into her bedroom and pray her rosary. There was a real danger to the crops from hail, rain, and wind during a severe storm. Thankfully, our crops were never seriously damaged.

The dining-living room contained a big table and chairs and the gramophone and a new battery radio. During the day, mom listened to The Happy Gang, and some soap operas like Ma Perkins, and other CBC programs, while after school I listened to Superman, Green Hornet, etc. In the evening, the whole family listened to the CBC news, Lux Radio Theater, Jack Benny, Amos and Andy, Bob Hope, Bing Crosby, Amateur Hour, Gang Busters, etc. When the battery ran low on power, my brothers were required to recharge it, that is drain it and add more sulphuric acid.

The first time they did it, I saw them hunched over the battery on the floor and carefully pouring in the acid. The light was very dim and they couldn't see the level of the acid, so Lou got a straw and placed it in the opening and sucked to check it. Suddenly, Lou got a mouthful of acid and spit it out with a scream, grabbing for the water dipper to rinse his mouth. Fortunately, he didn't swallow any, but the inside of his mouth was badly burnt. It was certainly not considered serious enough to call a doctor since nothing was broken. For weeks after, Lou only lived on a diet of raw eggs. I remember that Lou once was driving a load of grain to town, and he drove the wagon to the house first, where mom handed him a bag of raw eggs and a nail to punch small holes in each so he could suck out the egg yolks and whites for his lunch.

Lawrence chose to sleep and spend his rest hours in a small cabin (about 8 ft. by 12 ft.) about 50 yards from the house. It was on skids and contained a cot, a small table, kerosene lamp and a space heater. It was always called the "caboose". He came into the house for meals and often stayed a few hours for some family time.

Besides listening to the radio and phonograph, we played card games like cribbage and pinochle, did jig-saw puzzles, and read.

The well that we got our drinking water from was located in the barn yard, near the creek. The well had a pump which also discharged directly into a large water trough for the animals to drink. The fence separating the barn yard from the runway to the pasture was connected to the trough, so animals could drink from either side.

Dad and my two brothers (Emile and Julia didn't come to the farm, and I will cover that part of their story in a later chapter) built a big hip-roofed barn out of logs from the property and shingled it. There were three sections, each about twenty feet square, placed end to end: with stalls for cows at one end and stalls for horses at the other, and hay storage in the middle. There was a hole in the ceiling of this section to enable us to toss hay down from the large hay loft above. The spaces between the logs were filled with mud or fresh cow dung which dried, fell out, and had to be replaced.

Thinking back, I have to admire the work that went into the construction of the barn. First was cutting of the trees while the land was being cleared, selecting those that were suitable and sawing them into proper lengths, peeling them, hewing the two sides of each to fit flat on the logs above and below and end to end, then building the walls, about sixty feet long. The hip roof, about fifteen or twenty feet high, was built of lumber and shingled, and covered the full length of the barn, creating a huge hay loft. All this was done with the use of only very rudimentary tools, a hand saw, a swede-saw, hammers, level, and a framing square. I don't remember ever seeing a tape measure on the farm. There was something else that got a lot of use – an eighteen inch piece of railroad rail that was used to straighten old, bent nails for re-use.

Dad bought a big McCormick-Deering tractor for clearing the land, towing machinery, etc. It was quite large and slow moving, all steel with big rear wheels that had about four or five inch steel lugs all around them.

When we moved to the farm, Lou and Lawrence were about fourteen and sixteen years old, and their job, among many, and besides building the barn, was to cut the trees and clear the land, then help Dad with the tractor to pull the stumps and the roots, collect all of this into big piles and burn it. Most of the trees were alder and aspen so they had no value, except as firewood. That is, until years later, when it was discovered that the wood was excellent to manufacture a light colored hardwood paneling, plywood and chipboard. There were also quite a number of spruce and pine trees. While the boys were collecting the stumps and roots and burning them, Dad was busy breaking the land, using the tractor and breaking plow, and then getting it ready for planting.

The crop from the first planting on about 100 acres averaged about 60 bushels of wheat per acre, a yield never equaled until farmers began using fertilizer and weed killer many years hence. The family had a photo showing just the heads of the horses over the standing wheat as it was being harvested with the binder.

A couple years after we built the barn, we totally filled the loft with hay during the summer. A few days later, it was noticed that the barn was listing and was about to collapse. Dad had built it on level ground, but with no cement footings or foundation. Dad and my two brothers hurried to cut three trees for logs which they used to prop up the far side of the barn. I think the Lord had a lot to do with keeping that barn standing for as long as we lived there.

The pasture consisted of about sixty acres on the north quarter which Dad bought a couple years after we moved to the farm. It had been owned by a large Dane or Norwegian man, named John Heinie, who wasn't much of farmer, but was a good, strong, laborer who worked for Dad during harvest and he continued to occupy his little cabin with his wife, their baby son, and his brother-in-law. We always called it "the Heinie place". On that quarter section, Lawrence and Lou cleared about 100 acres - in two strips: one was about 30 acres along the south border adjacent to the home farm, and the rest along the northern edge of the property. The middle 60 acres was not suitable for farming so it was left to provide pasture. A strip about 20 feet wide next to the western border of the home quarter was fenced off to allow passage of the cattle between the pasture and the water trough/barn yard.

In one end of the barn were several stalls for teams of horses. There was also a stall for Lawrence's saddle pony, called Tony, which I'll talk about later.

The year after we moved to the farm, Dad traded one team of horses to a fast talker for a team of mules. Within days everyone in the area heard the news that Joe Benoit had been suckered. After freeze up, Dad and Lawrence travelled north with the mules, sleigh and fishing nets to do commercial fishing on the many lakes in that area. A few weeks later, someone started a rumor that Dad had fallen through the ice while crossing a frozen river and the mules' ears were seen poking through the ice at the far side of the river. Yvette was told the story at school by another student and she went into hysterics. The teacher sent us home, and two miles of crying later, Yvette told Mom the story. Mom, of course, was devastated and sent Lou into town to talk to the priest about what to do, because there was no way to contact anyone who could know the truth. The priest came out to the farm immediately and assured mom that the report had to be a false rumor for the very reason that no one could have been there to witness.

Dad came home a couple months later, safe and sound. He sold the mules because I guess he didn't like competition at being ornery. (Actually, Dad wasn't ornery, and was quite even tempered except for occasionally losing his temper.) He went north a couple more winters, once fishing with Lawrence, and, the last time, buying fish from other fishermen and hauling them to Prince Albert and Saskatoon to sell to wholesalers. Most of the fish were called "whitefish", usually two or three feet long but I've seen a couple, referred to as "Jumbo Whitefish" that were about five feet long, and the jumbos tasted super delicious.

That last winter, Lawrence went north by himself to work for someone who needed a capable fisherman and cook. He claimed to be a great cook, and he could bake bannock that was more tender and tastier than any trained chef. The menu was always the same: bannock, beans, fish and tea. While there, he met another man at the camp who had the most beautiful beaded buckskin jacket that he had ever seen and asked if the man would sell it. The jacket was made of the finest deer hide, properly tanned and very soft, with fringes and covered by the most intricate beadwork that you could imagine. After about two months of talking to the man, he finally agreed to sell it for about $100.00. When the man's sister, who had made it, found out she was furious because she had spent months making it. Along with his pony, Tony, the jacket was one his two finest possessions.

Back at the farm, after the cows were milked, the milk was put through the separator and was at first made into butter for sale to the Evans' General Store in town along with eggs from our hen house. Many customers in the store asked specifically for Mrs. Benoit's butter and eggs. Later, when the creamery opened in Prince Albert, we switched to shipping cream instead of making butter. Mom, of course, continued to make her own butter for the family, and continued to bake bread until she died. For breakfast, we would have cereal (hot porridge or cornflakes or shredded wheat, etc.) covered with thick cream: the cream was so thick that when you took a spoon full of it, it would be about a half inch or more over the spoon.

Mom was a fantastic cook: wholesome for the most part, but very rich, a combination of French and German recipes. She would use that same thick cream for cooking. For example, she always creamed the peas or corn when she prepared them - delicious. No wonder most of the family suffered from heart disease.

During the first few years on the farm, Mom also raised ducks, geese and turkeys just to provide a wider variety of meat. The turkeys were well fed at home, but for some reason the entire flock of about fifteen birds wandered off one afternoon and ended up in a neighbor's yard. The neighbor, a Russian lady, saw a great opportunity, so she collected fifteen of the scrawniest of her own large flock of turkeys and herded them over to our place. Mom was furious but couldn't prove that they were different birds. Mom fattened them up and got rid of all of them, along with the geese and ducks, just keeping a flock of chickens.

I was happy to see the last of the geese as they always frightened me. When we first moved to the farm, I was only four years old and whenever I was in the barnyard and anywhere near the geese, my brothers would pick me up and toss me into the middle of the flock. They attacked me, hissing and beating me with their wings while I screamed my head off. I was never injured, just scared.

Mom and Dad ran a tab at Ducluzeau's General Store in Meadow Lake. Once a year, after harvest and the grain was sold, Dad would go into the store and pay off the bill. Besides food staples like flour, sugar, coffee, etc., the folks would buy almost everything else there, including overalls, shoes, and other clothing, plus Dad's tobacco.

Before moving to Meadow Lake in 1917, our family lived in French speaking communities where everyone spoke French. In Meadow Lake, there was a mixture of French, English, First Nations and Metis, Irish, Scottish, Russian, Ukrainian, Polish, German, Swedish and probably several others. The only common language was English, usually badly fractured when spoken as a second language. So Dad decided we would totally integrate and we would speak only English at home. When French people came to visit and spoke French, Dad would explain that we only spoke English in our home. If they insisted on speaking French, Mom and Dad would only answer in English. Nevertheless, there were many exceptions when my parents didn't want us kids to know what they were saying and would speak French to each other.

When I was about seven or eight, one of the cows gave birth to identical twin calves. I asked Dad if I could have one for my own if I looked after them. Dad said sure. After the calves were weaned, Dad rigged up a pen for them in an empty stall in the barn. There was no door or gate to keep them in, so he tied a rope across the opening of the stall and then tied both calves to it, with short leads to that and with nooses around their necks. A couple weeks later when we got home from church, I went out to the barn to check on the two calves, only to find one of them dead on the floor. The calf had started walking in a circle and the lead had become twisted with every rotation until it finally choked itself. When I told Dad, he checked it and that was his explanation. Then I asked him whose calf it was that had died, and he told me it was mine. How he could tell the two identical calves apart, I never could figure out, but my Dad was always smarter than me.

Dad also raised pigs. He kept about twenty sows plus a boar. The sows normally each gave birth to a dozen or more piglets, occasionally as many as seventeen. The males were castrated when they were still quite small, and I still remember watching the process each year until I was about nine years old. One of the boys would grab a piglet, put it on its back, straddled it and hold it by the back legs while Dad performed the operation. There was much squealing by the pig and cussing by the holder as the animal kicked him in the crotch with its front legs. They finally found a solution, placing the little pig, head first, into an empty nail keg, which my brother could straddle and hold the hind legs in position while its beans were snipped. For a few years we would usually sell a couple hundred pigs every fall.

Every year, until the boys left home, the family butchered a steer and a pig. I found it exciting to watch. The steer was done in the late fall, after harvest. There were two trees in the barnyard with a beam fastened between the branches, and a big barrel of water was placed below, over a wood fire. A neighbor, Frank Williams, would come over with his high-powered rifle to kill the animal (one shot in the brain). The steer was hoisted off the ground with a pulley, cut open, and the cavity emptied and the usable organs were salvaged. The carcass was then raised and lowered into the hot water several times while the hair was scraped off. The meat was all cut up into manageable portions and taken to the house. The hide was scraped of any meat still on the surface, then dried and sold.

The pig was butchered in the spring following the same routine. Frank would again receive some meat in return for his help.

There was no refrigeration at that time so mom would can the meat or smoke it. She had hundreds of sealers (mason jars) of various sizes – pint, quart, 2-quart - and filled them every year with meat, vegetables, fruit, jam, and jelly. A family favorite was what mom called "boiled dinner" and was preserved in 2-qt jars. It consisted of pieces of lean beef, cut into cubes, along with fresh vegetables from the root cellar - carrots, wax beans, cabbage, and pieces of turnip. Heated, and served with mashed potatoes, it made for a very tasty meal, especially on a cold winter day.

After butchering the pig, mom would cut up the outside fat and skin to render down to make some lard/shortening, and the rest would be used to make lye soap. The rendering process involved placing the fat into big pans and heating it in the oven. It was not pleasant to be in the kitchen that day, because of the acrid odor, especially when she made the soap, which involved adding wood ashes to the boiling fat. When it was ready, it was removed from the oven, skimmed, and the soap hardened into a solid slab the size of the pan and about 1 1/2 inches thick. It was then cut into bars. It was used at first for everything, but when we were able to afford to buy Lifebuoy, the lye soap was reserved for only the laundry.

With such a store of good food in the cellar, mom never minded unexpected company, and they always were invited to stay for a meal. There were no phones, so company was almost always unexpected. There always were chickens available to be killed. I used to watch Dad, or one of my brothers, as he selected a hen or rooster, swung it around his head a few times till it was dizzy, placed it on the chopping block, and then chopped its head off. (When you make the chicken dizzy, it won't move for several seconds - at least not until it's too late to take evasive action.) The dead bird was tossed into the snow where it flopped around while it was in its death-throws. I felt pretty important when I was given the regular job of killing the chickens, and I was about nearly ten, after Lou and Lawrence left home.

Dad had built a small smokehouse which was used to smoke some of the meat, especially the pork - bacon, ribs, etc. The smoke was generated by a smoldering fire of sawdust. The top layer of sawdust was dampened with water to ensure it wouldn't catch fire. I remember one evening during dinner somebody looked out the window and saw the smokehouse was ablaze. When the fire was extinguished, we found that the meat was thoroughly cooked as well as smoked. Dad didn't bother rebuilding the smoke house because Lawrence and Lou left home the next fall, and we quit butchering our own animals.

Every winter, Dad cut and hauled into the yard a few loads of logs for firewood. He would call three or four neighbors to come and give a hand with sawing it up into stove firebox lengths. The advantage of cutting firewood in the winter was that it was much easier to split when it was frozen. A neighbor who owned a power table saw that was mounted on a sleigh would come over and, with the help of the others, would carry each log over to the saw and feed it slowly on a carriage through the machine. For payment, Dad would give each one some fresh meat.

I remember one afternoon when I was about seven or eight years old, I was hauling firewood from the woodshed with my sled and it tipped over in the deep snow. Dad had built a rack to attach to my sled, about two feet high by three feet long, so that I could haul enough to fill the wood box with about two loads. My Dad was splitting wood at the newly sawn pile nearby. Upon going off the path and dumping my load in the deep snow, I kicked my sled in a snit and cussed under my breath. Dad just watched my little temper tantrum, then he picked up a piece of frozen kindling about 18 inches long and gave me the only licking that I can remember getting from him. In spite of about three layers of clothes it certainly made an impression on me and I was always careful to not have a tantrum when I was near Dad.

The discipline that I did receive was normally administered by Mom, who used Dad's razor strop. The strop consisted of two strips of leather, one coarse and the other fine grained, each about two inches wide, and were attached to each other at one end with a metal swivel ring. It was used for sharpening his straight razor. When Mom swung it against my bum and legs the two pieces of leather would make the loudest smack, but without a lot of pain. I soon realized that it sounded a whole lot worse than it hurt. So, whenever I got a licking, I started crying before even the first swat, and continued throughout the spanking, accompanied by screaming promises that whatever I had done, I'd never do it again. About six or seven swats was usually all she could handle. I'm sure it hurt Mom a lot more than me, and I can't remember getting more than three spankings, and they were probably as punishment for lying, or for disobeying an instruction, or for disrespect.

Dad built an ice house, just a rough shed, which he filled with blocks of ice that he cut at the river and hauled home. To keep it from melting too fast, he first laid a thick layer of sawdust on the ground in the shed, and then he alternated 18-inch blocks of ice and 4-inch layers of sawdust, up to a total thickness of about 6-feet.

The ice was used mainly for making ice cream during the summer. We had a 2-qt ice cream container which fit in a wooden bucket with a crank mechanism attached to turn the container inside the bucket. Mom would fill the container with vanilla custard that she made with thick cream. The bucket was filled with shaved ice and salt around the container and about 20-minutes of turning the crank produced the most delicious ice cream you could imagine. Without refrigeration, we had no way to save any, so we had to eat it all at once.

Mom always had a big garden so the family had plenty of fresh and preserved fruit and vegetables year round. Dad's contribution was to dig the garden, which he did by pulling out a fence post to enlarge the gate opening, drove the tractor and plow in, and plowed and harrowed it and was finished inside an hour. It was about half an acre or more in size, and, man, did it ever produce a lot of vegetables – organic, and enough to last the year. This garden included enough little,"new", potatoes to last until the main potato patch was harvested. Mom did just about all the rest of the gardening, planting, weeding and harvesting. Besides the vegetables, the garden contained long rows each of red and black currants and raspberry bushes and rhubarb. (The dried rhubarb leaves provided a substitute for tobacco until I was about eleven. It was better than dried alder leaves.) Mom found a recipe for "marrow honey", a jam made from vegetable marrows, lemons, and sugar - it was delicious, became the family favorite, and each year she would can about twenty quarts of it.

I recall one afternoon my chum, Donny, and I decided to have a feed of fresh peas so I went into the garden and picked enough to stuff my shirt full. When I came around the house Mom was waiting and asked what I had in my shirt. I told her that I had some peas to eat. She said "fine, sit down on the step and I'll shell them for you." She shelled peas and made me eat them until I was almost sick. I hated peas for the next twenty years.

Besides the garden produce, Mom would preserve quarts of wild fruit: strawberries, gooseberries, blueberries, choke cherries, Saskatoon berries, and raspberries. I hated picking berries, but I was required to help, filling an enamel cup. Unlike the tame strawberries and blueberries, the wild varieties were very small and took me ages to fill my cup. Of course, the process took longer because I would be spilling some on the ground, and also eating at least half of them.

The main potato patch was about half the size of the main garden and was located in a different part of the farm. Dad looked after this garden by himself - planting and harvesting. After plowing and harrowing the area, he would then plow a furrow; I would follow behind, placing pieces of potato in the furrow. Then Dad would plow another furrow which would cover the seed potatoes I had placed in the first one, as well as create another trench for the next row. Before starting, Mom and I would cut seed potatoes from the previous year's crop; each piece contained one or two eyes, which often were already sprouted while in the root cellar.

I was required occasionally to work in the garden, hoeing and weeding, bur mostly walking between the rows with a tobacco can containing kerosene in which I deposited the many potato beetles that were crawling on the leaves of the plants. It was tedious work and I soon would tire and find something else to do.

The year after he bought the Heinie place, Dad bought another quarter section of land from another man, called Poirier, who couldn't prove his homestead. (The Homestead Act provided, free, a quarter-section (160 acres) of virgin land, with the stipulation that you must clear it and plant a crop of a certain number of acres within a certain number of years or it would revert back to the crown.) So Dad and my brothers were back to cutting trees, pulling stumps, digging up roots, burning everything and plowing it before they could start growing more crops. This, again, proved to be excellent land and produced bumper harvests.

In 1936, Dad bought a new Pontiac car, so we then were able to take family trips to Prince Albert to visit Mirelda and pick up Yvette from boarding school in June. Lawrence got to stay home to do chores but Lou would come with us. It took all day to get there because Dad only drove a maximum of 15-25mph - he was always examining all the crops along the way, estimating the yield, how many weeds were in the field, etc. (My kids were never forced to ride with me driving that slowly. Lucky Kids!!!) Driving in the city was quite a challenge for Dad, and he was all over the street looking for addresses or just plain gawking. Once he forced an oncoming car right off the road and across the adjoining railway tracks. The driver was pretty upset, and when Dad gave the excuse that we were from Meadow Lake, he said he could believe that.

On the way home we always stopped for a few days in Leask to visit Aunt Annie and Uncle Ovila Benoit and their kids on their farm. Uncle Ovila and Dad were brothers, while Aunt Annie and Mom were sisters, which made for really close cousins of which there were many - about 16 altogether. My cousin, Pat, was 10 days younger than me, sounded like me and, when we were kids, he looked like me. Everyone was really excited to be together again. There was always lots of good food (Auntie cooked like Mom!!). Pat and I would go out catching gophers and sometimes we walked into Leask, about four miles, or to another aunt, Emily, and Uncle Napoleon, about five miles away near Marcelin. On the way, we would throw stones to see if we could hit the glass insulators on the telephone poles. Pat always had to be home in time to bring in the cows and help with the chores. I didn't have to help because I was on holiday. Two of the cousins were really pretty girls, a few years younger than Lou, and were able to sing beautifully. They were a happy family, lots of jokes, teasing, and always singing by Yvonne and Silvia. Uncle Ovila, when he wasn't working on the farm, could always be found in the beer parlor in Leask where he had a chair reserved.

Mom was two years older than Annie, and they remained closest to each other of the family. Another two sisters of Mom, Angeline and Edme, married two brothers, Alex and Paulin Colleaux, and they will come into my story later on.

While staying at Aunt Annie's, we would go over to Aunt Emily and Uncle Napoleon Beaulac's farm in Marcelin for a meal. I once mentioned to Aunt Emily that my Mom always cut her pies in only four pieces and we were encouraged to have seconds. My Aunt Emily snorted and pointed out that I was not at home and to be happy with whatever portion I received. There were eight of us and she had only one pie, so it was easy to figure that there would be only one small piece for each of us.

At some point on the trip, we also visited two others of Mom's sisters, Aunt Edme and Uncle Paulin in Big River for a day, and a day with Aunt Loretta and Uncle Sam Bujold in Debden, some forty miles from Leask. All of these uncles figure into my story in later chapters. Aunt Emily's children were similar in age to my older siblings, and Aunt Edme's son was about three years older than me, so I didn't have anyone to play with at those homes. Aunt Loretta, always referred to as "Aunt Lala", had four children of the same ages as my older brothers and sisters. There were two sons and a two beautiful daughters, Claire and Estelle, all born between 1920 and 1927, so of about the same ages as Lou, Lawrence and Yvette. Their youngest son was Raymond, was only five days older than me, and we got along really well.

Dad and Lawrence and Lou decided one winter that they would buy some instruments and form a small band. Dad had a good ear for music and had been a really good fiddler at one time, and was able to play any tune that he heard. Unfortunately, he broke his little finger and wasn't able to play a fiddle any longer. Dad could play the mouth organ, though, and so he bought a new harmonica. Lawrence chose a ukulele and Lou got a guitar. The musical talent wasn't actually hereditary in our family and stopped at Dad, and so the plan fizzled and died.

A really big celebration in town was the annual Meadow Lake Stampede which was the second biggest in Canada to The Calgary Stampede. It was a three-day event and involved large prize money to the winners. We always attended all three days. Of particular interest was any event which featured a local competitor. I remember that the chuck wagon races took place in the evenings and attracted the largest crowds.

Before the chuck-wagon races, I recall watching one of the local drivers, named Josh LaRon, rope wild horses that had been used during the bronc-riding events during the day. He would hitch them to his wagon and actually control that unruly team in the races and won often.

Josh was a character who had figured out a system that worked for him, and I think the police and judge went along with it. In the late fall, Josh would steal something, like a few bushels of grain and try to sell it, be arrested, have a trial and then spend six months in prison at the Prince Albert Penitentiary. While in prison he had a regular job, looking after the prison's herd of purebred Clydesdale horses, and would travel all over the country competing in horse shows. He behaved himself and was rewarded with good clothes, ate good food, visited all the major cities, and stayed warm. He was a fantastic driver and horse-trainer. He would be released in the spring, just in time to hit the rodeo circuit again.

One afternoon during the stampede, my folks were seated in the grandstand watching an event, when some people came and stood in front of my Uncle Paulin who was visiting us with his wife, Aunt Edme. My uncle happened to be smoking a cigar and was quite upset that the woman wouldn't move from in front of him, after he had asked her politely. She finally got the message when she smelled wool burning and got a warm feeling on her back side.

We had a dog that we brought with us from the dairy. It was ginger colored and we called him "Ginger". He was just a mutt of medium size and was never allowed inside the house except during electric storms which really scared him, and even then, he was only allowed into the closed veranda. He was a good watchdog and whenever a chicken hawk flew anywhere near the barnyard, Ginger would be right there under it, barking until the hawk flew away.

One Sunday, Yvette was sick and had to stay home from church. Ginger started barking and she saw a man coming into the yard on foot. She was naturally afraid, so she hid in our parents' bedroom. Peeking out, she saw the man come to the kitchen window, then, not seeing anyone in the house, he headed for the barnyard. She watched as he looked into one of the storage sheds, so she went out outside and said "sic" to the dog. Ginger raced at the man, barking furiously. The man took to his heels, racing across the field with the dog chasing him and barking all the way to the road. It's a good thing that the man didn't try the door, because it didn't even have a lock. Also, I should mention that Ginger was quite old and was missing quite a few teeth, so he wouldn't have been much of a match if the man had turned on him.

Ginger often got into trouble during his night patrols, when some unwelcome visitor came by. At least once every summer, we would find Ginger with a bunch of quills sticking through his tongue and cheeks in the morning after he defended the farm from an attack by a porcupine. Dad always said to never kill a porcupine because the gentle creatures could be eaten raw by any person lost in the bush. Anyhow, Yvette always got the job of removing the quills from Ginger's month, a very painful exercise for both of them.

One afternoon, I took Ginger with me to get the cows from the pasture. We were following a path that ran next to the barbed wire fence, when suddenly, as I was stepping over a fallen tree, the dog jumped between my legs and I was knocked over, falling against the fence and all three strands of barbed wire gashed my neck several times. Although there was quite a bit of blood, my carotid artery was not punctured. I tied my dirty handkerchief around my neck and carried on with my chore of finding the cows and bringing them in. During supper, Mom asked if that was blood she could see on the handkerchief around my neck, and wanted an explanation. I put the blame for the accident squarely on Ginger, and he wasn't there to counter.

When I was about eight of nine, Ginger was attacked by a pair of grey-hounds that tore his throat open. He died the next day. The greyhounds were owned by Frank Williams' brother who was visiting Frank from his home in Alberta. The greyhounds were normally used to hunt and kill coyotes, so Ginger was no match for them.

We got another dog, a collie named "Sport", and he was able to do everything that Ginger could, but I just couldn't feel the same degree of affection for the new dog.

When I was about eight years old, I was in a pasture near the barnyard, about six acres in size, when I was nearly kicked in the face by Buster, the same plow horse that had kicked Lou on the knee, the previous year, breaking the knee cap in four pieces. I recall that I was just standing there, by a granary and the fence, when Buster came galloping towards me. Just as he went by, he kicked out both hind feet at my head. I suddenly saw those two huge hooves about six inches from my eyes. God was certainly watching and protecting me, because if he had connected I certainly would have died.

We still had old Ned that had pulled the milk cart while we were on the dairy, and I occasionally would ride him. He was so sway-backed that the saddle wouldn't fit him anymore, so I had to ride him bare-back, when I went to the swimming hole. He was so slow that Donny had no trouble beating him in a short race. Therefore, Dad just left him in the pasture to live out his final years. One day I realized that I hadn't seen Ned at the water trough for a few days, so I went looking for him in the pasture. I finally found him in a small abandoned log building that had been Heinie's barn. He had been dead for a couple days. I was sorry to see him end this way and I had a long cry over his loss. I went home and told dad about it and he said he would look after it. There was no way of getting his carcass out of the structure, so he just set fire to the building, cremating Ned inside it.

Our mare, Queenie, got pregnant by a big stallion that his owner brought by, farm to farm, to perform the stud service for various farmers during the early winter. I had been there to witness the process – a brief courtship and minimal love play, before the very sexy stud lost patience and made his conquest – about ten minutes from start to finish. Queenie was not very impressed and gave the stud a bite on the ass as he strode haughtily away. In due time, Queenie gave birth to a colt, called Prince, naturally, and I played with him often as he grew. He was about two years old at the time that Ned died and I decided that Prince was strong enough to carry my weight, (I wasn't fat, just a bit pudgy), so I brought him close to the rail fence and I climbed up and slid over onto his back. He didn't react, so I took him to the barn and put on the saddle and bridle, and then proceeded to ride him around the barnyard. That evening, I asked Dad if I could break Prince and ride him; he just looked at me and said, "I guess you've already done it eh?" I said yes, and then he said, "in that case, go ahead". I now had my own transportation, and Prince could run a whole lot faster than Ned or Donny.

Winters were brutal, with temperatures as cold as 45 degrees below zero and several blizzards each winter which would block the roads with snow drifts for days.

I remember going out with my sled on winter evenings with a full moon and zillions of stars that you could almost reach out and touch, and it was so cold that every footstep squeaked out loudly, and the northern lights would flash and swirl across the sky. Often we could hear the train whistle blow in town, seven miles away.

One day, I and all my schoolmates went to a funeral in town for a young girl in my grade that had died from tuberculosis. It was a bitterly cold day with fierce winds when we left the school. I could have ridden with the Browns in their enclosed, heated, sleigh but instead I decided to ride in the Williams' open sleigh with Donny and some other chums. It was even colder on the way home, and I finally walked into the house with my toes, cheeks and fingers frost-bitten. The conventional remedy at that time was to rub snow into the frozen parts, but the end result was still a good deal of pain and a propensity to be more easily frost-bitten in the future.

One morning, following a blizzard which left the roads blocked with 3-foot drifts, I insisted on going to school because I might miss something new, I slogged my way there, only to find the only other kid to make it was a girl who lived only a couple hundred yards from the school in the opposite direction. Because of us, the teacher had to mark every other student absent and I won a prize for perfect attendance that year.

On another occasion, my parents and I went to visit some long-time friends, Mr. and Mrs. Gran, to have dinner, play cards and have a few drinks. We went by horses and sleigh because the roads were closed by a snow storm. After we arrived, there was another snow storm, but fortunately it cleared about ten o'clock that evening so we were able to leave for home. Mom and I were huddled under blankets in the sleigh box while Dad was standing in front, driving. Suddenly, as were passing over a three-foot snow drift, the sleigh hit a dip in the snow and the sleigh slowly turned over, pitching all of us out into the snow. Mom was particularly upset with Dad for not being more careful and accused him of having drunk too much rum. It was sort of a D.U.I. road accident in slow motion. Anyway, we were only a little more than a quarter-mile from home so Dad unhitched the horses and we all walked home, silently, as Dad didn't have very much to say, not even to mention that the weather had now cleared and it was a nice night for a walk in the moonlight.

Dad didn't drink very much or very often, but I remember one winter day Dad took a sleigh-load of wheat into town to sell at the grain elevator. After his business was done, he bumped into Frank Williams who suggested they go into the beer parlor for a drink. That evening the family, minus Dad, were just finishing dinner, and mom was worried about Dad who had said he would be home by three, when one of my brothers spotted the horses and sleigh stopped in front of the barn door, with Dad slumped over on the seat, totally out of it. Fortunately, the horses had known their way home, even if Dad didn't in his condition. The boys put the horses in the barn and brought Dad into the house. Mom sent me to bed so I wouldn't either: a) see Dad in his "disgusting" condition; or, b) hear her giving Dad supreme shit. I had already witnessed some of both by that time. The final result was that Dad agreed that, in future, when he felt like having a drink, he would bring some beer or a bottle of wine or rum home and they both would have a drink. Dad stuck to his promise during the rest of his life.

Dad decided one summer day to visit an old bachelor about two miles away to borrow some western magazines. These were "pulp" magazines, cost ten cents, and all had the same theme: cowboys against the rustlers or the Indians and often included the odd maiden who, desperately, needed to be rescued. The boys had taken the car to town, so Dad decided to use Lawrence's pony, Tony, which was in the barn. He saddled up Tony but didn't bother with the bridle because Lawrence didn't seem to ever bother with it. Using just the halter, he rode to the neighbor's log cabin, talked for a while, picked out an armful full of magazines, and started for home. As soon as they turned onto the road, and as was his custom, Tony took off at a full gallop, with Dad yelling "whoa" as loud as he could, and leaving a trail of magazines all the way home, finally stopping at the barn door. Dad later told Lawrence to be careful in future while riding that wild horse. Lawrence had a good laugh at that.

A few weeks later, the same thing happened to me when I decided to ride Tony while going to bring the cows in for late afternoon milking. Tony was already saddled but only had on a halter, and I was soon headed for the pasture. My two brothers were stooking wheat at the far end of the north quarter, so I thought I'd take a long detour to show off my riding skills to them. At age eight, my legs were still not long enough to reach the stirrups, so I was just sort of balancing on the saddle. Just after leaving the boys, Tony took off racing for home, me screaming "whoa, whoa" all the way home. Tony didn't even slow down until, just as he reached the water trough, he suddenly placed both feet down together and skidded to a stop, with me going over his head. All I had time to do was grab him by the neck as I went over, and ended up with my feet swinging inches over the water. The boys killed themselves laughing as they listened to me scream-ing as the horse ran home. Lawrence later explained to me that whenever he wanted to stop Tony, he would reach over the horse's head and, with both hands, loop the halter rope over his nose and pull back; but I was too small for that. Dad and I never rode Tony again.

Another exciting time every year was harvest. During the first couple years we used horses. Cutting was the first part of the process and Dad drove the horses and operated the binder, while Lou and Lawrence were required to stook the sheaves for drying. When we got the new tractor and binder, it was so much faster, that we needed to hire more men to help with the stooking. John Heinie and Tony Zwollock were the usual men for that task. That's when Mom would have to bake bread and pies and cook from dawn to dusk. It also meant making big lunches of sandwiches and pies and taking them in pails out to the field for the men.

Threshing time followed in about three weeks, and involved a lot more men. The threshing machine was powered by a tractor or steam engine with a power take-off. I recall that in the early years, when Dad hired a man with a steam engine, I was so impressed with it: it resembled a railway locomotive with a wood fired boiler and huge steel wheels, (the rear wheels were about eight feet in diameter and the front were about four feet). As the vehicle crept along at about five miles per hour, you could almost feel the ground moving, steam and smoke belching from the stack.

The threshing crew consisted of the steam engine or tractor operator/ mechanic, a machine man to supervise the threshing machine, a loader to assist the haulers to feed the sheaves into the machine in a constant flow, about five haulers who drove their teams of horses and racks around the field to collect the sheaves, and a "field man" who went from hauler to hauler and helped to load the sheaves onto the racks. There was the big boss too, which was Dad.

For that many men Mom had to get a hired girl to assist her. She was usually not experienced or trained to even help. Often it would be the daughter of a poor local family and Mom was always reluctant to fire her, no matter how incompetent she might be, which meant that Mom would have to carry the extra load. The lunches were always similar to cutting time, except that Mom would get Dad to buy bread from the bakery in town, as well as sliced meats, for the piles of sandwiches needed. Because we always had home-made bread during the rest of the year, I really enjoyed the bakery product and looked forward to having it for about a week in the fall.

During the first three years, we didn't own the threshing machine and had to contract the service from a family, named Tony Kulcheski who farmed a few miles away. His crew included his four sons, a couple sons-in-law, and a few young local men who needed the work. These non-Kulcheski men said they would never hire on again if they had to eat Mrs. Kulcheski's cooking. I recall the crew as a bunch of young, burly, loud and happy men, who sat at the big table and suddenly became quiet as the food was served, and then swiftly shoveled the food into their mouths until their appetites were satisfied. Mom then served dessert, a full quarter of a 12-inch pie to each, and seconds to everyone. They drank their first cup of coffee from their saucers, it cooled quicker that way. The Kulcheski men all licked their plates and turned them upside down on the table, ready for the next meal. Mom muttered to herself all the time she was washing the dishes, something about uncivilized people.

That's not the only thing that upset Mom about the Kulcheski family. As we drove past their farm during harvest, we could see the whole family working in the field, including the old lady and daughters, stooking or loading sheaves on the rack. In Mom's estimation this was definitely not women's work. They certainly had a different cultural background.

About 1936-1937, Dad bought a new rubber tired tractor, one way disc, binder and threshing machine, and life became a whole lot easier.

When Dad got his own threshing machine, he had no trouble recruiting a crew, as the local men knew they would have the best meals they were likely to get all year.

On one occasion, our threshing machine broke down just before noon, so Dad asked the machine mechanic if he would work through the noon break to do the repair and Mom would make a special lunch for him at the worksite, so he agreed. Mom made a pail of sandwiches and on the top she put a whole 12-inch pie, and covered it over with a tea towel. When he opened the lunch, he could hardly believe his eyes, so he ate the entire pie first, to make sure he would have room for all of it, and then still was able to cram down a few sandwiches.

When threshing was completed and the equipment was put into storage, what remained in the field was a huge straw stack and, where the machine had stood, was a small pile of weed seeds that had been screened out of the grain. These seeds were always picked up with a shovel and fed to the pigs or buried where they wouldn't grow new weeds. One year, Dad didn't pick up the seeds and turned the cows into the field to graze. One of the cows unfortunately found that little pile of weed seeds and ate them all. That evening, at milking time, the cow was found to be all bloated up with gas and was in considerable distress. Not having a vet nearby, Dad asked me to call Frank Williams for advice. Frank's solution was to pour a bottle of linseed oil down the cow's throat. We didn't have long to wait before there seemed to be some sort of explosion in the cow's belly and the shit hit the far wall. A lot of it!!! Interesting!!! The cow survived and was back in production the next day.

"Old-Fashioned" Christmases were still "Modern" celebrations at that ancient time for our family on the farm. What a happy and joyful time we had.

The Christmas tree was selected from a 60-acre plot, (our pasture), and was always about 8-ft tall, reaching to the ceiling. The decorations included a bit of garland and tinsel and silver icicles, and a whole lot of strings of colored popcorn that we had made ourselves, and some ornaments, all used repeatedly and packed away for the next year. There were also a dozen little candles attached to clips, and because of fire hazard, they were only lit once or twice over the holidays. Always they were lit at midnight or after we got home from midnight mass and, again, after we had been asleep for a while, we were wakened to go see what Santa had brought.

When the weather was clear we would go to town seven miles away for midnight mass, using a cutter pulled by one horse. In the church there would be a manger scene with figures about two feet high, depicting the Holy Family, shepherds, magi, angels, and some animals. I was always very impressed. Following midnight mass we were faced with the long trip home, arriving about two-thirty or three a.m.

Before we went to bed, we would put out a glass of milk and a plate of Mom's Christmas cake (Santa loved Mom's fruit cake) and turn on the radio which played nothing but carols over the holidays.

I always stayed awake in my bed, listening for Santa's sleigh bells but I could never keep my eyes open long enough. When mom called Yvette and me to come and see what Santa had brought, the candles would be already lit, and the cake and milk gone except for a few crumbs.

For weeks before Christmas I would pour over the Eaton's catalogue picking out everything that I wanted, then shortening my list to about ten items. Mom would come by with a pair of scissors and tell me I could have them all (the pictures, that is), and all I had to do was to cut them out. I recall that one Christmas I actually got a sled, and another time I got my pair (?) of skates (they both were for the left foot) that I had picked out in the catalogue and drooled over for weeks.

Days before Christmas, Mom would be busy baking and freezing, pies and cakes, and making candy. We always had a wide variety of fudge: divinity, chocolate, cream, and maple, as well as pull-toffee, and often something from a new recipe. Mom would bake a whole lot of meat pies, called "tourtieres". The Christmas fruit cake was always made in November so it could age and absorb the rum. The pull-toffee was a favorite of the kids: it would come off the stove as a sort of pale yellowish liquid and was poured into a big cake pan which was sitting in a bed of snow to cool enough to be able to pull with bare hands. When it started to set, Mom would put butter on her hands and then start to pull it, stretching, then fold it over and stretch it again and again until it turned to a beautiful silver/white color. She then cut pieces off for each of us kids to pull and eat. It didn't seem to matter how thoroughly I washed my hands, my toffee always turned to gray soon enough. It still tasted great.

The Christmas after the boys left home, and Yvette was at boarding school, I was the only child still left at home, so it was pretty quiet. The folks asked me to get the Christmas tree from the pasture on the Heinie place. Feeling pretty important, I hitched a horse to the toboggan, got the axe and set out. The toboggan was home-made, about eight feet long with a wooden frame covered over with tin so that it would slide easily over the snow. I wasn't familiar with the operation of it, so it often would slide too fast and would hit the horse's heels. Fortunately, the horse didn't kick me, and only made half jumps forward, which caused the toboggan to ride up on his heels again.

I finally reached the pasture and began the search for the perfect tree. With only a selection of about a thousand trees you'd think it would be such an easy choice. I finally found it. It happened to be the top of a thirty-foot tree, and, from the ground it looked to be just right - symmetrical and lots of branches with no big gaps. I chopped the tree down, cut off the top eight feet, loaded it on the toboggan, and hauled it home. However, when we put it up, it was the worst tree ever. Mom, trying to make me feel good, said it would be fine, all we had to do was fill in the empty spaces with decorations.

After war was declared in 1939, the family fortunes turned. The price of wheat suddenly jumped and the farm became very profitable. Lou and Lawrence tried to enlist, but both were rejected, Lawrence because of liver or other internal problems and Lou because of his stiff knee. Both decided to leave the farm that fall after harvest, Lawrence to Prince Albert and Lou to New Westminster. Before the boys left, Dad down-sized the farm, getting rid of the horses, except for one team just in case of emergency, like being snowed in during winter storms. Also gone were all of the pigs and cattle, except one cow.

Dad needed help on the farm so he hired Harry, who had a small farm nearby. Harry wasn't much of a farmer, but he was a good mechanic and operator and he could follow instructions willingly. Just what Dad needed!!! Harry didn't have any machinery of his own, so Dad let him use ours in lieu of some of his wages.

Looking back, I guess the Lord was pretty pleased with our Little Joe Benoit, because we never once had a crop failure, were never hailed on enough to cause real damage, or had an early frost, unlike our neighbors who often had extensive damage on their farms. I remember one year that the Brown's crop was totally wiped out by hail, yet ours was not even touched, just across the road.

Mom and Dad were good Catholics, went to church every Sunday (twice, if the roads were good,) prayed daily and had the priest bless the seed grain before planting it in the spring. Dad always carried with him a small crucifix (small cross with an image of Christ nailed to it). On one occasion, Dad was driving the tractor in the field, standing beside the seat and pulling the one-way, when Dad fell backward off the tractor. Fortunately, his leg hooked over the bracket connecting the tractor to the one-way, and Dad dangled there just a couple feet in front of the discs. All he could do was pray for a miracle. The tractor continued on across the field, went through both fences between the cow path and Williams' pasture. It stopped when it hit the trees in Williams pasture. Dad was not even scratched but he was sore from being carried so far in such an awkward position. (I still have the crucifix and I keep it in my car, and it's still keeping me safe despite me doing some really stupid things while I was driving.)

With the boys gone and Yvette going to boarding school in a convent, life became very quiet on the farm, especially during winter. Dad milked the cow in the morning when I went to school, and I did it in the evening. That was only partly successful as the cat would always appear and I would feed it directly from the teat. The cat sat about eight feet away, opened its mouth and I would try to squirt milk at the target. Like I said, it was only partly successful, and most of the milk would drip down the wall. I would come into the house with barely half a pail, leaving another quarter pail somewhere on the barn wall. Mom wondered once whether the cow was drying up, but Dad said he was still getting three quarters of a pail in the morning so altogether that was all we needed. Dad was always wise enough to read the signs on the wall.

During harvest, when I was 10-12 years old, Dad used me to drive the tractor while Harry would operate the binder. This was the new rubber tired Cockshutt tractor that he had bought a couple years before and had a top speed of 20 mph. I kept sneaking the throttle up to the point where we were going too fast to cut the grain properly, so Harry often had to yell at me to slow down.

My parents and I spent most evenings by playing cards, reading, doing jig-saw puzzles and listening to the radio. We were especially interested in the war news after Lou enlisted in the army and then was sent overseas. Mom spent a great deal of time praying and crying with worry over Lou.

In 1943, when I was 12 years old, I went to Prince Albert to live with Mirelda and her family and take my Grade 8, at a separate school. This was followed by two years at a boarding school in a Benedictine monastery at Muenster, Sask. I came home for summer vacations and spent Christmas and Easter with any of Mirelda, Lawrence, or Aunt Annie in Leask, near Prince Albert. (I'll talk about those periods in a later chapter.)

While I was attending boarding school, my parents spent both winters on the West Coast and really enjoyed themselves - the first real vacations they had ever had. In the fall, Dad took the cow over to our neighbor, "Rock" Brown, and told him he could have all the alfalfa hay from the 2-acre patch; he just had to cut it and haul it. Dad then bought a quart of milk, from our cow, fed with our hay, for 10-cents per day when the folks were home.

By this time, Dad was renting land from Rock Brown, Harry the hired man, and Ed Kulcheski on a crop sharing basis. Dad gave each a third of the proceeds of the crops from their fields in payment.

When I was about eleven or twelve, Dad thought that it was about time that I made myself useful, so he asked me to take a wagon load of wheat to sell to the operator of one of the elevators in town. I jumped at the chance to do something important. When I pulled into the elevator I was told where to stop on the scale while the loaded wagon was weighed, I jumped down while the wagon was tipped to empty it. I watched as the operator marked down the weight and again when he weighed the empty wagon, calculated the net weight of grain and wrote a cheque for Dad. On the way home, I figured out the system and later asked Dad for the money for my ninety pounds of "grain" that I had contributed before I clambered off prior to dumping the load. Dad didn't agree because he didn't want me to start being dishonest in business. At that time, I hadn't developed a talent for planning but at least I could already recognize opportunities as they came by.

I had a short but profitable career in the fur business when I was ten and eleven years old. With the onset of World War Two, a market opened for rabbit fur to be used in the manufacture of felt liners for outdoor boots used by the armed forces. I set two trap lines, using snares made of copper wire, in our pasture and in the grove of alders located between our house and the road. I would set about fifteen or twenty snares, check them in the morning and after school, remove any rabbits that I had caught, usually two or three, and then reset the snares on another rabbit trail. After school I would skin them and stretch the hides over frames that I had carved out of cedar shingles, and let them dry for a few days. I sold them to a dealer in town every Saturday for nine cents per pelt. The first winter I made good money, enough to buy Mom a pretty new teapot and a package of fancy handkerchiefs for Christmas and Easter, plus some five-dollar War Savings Certificates for myself. The next year I only earned a few dollars before the rabbit plague struck. It was a disease developed and introduced in Australia to control their rabbit population, causing sickness and death of the rodents in seven year cycles. Years later, when Mom died, I found the handkerchiefs, still in the original box, in her dresser drawer, as well as the tea pot in the cupboard.

Brown or gray in the summer, rabbit fur changed color in the winter to white, and was quite soft to touch. Their use became popular in the manufacture of women's fur coats and was marketed as "Coney". I'm quite sure that none of my rabbit pelts ever ended up in keeping some woman warm, as they were needed more urgently for foot wear for the troops.

When I was 12 years old, I rode Prince to town in the summer for some reason. On the way back, I was galloping along and, as I was turning a corner, we hit a muddy patch in the road. (It had rained the previous night.) Prince's feet slipped out from under him and we landed flat on the ground, but I just had time to jump clear before we landed. I scrambled to my feet and rushed to see if the horse was injured. Just as I reached him, he rolled over and, too late, I saw his hooves coming straight towards my head. The blow knocked me on my ass, but fortunately I didn't lose consciousness. We continued on home at a more modest pace. That was another incident that Mom didn't need to be told about; although she did ask how I got all muddy on one side, and I told her that I was running and fell, which was at least partly true.

During the war, the federal government gave each farmer a certain amount of money for each acre that they left in summer-fallow in order to rest the land. My Uncle Poulin, (Aunt Edme's husband) was one of the persons hired to record the claims and verify the number of acres actually in summer-fallow. Without prior announcement, the number of acres actually planted to wheat that year then formed the basis of the quota of grain you were allowed to sell during the following several years. Dad was able to use the quota books of the farmers he was renting land from, with none of it in fallow, and so was able to sell all his grain each year before the following harvest. Some farmers had put too much land in fallow that year and now had unsold wheat carried over to the next year.

My summer vacations at home were now mostly unexciting. The spring planting had already been completed before my return, and harvest happened after I went back to school, so there wasn't much to do except a few chores and go swimming. I would saddle up Prince, and ride to the Hamilton's farm, about two miles away, where there was a five-foot deep swimming hole next to a bridge over the creek. It was the same creek that passed downstream through our pasture, but this was the only spot that didn't dry up during the summer. None of us could swim, so we each brought a 10-lb syrup can in which we punched a hole in the bottom with a nail, and threaded a piece of binder twine through, long enough to tie around our waists. By putting on the lid, we had some crude floats to support us as we swam. They worked fine for about a month until the twine rotted and frayed and then, just when I was in the middle of the pond, it broke and floated away. I had no choice but to swim for my life. And that's the way I learned to swim. Funny, the other four kids had the same thing happen to their floats that same afternoon or over the next few days.

One day in the summer of 1945, when Lou was home from overseas and had been discharged from the army, the folks received my report card from the college saying I had passed my Grade 10, but that I wouldn't be accepted back in the fall. It seems that, because I had no desire to enter the priesthood, they could use my place for another student who would like to be a priest.

Dad, shortly before this, had been notified by the government that he was required to pay something called income tax, which he had never heard of. What's more, it would be retro-active. Even worse, it cost him a lot of money to settle the whole business. He said he'd be stupid to work so hard to earn a decent income and then have the government take most of it away. He asked Lawrence and Lou if they wanted to take over the farm, and both said no, that all the hard work they had done was still too fresh in their memories.

Dad visited the real estate agent, listed the farm, and sold it within a week. The next week, Mom and Dad went to Saskatoon, bought a house and called Uncle Poulin, who was an auctioneer, to sell the other goods. Dad had bought a brand new self-propelled, 14-foot combine. It was still in packing cases and he had no trouble selling it as they were on back-order at all the dealers (the war had just ended, and factories had not yet switched back totally from manufacturing armaments to farm equipment and household appliances).

When Dad sold the farm the grain crop in the fields was about two-feet high, and it was a month prior to harvest. It was another bumper harvest. So, a month after the new owner took over the farm, he was able to pay off the total cost of it.

The last day on the farm was the auction sale. Everything was sold except for our personal clothing. Some of the equipment, like the tractor, one-way, plow, and car had already been sold privately. I do remember that there were hundreds of canning jars that Uncle Poulin kept hauling out, a case or two at a time, until it became a joke with everyone there. There didn't seem to ever be an end to them.

Farm House – Front

Farm House – Rear

Elmer, 5, with Dad

Elmer riding Prince - Barn & outbuildings in background

Chapter 4

EARLY CHILDHOOD FRIENDS

My first best friend was Donny Williams. He was just a month older than me and lived on the next farm, just across the creek - about 400 yards away. Between our houses there were about fifty feet of alder trees, the property line fence, more trees, their vegetable garden, the creek, and more trees. Their family included his dad, Frank, mother, who I only knew as Mrs. Williams, and brother, Victor, who was about three years older than us. They moved in a year after us.

The Williams' family was from Missouri and homesteaded next to us, but only half-cleared their property. Frank wasn't very successful in farming and supplemented the family income by going north every winter to hunt and trap. I guess he was pretty good at it, because he always brought home quite a load of fur pelts such as beaver, weasel, muskrat, etc., which he was able to sell at the fur auction in the spring. He also occasionally worked for my dad during the summer, stooking grain and on the threshing crew. Frank had a bit of a drinking problem, which contributed to the family's poverty. Mrs. Williams had been a school teacher before she came to Canada, and was a shy, pleasant, but very quiet woman.

Frank built a fairly large log cabin, about 20' x 15', and divided it about eight feet from the end with a rough lumber partition, six ft. high, to form the single bedroom. He then built two bed platforms of rough lumber, one for the adults and one for the kids. Mrs. Williams bought some cotton ticking and made two mattresses, filled with straw, which they changed every summer while the cabin was being fumigated to get rid of the fleas.

I recall one afternoon, Donny, Vic, and I were in the tent, just talking, when Vic turned onto his elbows and knees with his bum pointed towards the roof; he sucked in some air into his bum, waited a minute then farted the stinkiest bomb. He repeated this "farting-on-demand" routine for quite a long time, until it drove us out of the tent.

Vic was a very talented boy in some ways. When Vic finished school, he joined the RCMP. At that time new recruits had to be single and could not marry without express permission of the commanding officer and not until they had served at several different postings. Vic got married anyway and as punishment, he was posted to the Parliament buildings in Ottawa and served the country by standing guard and having his picture taken with tourists.

For several years, Frank walked over to our house every evening to listen to the news on our radio. After that he would discuss the news with dad and mom, and then walk home. You always recognized it was Frank's footprints in the fresh snow, because they were directly in front of each other and in a dead straight line; he was quite proud of his footprints. Frank finally bought a radio for the family, but it was restricted to listening to the eight p.m. news and Donny and Vic could listen to Superman and the Green Hornet after school, but always the volume was kept very low (you had to stand right next to the radio in order to hear it), so as to not wear out the battery.

Frank had built a small corral adjoining their log barn and inside it were a couple hay stacks to feed their two cows and two horses during the winter. Donny and I often would sit with our backs leaning against the hay stack and smoke or just talk big, just to impress ourselves. Occasionally, another neighbor kid, named Dennis Brown, who lived across the road from me, would come over to play with us. Dennis was a couple years younger than us and was not either as sturdy or smart as us. He was always quite impressed with our worldliness and therefore a real patsy for our pranks.

On one occasion, when Donny and I were about ten, we were sitting by the haystack chewing plug tobacco, (which Vic had stolen for us from the store in town). Dennis arrived and while we ignored him, it wasn't long before he asked to try some plug tobacco. We explained that giving him any chaw would be a waste because he'd probably spit out the "juice". (We had been doing just that, but not when he could see us). He promised he wouldn't spit out the juice, so finally Donny cut off a big piece and gave it him. He manfully chewed and swallowed for a few minutes until he started getting pale. We said "see you're getting sick" but he insisted he felt fine. When he started turning green, we started getting scared and finally convinced him to spit out the chaw, and then told him that he would feel better if he ran around the haystack as fast as he could. He made it around the haystack once and we urged him to keep going because he looked better. When he didn't arrive back, we went looking for him and found him throwing up his lunch. We sent him home with assurances that we all had had fun and he had done "good". That evening, Mrs. Brown came over to visit, and commented to mom that Dennis had a really upset stomach and vomited green stuff.

I remember doing the same thing to Dennis with green blueberries. I had been sent to pick wild blueberries in the pasture and came home with a large jam tin full of berries, many of them green. I was just starting to pick out the unripe ones to throw away, when Dennis arrived, and wanted to know what I was doing. I put a green berry in my mouth, tucking it in my cheek, and made a big show of chewing and smacking my lips. Dennis could hardly believe me when I told him the green ones were best of all because they made you smart. He ate quite a few before he eventually got smart and stopped eating them. Mrs. Brown came to visit mom the next day and commented that Dennis had been quite ill the previous night; throwing up more green stuff. She failed to mention whether Dennis seemed to be any smarter than before, and I didn't ask her.

There was a trail through the bush and creek bed between our houses and had a vee-shaped gate in the rail fence to be able to cross into the Williams pasture. During the frequent visits back and forth to play, it was always the macho thing to do to swing ourselves over the rail fence. The correct method was to run to the fence, put your hands on the top rail, and without breaking stride, swing your body over, landing on your feet and continue running. I seemed to have a mental block about half way through the process, and, too often, I came down hard on the rail. (Man. That Hurt!!!) I still think that's the reason I had to adopt my three kids - LUCKY ME!!!

Another neighbor, named John Dickewiski, who had emigrated from Russia, lived directly across the road from the Williams' farm. One day we were hanging around while John and Frank were chatting, and John started teasing Donny about Olga Kulcheski, a girl in our grade. Olga was one of about ten kids in her family who all had to work in the fields. The father, Tony, helped all of his kids get started in farming when they got married by giving each a half-section of land plus a team of dapple-gray horses, Tony's favorite color. So John says to Donny, "what you going to do when you grow up? Get married to Olga? Tony will give you farm and two hopple gray horses." Donny and I laughed so hard we fell on the ground just thinking of it. Olga would have needed much more than the usual dowry to entice a marriage proposal from either of us.

Another friend of the same age was Leo Owens, who lived about two miles down the road. Because it wasn't within easy walking distance, I usually only played with him at school or during family visits. Mr. and Mrs. Owens had moved to their farm about three years after us, and the family included an older son, Clive, and two daughters. Clive was the same age as Lou, and they became good friends. Our two families used to visit back and forth often. Their farm property adjoined a large slough (a shallow lake, about one or two miles across, with no stream in or out, and consisted of snow melt and rain) where the neighbors used to skate in the winter. I sort of learned to skate on that lake. I remember that I asked mom to buy me a pair of skates and was overjoyed when she bought me a pair for Christmas from the Eaton's catalogue. When they arrived they were both for the left foot. Because they were too large for me (provided room for me to grow, I put on two or three pairs of socks, and headed for the slough. Eventually, I managed to keep my feet under me and was making some forward progress and speed, when I spotted an air hole. (This hole was caused by methane gas constantly produced by rotting vegetation at the bottom of the lake and the hole stayed open through most of the winter.) I hadn't learned how to stop, and began to panic as I quickly neared the hole. Finally, in desperation, I threw myself onto the ice and came to a stop about eight feet from the icy open water.

One summer day when I was about ten or eleven, I saddled up Prince, got the 16-gauge shotgun, a pocket full of shells, and rode over to visit Leo. I wanted to go down to the slough and shoot some ducks. There was a rail fence that ran into the edge of the water that I was able to straddle and work my way out beyond the reeds to where I could get a clear shot. There were no ducks, only a few water hens which are not edible. I thought, "What the hell, better than nothing". So I stood up, aimed, and fired. The recoil knocked me almost into the water, and hurt my shoulder so much I had to go home. (Another secret I didn't dare tell Mom.)

A fourth friend was Eddy Zwollak, also my age, was the only child of Big Tony and his wife, and had just arrived from Poland, where Tony had been a soldier in the Polish army. Eddy had a tough time at school, which I'll touch on when I talk about my country school. However, I can tell you that Eddy later joined the army during the Korean War, was wounded (slightly) but was found to be an expert marksman, was transferred to the rifle marksmen team back in Canada, competed in and won top marks in many Bisley competitions. Bisley competitions pit top riflemen from all of the British Commonwealth and are held in England.

I had another friend a couple years older than me, named Robert Gran, who lived about a mile out of town. His parents, Martin and Marie, were long time family friends and Martin was my godfather when I was baptized. Martin had a government contract to operate an experimental station on his farm. That involved planting various strains of grain in small plots on his land. He also had to cultivate a small orchard which included a variety of trees, mainly crabapple, as well as berry bushes. Robert and I were not "close" friends, mainly because of our age difference. Robert eventually joined the RCMP and served in the Yukon or NWT.

One winter day, Mom and Dad invited Mr. and Mrs. Gran and their oldest daughter and her husband, the Pliskas, over for dinner and game of bridge. They also brought Robert and Johnny who was Pliskas' son, about a year older than Robert. Dad had bought a bottle of good rum and a gallon jug of Port wine for the occasion, which he mixed 1/4 rum to 3/4 wine to be served during the bridge game. Johnny located the booze in the pantry, so he and Robert suggested we play hide and seek; two would hide while the seeker would go into the pantry and count to a hundred or have a drink of booze and then go seeking. A couple hours later, Johnny and Robert were both outside, barfing in the snow bank. I hadn't drank very much so I didn't get a licking, and the others were too old for a licking, so they all packed up and went home.

Chapter 5

MEADOW RIVER SCHOOL

I started school in January, 1937, just before my sixth birthday. The timing was a bit unusual, but Donny who turned six on December 26th, had started school in September, and besides, we were the only two or three grade one pupils in the school. Also, it was on the suggestion of the teacher who was a family friend, and she boarded with us and she felt I could easily catch up.

The school was built of logs, with only one room and was located two miles from our home. Total enrollment varied between twenty and twenty-five, and encompassed grades one to seven. Grade 8 was available through a correspondence course but this was rare.

Yvette went to that school and was able to help me to get started. We walked together and, of course, there were always other kids on the way for us to join up with.

I remember that the night before I started school I began to cry, because I had just realized that I couldn't read, so I would be the dumbest kid in the school. Miss Poitras, the teacher, reassured me that I would learn soon enough.

The next September, we moved into a brand new, very grand school, with a new teacher, just a half-mile from home. Again, it was only one room, but it was built of smooth lumber, painted white, and had lots of windows, two walls of blackboards, with new desks and two cloakrooms, boys and girls. It had a big, 45-gal drum heater. We placed our lunch buckets around the heater during the winter months so that our sandwiches would be thawed out by noon. There was also a two-bedroom teacherage for the teacher to live in, a well, and a barn for horses and dog teams.

The teacher, Miss Speers, boarded at our home during the first year and then moved into the teacherage for the second year. She only lasted two years, as she was quite pretty and was quite quickly snatched up by one of the German butchers from town and got married.

My only vivid memory of Miss Speers was that she broke my nearly-new ruler. Donny's desk was right in front of mine, and he and I were caught flicking wheat, which we had brought from home in our pockets, at the blackboard near where she was writing. For some reason she found it to be very irritating. She marched over to Donny's desk, snatched his ruler, said "Stick out your hand" and when he did, she gave him a couple smart swats on his palm with his ruler. She then moved on to me, took my ruler, and said, "Stick out your hand", which I did. Quite unnerved by seeing what had happened to Donny who was still bawling, I pulled my hand back just in time, the ruler hit my desktop and broke. When we got home, Yvette told mom, and Mom scolded me, blaming me for the broken ruler, quite unfairly, for what the teacher had clearly done.

My next teacher was the best of all, Mr. Friesen, whose grandson played in the National Hockey League a number of years later; I think it was in the 1980's. Mr. Friesen lived in the teacherage with his wife and little son, and he bought a quart of milk from us every day, which I was supposed to deliver when I went to school.

Mr. Friesen was a star softball pitcher and helped the men's team from our district win most of the tournaments. He was a stickler for fitness and every day, even during winter, all of the students had to go outside during both recesses and the hour-long lunch break and play soccer; and in September, May and June we played softball. The only exception to the rule required a note from the parent, and also you had to actually look sick. As a result, our school of 23-25 students won the trophy at the annual sports day in town every year, competing against about six country schools plus three schools from town. Vic Williams won every event in his age group, plus he won the pole vault against the high school boys when he was 12 - 15 years old. Vic cut his own pole from a tamarack tree which was the right height and thickness and dead straight. He then peeled off the bark and laid it flat to dry and season, turning it often during the next year to keep it from warping. The result was a pole that was about 10-ft long and lighter and more flexible than the aluminum poles that the high school boys used.

Mr. Friesen's main fault was that he really hated it if somebody made him look mortal. While playing soccer at school, I remember that a couple times when I checked him, I was able to take the ball away from him, only to get a vicious elbow in my back. It only encouraged me and the other kids to keep at him.

I was in Grade three, probably, when Eddy Zwollack started at our school, newly immigrated from Poland and barely able to speak English. The kids found it so amusing to hear Eddy speak Polish that we would get him to count from one to fifty or to say different things over and over in his native language. Eddy finally got tired of this, (which I later realized was harassment) and fought back. Thinking he could beat me, Eddy grabbed me and wrestled me to the ground. I managed to get my legs around his waist and just held him out of reach of his fists. I was content just to hold him away and I don't think he laid an actual punch on me. Finally the non-battle ended after about fifteen minutes when the teacher rang the bell. Anyway, we stopped bugging him after that. That was probably the only fight I had with anyone except Donny, which I'll talk about in the chapter "Lawrence and Lou".

When I was about eight, on a really cold day during the noon hour one of the boys, Harry, about twelve years old, and who had a dog team and sleigh to ride to school, decided to harness them to the sleigh and give rides to the other kids in the yard. The lead dog was a vicious husky, and while I had my back turned and couldn't see because of my parka hood covering most of my face, the team came near me and the husky bit my arm. The dog team driver, Harry, had to choke the dog to get it to release my arm. I didn't feel any pain at the moment but went into the school where the teacher peeled off several layers of clothing - parka, sweater, shirt, and long underwear. Eventually, he was able to see the wound - about an inch long and a half-inch wide and a half-inch deep. Mr. Friesen took a bottle of iodine (the only antiseptic available at that time, besides alcohol), poured it in the hole and bandaged it. He asked if I wanted to go home, but there was still no pain so I decided to stay till "home-time". About a half-hour later, the pain started and then I ran home. Mom looked at it and asked me if I wanted Dad to take me to the doctor to have it stitched up. That sounded even worse so I declined and Mom cared for me until it was healed. She changed the bandage morning and night, and applied a home remedy salve called Zam-Buck that she got from a Watkin's travelling sales-man. I think rabies shots had not yet been discovered, but there was no infection and it healed in about a month. I have always been afraid of dogs since that event. I'm amazed that my mother never panicked in a crisis, and always knew how to treat every ailment.

About two weeks later, on the way home from school, Harry was fol-lowing another boy, Hilliard, who was crouched on a little sled about 3-ft long and being pulled by his two dogs, when that same husky bit Hilliard on the ass seriously. There was a meeting of the School Board quickly called and Harry was told he would have to keep his dog team sheltered during the day in an abandoned log barn about a quarter mile from the school. Harry lived with his family in a cluster of log cabins near the Meadow River, occupied by dirt poor people, about four or five miles away, too far to walk.

Harry was in grade two when I started school, then over the course of the next three years, he went back to grade one, back to two, on to three, and then alternated between grade two and three monthly or even weekly, until one day he wasn't present to answer roll call. The teacher asked if anybody knew if Harry was sick, and someone volunteered "he's 15 today". That was the end of Harry's formal education. He got a job with a local rancher and became a successful rodeo rider, winning his share of purses.

Every month, on a Friday afternoon, our school held a "Junior Red Cross" party when we would bring goodies and play games or have a talent show. Mom would buy a package of cookies for me to take to the party, and because Mom always baked for us at home, "bought" cookies were always a special treat. Having to share was really painful, because the older kids took most of them and I would be left with soggy blueberry sand-wiches when I finally got my turn. I complained once but Mr. Friesen gave me shit in front of the class for being selfish. I was, and I have tried to change.

I remember one occasion during a talent show, I had to stand up and perform. For my performance I decided to sing a song that Yvette had been singing non-stop for days. Anyway I didn't know all the words, and I guess I didn't come close to the actual tune, so after one chorus I had to sit down because the whole class was booing and laughing at me. What an embarrassment.

One other talent show stands out as a classic. A little grade one boy, named Alfred, stood up to give a recitation, which he had composed himself, and after bowing, in a loud voice he recited: "Listen, listen, the horse is pissing". He bowed again and sat down to wild applause from all the class.

Whenever we had a geography bee, the winner would always be Eddy Zwollak, the Polish immigrant kid who knew the names of all the cities, lakes and rivers in Europe and Canada because he had been there. I devel-oped a deep yearning to visit those places someday. I managed it, but not until I retired, more than fifty years later.

One spring day about six of us kids were walking home from school when a sort of truck came by and stopped to give us a ride. The truck was a homemade vehicle that the two men in it had put together from used parts. There was a used chassis and engine and a steering wheel but every-thing else seemed to be made of lumber: a wooden flat deck and bench for the driver and passenger. We all piled on the flat deck, just sitting on the deck, while the driver started off at a fairly slow speed. I was the first to get off, but when I called out to stop, he just kept on. A couple kids who knew the driver and his friend, told me both of them were deaf/mutes. I panicked and jumped. Fortunately, we weren't going fast so I only suffered a few bruises when I hit the ground and rolled.

The Christmas concert was always a big event in our school, attended by all the families in the district, whether they had children attending the school or not. There were always two or three plays, interspersed with several carols, and ending with an appearance by Santa who distributed candy to all the kids. Every student got to perform in at least one of the plays, while the carols were sung by the entire class in unison, more or less. I remember one year that Mr. Friesen called Vic Williams and I aside and quietly asked us both to just move our lips, because our voices were putting off the rest of the class. I was really crushed, and in fact, I've never quite gotten over it. I was never asked to play lead actor in any of the plays, either. I was always a reindeer or something else that couldn't speak.

When I was about nine, a new family moved to a farm about two miles from us, including a daughter and three sons, all of whom went to our school. The youngest was called Elmer, and was a very skinny, malnourished kid. The boys at school quickly decided that having two kids named "Elmer" would be too complicated, so we had to find a solution. Someone asked what my middle name was, and I told them it was Joseph. From that day I was called "Joe" and the other kid was called "Little Joe".

The school was rented out for public dances occasionally. Most of the school kids were able to attend the dances but I was never allowed because of the activities taking place outside in the school yard. It would be pitch dark in the yard, but that didn't seem to hinder the bootleggers and their customers, and certainly not the lovers who seemed to find the ground quite comfortable under the circumstances.

When the war started in 1939, the government soon began issuing instructions through the rural schools, on how to assist our country through various incentives. For example, to increase the crop production we were paid one or two cents for each crow egg and each gopher tail because both those pests ate quite a bit of grain. Most of the kids took part to some degree, a few cut off the tails of the gophers and set them free in hopes they would grow new ones.

Male teachers enlisted in the armed forces in such numbers that many schools soon were scrambling to fill vacancies. Unfortunately, our school was no exception, as Mr. Friesen was hired by the town school board to fill a vacancy at a much higher salary. I was 12 years old at the time and starting Grade 7. The Saskatchewan government found a temporary solution by granting a license to any Grade 12 graduate who took a 6-week teacher training course. These temps were required to upgrade their training to obtain a regular certificate within a certain number of years after the war ended.

By necessity, we were forced to hire one of these temps. A couple members of the school board were Ukrainian and one had a nephew about 60 miles away who the Board hired. He turned out to be an 18-year old, awkward, boy who spoke broken English, and was unable to exert any discipline, and was totally incapable of teaching the subject matter. After a month, Mom asked how I was doing and how the teacher was doing. I said I still hadn't learned anything new. A week later, Mom announced that it was arranged that I would go to Prince Albert to live with Mirelda and her family and attend separate school two blocks away from her home. More on that in the next chapter.

The school board had fired the young Ukrainian teacher a couple weeks after I left and replaced him with a young female teacher who was more capable but still not able to properly discipline the students. The boys were having a blast harassing her almost daily.

One noon hour, they went into the wheat field adjoining the school yard and which had been cut and stooked. As one boy would lift a sheaf of grain, mice would be revealed scampering for safety. Other boys would be ready to catch them and put them in a box. When they had collected about twenty mice, they brought them into the school and released them, some in her desk drawers, and others onto the blackboard ledge where they raced back and forth, looking to escape but too scared to jump. When the teacher came back from her lunch break, she got a real scare, especially when she opened her desk drawers. She already knew the ringleaders, so she called them up to the front of the class, and brought out her strap. On about the third kid, she was already getting tired, so she placed her feet firmly on the floor about two feet apart and swung the strap really hard. The boy jerked his back just in time and she ended up hitting herself on the follow-through, - right where it hurts the most. He and the others got suspended.

This lady teacher did provide some erotic entertainment though. When she was teaching the Grade 7 and 8 students, she would move her chair to the front of their row, facing them. It wasn't long before one of the boys dropped his pencil and bending down to pick it up, was able to take a quick look up her skirt and realized she wasn't wearing panties. Golly, there was so much dropping of pencils and erasers in that class, that none of the boys learned much. Or maybe they learned a lot. The boys claimed that she knew what was going on, because she kept smiling and never crossed her legs.

Anyway, she also was quite pretty, and soon had a young local farmer courting her. The school was on the open prairie, with not a tree within a half mile, so everyone in the district knew by noon every day if there had been a certain red pickup parked next to the teacherage in the evening was still there before eight in the morning.

When I came home from Prince Albert, during the next year's Easter holidays, I went to school one day to see all my friends. The teacher seemed very pleasant but didn't provide any special entertainment for me.

Chapter 6

SCHOOL IN
PRINCE ALBERT

In 1943, when I was 12 and starting Grade 8, my teacher at Meadow River School moved to a job in town and his replacement was an eighteen year old high school grad with only a six-week training course and wasn't able to handle either the subject matter or the students. At the end of September, I still hadn't learned anything new so my parents arranged for me to go to Prince Albert to live with my sister, Mirelda, and her family to attend separate school.

Mirelda lived in a 3-room duplex owned by a convent and was located on the grounds of the convent, the same one that my other sister, Yvette, had attended for several years. Already in her home were her husband, Francis, and three children, Mona, Marty and Louis, all under the age of five. The bedroom had a double bed for Sis and Francis, another for Mona and Marty, and a cot for Louis. I slept on the chesterfield in the living room.

Francis worked as a linotype operator for a weekly newspaper, The Prairie Messenger, which was owned by the Catholic diocese, and he was earning very low wages. It was therefore necessary for him to find low-rent accommodation and supplement his income further with odd jobs. Part of the deal for the duplex required him to borrow a flat deck wagon and horses from the orphanage four blocks away and haul firewood from a wood shed at the back of the property to the convent furnace room twice a week. I was required to help with this chore. At least I didn't have to haul it with my little sled.

The new school proved to be quite an adjustment for me. My class consisted of about thirty students, far more than the entire eight grades in my country school, but much more disciplined and with totally different distractions. I soon adapted though, and got into the routines of life in the city. My teacher was a lovely nun, named Sister Marcien, who was excellent and there were never any disruptions in class.

I don't have any particular memories about the subjects that were taught except art. We were required to purchase pastels and art paper. That was the part I did well; the actual drawing and coloring was a disaster. I remember once we were asked to draw an apple, and my version looked nothing like the actual apple on the desk. Not even the shape was correct as my picture looked like a very much bruised piece of fruit with no shading of colors, etc.

I made a few friends at school, particularly the Page brothers, Gerald and Raymond, who lived just a half block away. They had two older sisters, Jeanette who was a sweet but plain girl, and Madelaine who was a beautiful auburn haired girl that was very popular with all the young local men.

Another boy that I knew at school was about a year older than me, named Bobby McGrath, and for some reason he made an impression on me, because in 1963, twenty years later, I saw him sitting at a desk at Tide Bay Construction in New Westminster working on a tax audit and I called him by name. He said he had no idea who I was but sure hoped he didn't owe me any money.

The Page boys and I joined the Army Cadets and I was very excited to receive and wear a uniform for our weekly drill at the local armory. The drills consisted of endless practice in saluting and marching with wooden rifles, and some other useful skills such as map reading, use of a compass, and marksmanship using real rifles and live ammunition. The best part of the parade night drill was that before we went home, we were able to go into the canteen and buy all sorts of treats that were rationed or not even available to the public, especially chocolate bars. Besides the one evening per week spent at the armory, we often were required to go on marches in the country side on weekends, and actually use our map reading and compass skills.

The duplex we lived in had a very tiny bit of front yard which was meant to be lawn but was mostly just bare dirt, and fronted a driveway for the convent. Twice a day the convent girls were required to go for a half-hour walk in the neighborhood and started out on that driveway past our house. It was very seldom the girls had a chance to even see a boy and there was I, a very shy but, at least, a live specimen in their back yard. We used to wave to each other and if I was outside, we'd speak a few words if the nun wasn't watching. The convent girls used to whistle when they saw me in my army cadet uniform, proving that girls are always attracted to men in uniform.

During the winter, the local skating arena provided free skating one afternoon per week for all of the school students in the city. Both separate schools and the convent shared the same time slot. Naturally most of the convent girls wanted to skate with me and I recall often there would be a tug-o'-war between two of the girls with me in the middle. It certainly wasn't my skating prowess that attracted them; more the fact I was the only boy they knew. We would skate around the ice surface more or less in time to the music for the duration of a song, then change partners.

Mirelda and Francis used to go to the movies once per week and I would baby sit the three kids. The kids were only a few years younger than me, so there wasn't much discipline but lots of fun. I remember that I learned that if you put some vinegar and a spoon full of baking soda in a pop bottle, sealed it with a cork and shook it, the cork would pop off like champagne. Mirelda one day asked me if I knew how come we had all the round white stains on the kitchen ceiling. I certainly couldn't explain such an odd phenomenon, except possibly a miracle. Anyway, the round stains stopped manifesting themselves about that same time.

One evening when I was babysitting the kids and had put them to bed, they began jumping on the beds and horsing around. I finally went into the bedroom to give them the usual threats about what I would do if they didn't settle down, and as usual, was treated with ignore. So I got Louis a bottle of milk hoping that would help, which it didn't. The baby bottle consisted of a Coke bottle full of milk, with a nipple stretched over the top. Louis liked to grip the nipple in his teeth or in his fist and swing the bottle around. I lay down beside him on his bed to ensure they would settle down and in a few minutes everyone was asleep including me. Suddenly, Louis swung the bottle and hit me in the eye. Man, that hurt, and I woke to find Louis laughing at me. I wore a shiner for about a week and the kids at school were sure I had been in a fight.

Sis and Francis went to play bingo one winter evening and were really lucky, winning a whole lot of Pyrex bowls and cookware which they actually needed. It was a 3-night bingo event so they went again the next night and won more. I was babysitting for these nights out, and on the third night there was a bit of bad luck. The kids were playing tag and while they were crawling under the china cabinet, the first kid stopped, the others ran into him and they all tried to straighten up and bumped their heads on the bottom of the cabinet. There was the sound of falling dishware inside the cabinet, so they scampered out and quickly opened the doors of the cabinet. Out fell most of the Pyrex cookware onto the floor, breaking several of the items. When she came home with Francis, Mirelda was really upset and cried over the loss. Fortunately they had again won several more pieces of Pyrex cookware plus they had a good time being winners at least until they got home. I guess I wasn't the most dependable babysitter, but at least I worked cheap.

That winter, Francis got a part-time job unloading railway ties from the boxcars at the creosoting plant. I was able to help and also received part of the piecework wages. The boxcars were shunted onto sidings and the ties that had been cut in the woods were stacked inside right to the roof. They had to be unloaded and placed side by side in rows about forty feet long. After each row was completed we had to place a single row of ties end to end along one edge of the previous row and then place the next row side by side with one end raised off the previous ties to provide a space for air circulation. The ties were green wood and weighed a lot, so we dragged them from the boxcar along that uneven surface with the use of a pick which was stuck into the end of each tie and then pulled it into place. After the ties were seasoned, they then were transferred to the creosoting plant for treatment and then were used for rail line repairs. It was hard labor, but I worked with Frank at that job until the end of the school term.

Lawrence was married and living with his wife and daughter, Marlene, across town in Prince Albert and so I went to visit most weekends and often stayed overnight, sleeping on the sofa. They treated me nicely and I was naturally the butt of Lawrence's constant teasing and practical jokes.

I never even wondered where I would go to high school but fortunately Mom and Mirelda did. It was arranged that I would go to boarding school at St. Peter's College, the Benedictine monastery in Muenster, Saskatchewan, which Francis had attended during his high school and short-lived studies for the priesthood.

Elmer in Army Cadets uniform, age 13

Chapter 7

BOARDING SCHOOL

To start my Grade 9 in September, 1944, I left for St. Peter's College in Muenster, Sask., taking the train east to Prince Albert then south to Humboldt, about half way to Regina, and directly east of Saskatoon. It was arranged that one of the priests from the college would meet the train and drive me to the college, about six miles east. I arrived at midnight, getting off the train by myself and with no one waiting for me. The plan was already in trouble.

This was my first time travelling alone with no family to meet me and I didn't know what to do. I waited on the train platform for quite a while until the station agent came out to see if I needed help. After explaining that someone was supposed to meet me, the agent phoned the college and one of the prefects, Father Jerome, (afterwards referred to as "Jerry") who said he would be along shortly and I should just wait in the station. An hour later I began to fear that I had been abandoned and got scared, just thinking that I might never be rescued. The agent again phoned Jerry who again assured that he would be along soon and to just be patient. Jerry finally showed up at about eight o'clock in the morning, well rested, and without any apology, took me to the college where I spent most of the next two years. It was a bad start to my year and I missed my family terribly, crying myself to sleep each night during the first couple weeks and never anyone to comfort or reassure me. Many of the other young boys also had similar difficulties in adjusting to life away from family.

College life saw our days filled with activities and study. The school's main object was to prepare all students for the priesthood through superior standards of education in both secular and religious subjects. There were about eighty boarding students plus about ten day students who lived in the area, and consisted of mainly grades 9 - 12. The college had one of highest standards of education in Saskatchewan. About four students who had graduated from Grade 12 stayed on in the Second Arts program, which was actually a seminary preparing them for the priesthood and involved several more years of study.

The teachers were all priests. Two of them, Fathers Alfred and Jerry, were also prefects and were responsible for the daily supervision of the students. The whole college, along with the farm operation, came under the rector, a priest named Father Xavier, known to all students as "X". The top of the ladder, responsible for spiritual life, was the abbot. The large farm, which raised several grains plus cattle, chickens, pigs, etc., as well as large vegetable gardens and an apiary, was staffed by several brothers. The kitchen, laundry, mending and other similar work was done by a group of cloistered nuns. Being cloistered meant they were shut off from the outside world, never talked to or were seen by anyone that was not of their group.

Jerry was very stern and strict, but also kind of sneaky, always appearing out of nowhere at the most inopportune times. I guess he'd seen every trick in the book hundreds of times which kept him way out ahead of the students.

The main building was a four story red brick building with a bell tower on top. There were three student dormitories on the fourth floor, the main one having about sixty cots in two long rows, and the others each had about ten beds. The largest dorm had a set of four windows about every fifteen feet along the outside wall, with two walk-in closets between the windows. The closets were back to back and we stored our suitcases on the floor and hung our clothes on hooks on the walls of the closets. All of the windows were kept wide open at night, year round, to make sure we got enough fresh air. In the winter the air was so fresh it was positively insulting. In the mornings we found our facecloths were frozen onto the metal frames of our beds where we hung them the previous night at bedtime.

Our day started at 6:00 a.m. with the sound of a shrill bell that sounded like a fire alarm which rang for five seconds, which was four seconds longer than was necessary. But Jerry thought it was necessary, no matter that our heads reverberated for the next ten minutes. We had about half an hour to wash, dress and make our beds and get to the chapel on the third floor for mass every morning. After mass we went to the refectory in the basement for breakfast, then an hour walk, before starting our studies.

At 8:00 a.m. we filed into the study hall: it held all eighty students, each at a desk which contained all of our books and supplies, in about ten or twelve rows, with the prefect at a desk on a raised platform so that he could watch over everyone. We started with a few minutes of prayer, followed by study until 8:45.

We then went to our classrooms for three one-hour classes, followed at 11:45 by fifteen minutes of study, and then lunch. After lunch we had until 1:00 pm to go for a short walk. On Mondays, Wednesdays, and Fridays we went into the study hall for a half hour of study followed by two one-hour classes, then were free to play sports or whatever till 5:00. On Tuesdays, Thursdays and Saturdays we had study period till 2:00 p.m. then were free for sports, etc., until 5:00. We then had study until 6:00 followed by dinner. After dinner we were free until 7:30 then studied until 9:00 when we went to the chapel for evening prayers and then to bed. The study periods included doing lots of homework, but after 8:00 p.m. we were allowed to write letters or read novels.

On Sunday, after mass and breakfast, we had study from 8:00-9:00 a.m., attended high mass at 10.00-11:00, then were free till 11:45 when we assembled in the study hall before lunch. After lunch we had another hour of study before free time from 2:00-5:00. That's when the regular weekday routine till bedtime kicked in again, that is, study until 6:00, followed by dinner and free time until 7:30, then study until 9:00, then chapel and bedtime.

That worked out to about 24 hours of class time and nearly 30 hours of study time per week. With all that study and class time it's no bloody wonder the school had the highest standards of education in the province.

All students were required to take Latin, because so many of the Catholic rituals were in that language. My Latin teacher was Jerry, who, as I have mentioned was really strict and had no sense of humor. In fact, I'm sure he enjoyed watching us cower in our seats, worrying that we might not have the correct answer to whatever question he might ask. As a result, Latin became my best subject and I always received marks of at least 90% on my monthly report card. I was able to read and write Latin but never could speak it. Other subjects were not nearly as good, but I usually averaged about 75-80%. One of the older boys, named Bill Gray, was very helpful to me with my Latin and other subjects. He was in Grade 12 during my first year and stayed on for the Second Arts program, eventually becoming a very highly regarded priest. I learned that his mother had nursed my mother in the sanitarium when I was just a year old.

In the dining room, we sat at tables of six boys each, with the two prefects at a smaller table in the middle of the dining room where they could supervise everyone. Students waited on tables, one for each two tables. They ate after everyone else was finished and received extra food plus some other privileges.

On weekdays, for breakfast we had cooked cereal, either lumpy oatmeal, lumpy cream of wheat, or lumpy Red River Cereal. There was also bread and butter and honey or carrot jam with milk or coffee to drink. The coffee was heavily laced with saltpeter in order to diminish any sexual urges we might develop. The butter consisted of a slab about a quarter-inch thick cut from one-pound bricks. The piece was seldom sliced evenly, so we took turns at each table in dividing the slab into six portions as evenly as possible, with the boy who divided it getting the last portion. Sometimes the slab would be a half-inch thick on side, tapering to almost nothing on the other side. The cutter had to be a genius at geometry in order to ensure he was left with anywhere near an equal share.

At every meal there was a frenzied scramble to empty the serving bowls and rush the waiter back to the pass-through window from the kitchen in order to request refills. Usually we got at least one refill, and sometimes even a second. Often it was necessary to fill up on dry bread, sprinkled with salt and pepper. The jam, a teaspoon-full each, was home-made by the nuns from carrots and wasn't very tasty but was edible most of the time, although it occasionally became fermented and a new batch had to be prepared, lest we start enjoying it.

The carrot jam was a substitute for honey which the college produced from its own apiary. The college farm had several bee hives, enough to satisfy all our needs in most years, but that year there was very little honey produced for some reason, like a cold or wet spring and summer.

Sunday breakfast was a special treat, usually consisting of corn flakes, bread, butter, honey and milk or coffee. Again, the portion of honey for each of us was a teaspoon full. The best thing about the honey was that we could mix it with our little pat of butter and then have enough to thinly cover two pieces of bread. I still like the taste of the honey-butter mixture.

Bringing our own jam or peanut butter into the dining room was strictly forbidden and resulted in the loss of privileges if we were caught by the prefects. Nevertheless, many kids often did sneak a little container of something into the dining room. We had one obnoxious kid named Babich (but called "Baby") at our table, and he talked constantly and was disliked by everyone. He threatened to squeal on someone at the table if that kid didn't share his peanut butter with him, so he received enough to cover his slice of bread. The next morning Baby did the same thing and received a slice of bread covered with a layer of Exlax, which he ate thinking it was peanut butter. That was the last time he threatened to squeal because we threatened to punch him out if he did.

The kids always resented seeing the prefects getting all they could eat, while we often left the table still hungry. I don't mean we starved, but it's pretty hard to fully satisfy the capacity of the average teen-aged boy.

In my second year at St. Peter's College, my chum Donald Bubnick and I sneaked into Muenster to buy a loaf of bread and a jar of jam to eat in the dorm. As luck would have it, Jerry suddenly appeared on the path leading through the trees from the College. He just nodded and walked on, leaving us to spend all afternoon and night worrying what our fate would be. The next day at lunch time, we got the sentence: short bounds until further notice. Short bounds limited us to the small yard, a distance of about fifty yards around the building. The incident happened in early May and the sentence wasn't ever lifted.

Lunch and dinner usually consisted of potatoes, vegetables and stew with bread and butter. The stew contained one small piece of meat for each of us with a lot of gravy. We always covered slices of bread on our plates with gravy, as much as we could get, most often two slices.

We all believed we were being starved but when I got home in June my mom was amazed to see that the legs of my suit pants which were almost touching the floor in September were now just about mid-calf.

Parcels from home were allowed and deeply appreciated by many of the students. My pal Bubnick got a parcel every couple weeks and it usually contained a cake plus a lot of sweets and sometimes a pack of smokes. He always shared the cake with me because it might have become stale. Mom and Dad spent the winters in New Westminster while I was at college, so they were not able to send parcels to me, except for once, when I received one which contained about a pound of divinity fudge.

The first Christmas I was at college my folks arranged for me to spend it in Leask with my cousin, Pat, and Aunt Annie and the rest of her family. I had a good time, probably better than if I had gone home to the farm with just my parents for company. The next I spent in Saskatoon with my sister, Mirelda, and her family, now increased by one, Caroline. I spent one Easter with Lawrence and his family in Prince Albert, and the second I went home to the farm.

We never had ice cream at meal time at the college, but we were able to get a bowl of vanilla ice cream for working for two hours in the garden, weeding. Many of the kids spent many afternoons working in the garden. I once worked two hours weeding and when I got my ice cream, I could barely eat it because it was so bitter. It seemed that when the cows were feeding on new grass in the spring, it tainted the milk and hence also the ice cream.

We were often served hard boiled eggs, especially during Lent. Once, I opened my egg only to find a partially developed chick inside. That finished me with boiled eggs for about ten years, especially when served in the shell.

Food was often used as pranks in the dormitory after lights-out. Kids would sometimes smuggle a hard-boiled egg or two from the refectory and stash it in their closet in the dorm. After everyone was in bed, the egg would be hurled, glancing off the wall, and spraying egg and shell for twenty yards over everything and everybody.

Another stunt was to bring cornflakes from Sunday breakfast and use them to warn of the approach of Jerry when he did his patrols after lights-out. The aisle between the two rows of beds was about four feet wide and the floor boards squeaked when anyone stepped on them. Anyone, that is, except Jerry, who knew every board that squeaked and was able to walk the entire length of the dorm undetected. Hence, a light sprinkle of cornflakes across the aisle about thirty feet away provided ample warning to turn off your crystal set or hide your snack.

Bed time proved to be the favorite time for most pranks. It was seldom that at least one kid didn't climb into his bed only to find his sheet had been frenched (folded in half) and his feet would reach about only half way to the foot of his bed. Another trick after lights-out was to dump a pail of cold water on someone that was sound asleep. I was doused once during my two years at the college. It happened on a cold winter night and I thought I'd freeze before morning. I never learned who the prankster was that soaked me.

One student who wasn't the sharpest tool in the shed was doused with cold water at least once per week. He was a really tall, awkward, boy who suffered from a bad case of acne and used to sit in the study hall and pick his pimples with his compass point. One night, one boy doused him and as he sat up in bed another boy took his picture. Another student, who operated a film developing business on the side, developed the film and sold several copies to the other students. I'm sure he was the boy who took the picture because he was the only one that owned a flash camera.

There was very seldom any actual fighting, and I only once saw a blow landed. It happened one winter morning after breakfast when we were leaving for our morning walk. It involved Babich and another kid from my class, named Pat Rooney. Pat came from the orphanage in Prince Albert and he was quite short but a tough Irishman with a short fuse. Babich had been babbling all through breakfast and continued while coming out the door. Pat had had all he could stand and he warned Babich that if he heard one more peep from him, he'd punch him in the nose. Babich said "peep" and Pat punched him on the nose, making it bleed. Father Jerome had just come out the door and witnessed the entire incident. Jerry just walked past, smiling. It was one of the few times I saw Jerry smile.

We had access to the day room for about a half hour in the afternoon and again after dinner until 7:30 p.m. The day room had a small mantle radio on a shelf in a cabinet at one end of the room that usually had about ten boys huddled around it listening to modern music. The rest of the room contained three long tables with benches for the boys to play checkers or cards. The older boys were allowed to smoke in this room or outside. I was still too young to smoke so Bubnick and I had to sneak our smokes. Bubnick actually got a few packs of cigarettes in his parcels from home, and I was able to get an older boy to buy me tobacco from the tuck shop. During my summer holidays mom told me that the college had notified her that I was smoking and asked for instructions. She told them I had been smoking for a few years already, so not to punish me for it. Although she wished I wouldn't smoke, I should just try to cut back.

After Christmas, in Grade 10, my folks agreed to pay for me to take piano lessons. I never actually learned to play any tune with any degree of skill, but it got me out of the study hall for a couple hours each week. I had a lesson once per week in the afternoon, and I had permission two afternoons per week to go to a classroom where there was a piano on which to practice. I never could play more than a few bars of The Blue Danube, Celita Linda, and Flow Gently Sweet Afton; the last two were never recognizable by anyone listening. However, the classroom was next door to the Day Room, so I was able to sneak in there for a smoke and break the tedium, until one day when I found a man in there already having a smoke. He was a former RCAF pilot who had just been discharged and was completing his Grade 12 in preparation to attend university. We were standing in the dark by the door, watching for any approaching prefect, when I suddenly became aware of a hand on my groin. I suddenly got the heck out of there and right back to the study hall. When I confided to Bubnick what had happened, he just laughed and said "he finally got around to you, eh? He's already hit on most of the young guys."

Religion was naturally the most emphasized of any subject or activity. The first class of the day was always Catechism, and it included sex education for about two weeks each year which I didn't really understand because the words were not the ones I was accustomed to.

Every winter, about February, we stopped everything in order to attend a retreat. This was about five or six days to reflect on our futures and to consider if we were leaning towards becoming priests, as well as to repent our sins and plan how we could become better Christians. During this retreat we had to fast and to remain silent except for a few minutes in the afternoon. It was not a realistic exercise for me and I often met Donald Bubnick in secret for cigarettes and a chat. Many of the other kids did likewise.

In my second year, I found that some of the older boys also broke the rules. A couple days after we finished retreat, we were visited in the study hall just after studies began at 7:30 p.m., by the rector. He said that he had been advised by someone that had attended a dance in Humboldt one evening while we had been on retreat and had identified four of the college students who were there along with some girls. Nearly everyone gasped and/or snickered at just the thought of such a sacrilege. He then asked the guilty parties to stand up and admit their guilt and accept whatever punishment would be meted out. Nobody moved for about a half-hour. Finally, the deafening silence was broken by a series of gasps, when one Grade 11 and three Grade 12 students stood up and were ushered to the rector's office. What a scandal!!!

The next day we learned the sordid details. The Grade 11 boy had arranged with his older sister to meet them in Muenster with the family car and drive all of them to the dance, and to bring her girlfriend and a bottle of whiskey. After "lights out" at 9:30 p.m. they waited until Jerry did his patrol in the darkened dormitory. Then, about ten o'clock, they climbed down the fire escape from the dormitory to the ground, jogged into town and met the girls and the car, then proceeded to the dance in Humboldt.

The punishment varied among the boys following discussions with their parents. Two were expelled immediately and a third was allowed to stay until the end of the school year. The fourth was forgiven because his parents convinced the rector that he would become a priest (I don't think he ever did become a priest). The reaction by the students was mixed, some believing all four should be expelled while others thought they were some sort of heroes. Most of us thought the entire episode was just plain stupid and immature or funny.

A few of the students played hooky occasionally claiming they were too sick to get up for school. I once tried it on the advice of a friend who was a year older than me. Sure enough, we each received a breakfast tray in bed and afterwards I settled down with a library book. Jerry arrived later with a thermometer. I knew we didn't have fevers so my pal showed me how he shook the thermometer enough to indicate an increase of a few degrees. I had never used a thermometer before or read it, and so I shook it pretty hard. Jerry acted quite concerned and told me he would check it again in an hour and if it still was as high, he would call an ambulance to take me to the hospital in Humboldt. When he came back an hour later we both were relieved to learn that I had made a complete recovery and I would be able to get up for lunch. I never played hooky again.

Every year, in February, the college put on a concert which ran for three nights and invited the public as a fund raiser. The concert included a three act play, plus two violin renditions of classical music by Father Paul, who was a fantastic musician. One of the students, Bernie Feehan, was a great comedian who would recite a funny monologue and tell some jokes. All three performances were usually sold out with just standing room for the students on the one night we were able to attend.

22Hockey was naturally the favorite sport during the winter. We had a regulation size outside rink, complete with a change room heated by a wood-fired space heater. Father Jerome was responsible for the hockey program. When the weather turned cold about the end of October, Jerry would flood the rink and then build up the ice surface and paint the lines and then every morning he would repair cracks or gouges with the water hose. Of course, spraying to the outside edge resulted in about a half-inch buildup of ice all around the bottom of the boards.

While playing hockey during my second year one day I got the puck on a breakaway and headed for the goal. An opponent managed to reach me with his stick, tripping me, and I ended up on my back, sliding head first into the ice-coated boards. I was out cold for a few minutes but I recovered and was left with a damaged spine, both neck and lumbar areas.

Jerry listed all the kids, assigned them to teams, and the teams to three leagues based on skill levels, and prepared a schedule that ran until spring, including playoffs. My brother Lou came to visit me at the college in 1946 when he arrived back from the war in Europe. We went for dinner at the hotel in Muenster and went back to college where I had to play hockey in a play-off game. I was never very good at hockey but Lou made me feel good by telling me he was impressed.

My skates were hand-me-downs given me by Francis who had got them second-hand when he attended St. Peter's about fifteen years earlier. They were suede and really shabby, and too big for my feet, necessitating at least two pairs of socks in order to keep them on. The result was that I looked like I was almost skating on my ankles. A priest named Father William was watching us play one day and he called me over and asked me if I was wearing Frank Sader's skates. I asked him how he knew and he replied that about fifteen years earlier he had been Frank's coach and the skates still looked the same.

The college included a team consisting of the best hockey players, mostly Grade 12's, who competed in the Saskatchewan Junior League. The team was called "The Squad", and played against teams from Prince Albert, Humboldt and other places within a couple hundred miles radius. One of our players was signed by an NHL team but was cut during his first training camp. I guess he had spent too much time studying and not enough time playing hockey.

There was a locked room in the basement in which there were stored a lot of pairs of skis which we could borrow for a few hours in order to do cross country skiing. The main problem with them was that they had no bindings, just a loose strap that went over your foot. The result was that your feet were constantly twisting and sliding off the skis causing falls, and sometimes bruised egos.

One afternoon, I was skiing along the creek bank about a mile from the main building when the trail I was following turned down the bank and between some trees and bushes. One of my skis caught on a tree and I fell backwards, my coxyx (tail bone) hitting a rock that was under two inches of snow. I would have needed about two feet of snow over the rock to prevent serious injury. Man!! That hurt. I just lay there until the nausea eased, then made my slow and painful return to the college. It was still really sore when I returned to playing hockey about a week later and that's when I fell on my ass and hurt it again.

The college built two double handball courts for us about three blocks away from the main building. They each consisted of a large cement pad divided in the center by a brick wall in the form of an "H". It hurt the hands a lot because I didn't have gloves, just winter mittens. It hurt our knees even more when we fell onto the concrete base.

I enjoyed tennis and played quite a bit of it over my two years at the college. There were two paved courts and were in good condition.

Swimming was in the creek which had been dammed on the farm north of the College to form a little lake about 200 yards in diameter and which had a diving platform. The water was about 10 or 12 feet deep in the deepest part. I was dog-paddling in the deep area one afternoon when one of the bigger kids pushed me under. I came up spluttering for air and he dunked me again. I thought I was going to drown, and would have, except that another kid pulled me out. Because the pond had no drainage or intake except during the early spring, the water became stagnant and everyone got swimmer's itch.

One of the neighbors about a half-mile to the east had a large dugout that he maintained for a water supply for his cattle. About ten or more of us went there to swim most afternoons during my last year there. My problem was that I was still confined to short bounds and had to ask Jerry's special permission to go swimming. Asking to go to the neighbor's dugout would have been ridiculous (the neighbor had a gorgeous teenage daughter and Jerry, I'm sure, would have wanted to protect her), so I just asked if I could go swimming. Donald Bubnick and I would leave with a group of boys for the dam. Then after crossing the tracks, Bubnick and I would crouch down and run till we reached the neighbor's fence line, then cross back over the tracks, and run along a ditch until we reached the dugout. After our swim we would casually walk past the neighbor's house, then down the lane back to the college.

I'm sure sneaking was a wasted exercise because Jerry used to go up into the bell tower and with his binoculars could see everything and everyone for miles, including us smart guys who thought we were getting away with something.

Every month we received a report card, with a copy sent to our parents. If anyone received a mark of "III"(60-70%), or "IV"(50-60%), in any subject(s), the student was required to see the rector, Father Xavier, to determine what the problem was. I was required every month to see X. After discussing whatever subjects I might be having a problem with, X always asked me what I wanted to be when I grew up. I always thought I'd like to be something different from the last month, and it would range from pilot, Mountie, sailor, or store keeper, etc. Then he would ask whether I would like to be a priest. I always answered NO!!! Then he would ask me to ponder about my future and he'd see me again the next month.

Most of the students said they were leaning towards the priesthood and I think all of them were welcomed back the next following year and a few actually became priests. However, in July, my parents received word that I would have to go elsewhere for Grade 11. I know it sounds like I got into a lot of trouble at College but I was in about the middle of the pack and I'm sure I would have been encouraged to return if I lied about wanting to be a priest. I know that Bubnick always told X that he planned to become a priest and he returned every year until he finished his Grade 12. He then became a teacher in Esterhazy, Sask. Becoming a priest is a desirable calling, and Mom would have been more proud of me, but I just couldn't visualize myself serving God in such a manner. On the other hand, the college was right in wanting to reserve the few spaces available for students that may be destined for the priesthood.

As it turned out, Dad decided to give up the farm and retire in Saskatoon where Mirelda was now living. Everything seemed to turn out okay.

Boarding School - St Peter's College 1943-1945

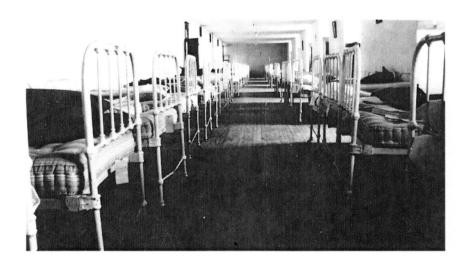

Boarding School - Dormitory - 80 beds

Boarding School - Elmer 13/14

Chapter 8

HIGH SCHOOL IN SASKATOON

When the farm was sold in 1946, my parents took a quick trip to Saskatoon and bought a bungalow on the south side of the city in a newer area, called Nutana. I enrolled in the Nutana High School which had several hundred students, about eighty or ninety in each grade.

On my first morning at school I was assigned a home room and that's where I was greeted by a student, named Bill MacDonald, who welcomed me and we immediately became fast friends and remained so until I left Saskatoon for good in 1954.

Being in such a huge school was a big adjustment for me and it was some time before I felt really comfortable with the new routine.

First was the fact that it was co-ed, and I couldn't believe it when a cute girl, named Althea, made eyes at me. After a couple weeks I asked her to go to the movies with me. The date didn't go too well for me, being a farm boy, and I wasn't used to being with a girl after two years in an all-boys boarding school. In the following week, another girl invited me and Bill MacDonald to a party at her home on the Crescent, a street of beautiful houses across the street from the river. Her father must have been wealthy. Bill was pretty excited about it because this was a very exclusive clique and he had been hoping to get into the group since Grade 9. Bill and I went together to the party; and, low and behold, there was Althea, obviously the reason I had been invited. The kids played some games and danced to some of the modern music of the time. I didn't know how to dance so they taught me to do the "Nutana Shuffle", a modified jive. At the end of the party, we played a game ("fixed" by the girls) to select partners to walk the girls home and I ended up with Althea, naturally. I was stuck with Althea, it seems, even if I didn't much care for her. I continued to be included in the house parties until we moved across town at Christmas. About the end of October, the school put on a Sadie Hawkins dance and another girl that had caught my eye in class asked me to go with her. Even Bill was envious of my good luck. I only went out with her once because I couldn't afford steady dating.

School was a mixed bag for me. I was taking Latin and found that when I was in Grade 10, at St. Peter's College, Father Jerome had covered all the Grade 11 material we would be taking till Christmas. Also, it seemed that I knew more Latin than the teacher did. The result was that the teacher passed all the questions in class to me for answers, if he didn't know them. Secondly, because my homework was usually correct, all the boys borrowed my paper to copy before I handed it in. By the time I did hand it in it was always crinkled up and dirty. At the same time, I was copying Bill's answers to the Math homework. On our Christmas report cards we were not surprised to learn that Bill and all the other boys had flunked Latin and I had flunked Math.

My Math teacher had returned from the war and was in poor health and was in a lot of pain, hence he had a mean disposition. He just had to ask me a simple question and I became scared and tongue-tied. One day, one of the students had his dog follow him to school and "Army" Armstrong, the owner, had got him to lie quietly in the far aisle, which happened to be next to me. During class, the dog started to scratch a flea, making a loud thumping sound as his leg hit the floor with every scratch. The teacher turned around from the blackboard and looked directly at me. The dog chose that very moment to stop scratching. About two seconds after the teacher had resumed writing on the blackboard the stupid dog started scratching and thumping on the floor again. I started sweating and wondering how I could get out of the room without a beating. The dog stopped again just as the teacher headed down the aisle towards me. Fortunately the dog started scratching and thumping again just in time. The teacher then spied the dog, asked if it was mine and I said "no". Army said it was his dog, and the teacher merely told him to leave him at home in future. Army had a big laugh at me for nearly being kicked out of class. That teacher reminded me a lot of Father Jerome, and they were the only two teachers I ever feared like that.

Altogether, I quite enjoyed school at Nutana, but Mom and Dad decided to move across town to the Caswell Hill district at Christmas and bought a cute little bungalow three blocks from Mirelda and her family.

After the Christmas holidays, I enrolled at Bedford Road Collegiate, which was about eight blocks from our house, and only about three blocks east of Mirelda's. The high school had been built during the war and was used by the army for instructing the troops in technical training. A noted politician, Roy Romanow, who graduated from Bedford two years after me, later became the premier of Saskatchewan.

I really enjoyed my nearly two years at Bedford and made many good friends, including a few that I regained touch with many years later out in BC.

One such friend was Eugene "Homer" Hearne who was in Grade 12 and a year older than me. He was a boy I had met during my previous Christmas visit to Mirelda, and was a mutual friend of Bernie (Bono) Feehan from college and whose home also was in Saskatoon. Through my friendship with Homer, I became a member of a group of about six guys who hung out together, playing sports, pool, dancing and partying. We all smoked but none of us drank liquor because it might hurt us in playing sports. In the next few years after high school we all caught up with all the beer drinking we had missed.

Homer was into competitive speed skating and belonged to the Saskatoon Speed Skating Club. They had a speed skating oval and club-house on the west side of town and I used to go with him often to practices and local competitions. Afterwards, several of the skaters and I would stay for a while, playing cards or rumoli. Homer gave me a pair of his skates that he had replaced with better ones, so I used to practice speed skating when the rink was not in use. I was never fast enough to compete. Two of the boys were on the team that went to the Olympics to compete in 1948.

In the spring, Homer and another friend, named Jim Moore, and I spent several Saturdays at the University Of Saskatchewan grounds snaring gophers. We'd each pack a lunch and spend the day there. There was a small pond nearby so that as a last resort we could drive them out of their holes with water. We would separate and see who could catch the most gophers. Moore could crouch beside a gopher hole for hours without ever making a sound. As a result, he earned the nickname "Silent" which stayed with him for years.

That same day, Homer came looking for me and found me near a patch of bull rushes by the pond, and I got the nickname of "Moses" (as in "Moses in the Bull Rushes"), and that has stuck with me all my life.

Another friend in my class was Ken Ross who had an evening job in the park near my house, playing music for a couple hours at the free outdoor skating rink. Ken would bring a bunch of his own records, which would be mainly jitterbug, jazz, ballads and other modern music. These supplemented and out-played the records that the park supplied, like "The Skaters' Waltz" and other classical numbers. The little office at one end of the skate-change room was nice and warm and we'd spend most weekday evenings there during the winter.

One afternoon, a friend from high school, came over with his parents to visit for an hour or so and when they were leaving they asked if I would like to join them while they went to see some other friends down the street. I said sure, because the friends they were referring to were the Howe family. That's how I got to meet the great Gordie Howe, who had just completed his rookie season in the NHL and was already recognized as a future all-star.

One evening there was a concert and dance downtown starring Louis Armstrong and Jack Teagarten, who were world renowned jazz musicians, and our entire crowd planned to go. This was in the winter of 1947, the year after Jack Teagarten became the first white musician to ever play in a black band, Armstrong's, and it also was the year after Jackie Robinson became the first black person to play for a major league baseball team. Both of these events are recognized as milestones in the battle for equal rights for black people. Louis Armstrong was later named a special US goodwill ambassador.

My only problem was that I couldn't jive properly. On the Saturday evening prior to the concert, we were at a house party, and on the way home I told Homer and the other guys of my problem. Homer said no problem, he'd teach me right now. So we stopped under a street lamp and he showed me the basic moves without worrying about my feet. As Homer explained it, the dance hall would be so crowded that no one would be able to see my feet, anyway, and I could work on that part later. Sure enough, the dance was great, the music was great, and I had a great time.

After Grade 11, during the summer of 1947, Homer and I got jobs at a concession booth at the exhibition. This particular booth had a large bunch of young men who carried trays of about 30 or more ice cream cones to sell in the grandstand. Homer's job was scooping ice cream to fill cones and my job was washing the trays. The concession stand operated during the horse races in the afternoons and again during the grandstand shows in the evenings. In the afternoons we were able to watch some of the races and won a couple dollars on the last day betting on a horse we picked to win. For a week of backbreaking work we each received fifteen dollars.

With my fifteen dollars I decided to travel. First, I took the bus to Meadow Lake where Yvette and her husband, Albert, met me and took me to Goodsoil, about thirty miles northwest where they lived. They were operating a small grocery store there and Yvette was teaching in the local elementary school. I spent a week with them and during that time we went camping for about three or four days at a lake about four hours away by horse and wagon. It was a beautiful lake and totally isolated. Our group also included Albert's twin brother, Herman, his younger sister, plus two cousins, a young man about the same age as Albert, and his sister, Annemarie, who was my age. The fishing was good – pickerel - and the scenery was fantastic.

From Goodsoil I went back to Meadow Lake and caught a ride on a truck hauling freight to Ile a la Crosse, about 150 miles north, an all day trip, to visit Emile and his family. Other passengers included a trapper and his wife who had brought their furs down for sale at the fur auction in Saskatoon and had invested their earnings in liquor and were now heading back to their trap line, nursing the grand-daddy of all hangovers. They were good friends of the trucker (had often partied together), so they sat in the cab with the driver. The other passenger was a young man returning north from a visit to town. He and I sat in the back of the open truck, perched on the load of freight; not the most comfortable seating.

It had recently rained, so the dirt road was full of muddy pot holes which made the ride that much more uncomfortable. In late afternoon while driving through a big, deep, mud hole, we got stuck. While trying to get out of the hole, the rear axle broke. That meant the trucker had to walk about 10 miles to where there was a small sawmill to arrange for a machine to tow us out of the mud hole. By the time that was done, it was too dark to replace the axle. Never willing to pass up an opportunity to party the three in the cab had a bottle of rum to keep them amused, and they had great time till about midnight. That left me only a few hours of trying to sleep, while leaning against the freight, and with millions of mosquitoes tearing at my skin. Also, I had eaten all my lunch at noon so I was starving and would continue to starve until our arrival at noon the next day in Ile a la Crosse.

The last stage of the trip involved loading the truck onto a barge and crossing the lake to the settlement of Ile a la Crosse. That was the nicest part, seeing the village come into view: including the mission, hospital, Hudson Bay Trading Post, and Benoit's Hotel.

I spent over a week there and I have so many nice memories of my visit which I will tell you about in a later chapter entitled "Emile".

When it came time for my return to Saskatoon, Emile arranged for me to fly to Prince Albert and supervise my two nieces, Anita and Muriel, who were returning to the convent in P.A. for another year of school. There were a couple other young girls on the plane, also returning to boarding schools.

We travelled in a small bush float plane which made several stops, delivering mail and small items of freight to small villages and camps on the shores of various lakes all over Northern Saskatchewan. There are hundreds of lakes up there. Before boarding the plane all of the kids made sure they each had a jam can held ready for when they got air sick. They were certain the operative word was "when", not "if", because they always got sick. Our first leg was about two hours north to Snake Lake, where we stayed about an hour and remained on the plane. Next, we flew about an hour northeast to a camp on some lake where one of the passengers deplaned. After only a few minutes, we were again in the air for about a three-hour flight south to Lac la Ronge. There we deplaned and had about an hour on shore where we could get snacks and stretch our legs. I went into the restaurant and for the first time saw that moose and venison were the only meats listed on the menu other than wild duck and goose. We finally arrived in Prince Albert about five pm; about nine hours after we had first took off from Ile a la Crosse. The flight had been really calm, much to the disappointment of all the children who had been looking forward to filling their jam tins. Anita had almost been lucky at one point but, despite a great deal of heaving and retching, all she could manage to throw up was a bit of her sandwich which, I think, had been lodged in the back of her teeth.

After an overnight with Lawrence and his family I finished my holiday, returning to Saskatoon just in time to start my Grade 12.

Throughout my time at Bedford Road Collegiate, I had a steady job, one or two evenings per week, babysitting Mirelda's kids, which now numbered five. The youngest then was Diane who was born in 1946, just before we left the farm. I was named her godfather when she was baptized. Even when I wasn't babysitting, I would often stop by their house after school to visit, play with the kids, and hold Diane. When babysitting, I always wore a particular tie that she liked to hold and chew on. Mirelda and Francis paid me a dollar for one night of babysitting and fifty cents for a second night, if in the same week. With that amount I was able to buy myself a small radio for my bedroom, paying The Bay $27.50, in instalments of two or three dollars per month.

I participated in several sports at school: basketball, volleyball, and tennis, but wasn't good enough to make the interschool teams. I played football with my friends on many Sunday afternoons. A bunch of us would climb the fence at Griffith's Field for a game of pickup, forming two teams of six to eight players, all with different skill levels. I had never actually played football so I had to play as a lineman, both offence and defense. There was always this one huge, dumb, but vicious guy who insisted on lining up opposite me. He just ran over me on every play, pushing me down to the ground and then stomping on me. He enjoyed watching me painfully crawl off the field and occasionally recover enough to go back in, only to have him repeat the stomping on my body.

Dad was loaning money on second mortgages to people who wanted to borrow for down-payment to purchase a house or for improvements. The usual interest rate on second mortgages at that time was about eighteen percent and there would be a penalty for early payout of three months interest. Dad paid me two dollars per week to do the record keeping and issue receipts. This, together with baby sitting and my fifty cents allowance gave me about five dollars per week for spending money - plenty to buy cigarettes, play pool on Saturday afternoon and go to the teen dance at the YMCA on Saturday night.

The Saturday night dances at the YMCA were great with music played on a juke box with a nice mix of fast and slow tunes. The boys and girls went on their own and then often couples would hook up for the home waltz and would go home together on the street car. Half way through the dance there were be an intermission and we could buy cokes and dough-nuts. On Sunday evenings we went to teen dances at the separate school downtown which had a similar format.

Except for the two dates I had in Nutana, I only had one other date in Grade 11. That was the sister of one of the guys I had gone to school with at the boarding school. She was really cute and I took her to the Sunday night dance at the Catholic school. When I went to pick her up, her mother invited me to come in and wait till the girl finished getting ready. I was told to sit in a particular chair in the living room while the mother then proceeded to ask for my family history. When she asked me what my father did for a living, I said he was a retired farmer. The mother suddenly became quite brusque and she stopped asking. The date was okay, but when I called her the next week for another date the girl said she was busy and didn't know when she might have another free night. I had always been quite proud that my father had been as successful at farming that he could actually retire in his sixties.

I continued to struggle with my math, especially Algebra. In Grade 12, I flunked my Christmas exam in Algebra (got 45%) and was feeling pretty desperate on the day before my Easter exam which promised to be even worse. However, the Lord was merciful again. I had started dating a girl named Mary in February and she was both beautiful and smart - in fact, she was a straight "A" student. She was my first steady girlfriend. Anyhow, when I told Mary that I had no chance of passing my Easter Algebra exam the next day, she offered to tutor me that evening. I jumped at the chance, and arrived at her house at seven o'clock, met her parents, and the two of us got together at the kitchen table. My problem in Algebra was in solving equations involving two or three unknown values. She explained the logic in such a way that almost immediately I understood the entire concept. I spent the next hour practicing solving problems. The next day, I got 96% on my exam and was actually expecting 100%. Mary got her usual 92% but was really pleased for me. Because I had flunked Algebra at Christmas, I still had to write the government exam in June, but I had no trouble with it.

I was taking three science courses in Grade 12, one more than required, just in case I might have trouble in any one. My physics teacher missed about two-thirds of the classes because he was coaching the interschool football, basketball, and baseball teams which competed against the top teams at the other three high schools. The physics course covered complicated subject material such as radio and electric circuits. My teacher's final instructions, before he skipped the last class, were: "just read your text books and good luck". We had only covered about a quarter of the material. I got 38% on my exam.

It turned out that my French teacher at Bedford was the wife of my very mean and miserable math teacher at Nutana, who died just after I left for Bedford. I found her to be the sweetest and prettiest teacher since Sister Marcien in Grade eight.

In June, 1948, I graduated from high school, at the age of seventeen.

The counselor at school asked me if I would be interested in going on to university because there was a bursary available for use at a Catholic university, but I said no, I'd had enough. Besides, my dad had only had about six months of schooling altogether, and he claimed that if I got my Grade 12 there was no limit to what I could accomplish, certainly I'd never have to work outside in the cold and rain. In the end he proved to be pretty successful.

I wasn't expecting any awards or prizes so I didn't even attend the graduation ceremony. My parents had moved to New Westminster at the end of May, so I stayed with Mirelda until I finished school at which time I also went to New Westminster.

The following eight chapters are devoted to my parents and to each of my brothers and sisters. Each chapter includes certain items of particular interest to them and their families or to us.

Elmer & Mary at graduation, 1948

Elmer - Graduation, age 17, 1948

Chapter 9

MY PARENTS IN RETIREMENT

I can't say my parents were really happy in their retirement years, and certainly they seemed content; they didn't seem unhappy and didn't complain. I guess what I mean is that they didn't do anything exciting like travelling to interesting places and didn't go visiting friends mainly because they didn't make new friends after they left the farm and dad was disabled.

Dad would have loved to travel, but they managed to take only two trips to New Westminster to spend a couple months during each winter while I attended boarding school in 1943-1945. During the following year, after we moved to Saskatoon and had later re-located in the area near to Mirelda, Dad had a serious stroke which left him paralyzed on the left side of his body. He walked with a cane and his left hand and arm hung loosely.

In 1948, just before I finished high school, Dad decided he had had enough of the cold prairie winters, so he sold the house in Saskatoon and moved to B.C. The folks made a trip to Saskatoon to visit family in 1953 and I will recount that in a later chapter.

They bought a two-story house in New Westminster and hired Lou and Margie's friend, Gordon McKellar, to make some alterations to provide a couple light housekeeping rooms to rent out to single girls in order to provide some regular income. The coal-burning furnace was

---

---

the BOY FROM MEADOW LAKE

converted to oil and the coal storage room was converted to a bedroom in the basement.

The front first floor room was rented to a French Canadian girl named Vi Belcourt, who stayed until after Mom died and the house was sold, many years later. The girl was very quiet and didn't have any boyfriends, although she was quite attractive. Mom baked bread and cinnamon rolls every week and shared them with the girls that rented the housekeeping rooms.

Dad would have loved to go to Hawaii, but Mom said no, it would have presented too many problems: at the airport, on the plane and at the hotel. At that time, planes were boarded by climbing steps from the ground, some distance from the terminal, and there were few facilities to assist handicapped people. He couldn't go by himself because, due to his stroke, he was unable even to dress himself.

Each day, Dad would have Mom help him to get dressed in his suit, dress shirt and tie and his well-polished shoes. He was seldom ever dressed "casual" which would mean no-tie. After lunch, if the weather was good, he would go out for the afternoon to various locations. He would go out of the door to catch the local bus which passed in front of the house. Often, the bus would be coming down the street and Dad would hold up his cane, the bus would pull into the curb in front of the house and Dad would get on, with warm greetings from the driver and other passengers, all of whom seemed to know him by name. He would sit near the front and would talk to the driver and anyone else sitting nearby.

Sometimes he would get off on Columbia Street, in front of the Post Office where there was a bench on the sidewalk, and visit with anyone that stopped. Some days he would walk to one of the two theaters across the street and go to a matinee movie. I met him one afternoon when I was on my way to work and walked with him to the theater where the ticket cashier greeted him by name and made a big fuss over him. She happened to be the most beautiful blonde I had ever seen, and so I got right close to Dad and said something so that he would introduce me, but they both completely ignored me and the opportunity was lost.

Other days, Dad would take a series of local buses, transferring from one to another, arriving in downtown Vancouver where he would find a bench in the little park at Victory Square. I walked past the square on my

89

way to work and would often see him there, sitting and talking to some-body. It could be a well-dressed business man or a bum, an office girl on her lunch break or a hooker, in fact, any person that would talk to him.

Dad got into a bit of trouble when he discovered a new way to pass his afternoons. He wandered into a real estate office and asked if they had any good listings for income properties. They were only too happy to show him houses that would make him rich. In the following week, he would go to a different realtor with the same line. There came a time when he hit an agent who was a bit sharper and talked Dad into putting a down payment on a property. When he got home and told Mom what he had done, she hit the roof and insisted she was not moving. The realtor insisted that he would keep the down payment and only returned it after Lou or Emile intervened. That was the end of that type of stunt.

Dad did get to see pretty much every part of the lower mainland, or at least every area that had bus service. The nice part was that it never cost him more the one fare per day, since it was always a round trip, transfer-ring back to his home

Mom seemed to be happy and content, especially in the non-winter months, when she was able to spend hours each day in her beloved garden. In Saskatoon, the garden was small, and the neighbor had a huge tree located almost on the property line dividing the two back yards. The tree had a vast root system that extended through most of our back yard and sucked all the moisture from Mom's garden. It was a problem during the first year, but a small bag of salt buried near a large root extending into our garden seemed to cause the tree to wither and die suddenly.

The house in New Westminster, besides having the usual size yard, also owned the big inside core of the block, probably 50' X 80'. In addition to having a nice apple tree, three plum trees, a pear tree, she had now more vegetable garden space than she could handle. At the back of the house was a grape arbor of 10' X 10', under which you could sit, with more grape vines against the back porch, and a couple of peach trees. Mom's only problem was getting her sons, Lou and me, to pick the darn fruit; there was so much, and nobody wanted it.

Mom was quite content to spend hours in the vegetable garden daily and all summer long she was able to have plenty of fresh veggies on the table. Her favorite lunch was a slice of home-made bread and butter with fresh green onions and radishes.

Their house was about four long blocks from St. Joseph's Catholic Church in New Westminster. Every day, unless it was snowing, Mom got up early and went to early mass and took communion.

The folks occasionally had extended family members who stayed for several days at a time, and involved a great deal of feasting and laughing about events that had happened in their younger days. There was always teasing and tricks played on each other. I think the best one was perpetrated on Uncle Harvey, Mom's only brother.

In the mid 1950's, Mom got the brilliant idea to invite all of her sisters and brother to a family reunion at the house in New Westminster. Some of the sisters had already passed away, and some of the siblings hadn't seen each other for probably forty or more years. It was to be held in July or August, and was to last for a week. Uncle Napoleon and Aunt Emily arrived a few days early, followed by Uncle Poulin and Aunt Edme and Uncle Sam and Aunt Lorette. The last two were coming from their homes in the States, Aunt Mary from Minnesota and Uncle Harvey from eastern Oregon.

Mom asked Lou, who had a car, to drive Uncle Napoleon and Dad to the train station to pick up Uncle Harvey who was the last to arrive. Uncle Harvey got off the train, quite a short, bald man, but a very jovial person and still recognizable, despite the decades that he hadn't been seen. They collected his bag and got into the car, and headed for Mom and Dad's house. After a few blocks, Uncle Napoleon remarked that he was feeling pretty horny, and maybe they should stop at a house where there were some "Rosies" that would give everyone a good time. "It'll only take a few minutes and then we'll go to see the sisters. Okay?" Dad just smiled and nodded, But Harvey got very excited and said he never did that stuff and that he was a good, clean-living Christian.

When Lou parked in front door of our house, everyone got out of the car except Harvey, who said he preferred to wait in the car. The others said nonsense, it was too hot outside and if he came in he could have a nice cool drink while he waited for the others. He finally agreed but insisted "If I come in, I won't do anything. You can't make me do anything." They assured him that nobody would be forced to do anything he didn't want to.

The four men climbed the steps to the porch and after a bit of milling about they managed to get Harvey into the front and pushed the doorbell. Seconds later the door opened and five old ladies burst out, all grabbing at Harvey and wanting to kiss him and hug him. Meantime, Harvey was yelling "no, no!!! Get away from me, I don't do that", and slapping at them. The other three men were having the best laugh in years. After a minute, Harvey realized they were calling him by name and were in fact, his sisters, and were not particularly sexy either.

After the week-long reunion was over and the sisters started to depart, the noise level in the house dropped considerably. Napoleon and Emily and Harvey stayed on for a couple more weeks and that provided Napoleon plenty more opportunities to play tricks on poor Harvey.

Most days the men would go for a walk in the neighborhood and, as was the fashion in those days, they wore hats. Harvey first found that his head was either growing larger or that his hat was shrinking, then the trend reversed, and then again his hat became so tight that he thought he would have to buy a new, larger hat. Finally, he examined the hat and found that the inside sweat band was lined with broken match sticks. Napoleon was either putting more sticks in or taking some out of the band each day.

I've already mentioned that Mom was a great cook, but she was particularly fussy about the food that she bought. After I bought my first car, I once drove her to Woodward's store to do her grocery shopping. In the meat department, where she wanted to buy some ground beef, she didn't look at the pre-packaged meat on display, but sorted through the round steaks and, in disgust, called the butcher and asked him if he didn't have any decent steaks which didn't have so much fat. He went into the cooler and came out with a fresh piece and cut off a couple steaks and brought them to her. She checked them over, had him remove a few bits of fat, and, resignedly, said they would have to do. "Now, will you grind them up to make my ground beef."

Mom had owned a canary for some time on the farm and enjoyed listening to its chirping. So, it wasn't surprising to find a budgie in the kitchen, followed by others over the next several years until she passed away. Dad also got quite attached to them and it was nice to see the folks teaching the bird to talk. It bothered me when I dropped by to visit and the bird was out of its cage and it would be flying around. I especially didn't like it loose when I was eating. Dad enjoyed having the bird come into his little bedroom and perch on his chest or even on his chin when he wakened in the morning and they would talk to each other.

Dad was fiercely proud of his children. One day an old acquaintance dropped by and started bragging about his children: he said that one was a lawyer and another was a doctor, etc., etc. Dad replied that his kids were doing even better, I was a psychiatrist (actually, I was a student psychiatric nurse), Lou was one of the head men at Essondale (actually, a cooking instructor) and Emile was a top man at the Vancouver Post Office (actually, he was a mail sorter). After the guy left, Mom said: "Joe, how could you lie like that about our sons?" Dad just smiled and replied: "if he can lie about his sons, I can lie better".

In June, 1957, my dad had another serious stroke and was taken to Royal Columbian Hospital, where he was mostly semi-conscious and was in an oxygen tent. He lasted only a few days until he passed away on June 22nd. Mirelda and Francis, Lawrence and Doreen, and Yvette and Albert came for the funeral from the prairies, and, of course, Emile and Julia, Lou and Margie, and I and Rose were present. During the ceremony, I looked around and was amazed that the church was full, well over two hundred people, and almost all of them were strangers to the family. My Dad had certainly touched a lot of people in the nine years that he lived in the community. During the ceremony, I recall sitting there in the church, thinking of how I could have done much more for him, like visiting more often or even taking him for rides after I bought my first car in 1953. I'll touch more on that in a later chapter.

After Dad passed away, Mom was very lonely, but she still carried on in the house and spent hours in her garden and still attended church for mass at seven or eight a.m.

Mom always walked to church, taking a short-cut through the little park at the north end of the City Hall, saving almost a long block in the distance. One rainy winter morning, while walking on the path through the park, she was attacked by a man who attempted to sexually assault her. As he tried to raise her dress, she beat him with her umbrella and screamed. After a half-minute of scuffling, the man ran away. Mom was quite shaken by the attack and made her way to the nearby police station, which is located at the rear and north end of the city hall. She could give only a brief description of the man and he was never arrested. After that, she had to stay on the sidewalk all the way to church until the days grew longer and visibility was clear among the trees.

A few months after Dad died, she asked Aunt Edme, her younger sister, to come and live with her. At the time, Edme was a widow and had been left pretty much destitute, as Uncle Poulin had never accumulated any property or savings. Aunt Edme was a jolly, plump, little lady who smoked in an unusual way; she would light a cigarette and puff at it quickly about twenty times, not inhaling, and not taking a breath into her lungs. Then, she would take a deep breath and then repeat the puffing. Her head would be in the cloud of smoke until the cigarette was finished. Aunt Edme was a good companion for Mom and they got along well, keeping each other from getting too lonely.

Aunt Edme refused to eat any bread other than rye, so Mom bought rye bread for Auntie and still made her own white bread, along with the cinnamon buns, which she shared with Vi, the light-housekeeping renter.

In the spring of 1962, Mom was constantly feeling fatigued to the point that she could hardly work in her garden and had huge black and blue bruises on her body. She finally agreed to go to the doctor. He diagnosed it immediately as acute leukemia and sent her to Royal Columbian Hospital with a prognosis of ten to thirty days to live. They let her believe it was only a bad case of anemia and that she would soon be able to go home.

There was very little known of the disease at that time, certainly not even the value of blood-transfusions to slow the progression of the condition, and chemo-therapy had not been discovered.

Rose and I were living in Sapperton at the time, just up the hill from the hospital, so I would go in to see her in the afternoon and take my portable tape recorder with me. I had a tape recording of "Yellow Bird" which was her favorite song and I would play it a few times for her each day. The evening visiting hours would see her private room jammed with visitors. The days and then weeks passed, and she was still with us. My annual vacation was due in the first two weeks of August, so Rose and I left with our friends for a camping trip at Wood Lake, north of Kelowna.

Upon our return, we found Mom still very much alive but very weak, and she was requesting a transfer to St. Mary's, operated by the Catholic sisters, in New Westminster.

That was when I decided to run away from Rose, so I packed my clothes into the car and drove across town to Mom's house and moved into her bedroom, and became man of the house.

Mom finally passed away on September 17, 1962.

I continued to live in the house with Auntie for about a year, until I started a job at MacMillan & Bloedel Ltd., and I moved to Vancouver. The house was sold in 1964, just after I was transferred to the paper mill at Port Alberni.

Dad & Mom - Just retired, 1946

J. Elmer Benoit

Back (L-R) Elmer, Emile, Lawrence, Lou; Front (L-R) Yvette, Mom, Mirelda

Mom - Blair Family Reunion

Chapter 10

EMILE

My oldest brother, Emile, was born October 16, 1911, at Marcelin, Sask., exactly nine months and two days after mom and dad got married, and about twenty years before I made my appearance in this world.

Because of the great difference in our ages, I don't have any first-hand memories of his early years. I know that he was about five and a half years old when the family moved to Meadow Lake and he later was educated at a Catholic boarding school in Edmonton. I don't know how many years that involved, but it was at least Grade 12.

Following school, he returned to Meadow Lake, and I don't know exactly what he did to earn money until we started the dairy, but he was able to court and eventually marry Julia (Juliette Marion) in 1933.

Mr. Marion, Julia's father, was the Liberal Member of Parliament for Meadow Lake and Northern Saskatchewan for many years. She had three brothers, Archie and Bert (nicknamed Swede and Sonny) and Marcien, and two sisters, Camille and Theresa. One of the brothers was a professional gambler who eventually moved to B.C. and made his living by travelling up the coast on the boats which carried freight and passengers between Vancouver and various logging communities. He was a card shark and he would clean out the loggers of their cash while they were travelling out on their annual vacations. George Reichart, my landlord in the 1950's in New Westminster, had been a professional gambler and he remembered

Marion because Marion used to come back from a trip up the coast, flush with cash that he had taken from the loggers, and he would want to get into a big stakes poker game with George and his friends. George said Marion always lost because he wasn't a very smart poker player, but mostly because he couldn't cheat the very good players. Another of Julie's brothers operated a general store in Ile a La Crosse. Emile didn't hang out with his in-laws very much.

While we operated the dairy, both Emile and Julia worked in the family business. My other brothers claimed that Emile's only contribution consisted of driving the horse and milk-cart to deliver the milk. He would collect what he could, which often was very little during the Great Depression. Because most customers had children we sold them milk on credit, thus accumulating huge bad debt write-offs, but then nobody paid income taxes anyway, at least not in Meadow Lake during the depression.

Julia had a beautiful voice and always sang in the choir with Dad at church. Their voices blended well and people would often comment about their duets. When they weren't in the choir, even more people would comment about the choir's singing.

One Sunday during mass, Julia was kneeling in the front row of the choir loft and was looking straight down at some man's shiny bald head. Without realizing what she was doing, a fair sized drool formed in her mouth and suddenly it escaped her lips and landed splat on the guy's bald head. Before she could pull her head back out of sight, he looked up and their eyes met. Julia was totally mortified and sneaked out before the service ended. She had many laughs about that.

While living on the dairy, Julia acquired a mortal enemy in the form of a little red Bantam rooster. The rooster would lurk around the corner of the house waiting for Julia to come out to go to the outdoor toilet. Julia would check first to ensure the bird was not in sight, and then she'd open the screen door and dash for the toilet, with the bird squawking at her heels. She would reach the toilet just in time and quickly shut the door. The rooster then would stand by the toilet door and crow. It then again would hide behind the toilet for her to eventually come out. After waiting till she was sure the bird had lost interest in her, Julia would finally burst out of the door and race for the kitchen door with the red rooster hot on her heels to the accompaniment of her screams and the rooster's squawking. She would just make it in time, slamming the screen door closed behind her. The darn rooster would then strut around on the porch and crow triumphantly several times more, just to rub it in.

Julia was terrified of thunder and lightning storms to the extent that she would crawl under the bed with her head buried in a pillow. She never got over that fear.

In 1935, when the folks sold the dairy and we moved to the farm, Emile and Julia moved about 150 miles north to Ile a La Crosse where they operated a "stopping place" where travelers, commercial fishermen and government workers, etc., could rent a bunk, buy meals, as well as get food and shelter for their horses. The sleeping accommodations consisted of a large bunk room holding about a dozen or more wooden bunks, with straw mattresses, on which the guests put their bed rolls and spent the night. Julia was a great cook and could handle that part of the business efficiently and profitably.

Besides Emile and Julia's stopping place, the village included the Mission staffed by the resident missionary and a few nuns, the hospital which was operated by the federal government and staffed by a doctor and two or three nurses, and the Hudson's Bay Company Trading Post which was managed by the factor, plus his family. The majority of the residents were First Nations people and they lived in harmony with the white residents although there was not much mingling socially with each other.

Julia gave birth to daughters Anita, in 1937, and Muriel, in 1939, in the hospital which was mainly there for the care of the First Nations population. Several years after the girls were born Julia asked the doctor how come he had never sent them a bill. The doctor just smiled and said he had registered them as Chipwean births and the government had paid him. Therefore, Anita and Muriel could have, in later years, moved back to Ile a La Crosse and claimed land to settle on and then collected treaty money.

When I was about nine years old Mom, Dad and I went to visit them at their stopping place in the winter and we had a nice trip. Dad put the hay rack (sort of a flat deck) on the sleigh, and on that he built a little cabin with a slot under a window in the front end for the reins and left room at the rear of the rack for storing hay and oats for the horses and fire wood.

We had a wood-fired space heater in the cabin that Mom was able to cook on and provided warmth. It took us three days to reach Ile a la Crosse. There were no maps or road signs, so it was only Dad's familiarity with the terrain that kept us from getting lost. Also, it's not like there were a lot of intersections. At night we used stopping places to shelter the horses and stayed in our cabin to eat and sleep. During the long days of driving, Mom and I played "I spy" and card games like "fish". One afternoon when I felt particularly restless, I asked if I could get out and run behind. I put on my parka and started running while holding onto the back of the rack. Things went pretty well for a few minutes while the horses were trotting along. Then I started getting tired and was about to jump onto the back of the rack when suddenly we went over a bump and I lost my grip and fell on my face. I struggled to my feet and tried to catch up, only to see the rig leaving me farther and farther behind. I yelled but Dad couldn't hear me and they kept gaining on me. He finally stopped and I was able to get back into the cabin, never to try that exercise again.

One of my few memories of that visit was of Emile playing a trick on Julia with not good results. Emile opened a box of Cracker Jacks and the prize inside was a nail bent to fit around your finger and a piece of red stained gauze bandage. He fitted the nail around his finger and wrapped the bandage around it and showed it to Julia, telling her he had run the nail clear through his finger. She took one look at it and promptly fainted. That's one practical joke that turned out flat.

On another occasion I went with Anita to visit the home of one of her little friends. The lady had put a frozen Jumbo White fish on the back of the kitchen stove to thaw out. The stove was a Renfrew Range, the same as Mom's, was about five feet long and the fish measured the full length of the stove. I'm sure I have never seen a bigger white fish. I just stood and stared at it in awe.

Emile and Julia then moved to Yellowknife where they were employed by an airline, CPA, to operate its living facility for the pilots and to service the planes during their lay-overs, and handle paper-work such as tickets, freight shipments, etc. Emile was also required to refuel the planes. During the winter, the planes were equipped with skis for landing on the frozen lake; and after spring thaw the planes were converted to pontoons. They left Yellowknife after just a couple years and returned to Meadow Lake.

Emile got a job at Fred Clarke's general store and built a little house in town, but they stayed only for a short time.

They then returned to Ile a La Crosse where they built a hotel which had about eight rooms, a cafe, and a pool room with two tables. One of the tables was a nice regulation-sized snooker table, and the other, more popular, was a small, Boston pool table. Emile also bought a Wurlitzer juke box and arranged with a record store in Saskatoon to send him two new records every month. That juke box produced at least a hundred dollars a month of net profit, at five cents per play. Emile was also the airline ticket agent, sold insurance, and was the government liquor agent for all sales of alcohol.

Julia was a fantastic cook and the locals especially liked her pies. One of the locals once bought one of her blueberry pies to take home. It was winter and he didn't want to have his hands freeze, so he just folded the paper plate over with the pie inside and shoved it all into his parka pocket and left for home. He had earlier drunk quite a bit of rum so I don't think that there was much fear of frost bite. But his parka was a terrible mess.

On another occasion, an old trapper was craving some mincemeat pies so he offered to buy a big pail of mincemeat for Julia if she would bake pies and give half of them to him. So she ordered the mincemeat, he paid her for it, and she baked his pies. He took his pies home and that was the last time anyone saw him alive. About a week later somebody checked on him and found him dead in his cabin. Julia was teased for a long time that her pies had done him in.

When I was sixteen, I went north to Ile a La Crosse by freight truck to visit Emile and his family during my summer vacation. What a wonderful experience that was.

The village had grown considerably from my visit six years before. Besides the buildings that had been there on my first visit, there were now a Department of Natural Resources office with a couple employees, an RCMP officer, and a regular store owned and operated by one of Julia's brothers and his wife. There were also several new homes for the additional white people and for some more natives who had moved into the village. While I was there we had quite a few planes arrive with people who worked for the government or on business.

I soon found myself with lots of chores to help out. I carried water from the well next door, made Kool Aid in half-pint bottles that we sold in the cafe (pop wasn't available because of the high cost of freight), waited on tables in the cafe, and relieved Emile in the pool room.

The favorite pool game was 7-ball, played with numbered balls. Players paid five cents to play and were issued numbered "peas" which determined the order in which players shot the balls in numerical sequence, with the winner being whoever sank the 7-ball. The winner collected the total pot and paid the five or ten cents cost of the game. Usually the winner would sink the 7-ball by deflecting it off the ball they were shooting. The games only lasted a matter of seconds to a couple minutes. Often I wouldn't have time even to sit down before I would have to rack the balls again.

While I was there, the First Nations trappers received the final payment for their furs, mostly muskrat, that they had trapped during the previous winter and which they had shipped to be sold at the spring fur auction in Saskatoon.

With their sudden wealth they all ordered liquor, the maximum number of bottles they were allowed, from Emile. They celebrated in the pool room and cafe until the liquor arrived. The pool room was kept open until about 3 a.m. for about three days until it arrived. It arrived on a special flight, the bush float plane fully loaded with cases of booze. I helped Emile and the pilot to haul it from the dock, about a hundred yards, to his office. There was hardly room for Emile to get into his office.

People had been watching for the plane's arrival so it was only a few minutes before they started arriving. They filed into Emile's office, one by one, signed their names and were given their booze. Each person opened his bottle and offered Emile a drink. To refuse any such offer would be considered an insult and disrespectful, so by dinner he was pissed and had to go to bed. I was therefore required to run the pool room until about one a.m. when Emile was finally able to relieve me and I went to bed, absolutely pooped and suffering a splitting head ache because the juke box had been going steady for three days.

The music was mostly country, as in "cowboy" and the customers, it seemed, would only play a couple favorite tunes over and over again. I remember (how could I forget!!) the two they favored that month were "My Filipino Baby" and "Detour" by Hank Williams or Hank Snow.

During the mornings, before the pool room opened, I would play pool with Anita and Muriel. My two nieces were pretty good, because they would play often. The table came to just under Muriel's shoulders so she would extend her arms straight over the table to shoot.

We went to a movie one evening in the community hall. The room had rows of wooden benches and the projector, located in the middle of the room, was an old-fashioned type on which the reels of film were loaded and made quite a noise as they turned. The fifty or so people who came seemed to really enjoy it.

One afternoon, Emile and Julia shut the hotel and we all went on a picnic. We went in Emile's motorboat, a beautiful, sleek runabout with a good sized motor. We went to their favorite spot on a little island in the lake, a lovely isolated location, with no sounds except the birds singing and the breeze rustling the leaves.

On another day, one of the local residents butchered a steer in the middle of the village. I went over to watch the event with Anita and Muriel. When the butchers drained the blood from the artery in the animal's neck into a bucket, it totally grossed out the two nieces. They swore to never eat blood sausage for as long as they lived.

After about two weeks, I flew back to Prince Albert, accompanying Anita and Muriel as they returned to the boarding school at a convent at Duck Lake, some fifty miles southwest of P.A. I took the train from P.A. to Saskatoon.

Emile and Julia used to take separate holidays, going south for a couple weeks of partying while the other one remained to look after the hotel. I recall that Emile was a terrible cook, and while Julia was away he nearly starved, just living on beans. One day he decided to make French crepes for his dinner. Remembering that Mom always started with a bowl of flour he added some water and when he couldn't think of any other ingredients, he put that mixture into the frying pan. It resembled fried wall paper paste, which it actually was. On another occasion he wanted a change from plain beans so he added a bunch of wild blueberries. He claimed that was the worst meal he ever cooked.

About 1954, Emile and Julia sold their hotel in Ile a La Crosse and moved to New Westminster so the girls could finish their high school. The girls had got kicked out of nearly every convent in Saskatchewan because they didn't like so many restrictions and had decided that if they rebelled enough, no convent would accept them back again and then their parents would have to move to the city. Their plan worked!!! Emile didn't get a very good price for the hotel, but did receive a new Vauxhall car as part of the deal.

Emile got a job as an aide at the Riverside psychiatric hospital in Coquitlam where he worked for a few years during which his daughters completed their high school. His next, and last, job was with Canada Post as a mail sorter in the main post office in Vancouver. Each year Emile was required to re-qualify for his job. That entailed writing a test which demonstrated an accurate knowledge of all of the post office regulations, rates, etc., plus all of the mail delivery routes, or "walks". He would study for hours and worry himself almost sick before each test. He always aced his tests, the only sorter to do so. He got 100% every year for about fifteen years; then the post office installed automatic sorting machines.

While working at the post office Emile and Julia rented an apartment in the Kitsilano area of Vancouver for a few years. They then lived in an old farm house in Richmond where they cared for an old lady while earning a small salary and free rent. After a couple years, they bought a nice bungalow on about 2 acres of property which contained many fruit trees, mostly plum, and a big vegetable garden.

Their neighbors kept about ten chickens in their back yard and they came to feed on Julie's garden. After several complaints to the neighbors were ignored, Emile bought a trap and they had a couple free roast chickens before the neighbor learned that "free range" didn't include your neighbor's garden.

Julia got her practical nurse's qualification and worked for several years in a Care Center in Richmond and was loved and appreciated by the old people that she cared for.

Emile loaned money out on second and third mortgages to people who needed down payments to buy or improve their homes. The interest rates were exorbitant, but at that time bank loans were difficult to come by and people who needed money for down payments or for repairs were grateful. He had very few defaults, and the loans were usually no more than $3-4 thousand each.

When Dad died on June 22, 1957, Emile was the executor of our parent's estate and then he looked after Mom's affairs until she passed away five years later, on September 17, 1962. Settling the estate was a lengthy and frustrating period for Emile because the house proved to be hard to sell at a decent price.

Following their retirement, Emile and Julia travelled to Yuma, Arizona, every fall where they bought a small house trailer in a trailer park and spent their winters there until a couple years before he died. They really enjoyed their winters down south with many family and friends. Others who stayed in the same little park were Mirelda and Francis, Lawrence and Doreen and cousins Les and Grace Colleaux. Cousins Maurice and Margie Beaulac used to rent an apartment in Yuma and would come over every day, as well as friends of Maurice. Phyllis and I and other family members and their kids, as well as other cousins occasionally would also come for a month or so.

After their retirement, Emile and Julia moved to Keremeos in the Okanagan, where they bought a house trailer. They lived there for a few years and then moved to a trailer park in Penticton where they lived until he died in March, 1993, at the age of 83.

I recall going to their 50th wedding anniversary in 1983 in Penticton along with several relatives and friends. The highlight of the night for me was hearing Julie singing a love song to Emile. She still had a really beautiful voice, and there wasn't a dry eye in the room.

Following their graduations, Anita and Muriel worked for a short time in Vancouver before they decided to move to the United States. Muriel left first and got a job in San Francisco where she met an American sailor and they became engaged. The sailor's parents lived in Washington State and just before the wedding they agreed to host a weekend party for all of the wedding party to get acquainted: the groom, his best man named Bob Stewart, Muriel and her bridesmaid, Anita. Things didn't work out as planned: Anita and Bob hit it off and in 1957 got married. Muriel broke up with her guy before their wedding.

Muriel was a computer operator at PG&E for many years, and during that period, in 1965 or 1966, Pat and I drove to San Francisco and spent a week with her. She showed us all of the usual tourist sights and one day we drove to Reno for a bit of gambling and the free shows. I recall that Harry James the famous big band trumpet player and band leader was scheduled, but he didn't come on until midnight. When James came on stage I was so disappointed because he really looked like a has-been that had suffered from too many years of smoking and heavy drinking. We then had to drive back to Muriel's apartment in Oakland, arriving about 6:00 a.m.

Muriel later switched to a big university in San Jose where she became the head of their budget department. Soon after her brush with matrimony, Muriel became a lesbian, had several relationships but had a difficult time coping with the resulting stresses. She committed suicide in about 1990.

Anita and Bob lived on the US Naval base in Bremerton, Wash., where he was stationed and in 1958 she gave birth to a son, Kurt. Bob was later moved to the naval base in San Diego and they divorced soon after, with Anita keeping Kurt. Kurt was a brilliant sound technologist. Unfortunately, he inherited Bob's lack of social skills and has never married. Anita worked until her retirement for a big aviation supplier to the US Air Force. They have since moved to Prescott, Arizona.

Chapter 11

MIRELDA

My oldest sister was born on July 5, 1915, at Marcelin, Sask., and was not quite two years old when the family moved to Meadow Lake. Her birth name was actually "Esmirelda" but she was never called anything but Mirelda.

I don't know any details of her childhood until I was born, at which time she was 15 and probably in Grade 9 or 10. About a year later, when we had started the dairy, Mom got sick with pleurisy and spent the next year in a TB Sanatorium in Prince Albert. That required Mirelda to stop school to look after me and be the mom for the family which now included her five siblings plus Emile's wife, Julia. That meant cooking, cleaning, gardening and doing the dairy chores like washing bottles, and helping to fill and cap them. That was a hell of a load to dump onto a 16-year old.

My sister was quite pretty, and had a beautiful, clear, complexion, and a happy, cheerful disposition. Before Francis, there seemed to be no end of boyfriends calling on her, despite having to include me on every date, even for short walks. One boyfriend even had extra pockets included in his new tailored suit just to hide candies for me to find when he came to call on Mirelda (and me). It seemed clear that if he was going to curry her favor, he was going to have to go through me. I never considered that I had such power even in those days.

Mirelda moved to the farm with us and later went to Prince Albert to work at the Catholic hospital where she decided to become a nun. She had been courted casually for a few years by Francis Sader, who was attending St. Peter's College, the monastery in Muenster, Sask., where I later took my Grades 9 and 10. He had entered the seminary and was headed for the priesthood when the teachers there questioned his commitment and then recommended that he change direction and marry Mirelda. Mirelda at the same time was getting similar advice from the nuns. Both returned to Meadow Lake and resumed courting.

Francis got a job at the new weekly newspaper, The Meadow Lake Progress, which was located in what had been the house in which I was born. Francis worked as a linotype operator as well as assistant pressman. I think there were only two people involved in the business: Francis plus the owner/reporter/photographer/editor/senior pressman.

Mirelda helped out on the farm and bided time until their marriage. Every Sunday, Francis walked from town to visit her and was always asked how long it had taken him. It was seven miles by road, but he could take a shortcut through the Indian Reservation and that reduced the distance by about one mile. His times became faster and faster and he finally admitted that he was running most of the way, thus incurring much teasing from her brothers.

Francis often would bring his golf club (a No.2 iron) and a ball with him in the afternoon and would hit the ball towards the barn so that he wouldn't have to look for it. Frank kept that same No. 2 iron forever and never used anything else for years, even for putting. (He and our cousin Maurice Beaulac often went golfing in Saskatoon in later years, each of them using only a two-iron. At least they each had a club and didn't have to share one.)

Francis and Mirelda finally got married in February, 1938, in Meadow Lake and had a reception at the farm. There were probably about twenty people for the occasion and after a big feast we had a fiddler and guitarist play some "old time" music for dancing. Dad played a harmonica. I recall Mr. Poitras (the father of my first teacher) got up and did a gig.

Dad and Mr. Gran played a practical joke on our new hired man. The hired hand wasn't a very likeable person and, although he hadn't been invited, he crashed the party. To test his skill, Dad had the guy stand in front of everyone, holding a funnel inside the waistband of his pants and a coin balanced on the tip of his nose. The object was to tip his head and drop the coin into the funnel. Just before the instruction to drop the coin, Dad poured a glass of water into the funnel. This was a bitterly cold February evening in northern Saskatchewan so the poor guy must have frozen his privates.

The following December 22, their first daughter was born in Meadow Lake and was named Mona Noella. Things started moving fast. They moved to Prince Albert where Francis got a job at a Catholic weekly newspaper making very low wages. Martin (Marty) was born in 1940. Frank was able to get very cheap rent in a duplex owned by the convent in exchange for hauling firewood from the woodshed to the furnace room, a distance of about a quarter mile.

Louis was born in March, 1942, and in 1943 I went to live with them while I attended the separate school for my Grade 8, a period I covered in detail in a previous chapter.

Francis got a better job at the Prince Albert Herald, a daily paper where his brother Johnny worked, and in 1944 Caroline (Carol) was born.

They moved to Saskatoon in the following year where he started his final job at Modern Press which published a weekly paper called the Western Producer as well as several "house organs" such as the Co-op paper, and various corporate newsletters. Diane was born that year, 1946, and I was her God-Father when she was baptized.

We thought Mirelda had stopped having kids when there no new birth in 1948. However, Sally was born in 1949; the last of her six children, and a great sigh was heard from the rest of the family and an even bigger sigh from Mirelda herself, when the "Finished" sign was nailed to the bedroom door.

The cost of raising such a large family was almost overwhelming but both Mirelda and Francis took on additional activities to earn extra income.

In a previous chapter I told about Francis unloading and stacking railway ties from boxcars while I lived with them in Prince Albert. Soon after moving to Saskatoon, they started taking in boarders, renting out a few rooms at $10 - 12 per week with two men per room. They also then began offering just board to single men living in the area. At one time they were feeding at least twelve men. Francis later started a janitorial business, aided by sons Marty and Louis, cleaning office buildings, and the project lasted a few years. I always admired Francis because, in spite of having such a large family, he took full responsibility for looking after them, without ever complaining, and he did a fantastic job.

About 1960, they bought a new house in the Nutana area, in the southern part of Saskatoon, and began taking in female mental patients who had no place to live after the Saskatchewan government closed the mental hospitals. They would have as many as six former patients at any one time.

When they were operating the large boarding house on 5th Ave. Francis worked at his regular job on evening shift and was therefore able to help with the cooking and cleaning during the day. Every afternoon you could find Francis vacuuming the house while listening to his collection of Mario Lanza songs. He had about five or six Lanza records and played them over and over and over again.

When they had an ad running in the local paper to fill a vacancy in the boarding house, Francis usually phoned during the evening, disguising his voice, and enquiring about the vacancy. One evening about the regular time for Francis to be having his lunch break, Mirelda answered the phone and, thinking it was Frank having his little joke, she told the caller about all the extra services that she would provide besides the three meals per day, all for only $14 per week. The man said that what he had in mind was a more traditional board and room arrangement and hung up. A few minutes later Frank phoned and swore he hadn't called previously. Mirelda just prayed that whoever had phoned for the vacancy wouldn't come by to look her over.

Meal time was hectic with two sittings of hungry men all wanting to be fed as soon as possible. The racket in the kitchen was more like a barroom. The three older kids had to do dishes. Mona would wash and the boys would dry. Louis would pick up a dish and start to dry it, wiping it with the towel over and over, moving slower and slower until he finally stopped and just looked into space, until Mona would yell at him, which only started him drying the same dish again. My family said that Louis had taken my laziness to the highest level. I didn't know who should be proudest, Louis or me.

The kids were all very industrious and were always looking for some way to earn (???) a few cents to supplement their allowances. They often put on concerts in the basement. They would make benches for the audience out of three or four boards resting on blocks of wood and invite all the neighborhood kids to come, selling tickets at five cents each. Each was shown to a seat and given half the ticket to allow them to return after trips to the bathroom. Kool Aid was sold at five cents per glass or less.

Mona was always the producer/arranger/writer/director/emcee/and star. The concerts would be variety shows and include at least one magic act, a drama, some songs, jokes and lots of lengthy explanations of what you would see next. The audience of a half-dozen kids never complained and seemed to enjoy the entertainment.

They pitched a tent in the back yard every summer and smoke was often noticed coming from it, although Francis always claimed his kids didn't smoke. They dug snow tunnels in the back yard and then Francis made them fill them in before they could collapse with a child inside. They also organized and led kids' parades down their street, with everyone wearing costumes and beating on pails and pots.

Saturday morning was when the kids received their weekly allowances, and I was able to witness this collective shakedown of Francis several times. They started with the base allowances, subtracted their demerit fines for various misdeeds during the week and were paid the net amounts. As each kid received his or her money, another would remember they had bought a pencil, eraser or some other school supply and hadn't yet been reimbursed for it. Each child had at least two or three such recollections every week and Francis couldn't keep track of all the reimbursements. Each kid seemed to be able to get an extra dollar per week, while all Francis got was a headache from all the six kids yelling at the same time.

The Sader kids took organization to a whole new level at Halloween. They planned their route according to the profitability in treats from previous years' routes. They placed a huge cardboard carton on their wagon and as one child pulled it down the street on their route the others were knocking on the first door at exactly six p.m. They kept yelling trick or treat as they ran from door to door, not waiting for all to receive their treat and as each one got his treat he or she immediately left for the next house. As the fastest runner filled his pail first, he or she ran to the wagon to empty it. As soon as the kid pulling the wagon saw the other approaching, he or she left the wagon and took up the gauntlet while the first emptied his pail and pulled the wagon. A minute later the next kid would be arriving with a full pail. Again, before reaching the wagon, the other would already be on his way. By the end of the evening, they had collected a massive amount of treats, certainly enough to last until Christmas.

The kids attended Catholic separate schools right through until their high school graduation. During those years they participated in every Christmas concert; and always it seemed that they starred as the Holy Family in at least one play that included the birth of Jesus in the stable. They always looked so saintly. Their classmates would groan at the thought, I'm sure.

The kids were very generous with each other. One Christmas, when Diane was about six years old, she wanted to buy presents for all the family but didn't have enough money. She started loosening her front teeth until she was able to pull them out, one per day. She pulled about four teeth, and the money she got from the tooth fairy plus what she had saved, enabled her to buy presents for the whole family. While looking for the best deals, she must have walked at least five miles that Saturday. She covered every second hand store on the west side of Saskatoon.

Louis was a very quiet boy, by comparison, and loved playing by himself with his Mechano Set, building all sorts of models: ships, planes, buildings, and heavy equipment.

Francis worked at The Modern Press until his retirement at age 65, still operating a linotype machine. I think he was the only linotype operator in western Canada for the last several years as every other print shop had been converted to lithograph. I believe the company told him he could keep his job as long as he could keep his machine functioning. I'm sure his linotype machine was over 60 years old when they both retired.

When they retired, they sold their home in Saskatoon and bought a motor home and two house trailers, one in Penticton and a smaller, park model, in Yuma, Arizona. For many years they alternated between the two places – five months of winter in Yuma, followed by seven months in Penticton.

Mirelda and Francis did a fair amount of sight-seeing during their annual migrations between Penticton and Yuma and fully enjoyed their retirement years, and made several side trips to visit other family members and friends.

They spent many hours on their hobbies, Mirelda braiding coat hangers and Francis listening to his Mario Lanza records. Those records had been played so many times you could almost hear the flip sides because the grooves were worn so deep, and the music was then transferred to audio tapes.

There came a point when they could no longer go to their winter home in Yuma and then Francis lost his driver's license because of his age. He got rid of the motorhome and car and bought a motorized scooter that he was able to ride to the supermarket and occasionally to the take-out window of MacDonald's restaurant a couple blocks away. Francis had been troubled with sore knees for years due to arthritis and finally had both knees replaced.

They finally had to go into assisted living facilities in Penticton and Summerland where Mirelda passed away. Francis was later relocated to a facility in West Kelowna where he lived for a few more years until his death.

Mona married Mike Lozinski in 1958 and they had three children: Mike, Pat, and Cathy. Mike and Mona first operated a business school in Saskatoon. The marriage didn't last and Mona moved with her kids to Trail, BC, where she met and married a really nice man named Bob Cruickshank in 1968. Bob and Mona had a daughter named Karen in 1975. Bob was an Ironworker at the smelter in Trail, and Mona had several jobs, including insurance agent or sheriff. Bob and Mona celebrated their 25th anniversary in October 1993. Less than two months later, both had passed away, Mona from a lengthy battle with cancer on January 3rd, and Bob on January 16th.

Marty and Louise married in 1964. They had two children, Tim and Lisa. Marty was in the RCAF, working as a fireman when they married, and was stationed for a time at a Canadian forces base in Germany. After returning to Canada he left the Air Force and for many years had his own business supplying and installing eave troughs in St. Paul, Alberta. They then moved to White Rock, B.C. where they operated a coin laundry until they retired and have since managed an apartment building in White Rock.

Louis and Carol also married in 1964, just three weeks before Marty. Louis and Carol had two children, David and Susan. Louis was a teacher in various schools in Saskatchewan, mostly in Prince Albert. Following his retirement, they moved to Nanaimo, BC.

Caroline and Walter O'Dell married in 1965 and had two children, Joann and Jayson. Most of Walter's working years were spent as a pipeline welder and Caroline did office work but mainly just travelled with him, living in motorhomes and enjoying life as a "kept" woman, as I guess you could call it that. Anyway, they did have one fairly lengthy project on a pipeline in Australia. For a number of years they operated a campground at Sylvan Lake, Alberta. Towards the end of Walter's career, he worked as an inspector on pipeline construction. They have retired on their property at West Kelowna.

Diane and Gene Koopman were married in 1964 and they had four children: twin daughters Sherry and Sheryl, and two sons, Geno and Shane. They operated a small cattle ranch at Fort McLeod, Alberta, for several years and then moved to Black Diamond, southwest of Calgary. There they had a Subway Sandwich restaurant and a garage which were managed by Gino and Shane, respectively. Gino has since sold the Subway and is now building pre-fab houses. The twin daughters both married and each had five or six children. All are well to do and get along beautifully.

Sally married Basil Ciepliski in 1968, and had four children: Stephanie, Dustin, Jeremy and Aaron. Sally went back to university with Stephanie and both graduated together, Stephanie in the College of Nursing and Sally from the College of Education. Sally was congratulated for only taking twenty five years to attain her degree after finishing high school. Basil was a graduate in engineering and worked for many years at Sask Tel, taking early retirement as general manager of the mobility division. Basil retired again about fifteen years later from a job working for a consulting engineering company in Saskatoon. He and a brother bought his parents' farm in Bien fait, Sask. where Sally planted an orchard of Saskatoon berry bushes along with other lesser crops. On the same farm, Jeremy, with Basil's help, built pens and enclosures to raise wild boars at a time that wild meat commanded very high prices. Unfortunately, the high price of wild boar meat didn't last, and Jeremy decided on a new career as an electrician. At that point, Aaron decided to take over the facility and raise alpacas and is doing very nicely. Sally is doing well with her berries, at least when the weather cooperates. Along with Aaron and his wife, Mel, they have quite a thriving business with Saskatoon berry products, called Prairie 'Toons and

Bakery, selling pies, jam, berries, perogies, etc., as well as alpaca fiber socks and mittens, at farmers' markets in the area. Basil took a two-year contract to manage the telephone system in St. Thomas in the US Virgin Islands, and is now a semi-retired farmer.

Chapter 12

LAWRENCE
AND LOUIS

This chapter will recount my two brothers and our interactions until they both left the farm. I'm doing this because our three lives were so intertwined through all those years that if I wrote about them separately, I would be repeating many of the same words for each of them. Besides, I never knew which one was the master mind of the various pranks they played on me.

Lawrence (Larry) was born at Shell River, near Prince Albert, on March 23, 1917, and was only two months old when the family moved to the Meadow Lake area. Four years later, on Easter Sunday, March 21, 1921, Louis (Lou) was delivered by the Easter Bunny while the family was ranching at Crowesford, (referred to as The Big Swamp). Two months later Dad got a homestead just south of town and moved there. In 1922, the family moved to town so that Emile and Mirelda could go to school. About that time, the Red Cross began operating an outpost hospital in town.

Of course I have no direct memories until I was at least three years old. But I have been told that the two boys had major difficulties at school, first involving fighting with the First Nations school boys while reaching, and again when leaving, the school; and then with the teacher, Mr. Carpenter, which I described in the chapter "The Dairy".

Larry was a rebel and felt all through his life that he was being persecuted in many ways; and he had just cause for many of those beliefs. He also had a quick temper, and would fight if provoked by any perceived insult or other slight.

Lou, when he was just a lad, had a speech impediment which earned him the nickname "Dutch", because other kids couldn't understand him, and so they said he spoke Dutch. On one occasion, Mom sent him to the store to buy a bag of rice. He told Mr. Ducluzeau that his Mom wanted a bag of "wuz". After a half-hour of guessing, the storekeeper sent him home to get a note from Mom.

Larry received the nickname "Penny" because of his small stature. However he was sensitive to variations of the name. One night at a barn dance, he fought a much bigger man, named Buster Bird, because Buster called him "One Cent". Both were very inebriated at the time.

Lawrence had a bit of a bump on his nose, which resulted from hitting it on a rock and breaking it while diving from a boat in the Meadow River. It happened one afternoon when he was playing hooky, so no details were mentioned to Mom, except that he got a bump, and no one even thought of taking such a minor thing to the doctor.

Lawrence had a brilliant mind when it came to learning schoolwork. He wouldn't study or do homework, but he absorbed enough just listening to the teacher explaining to the class, so that when exam time came around, he answered enough of the questions to get fifty percent plus a few extra (just in case), then handed in his paper and went swimming. Another example was that after he started working as a plumber, he read the instructions on how to do "lead wiping" and then just did it. He apparently was the only plumber in Prince Albert that could perform that particular technique at that time.

Larry and Lou both bought BB guns, which were pump action air rifles that were not powerful enough to really injure except if struck in the eye. Larry and one of his chums, I believe he was the son of Percy Twidale, the post master, who also had a similar air rifle, used to have battles. They would race around the town, firing at each other and with a lot of yelling of threats; and cheering when one of them actually landed a lucky shot.

In the chapter outlining life on the dairy, I described how the boys had to fight their way to school and then got a licking from the teacher for fighting and then another licking from dad for getting a licking from the teacher. Therefore, when we moved to the farm, Lawrence was relieved when told he would have to quit school in order to work on the farm. He was nearly 17 and Lou nearly 14. I believe that Larry was in Grade 10 and Lou in Grade 8.

There followed four years of backbreaking labor for my two brothers. They cleared about 460 acres of virgin farm land, all of it covered by mostly poplar trees - aspen and alder. After cutting the trees, they had to help Dad remove the stumps, dig up the roots, and haul everything into huge piles and burn it.

After working all day at clearing the land, they still had to bring the cows in, milk them, run the milk through the separator, chop and bring in firewood and water from the well, and feed the pigs and perform many other farm chores.

Lawrence resembled Dad in stature, about 5'7" and was slight in build. All the fights he had as a child took a toll on his body. He suffered liver damage which caused him to lose pigment in his skin, resulting in him having blotchy patches on his neck and body which never tanned. Throughout his life he never complained about his aches and pains, even though he must have suffered a great deal. A doctor predicted that he wouldn't live past forty; he made it to 91, and will probably outlive all of his family.

Lou was a husky, strong boy and already out-weighed Lawrence before we moved to the farm.

Our friend, Mr. Gran, who operated the government experimental farm, obtained a pure bred Charlebois bull, which it was hoped would improve the quality of cattle in the district. The breed originated in France, was all white and was well proportioned and a nice looking animal. Unfortunately, it looked like a midget compared to the common breeds, equivalent in size to a two year old Hereford, Holstein or Angus bull. Mr. Gran offered his bull to service our cows that winter and Dad asked my brothers to look after the project.

The little bull was very interested in the cows and took his job seriously, but unfortunately he was too small to mount the cows properly, which resulted in terrible frustration for the bull and a look of scorn from the cow. The boys thought that if they built a platform for the bull to stand on, he might have more success. They came up with a brilliant solution to the problem and took the bull, cow, and a couple shovels out to the manure pile which was frozen solid and covered with snow. They dug down to the correct height for the bull, and then dug a "U" shaped section in front for the cow. They got the cow and bull all aroused again, backed the cow into the slot and led the bull up to her rear. The bull was so excited he couldn't wait to take proper aim, and just lunged onto the cow while he was off balance. The bull lost his footing, fell off the cow's back and landed in the trench beside the cow and looked up at the boys and uttered the saddest "moo". Larry and Lou were just killing themselves with laughter, while the bull hung his head in shame and the cow stood looking disgusted and had already totally lost interest in the whole exercise.

Like all of my family, the boys liked to tease the others, and sometimes with bad results, like crushing another's ego or self-confidence. They often fought with each other, but made up soon, and were always ready to go to the Saturday night dances together.

I was always happy to be with my brothers, no matter what they were doing, or how much they teased me. When we first moved to the farm, Mom had a flock of geese, and the boys delighted in grabbing me and tossing me at the geese; and as the birds hissed and pecked at me and beat me with their wings, my brothers would laugh their heads off.

One day, when I was about seven or eight years old, I was wandering around the barnyard, while the boys were cleaning the barn, shoveling the manure from the stalls onto the "stone boat", just outside the barn door. The stone boat was a small wooden platform on skids, about twelve inches high and six by eight feet, which was used to haul the waste to the manure pile whenever it had a full load. The boys called me to come to the barn to see something, so I came running. Lou was watching my approach through a chink in the log wall and just as I was about to appear in the doorway, I heard "now" and then a shovel full of manure hit me in the face. Because of my inability to breathe through my nose, I ended up with a mouthful of horseshit. I naturally went screaming and spitting to the house yelling for Mom. The boys swore it was an accident but I knew otherwise: the word "now" clinched it. The boys later tried to cheer me up; pointing out it was only horse manure, whereas it could have been a lot worse if it had been fresh cow dung.

For several years I believed in the Easter Bunny as well as Santa Claus. At Easter, Mom got me a colorful basket filled with equally colorful "straw" which I put on a ledge in the veranda and waited for frequent visits by the Bunny. There wasn't a lot of money for chocolate eggs, so Mom would only put one small egg and a few jelly beans in my basket at any one time. More often, I was called by my brothers who claimed to have seen the Bunny just leaving the veranda. I would dash to see what had been left for me, only to find my basket contained just a handful of rabbit turds. The boys would go out into the woods beforehand and gather a large quantity of the little frozen pellets which littered the snow in great number, and which they apportioned to many deposits in my basket throughout the day. I soon realized that the rabbit was innocent and that my brothers were having another sick joke at my expense. At the end of the day, we all went to bed happy.

Lawrence took pride in his following the "Code of the West", a moral standard as described in western magazines and cowboy movies. The main principles were that you didn't hit a man when he was down on the ground, you didn't fight dirty, and you defended yourself when someone insulted you, and you were always honest and truthful and you saved maidens in distress.

Lou took delight in baiting Lawrence, using those standards against him. For example, while they were working in the field and stopped to rest and were sitting on the ground having a smoke, Lou would say something like "if you were stronger, I'd (do something to you, like) beat you in wrestling". Immediately Larry would issue a challenge: "stand up like a man and say that!" Lou would just lie on the ground and laugh at him, thus making Lawrence madder and madder. Lou would then say "I don't want to wrestle you because you always get mad when I beat you". Lawrence would deny ever getting mad, all the time just fuming. Larry would hurl the worst possible insults such as "dirty, yellow snake", which any honorable man was supposed to defend against. Lou would just laugh at him until Larry would beg him to stand up like a man. Finally, Lou would stand up and wrestle Lawrence to the ground with a secure hold on him.

Larry refused to admit defeat and would struggle to get free. There would then follow a series of warnings about breaking the rules of fighting fair: "no pulling hair", "no nose holds", "no eye holds", "no pinching", "no head butting", and "no elbowing", etc. Lou would have to hold him down until he conceded defeat. On more than one occasion Lou would have to choke him until he passed out. When Lawrence came to, he would struggle to his feet and challenge Lou to a fist fight.

My chum, Donny Williams and I were often the butt of their teasing. Occasionally, when Donny and I were five to six years old, we would go out to where the boys were working in the field. We all would sit together on the ground, chatting, and soon one of the boys would wonder if Donny or I could beat the other in a fist fight. The boys would argue, as arranged by them privately, until one of them would ask Donny or me who would beat the other. Before either of us realized it, we would be fighting just to settle the phony argument between my brothers. Eventually one of us would land a blow and the other would run home, crying, while my brothers would have a good laugh and then go back to work.

After dinner, when the last of the chores were out of the way, the boys often played pinochle or cribbage. Lawrence usually left early in the evening to retire to his cabin, about 50 feet from the house where he read magazines and slept. He loved me and teased me a lot but didn't like to roughhouse or play with me.

Lou on the other hand spent a lot of time with me, wrestling, and playing cards. We had a card table that we converted to a pool table by wedging playing cards around in the wooden trim, leaving spaces for "pockets" and using marbles for balls and broom handles for cues. It didn't work very well because the least bump would send the marbles rolling all over. Nevertheless, it consumed many otherwise boring winter evenings.

Lou and I shared a double bed in the boys' bedroom. On Saturday nights during the winter, the boys went by horseback to dances in the district. I would lie on Lou's side of the bed to keep it warm for him and when he came to bed I would move over and then cuddle him till he was warm. He always appreciated that act of kindness.

Lou was my idol and he always loved me and was proud of my few accomplishments. However, there was one incident when I was about six that I was the recipient of his temper. The boys were going out to the barn yard and had just stepped off the veranda steps. I was standing on the steps with Mom, and I was carrying my BB gun that I had just inherited. I thought I would test fire it against a moving target and was dead eye accurate, hitting Lou on the arse. I remember him jumping about a foot off the ground and I only had time to turn before I get the worst boot ever on my arse. It lifted me at least two feet off the ground. Fortunately, Mom was standing right there and was able to prevent more punishment to my body.

About 1936, Lou was mounted on one of the horses and was herding the other horses in the small pasture adjacent to the barn yard when a big horse, "Buster", kicked Lou on the knee. It broke the knee cap in quarters as a "+". He was transported to Prince Albert on the following Thursday train and met by Mirelda and Frank who arranged to get him to the hospital. Fortunately, he was put under the care of a modern thinking doctor who, instead of fastening the pieces together with steel pins, causing a permanent loss of mobility, he tried a new technique: he tied the pieces together with cat gut which would dissolve after the bones were knitted permanently. Lou returned to the farm on crutches and walked with a stiff leg until it loosened many years later while marching during the war.

Larry had a strawberry roan colored pony, called Tony, which he kept for his own personal use. Tony was fed a regular diet of oats and hay, so that he would have the speed and stamina to carry Larry at a full gallop for long distances. Larry was a natural horseman, could do tricks on horseback, and was the best rider in the country. He would go to dances every Saturday night, standing on top of the saddle so as to not wrinkle his suit, and galloping at a good clip. Following the dance he would climb into the saddle, usually drunk, and tell Tony "home", and the horse would find his way home, racing at full speed.

One night Larry rode Tony to a barn dance in the Dunfield district, about ten miles east of the farm. Before the dance started he met Josh, the bootlegger who frequented the dances. The bootlegger made a deal with Larry to be his assistant for the night. In return for helping, Larry was to receive as much wine as he could drink. Josh had bought several gallon jugs of wine which he used to fill empty beer bottles, and were then sold for fifty cents per bottle. Larry's job was to go into the dance and lead any customer to where the bootlegger was located. The location changed often during the course of the dance in case a police officer might be checking for that type of activity. The night's business went smoothly and ended with Larry, Josh and Buster (who that night had been a frequent customer) sitting behind some willow bunches, and drinking whatever wine was left, which amounted to several beer bottles. The only proper way to ensure that everyone received an equal share was that Josh would open a bottle, mark the bottle with his thumb a third of the way down, drink till he reached that level, then passed the bottle to Lawrence who did the same thing and then passed it to Buster. After they drank a few bottles, Buster passed out and couldn't take his share. The only fair way to make sure that Buster got his share was for one to force his mouth open and the other to pour the wine down his throat. When they had finished the wine they all were totally drunk. They loaded Buster into Josh's buggy and he drove him home. Buster was too sick to work for a week.

Larry managed to climb into his saddle and Tony headed for home at a full gallop. After a few miles, he partly wakened and saw he was along the river bank and thought he was at the ford so he signaled to Tony to turn. Unfortunately, Larry had misjudged the location, and Tony jumped from the six-foot bank into about eight feet of water covered by about a quarter-inch of ice. Tony swam across the pool, followed the other bank a hundred yards to where the road continued from the ford, and resumed his gallop home with Larry still in the saddle but soaking wet and gradually freezing. Lou found them in front of the barn door when he went out to milk the cows in the early morning and he got Larry undressed and into bed and Tony into his stall.

A neighbor, John Dickewiski's son, Alex, admired Lawrence and his pony, Tony, and asked John to buy him a good, fast, horse also. John found one for sale about sixty miles away and bought it, along with a fancy saddle and bridle. Alex was really proud of his new horse and rode to town regularly and all over the countryside. It wasn't long before Alex challenged Larry to a race to the school corner and back, a distance of one mile. At that time, Larry was about twenty years old and weighed about 140 lbs., while Alex was about eighteen and weighed about 190. Lawrence easily won the race and Alex was crushed, claiming his horse was no good in spite of costing his dad a fortune. Lawrence offered to switch horses for another race. Larry again won easily, proving the advantage of less weight of the rider made a big difference. Superior horsemanship also made a major difference, although Larry modestly didn't mention that fact, so Alex went home happy.

I have previously mentioned that the big penitentiary was located in Prince Albert, and people sentenced to jail commonly referred to it as: "going to Prince Albert for 30-days, or six months," etc. Lawrence once returned from a month-long holiday at Mirelda's, and as he got off the train, a lady friend of Mom's asked him where he had been. The rascal just said "thirty days in Prince Albert", and walked away. Of course, the story quickly spread and Mom was most upset when people in town sympathized over her "jail bird" son.

In 1936, Dad bought a new Pontiac car, trading in the old Model "A" Ford. This was real luxury, and besides, both boys could now go to dances and attract girls to take home. They made a deal with Dad that, in return for their labor on the farm, they would each receive five dollars per week, plus guaranteed sole use of the car on Saturday night, plus a tank of gas. Dad agreed and so Tony was relegated to the pasture, except for occasional trips when the roads were impassable.

I have only slow motion memories of that car; Dad drove about 10-15 mph whenever we went anywhere. It took us a half hour to drive seven miles to town for church or shopping or the movies, because Dad would be busy, checking the condition of every field of grain we passed: yield (estimate of bushels per acre), new or increases in the size or species of weed patches, time 'til ripe enough to harvest, recent hail or frost damage, etc. Through all of this "downtime", I would be sitting between Larry and Lou watching whatever Dad would be pointing at. I should mention here that I suffered from adenoids and tonsils which caused me to breathe through my mouth instead of my nose. Soon after leaving home, as I sat with my mouth open, one of my brothers would stick his finger into my mouth and quickly pull it out. I would pound him until he said he was sorry and wouldn't do it again. I'd watch him out of the corner of my eye and then the other brother would do the same thing to me. I'd pound on him until he too promised not to stick his finger in my mouth. A half minute later the first brother would do it again and we'd continue all the way to town. In the meantime, Mom would be telling the boys to quit teasing me and Dad would ignore us and the noise and just continue commenting on the crops and still driving slowly along.

The boys on the other hand, and particularly Lawrence, had no trouble in getting from A to B in the shortest time. I remember that once when Mom had forgotten that she was supposed to catch the nine o'clock train to Prince Albert for an X-ray and check-up for her lung condition, she had only 10 minutes to get to town. Dad said he'd get the car and Mom said, "No!! Lawrence will drive me". They made the train with three minutes to spare. Mom was praying her rosary the whole, short trip.

One Saturday while Mirelda was visiting for a week, she suggested she and the folks go to a movie that evening. The boys said they were sorry but they had plans to go to a dance. There was a big argument as Mirelda claimed she outranked them in terms of age and importance. It ended with the boys threatening to pack up and leave the farm. With that, Dad agreed with the boys, and my two brothers took the car and went dancing.

The Second World War started in 1939. Right after harvest, my two brothers went to town to enlist in the army. I went along with Mom and Dad and I recall my parents relief and the boys' disappointment when both were classified as 4-F: Larry because of his liver and stomach problems and Lou because of his stiff knee. Both brothers were crushed; I don't think it was totally because of their desire to serve their country, but more so because of being faced with more years of heavy labor on the farm.

In any event they returned to the farm to consider their options. After a couple weeks, they made their decisions: Lawrence decided to move to Prince Albert to find work and with so many men quitting their jobs to enlist, there were lots of opportunities. Lou talked to his chum Clive Ewing, the son of our friend, Mrs. Owens, and the two of them decided to move to New Westminster, B.C., with similar expectations.

With Yvette attending high school at a convent at Duck Lake, Sask., that left only Dad, Mom, and me on the farm. It was a lonely time that winter as the boys were not great at letter-writing.

In the two following chapters, I will tell, individually, of their lives after they left the farm.

Chapter 13

LAWRENCE - AFTER THE FARM

When Lawrence left the farm in 1940, he went to Prince Albert and got a job in the Avenue Hotel, as a beer parlor bartender/waiter/bouncer. The hotel supplied him with a room and board. He didn't eat many meals, but he sure drank a lot of beer.

From there he went to work at the Marlborough Hotel, doing the same thing, except more of it, if that was possible. He once demonstrated to me how fast he could drink a bottle of beer: he opened his mouth and just poured the entire beer down his throat without even once swallowing.

Thank goodness, he cut down on his drinking before it was too late. He met Doreen Lockwood, who was the office girl at Fletcher's Plumbing, and she soon got Lawrence a job in the shop where he started his apprenticeship. With his keen mind, he soon qualified and became one of the best plumbers in Prince Albert. As foreman, he was called on to do major projects all over Saskatchewan: hospitals, schools, commercial buildings, etc.

Lawrence married Doreen in August, 1941. Doreen continued to work at Fletcher's until May, 1944, when Marlene was born. Lawrence was now most often called Larry by his workmates. In his spare time, Larry built a cute little house for his family. I should mention that Doreen's parents owned and operated a second hand store, so the young couple had no trouble filling their house with good, used, furniture. There were included several heirlooms that they kept and, eventually, handed down to their kids. One item I recall was an organ that was probably already an heirloom when they got it and I believe Marlene still has it. The little house was so full of furniture that every item was touching something else from doorway to doorway. It certainly gave a feeling of coziness.

Lawrence and Doreen lived across town from Mirelda. That was only about ten blocks, because Prince Albert wasn't very big at the time. During my Grade 8 school year in which I stayed with Mirelda and her family, I often went to spend a weekend with Lawrence and Doreen. Of course I was subjected to Larry's practical jokes as well as constant teasing. One evening after a large dinner I fell asleep on the sofa. Larry held a teaspoon of red pepper under my nose and marveled at how the pepper just lifted off the spoon, up my nostrils, and how my whole body lifted off the couch even faster. It was a really nasty prank.

About 1945, Lawrence and Doreen bought a much larger house in Prince Albert. They rented out a couple bedrooms to railway workers in order to pay some of the expenses.

In 1945, after Dad had sold the farm and we were in the process of moving to Saskatoon, Lou, Margie and I spent a few days with Larry and his family, while Mom and Dad got the new house comfortable. It was a bit like the old days on the farm, my two brothers teasing me constantly.

Doreen was told by her doctor that she wouldn't be able to give birth to any more children, so she and Larry adopted a sweet little five year old girl, named Marion, in about 1952. Lawrence adored her and thoroughly spoiled her. Doreen was accustomed to keep several dishes of candy on the coffee table and end tables, and because it had always been there, Marlene seldom bothered with it. However, Marion wasn't used to having as much candy as she wanted in foster homes and so she ate it as fast as her Mom could refill the dishes. Besides the two or three pounds of candy per month, Lawrence took her to the store every day when he arrived home from work and bought her a Popsicle. He called her "Popsicle Pete". Naturally she soon developed dental problems.

In November, 1954, I received a letter from Lawrence and Doreen telling me that Doreen had given birth to a baby girl, named Rita, and that I was to be her godfather when she was baptized. Doctors don't always know all about the possibility of pregnancies.

They leased a small lot from the local First Nations tribe at Emma Lake about twenty-five miles north of town, and Larry built a small cabin on it. There were aspen trees along one side of the property line and when I came for a visit, I loved to listen to the relaxing sound as the wind rustled the leaves as I fell asleep. The lake was small, had a nice sandy beach, and was shallow enough to make it ideal for children. The family moved to the cabin for the entire school vacation every year.

Lawrence took up sport fishing and he bought a small aluminum boat with a 7-hp motor and trailer, just right for the small lakes in the area. He would pack a lunch of six chocolate bars and a case of beer and spend all day catching and releasing fish. He usually would bring home a couple nice pickerels for dinner. Fishing became almost an obsession with him for several years.

Eventually, Larry did tire of fishing and took up golf, which then became his next obsession. There was a nice golf course near the cabin, and he bought a membership so he could play a round of golf before work, and another in the evening before it got too dark to find any "lost" balls. Larry had several five-gallon pails full of "lost" balls that he had collected and kept in his shed, free for anyone that wanted some.

A funny thing was that when he quit fishing he refused to ever fish again, even when I took our kids to visit one summer, about 1979. I asked him to go out with us and he said "no" and that was it.

Lawrence went into the plumbing business in partnership with two or three other plumbers in Prince Albert. Larry was responsible for jobs out of town while the others looked after projects in town. The partners insisted that they should all lease big cars and live it up at the company expense. It wasn't long before Lawrence realized that while he was working his buns off, the others were just living it up. When Larry found they didn't want to apply themselves to business, he just walked away, and swallowed his losses.

About 1952, Lawrence and Doreen sold their big house and bought a small home about two doors down the street. He raised the house off the foundation and dug a full basement under it by hand. In the basement he installed a furnace, laundry room, and a couple bedrooms for the girls.

During the next year, Rose (my wife #1) and I took the train from Saskatoon to Prince Albert and spent a weekend visiting. Larry and Doreen scattered sugar between the sheets as a trick. It is supposed to melt with your body heat and make you feel sticky. I just assumed it was soap powder that had not been rinsed out of the sheets properly during the last time Doreen did laundry, so we just slept on top of the top sheet. In the morning they kept asking if we had slept okay. We always said "fine" until they finally wondered if we hadn't noticed the sugar. Doreen was a little upset when we told them we thought she hadn't done a thorough job of rinsing her laundry. That was one of the few times Larry's prank fell flat.

While Lawrence was working out of town, installing plumbing and heating systems for most years, Doreen had to manage the house and raise the kids pretty much on her own. She did a good job because the kids turned out fine. During the school years she had several hobbies which she used to not only pass the time, but to earn spending money by selling the crafts to neighbors etc. I remember receiving several as Christmas gifts. She started with plaster ornaments, then copper tooling, and finally oil painting. Doreen actually was quite talented, always had a pleasant disposition and she was very helpful to others.

Lawrence enjoyed driving good cars and had a succession of Buicks and Pontiacs, all loaded, powerful, and comfortable. Also he kept them well serviced and maintained. He spent most evenings reading western novels and had a large collection of western paperbacks.

When he retired from his job, he and Doreen sold their house in Prince Albert, went down to Yuma for the winter, and while there they bought a park model trailer and built a closed-in patio along the full length of it to provide shelter from the wind and occasional rain. He furnished it with a couple couches and stuffed chairs and about fifteen folding chairs with cushions, made by Doreen, to accommodate the many family, relatives, and friends that congregated every afternoon and evening for happy hour and for games. Whenever Phyllis and I were there, I recall at least 10 or more other people were usually present. Dinner was either a "pot luck" or everyone went to the Golden Horseshoe Restaurant, for the "early bird", which saved you $1 until 4:00pm.

During the winter, Larry often went out to the orchards after the fruit had been harvested and picked whatever had been left on the trees or fallen to the ground but not damaged. He was able to fill his car trunk with oranges for a couple dollars, which he brought back to the trailer park and shared with his friends, family, and neighbors. Lawrence kept a large pitcher of fresh-squeezed orange juice in his fridge and would drink six to eight large glasses of it every day. When he got home to Prince Albert he went to see his doctor to find what was causing his skin to look yellowish. After some blood tests it was determined that he had Type 2 diabetes, and the skin color was from too much orange juice.

Another hobby for Larry was going to the flea market at the dog racing track in Yuma on Saturdays and shopping for good deals on miscellaneous items, usually not needed. He was particularly interested in belt buckles, and bought dozens every winter, and leather work, which he took home and gave to his sons-in-law and grandchildren.

Lawrence was partial to cowboy apparel and wore shirts that had fancy stitched yokes and studs instead of buttons, western cut pants, leather vests, and cowboy boots. He had several pairs of beautiful boots, including snake-skin and embossed steer hide. His clothes were always nicely ironed with sharp creases in his pants.

Larry loved to haggle over prices, particularly in the shops in Mexico. They went to two border towns often, San Luis Rey and El Guiteras, where they bought blankets, leather travel bags, and duty-free booze. He often didn't buy anything, just haggled. For example, if a leather tote bag was marked $25, he would offer $5. The shop keeper would begin explaining how he needed to feed his wife and many children, all the medicines and operations they needed, how his rent was so high, etc., etc. The shop owner would then beg for at least $20. Larry would counter with an offer of $7.50. The price would finally come down to $15, which was all that was expected in the first place by both sides. Lawrence might buy it at that price or else he would leave and return at a later date to go through the haggling process again. On his last visit in the spring he would haggle really hard, remind the shopkeeper he was leaving for Canada and when the merchant agreed to a ridiculously low price, Larry would pay the full amount and laugh when the shopkeeper realized he'd been fooled all along by all the haggling.

Lawrence and Doreen spent their summers at Emma Lake where they again remodeled and enlarged their cabin and made it a little less rustic. Larry was able to golf pretty much all day as well as to entertain family and friends who arrived in droves to visit and enjoy the beautiful beach.

Unfortunately, their idyllic lifestyles took a bad turn in 1997, when Doreen suffered a serious stroke which left her paralyzed in her right side and unable to speak. The stroke occurred during the night, so it was many hours before she was discovered and taken to hospital in Prince Albert, some 25 miles away. As a result of the lengthy delay, very little improvement could be achieved.

When Doreen's condition stabilized and she was able to be transferred, Lawrence was able to move her to a care center operated by the Roman Catholic Church, where she had a private room and good care. The staff would transfer her back and forth between her bed and wheel chair and Larry brought in a TV and other items such as photo albums. The loss of speech was devastating for her as I'm sure it would be for anyone. She lasted for several years until she finally passed away in 2003. During that entire period, Lawrence spent every afternoon and evening with her and did everything that he could to make her life easier. I was extremely proud of Larry for the loving care he showed Doreen for all those years.

When we went to visit for a few days, it was funny to watch Larry when he came home for dinner. Everything was planned and every step was precise: he opened the front door, went directly to the freezer and removed steaks for each of us, also bags of frozen tater tots and green peas, and without breaking stride, he turned on the oven and one stove top burner, then out to the patio where he turned on the gas barbeque. Back to the kitchen to pour peas and water into a pot on the stove, then poured tater-tots onto a tray and into the oven. Then back to the patio to scrape the grill and put the steaks on. Almost before we had time to pour drinks, our food was on the table. I think Larry had the same dinner every night for years, except he occasionally would go to a restaurant for a meal of pork chops and mashed potatoes.

After Doreen passed away, Lawrence moved to Prince George, BC, to be near to Rita and Marlene, and their families. He rented an apartment located between the two daughters and lived there quietly until his death in 2006.

Marlene became a school teacher and her first job was at an elementary school in Coquitlam, B.C., right across the street from where Phyllis and I would later live in a condo. She later moved to Prince George, BC, where she continued to teach until her retirement. She married Bill Hood in 1969. They had two sons: Trevor, born in 1973, and Matthew, born in 1975. Marlene and Bill divorced and she married Peter Cailles in 1992. That didn't last long and after several years she again remarried in 2008 to Stan Aksinchuk, who had a real estate and property appraisal business in Prince George. Presently, he does only property appraisals.

I was particularly close to Marlene and we visited each other often, especially since my retirement. I recall getting together at her home in Prince George, next to the Nechaco River, where there was a bonfire every evening in the pit on the river bank. A little red fox came by about three times each day to take a fresh egg from Stan's hand and trotted off to wash it in the river and then continued on his way. Each time we came to visit, would be reason to have a family get-together.

Marion married Reg Burch in 1977 and they had a daughter, Michelle, in 1978. They live in Saskatoon where Reg worked as a heavy equipment salesman for a dealer and Marion worked for the federal government from the time she finished high school until her retirement. Lawrence willed the cottage at Emma Lake to them and they have since again enlarged and remodeled it.

Rita moved to Prince George after she finished school and later met and married Don Klausen in 1974. They had two children: Doug, born in 1974, and Kim, in 1977. Don worked in a local sawmill until he had a serious heart attack, and was placed on long term disability until his retirement and still works part time for a car rental company. Rita worked in a doctor's office.

Chapter 14

LOUIS - AFTER THE FARM

Lou left the farm in late fall, after harvest, accompanied by his chum, Clive Ewing, who lived on a nearby farm. (Clive was a half-brother of my friend Leo Owens.) They arrived in New Westminster, rented a light-housekeeping room, and soon found jobs unloading hides for Swift's Meat Co.

It was a terrible job. The hides arrived from Swift's various plants in boxcars, and were raw, having just been removed from the cattle and had just been thickly coated with salt in the first step in the tanning process. The boys had to shake the salt from the hides and then transfer them to the next station. They were not supplied gloves and I don't think that would have helped much because the hides were stiff as boards, and so their hands immediately became dried and cracked and bleeding.

They soon found other jobs at the Canadian White Pine sawmill in Burnaby, BC, and they worked there until they enlisted in the army.

The folks and I were really amazed to receive a photo in the new year of Lou and Clive, taken on Christmas day, lying on the grass in the little park at the New Westminster end of the Pattullo Bridge, in their shirt sleeves in bright, sunny weather. Our Christmas had been celebrated in the traditional way with a feast and then sitting around our tree, and with about three feet of snow on the ground outside.

Lou had met a lovely girl, Margie Bowes, who worked in a local department store, and they eventually married after the war. At the same time, Clive met a girl named Delores, and the two couples double dated often. Margie loves to tell the story about the boys making dinner for the girls not long after they met. The boys proudly presented a dinner of boiled wieners, sauerkraut and mashed potatoes. The girls rolled their eyes and tucked in, and didn't let on that they were not impressed with the menu. Lou and Clive thought you couldn't go wrong with a meal like they had cooked. (It is still one of my favorites, though not often.)

The boys again tried to enlist in the army, and this time they were both successful. Lou was accepted for duty in the signal corps where his stiff knee wouldn't be as much of a handicap.

He was sent to the Army base in Vernon, BC, for a couple months of basic training and he told a story about being on maneuvers with full battle gear in the hillside area between the highway and the Kalamalka Lake shore. A buddy was crawling along, just ahead and to the side of Lou, when he heard a ping on his helmet. The man looked up to see a rattle snake staring into his eyes. He screamed, leaped to his feet and dashed down the hill, scattering his rifle, helmet, backpack, canteen, ammunition pouches, etc. in his wake. The soldier finally calmed down and completed his training and was sent overseas where he went into battle, but was later sent home suffering from "battle fatigue", a term used to describe a mental breakdown. I wonder if it started on that hillside above Kalamalka Lake.

Lou went on every route march and completed every one, despite the pain in his knee, and watched many able-bodied comrades dropping out over the twenty miles course. As a result of his decision to never give in, the knee joint loosened and his limp disappeared, although the knee was never pretty to look at.

My brother completed his training and we were notified that he was to be granted embarkation furlough prior to going overseas. He chose to spend it with Margie and so we weren't able to see him from the time he left the farm until he returned in April, 1946. It was particularly difficult on Mom as she was so worried about his safety and his letters were few. She prayed for his safe return constantly.

Clive completed his basic training at a different base and was transferred to the Intelligence Corps, for additional intensive training. During his embarkation leave, he and Delores returned to Meadow Lake to be married. Their wedding reception included a big feast, served outside on the lawn, with several friends from nearby farms, including Dad, Mom, Yvette and me. There was some music, courtesy Dad, Clive and his sister Yvonne. After the war, Clive remained in the army for some time and was stationed somewhere back east. I guess their marriage broke down, and one day he just didn't come home. Delores came back to New Westminster, while she waited for news of what had happened to him. After 7 years, she had the court declare him "presumed dead" and she remarried. A few years later, Lou was in Prince Rupert on business and, while passing time in his hotel room, he checked the telephone directory and, by chance, found Clive's listing. He phoned Clive and was invited to come over for a visit. Clive greeted him casually but didn't offer any explanation for his disappearance and for totally cutting himself off from all his family and friends. He had remarried and had a couple kids. Strange!!!

After returning home from overseas, Lou told me of several experiences that he had and I'll recount a few.

The most bizarre occurred when he was in Alsace, France, when the Germans started retreating from their positions. Lou had the most vivid dream one night of walking back to his tent from mess and there was an air raid. He dreamed that he dove under a troop transport truck and witnessed the most devastating bombing attack: people being killed, others badly wounded and screaming and bombs exploding all around him. He awoke in a sweat and lay awake for the rest of the night. Two nights later, the same attack actually took place and he lay under the same truck, watching the entire event taking place right before his eyes. Sadly, the bomb attack was performed by allied planes. A tragic mistake by the navigators!!!

On another occasion, while just back of the front lines, his unit was ordered to continue forward to the next village, not aware that the fighting force had been ordered to return to a previous position. Lou was laying line to a particular building which was to be the new command post. He was in a dimly lit building when he realized there was a German soldier holding a rifle right in front of where he was reaching. He just froze and waited for the shot. It didn't happen and after a few moments, he brought up his flashlight and found that the German was dead.

Lou's unit was close to the front, all the way from the invasion site in France, through Belgium and far into Holland. Everywhere they went, they were treated as heroes who had liberated the people who had been living in terror of the German invaders and suffering from extreme food shortages for years. Lou made good friends with the locals, particularly in Belgium and Holland.

It was in Holland that he suffered a back injury, I think from too many winter nights sleeping on the cold, damp, ground. I believe a disc ruptured in his spine, causing severe pain. He was sent back to England to a hospital at Aldershot and remained there until the end of the war. After a few weeks of bed rest, the inflammation in his back eased and he was able to get day passes and take the tube into London, returning to the hospital before his curfew each night.

Whenever Lou wrote home, he always asked the folks to send cigarettes. The cigarette manufacturers in Canada had special prices for armed forces personnel. Besides free shipping and being duty free, the prices were greatly discounted. The cigarettes were a hot item on the black market and in England they were worth far more than the regular retail prices. Part of the reason was that cigarettes were severely rationed and even if you could buy them, the British smokes were of very poor quality. People in Canada could place a standing order for a regular delivery each month of, say, 500 or 1,000 or more, to a particular service person. Margie and her parents were also regularly sending several cartons to him. Lou also was a very good cribbage player and when in the hospital he played with several other patients, always with the stakes for each game being a certain number of cigarettes. He won many more times than he lost.

He would pack a few cartons into a small back pack and take the tube into London. There would always be a couple black market operators at any station where he would disembark in the downtown area, eager to take any cigarettes or other contraband from anyone at the regular black market prices.

Meanwhile, back in New Westminster, Margie met a very nice man who, with his father, owned a good-sized construction company, specializing in road building and paving. Margie soon endeared herself to the young man's family and she became engaged to Jack, of Cewe Construction. This, of course, necessitated a "Dear Lou" letter to my brother, who was able to take the sad news in stride because he wasn't suffering loneliness to any great extent.

At about the same time, Lou met a lovely girl in London and he soon became a big time favorite of her family. Of course, the fact that Lou was able to supply the family with meat, sugar, cigarettes and everything else that was strictly rationed helped to endear him to the whole family. On his way out of camp, Lou would stop by the kitchen and trade cigarettes for the meat, sugar, etc., that he would provide to his new girlfriend and her family.

The war in Europe was nearing an end and Margie decided that Lou, not Jack, was the man that she wanted to spend her life with. There then was a remorseful letter of apology to Lou, begging him to forgive her and come back to her after the war. He explained that he had met a girl in London and he was considering marrying her. After a few more letters back and forth, he decided to come home before making a decision.

The war finally ended in Europe and the troops were ready to return home. The war with Japan was still in progress and the request was made for any troops in the European theater to transfer to the Pacific. Lou declined. As a result, the war in Japan ended a few months later with the atomic bombing of Heroshima and Nagasaki. The personnel who had requested a transfer to the Pacific hadn't yet left Europe, and were put on the first boats going home.

Lou finally arrived home in about March, 1946, and first called to see the family. About mid-April, he came to Muenster where I was attending the boarding school and seemed pleased with the way I had grown and had changed from being a shy little kid to a shy big kid. He was able to watch me play hockey in a playoff game and then we went to dinner at the hotel in the village.

He returned to the farm and was joined there by Margie a few weeks later. I don't know if he decided it was going to be Margie before or after she arrived but it was certainly before I arrived home from boarding school in late June. Within a few days I was totally smitten with her and would have married her myself if Lou didn't have seniority. Also, I was only fifteen at the time.

I remember arriving home on the train and Lou and Margie were there to meet me. They went to a dance in Meadow Lake straight from the train station and I waited in the car while they danced. I wasn't permitted to go to dances yet because of what I might see (Mom's orders). Margie was wearing a new pair of shiny gold shoes that she had bought that day, and I recall her being furious because she saw another woman at the dance wearing identical shoes. Margie had arrived in early June with enough clothes to last her all summer - several suitcases and a trunk full of shoes, some sixty pairs. She soon won the hearts of all of us.

I took Margie riding to visit the Owens family one afternoon. Prince was really rough to ride, even with a saddle, so I thought it would be better for Margie to ride Queenie which was as smooth as riding on air. Queenie was so round and fat that the saddle didn't fit. Margie was so tiny that her legs stuck out almost straight and required a real skill to balance on Queenie's back. Margie rolled off onto the ground once but was unhurt and we carried on to Owens with much laughing.

That summer was a very exciting time for me. As I have previously described, my parents were notified by the boarding school that I wouldn't be accepted back for Grade 11, the farm was sold and we moved to Saskatoon.

Lou and Margie came to Saskatoon and stayed with us for a couple weeks before leaving for New Westminster where they were married in the presence of Margie's parents and all of their friends.

They decided to open a fish and chips shop in Sapperton on East Columbia Street, just a half block from the Royal Columbia Hospital, and rented the upstairs suite in a house directly across the street from the shop. The shop, called the Bow-Ben, was a short-lived financial success and people lined up at the door for one of the few tables and the take-out business was even better. The menu featured two pieces of cod with a scoop of chips for twenty-five cents, three pieces of cod and two scoops of chips for thirty-five cents, deep fried oysters with chips, and pastries, etc.

In May of the following year, 1948, they had their first daughter, Wendy. Earlier that year, they closed the shop for a month and hired their friend, Don McKeller, to remodel and enlarge the shop. It was a bad decision because during that month their customers started going to a new cafe in the next block, a hamburger joint called Spots. The Bow-Ben re-opened, but the crowds didn't return and their income suffered.

Things got a whole lot worse financially. Margie was spending her time looking after Wendy, so Lou had to hire waitresses, but wasn't able to find the right type at the wages he was able to offer, which didn't improve the bottom line. Then in June, there was a terrible flood and the entire Fraser Valley was under water for several weeks. The flood waters receded in time, but the rains continued through most of the summer. Because of the wet farming conditions the potato crop suffered a condition called "blight" which left the potatoes scabby and, when they were deep fried, the chips immediately turned from golden brown to dark brown then to black and became mushy. After a few sacks of these spuds, Lou had to start purchasing white potatoes from California at a much higher cost.

I arrived from Saskatoon at the end of the school year and I wish I could say I arrived as a hero to save the day, but I didn't. I arrived on the third train to travel through the Fraser Valley on the CNR line after the flood and I remember looking out from the train onto a view of water from the mountains in the north to the mountains in the south. We crawled along at a speed of about five miles per hour for hours, with all the passengers sitting on the edge of their seats and looking very anxious.

I didn't have long to settle in as I had a job already waiting, working at the Bow-Ben, cooking fish and chips, peeling and dicing potatoes, mixing batter, waiting on tables, and serving customers with a bit of cleaning thrown in. Lou usually opened the shop and would have the coffee on when I arrived. We would start with breakfast of bread and peanut butter and coffee. We would have a short spurt of activity - delivery men and a few customers. During our next quiet break we would have our lunch of bread and peanut butter and coffee. Life can't get much better than that!!! (Actually, Margie's dad, Andy, was the charge cook at Woodland School, so he was able to pick up more than one 50-pound pail of peanut butter for us from work.) It would be quiet then until about 4:00 pm so Lou would go home to spend time with Margie and Wendy. When the first customers or phone orders started for take-out, I would slip out the back door of the shop and call Lou for help. After the dinner rush finished, Margie would bring over our dinner in pots, consisting of meat, potatoes and vegetables. On Fridays, Margie would join us for fish and chips, the only time in the week that we ate them. After dinner, Lou would go home until it was time to close the shop at 10 or 11pm.

Lou and Margie had many friends and seemed to attract more as time went on. It was unusual if at least one or two couples didn't drop in every night to visit and stayed for an evening snack. Snacks most often were do-it-yourself Dagwood sandwiches. That consisted of three slices of bread with at least four or five fillings, such as devilled egg, salmon, sliced meats, cheese and anything else that was in the cupboard. Margie always served tea, and she liked it weak. She had a large Pyrex tea pot that she would fill with boiling water and drop in one tea bag, causing a great deal of teasing about the weak tea. Saturday evenings usually saw a dozen friends crowded into that little three room suite, but still only one tea bag. Once a month, somebody threw a party, the only time anyone could afford to buy a bottle of liquor.

Lou had a plan that after I was trained in the business, he would sell the shop, I would get a loan from Dad and we would open a fish and chip shop in partnership in White Rock where we could make a pile of money in the summer and then take winters off. However, Dad didn't have a great deal of confidence in me, so that plan fizzled.

The next year I enrolled in a business course; and Lou, after running the shop alone with part-time waitresses for a time, decided to get out of the business.

With the aid of a reference from his father-in-law, Andy Bowes, Lou was able to get a job cooking at Riverview Hospital (known at the time as Essondale). His duties consisted mainly in supervising patients who, through long term service, were quite capable of cooking.

During his training period, he was assigned for a couple months, to the Borstal (Reform) School for boys and found it interesting to learn how so many kids could get into so much trouble at such an early age. Two of the youngest, about eight years old, were in for stealing a car. Neither being big enough to drive, one sat on the floor to operate the clutch, brake and accelerator while the other knelt on the seat and steered. They made it a couple blocks before the crash. It wasn't their first scrape with the law, so both were locked up.

Sherri was born in 1951, another beautiful child.

After a number of years at Riverview, Lou found the surroundings to be too depressing, so he quit and went to work for Jack Cewe in his paving business as a salesman. He tried very hard but found that the politics was not his cup of tea. It sounded to me that it involved getting contracts in competition with other companies based on which was most willing to grease the palm of the civic officials. Also, he hated being away from home so much, and he left after about a year.

He soon found a job as a cooking supervisor at the Okalla Provincial Prison in Burnaby. This was similar work to what he had been doing at Riverview, except the surroundings were different. The inmates did the actual cooking with very little supervision by the staff. The inmates were usually fully trained cooks before they were released and were immediately replaced by other fully trained convicts who returned from a few months of freedom. Lou remarked that it was amazing how little justice seemed to exist in Canada, because all of the inmates claimed they were innocent of their crimes and had been framed. Because he was again working for the provincial government, he was able to repay his pension contributions that he had withdrawn and, with credit for his years in the armed service, therefore when he retired he was able to draw a full pension.

Life continued then pretty much the same until he retired. They had many very happy years as they had hundreds of friends who dropped in to visit and drinks, and parties were frequent and were noisy affairs, and many trips all over the world. During their later years they renewed a friendship with a couple that Margie had been friends with at school. They owned a private fishing lodge on the Euchiniko River in the interior of BC, west of Williams Lake. The only way in was by float plane. It was a beautiful place and they enjoyed themselves immensely and it was there that Lou passed away in October, 1983, at the age of 62. He was sitting in the boat and Margie was nearby on the shore when his heart suddenly stopped. Even if an ambulance service and a hospital had been close at hand, there would have been no chance of his survival.

A few months after Lou's death, Margie started a relationship with a mutual friend, Rolly, who had lost his wife to cancer in early 1983. They have maintained separate residences and seem to enjoy the freedom that allows. Margie has been able to maintain old friendships and vacations with her long-time girlfriends.

Wendy married Rick Borsuk in 1970. Rick worked in his dad's freight business until it landed a huge contract to haul freight to the construction site of the W.C. Bennett hydro dam, and the company was sold to a competitor. Rick worked for a short time with the new owners as manager of their fleet maintenance department. He quit and went into the construction business on his own and then diversified as a property developer with a partner and was very successful. Wendy and Rick had two daughters, Carlee and Kerri, and a son, Kameron. Unfortunately, Carlee died in a car accident at the age of two, and Rick passed away in 2012, the result of cancer.

Sherri married Marshall Borden in 1980. Marshall was captain of a supply ship serving the off-shore oil rigs in the Arctic Ocean. They also had two daughters, Bristol and Bailey, and a son, Sterling.

Chapter 15

YVETTE

The younger of my two sisters, Yvette, was born on October 9, 1925, in Meadow Lake.

She was a plump little girl, suffered a weight problem all of her life, and her brothers, as well as other kids at school made her life unbearable because of it. It wasn't until she reached her teens that she stopped being teased. I have to confess that as a child, I was just as guilty of being mean to her, and I have felt sorry ever since.

I remember that when we came home from school, we would have a snack. Her snack would consist of a thick slice of home-made bread and butter, covered with a thick layer of cold boiled potatoes with salt and pepper. People in those years never considered the implications of the number of calories or the difference between proteins, starches, or carbohydrates.

Yvette was generally a happy little girl and was mostly content with her dolls and was always singing. That was actually her way of bugging me. Instead of singing wholesome, he-man cowboy songs when she was near me, she insisted on singing those popular "sissy" songs that she learned from the radio.

I don't remember a whole lot of our childhood years together because I spent most of my spare time playing with my chum, Donny, while she was mostly left on her own. I remember one occasion when I was in Grade

I and she was 11 years old, that a boy tried to sexually assault her on the way to school and, although she fought him off, it left her scared to walk the mile-and-a-half. Whatever the reason, our parents then sent her to a convent for schooling until she finished her high school.

Therefore, I only had her company during our summer vacations. I recall that during the summers, we spent many days picking wild berries. The first crop would be strawberries and the wild berries were only the size of a pencil eraser. Then came pin cherries, choke cherries and wild blueberries. All were tiny, and picking was frustratingly slow. Yvette was the best berry- picker in the family and would be quite happy just sitting in the berry patch and picking and singing for hours at a time.

Yvette graduated from Grade 12 in 1942 at age 17, and because there was such a shortage of teachers, she was able to take the teacher training program that was only six weeks long, and she started teaching in a country school near Meadow Lake that fall. She was only about 5'2" and was much shorter and younger than many of her students. Her first school was in the district of Doreme. (The nearby districts of Fa-Sol-La, and Ti-Do were never settled and therefore have never existed. My bad musical joke!!)

She was a super teacher and was much loved by her students. She transferred to a larger school at Goodsoil, a mainly-German area about 50 miles northwest of Meadow Lake, and remained there for many years.

Not long after her arrival in Goodsoil, she met a man named Albert Bundschuh, and they were married on January 2, 1947. On the day before the wedding, they were walking from our house to Mirelda's when Yvette slipped on the ice and fell on her face, blackening both eyes and severely bruising her nose. Before the small ceremony, the priest enquired if Albert had already demonstrated his desire to be boss.

While Yvette was teaching, they opened a little grocery store in Goodsoil and Albert operated a small farm. Albert was a lousy store manager and not much better as a farmer. His true calling was as a lover, siring eight children with Yvette and nearly as many with a mistress that he alternatively lived with while Yvette was busy having a child. Yvette finally left Albert in about 1973 and moved to Chilliwack, BC, with her four youngest children.

Yvette suffered from many health conditions and passed away on January 28, 1977, at Invermere, BC, where she had recently moved from Chilliwack. Phyllis and I drove up to the funeral with Lou and Margie and had a lovely visit with all of her children. They were nice kids and a credit to Yvette and the lessons she taught them.

The eight children are Harvey, born 1948; Mary, 1950; Susan, 1951; Joseph, 1954; Phillip, 1957; Glen, 1959; Lorne, 1962; and Ernest, 1965. After Yvette's death the two youngest, Lorne and Ernie went to live with Mirelda's oldest daughter, Mona, until they finished school and then went to live with their older siblings.

I'm sorry that I have not maintained contact with any of this family of nephews and nieces, because they didn't have the easiest lives but still managed to keep positive attitudes, a credit to the love and countless hours of caring motherhood by Yvette who received little support from her brothers.

Chapter 16

MY FIRST JOBS -
AND HELLO ROSE

When I graduated from high school in Saskatoon, I had a job waiting for me, working for my brother, Lou, in his fish and chip shop in New Westminster, serving customers and cooking.

My wages started at $10 per week, plus my board and room, with Mondays off. After a couple months, after I had learned to cook and perform the other functions, I got a raise to $15 per week. I slept on the couch in the living room of Lou and Margie's suite across the street from the shop.

Lou started work at about 8:30, cleaning the place and getting the vats of fat (beef drippings) heated, and receiving supplies of fresh fish, potatoes, bread and pastries, and opened the shop at about 9:00 a.m., when I would arrive in time for fresh coffee and breakfast. Lou would leave me alone in the shop in the afternoons and evenings, when it wasn't busy, and go home to spend time with Margie and Wendy. If several customers suddenly came in, I would go out the backdoor and call him.

While I was alone in the shop in the early afternoon, often some old men would come in for coffee and to talk. This was 1948, so their memories were vivid of the period from 1870, through the Great War of 1914-1918 and the Great Depression, as well the Second World War.

The city was actually founded in 1859 and the first settlers were the Royal Engineers from England, referred to as The Sappers. With completion of the CPR in 1885, the city provided a port enabling shipments in and out of western Canada to the world, and the town boomed. Columbia Street became known as "The Golden Mile". Most of the city's business area burned down in 1898. New Westminster was once considered to be the provincial capital. The city was later given the choice of that or as the site for the provincial prison. The city chose the prison and so it still became the home for crooks. The prison was torn down in the 1980's, I think, and was redeveloped for housing.

The oldsters talked about when they were young and how, every winter, the Fraser River froze over and people crossed back and forth on the ice with horses and sleighs until the Patullo Bridge was built in 1937. I should note that by 1948, although we had lots of snow in many winters, the river remained ice-free every winter.

Later in the afternoon, girls from the high school would drop in for cokes and I would chat with them. One of them told me she was good at knitting socks and would knit a pair of white ones with a cable stitch for me if I paid for the wool. When I got them I saw that they were equal in length, but one had a foot that was about 14 inches long and a leg of 3 inches while the other had a foot about 3 inches long and a leg of about 14 inches long. They were nice girls though. I dated a couple of the girls but only once each.

I made friends with two guys, Bob Fenton and Art Burrows. Art was a year older and Bob was about three years older than me. Bob had a car and worked as a delivery man for a laundry down the street. He got a girl-friend, though, and I didn't see much of him after that. They got married and had a family.

Art played junior lacrosse on a good team and I went to some of his games. He got knocked unconscious four times in the first three games of the season, so I didn't want to try to play the sport. Art joined the army and served as a tank operator in the Korean War. I used to visit his mom, an odd little English lady who doted on Art. On winter days, she would put Art's socks and underwear in the oven to warm before she woke him, and served him a cup of hot tea and a doughnut before he got out of bed.

One morning I arrived while he was still asleep, and she insisted on going through the regular routine while I was there, much to Art's embarrassment. He served through the entire Korean War. On occasion, when he was home on leave, he confided to me that he had been knocked about by his mates because he had difficulty adapting to army life, (complaining about the food, cold underwear in the morning, having to dress himself, - my joke), and the absence of other pampering. However, he soon adapted to army life and fitted in.

The weather was anything but pleasant during the first two years; it rained all summer and snowed all winter, it seemed. There was a lot of pea soup fog during the winter, because most people burned sawdust exclusively for cooking and heating their homes. In Lou and Margie's suite, there was just a kitchen stove which had a hopper attached, and held a ten-gallon bucket of sawdust. The hopper opened at the bottom to allow a steady flow of sawdust into the firebox. It was almost impossible to get dry sawdust, which would permit the fuel to flow steadily into the firebox. What we got was moist and stuck together. Every few minutes someone would have to give the hopper a swat and a clump of sawdust would drop into the firebox, the sudden input of fuel would ignite, the air pressure would lift the lids on the stove and we were treated to a blast of heat. It was a hell of a job to regulate the oven temperature and gave Margie fits when she was baking. She once baked a chocolate cake for someone's birthday, and the cake came out of the oven cooked around the outside, but raw in the middle. She took out the uncooked part and filled in the hole with icing. That evening there was the usual crowd of friends and she served the good part of the cake. Anyone that wanted seconds was served a two-inch thick square of mint icing. Lots of laughs!!!

The following spring, when Dad refused to co-sign for me for a loan to open a fish and chip shop in White Rock in partnership with Lou, I had to make plans for a new career. Lou had been talking with the chartered accountant who did his accounting, and was impressed by how much money he was earning as a CA, so he suggested I take a commercial course and then join a CA firm. It sounded good to me, so I discussed the matter with my parents and they agreed to pay for my school tuition and give me free board and room for the several months involved.

I enrolled at The New Westminster Commercial College in the spring of 1949, and was required to take the full course of studies, including bookkeeping, typing, business English, filing, etc. Soon after starting my studies I realized that I was wasting a lot of time on things I would never need as an accountant, such as typing, and I could be using the extra time better on the bookkeeping course. Therefore, I only practiced my typing when really required and my weekly typing tests attested to that fact. After six months of business school, I was only able to type 15 words per minute, after deducting mistakes.

I made several friends while at the business school. Cliff, Howard, and Slob (I can't remember his real name) were friends who had gone to high school together and were chums. Slob was an interesting kid who had broken his leg or hip and walked with crutches. The crutches were the type that didn't extend to the armpit, so all of his weight was supported strictly on his hand holds. He walked up and down the Sixth Street hill every day to school and, often, again in the evening to go to the pool hall. His chest, shoulders and arms were massive. Cliff and Howie picked on Slob regularly, teasing and ridiculing him. Much of it was deserved because Slob often did act like a slob.

One incident stands out in my memory. Just before I met them, they were hanging out at Howie's house and, just for laughs they tied Slob spread eagled onto a four poster bed. Howie's parents kept a flock of chickens in the back yard, and the boys brought in a handful of grain and a chicken. They opened Slob's shirt and pants and sprinkled grain over his belly and then set the chicken on him to peck away. Slob thereafter claimed to have frequent nightmares of monster chickens attacking and clawing at him.

I made another friend at the school named Bernie Martineau, who became my first best friend, someone that I would have given my life for and we had no secrets. He had enlisted for a two-year stint in the peace time army but, after a year, he couldn't stand it any longer and bought his way out. He was now embarked on a new career path.

While at the school, all of the boys used to go into the corridor at recess to smoke and talk. When doing this, we met a young guy named Roauld Anderson, who was working as an apprentice in a dental mechanic's shop next to the school. He later became a psychiatric nurse and I later worked with him occasionally in the hospital. At that later time, he was operating his own dental mechanic business on the side and made my first set of dentures and also arranged to have all of my teeth pulled. The cost was $100 for the dentist and $75 for both upper and lower dentures. That was in 1960 and I had them until 1990.

While at business school, Bernie met a bookie who knew somebody who knew somebody who knew a jockey who was in on a ring of crooked horse people that fixed races. The deal was that you got a tip in the morning, made your bet and collected and then paid the tipster 50%. The plan worked like a charm for three bets. Then on Saturday, Bernie got the tip and decided to go to the track in person and to be there to collect big time. The tip was for "Red Star" to win, and Bernie put $100 on the nose. He got really carried away with the race and the commentator announcing the race, and was cheering wildly as the winner was announced as "Star Duster". All of the sudden he realized that it was the wrong horse. Monday, at school, Bernie was able to tell the whole story about how he had been cheated, while he was supposed to be the one doing the cheating. He swore off gambling.

Although the business course was supposed to take ten months, I completed the bookkeeping part in six months and was anxious to get started on the CA program; I made an appointment with a CA who was advertising for a new employee. I was crushed to learn that the starting wage was only $55 per month and it was a four-year apprenticeship. I would have to pay Mom $45 per month for board and room and $35 per month for bus fare. I would need to get a monthly loan; and that didn't leave any money for necessities like beer.

I went into the Commercial College that afternoon and told Mr. Etherington, the owner/principal, the sad news. He said that he had received a call from a prior student (35 years prior), named Murphy, who was Vancouver bureau chief for the radio news section of The Canadian Press, a major wire news service, and he was looking for an assistant. I said that I would love a chance, so he set up an interview for me the following morning.

I found the office above a bank on the corner of East Hastings and Cambie St., across the street from Victory Square. Mr. Murphy showed me around, and I was very impressed with about six teletype machines, all clacking away and spewing news from all over the world, about three teletype operators key punching and another three or four men busy on typewriters re-writing news items. During the interview, I confessed to Murphy that my typing skills were sadly deficient, but he said "don't worry; you won't be thinking any faster than you can type. Also, don't worry about spelling mistakes, just re-type and cross out the mistake with your pencil". He offered me $25 per week, with $2 per week for working the evening shift. I was to have every second Saturday and Sunday off, all day, and every second Saturday that I worked would be on day shift and I'd have the night off.

On the Sundays that I worked, I was alone in the office and was required to operate the teletype machine. If you aren't familiar with the teletype, it had a keyboard rather similar to a typewriter, but there were several differences in the keys, (it only printed in capital letters and the upper case produced various symbols and other characters and numbers) and it punched little holes in a paper tape. You put the tape on a sending machine and it was transmitted to the various radio stations' news rooms. I was only given about a half hour of training on it before my first Sunday on duty, and that was a disaster. The teletype mechanic was supposed to set up the re-perforator machine on Saturday night before he went home, to receive the forecast from the weather office so that I could put the tape directly on the sender. The weather was received as hard copy, and the re-perforator machine reproduced it in tape form, and our office sent it to the radio stations without having to re-punch it. However, he had been drinking too much at work and didn't properly set up the machine. The result was just two long pages of gibberish, and I was now faced with having to re-type it. The problem was that you couldn't see whether you made a typing mistake until later, when it was being sent. I spent about two futile hours in trying and re-trying to send a legible copy until one of the radio stations' editors phoned and told me the weather was lovely and to just give up.

The Sunday shift started with a visit at seven a.m. to the Vancouver Police Station to pick up any overnight news items. There were usually only a bunch of drunk and minor charges for assaults and family disagreements, but occasionally there were more serious problems such as murders, fatal accidents, etc., or even something humorous. I recall once when there was a fight in Chinatown between two Asian gentlemen, and one was stabbed in the groin and had to be taken to the hospital. The victim's name was "Won Hun Lo". I wrote the story and then waited to be called by some radio news editor that might have used the story and who didn't clearly pronounce the victim's second name (as in "Hung").

I also had to call the hospitals later to see if they had received patients who had been injured in accidents or fires. There seldom were, but it gave me a chance to chat up the nurses and resulted in a couple dates with one nurse from the Lion's Gate Hospital. She had a little girl and was looking for a husband, so I didn't pursue the relationship (I was still only 19 years old and earning $27 per week).

On weekdays I worked from 3 to 11 p.m. and had barely time to catch the last bus home at 11.30. The job consisted mainly in re-writing and adapting news articles from the Vancouver daily newspapers. We had several regional splits when the national office in Toronto would shut down so the various regional bureaus could file our local news. After sending our batch of news items, we were able to relax and play rummy, drink beer, etc.

The company policy was that drinking beer in the office was permitted as long it didn't interfere with your work, and we interpreted that to mean not falling off your chair. We got our pay checks every Thursday afternoon, took them to the Carlton Hotel beer parlor across the street to cash them, have a few glasses, and buy a six-pack to take to the office. After a beer and a couple hours of serious work it was time for lunch. That meant going back to the Carlton for more beer, followed by a game of gin rummy with 10-cent limits. By Monday, we were too broke for either beer or rummy.

I had a particular friend in the office, named Marcel Belair, who was a teletype operator that could type perfect copy at ninety words a minute while being so drunk his eyes were mere slits. On Friday nights, we would leave the office in his car, stop at Sai Woo's café in Chinatown, pick up some chow mien and sweet and sour pork and go to his home where his wife, Helen, would have steamed rice ready. After eating, Helen would phone my Mom and tell her that I would be sleeping over and not to worry. Helen would move one of their two sons to share the top bunk and

I would crawl into the bottom, only to be wakened early the next morning by two excited little boys who thought it was such fun to jump on me and tell me everything they had done in the past week.

Marcel had a particularly interesting background. He was French Canadian, raised in Winnipeg and later moved to Toronto with Helen and worked in the company's head office bureau. During the war he was conscripted and reported for basic training in the infantry. He was about 5'10' in height and weighed about 115lbs. He didn't like carrying a heavy rifle while marching many miles and accidentally dropped it several times every day when on parade, which upset the sergeants and officers. He was considered to be a danger to everyone, so he was transferred to the army base post office. In the meantime, Gillis Purcell, the general manager of The Canadian Press, was having trouble keeping staff and so he contacted Marcel to see how he was doing. Marcel explained his troubles, and it only required a phone call to somebody in the Defense Department and Marcel was out of the army and back at work.

Purcell, called "Perky" by all the staff, was an old-time newsman who knew how to party. Every winter he arranged a hockey game in Montreal between the Toronto and Montreal bureau staffs. Everyone attended and there was a great party afterwards in the biggest hotel in town. On one occasion, Perky and others rolled up a huge carpet from the floor in a banquet room and staggered off with it to the train station. Part way on the return trip to Toronto, the train was stopped by the police who retrieved the rug. There was never any suggestion of charges. The power of the press!!!

One evening, near the end of my shift, a big fire broke out in a Vancouver warehouse that was used to store new cars in the False Creek area by one of the big dealers. Pop Finley, the night editor of the newspaper wire service, asked me to go over and phone him the details. As background, I should tell you that for the previous several weeks the Vancouver police were undergoing attacks by the press for corruption. Several people claimed that their valuables disappeared while they were locked up for drinking, etc. The issue became very intense and all the police were very upset with all the reporters.

I had identified myself to the police at the scene and was standing in the middle of the street watching the fire, when the crowd moved forward to where I was standing. A big police sergeant came along and told everyone to move back, so I was moving slowly back. He put his hand on my chest and gave me a shove and I stumbled backwards over several fire hoses. I said "Okay, I'm moving". With that, he grabbed me, said "I'll show you, you smart reporter", and marched me to a call box and ordered a paddy wagon. I was driven to the police station, booked and put into a cell by myself and spent a couple hours wondering how things had gone so wrong and how I was going to get out of the big mess.

Fortunately, a reporter from The Province, named Bruce Hutchinson, had seen the entire event and came in to bail me out. Bruce later became well known as a newspaper columnist. After leaving the jail, I had no choice but to go back to the office (it was the middle of the night, the buses had stopped running, and I had only a couple dollars). I lay on my desk, but wasn't able to sleep. The following morning, I was called into the bureau chief's office and was assured that a lawyer would handle the matter for me. One of the other staff went with me to the police courtroom for my trial at 10.00 a.m. A few minutes before we went into the courtroom, my lawyer came over to me, followed by Sergeant Washbrook, a cop the size of a sumo wrestler who had accused me of resisting. The lawyer asked me to shake hands with the officer, which I did after being told it was only a formality, and I was led into the courtroom and seated next to the Sergeant in front of the railing which separated the judge and court workers from the gallery where all of the other defendants were seated with the visitors. I felt more uncomfortable than important by the special treatment. When my case was called, the clerk read the charge and, in the same breath, said that I had apologized to the officer and he was therefore requesting that the charge be withdrawn. Almost before he had finished saying that, the judge said "Granted. Case dismissed", my lawyer grabbed my arm and pushed me out of the courtroom door before I could even say "what the hell". The lawyer was named Thomas Dohm, and he became a long-serving judge in Vancouver. They had all been able to take advantage of my naivety so easy and inwardly, it bothered me for years.

Through my time at the Commercial College and all of my nearly two years at The Canadian Press I continued my close friendship with Bernie. He became the favorite of all of my chums with my Mom. He was a French Canadian, from the Maillardville area of Coquitlam, was hand-some, suave, and always the perfect gentleman. Bernie also enjoyed young man stuff, like drinking beer, and chasing girls. (He was my kind of pal.) On Saturdays, he would pick me up in his car after dinner, and we would go to the Russel hotel downtown for a couple beers, then the Terminal Hotel in Maillardville, then the Commercial Hotel in Port Coquitlam, then about two miles east to the Wild Duck Inn, then on to the Maple Ridge Hotel where we drank another couple glasses of beer and bought a six-pack to get us all the way to Mission, about 20 minutes. By the time we got to the dance in Mission or Matsqui, we were scarcely able to dance, but the dance would be nearly over anyways. We usually managed to get a couple girls to take home. While parked somewhere on the way home, I would listen to Bernie go through the funniest routine, much of it in French, to a very impressed girl who thought he was giving her compli-ments, but was actually calling her a little cabbage whose eyes looked like piss holes in the snow.

After getting home in the early morning, if the weather was good, we would pick dew worms on the lawns of nearby homes and then, after one or two hours sleep, we would go fishing in the Fraser River near Fort Langley. I don't remember ever catching any fish, except bull heads.

One Saturday evening, after leaving the Russel Hotel, we went to a dance hall about a block away, arriving about half way through the dance. Bernie met a blond girl, named Mary, and she proved to be more than a match for Bernie's smooth line. After having something to eat, he took her home and casually asked her if she would be at the next Saturday's dance. She, just as casually, said "maybe". On the following Saturday, when Bernie asked me where we were going, I said "don't you want go to the Hollywood Bowl?", and he said "why?' and I said Mary's probably expecting you. We argued for a while and he finally agreed, as I knew he would. Mary was at the dance and avoided looking at him until he finally went and asked her to dance. On the way home, Bernie mentioned that he and I were going fishing in the morning. She asked if she could come and Bernie agreed, but only if she brought lunch for us. She agreed and we were later pleased to see her bringing out two big bags of food and a couple thermoses of coffee. We were both impressed at Mary's talent. It was weeks later that she admitted that she had got her mother out of bed and the two spent an hour making the lunch.

One of the perks of my job was that, as a CP newsman, I got free train passes on the railways. I took advantage of that and went back to Saskatoon both years that I worked at The Canadian Press. I should mention that the weather had been terrible ever since I arrived in June, 1948 – heavy snow and fog during the winters and almost constant rain through the rest of the years. Then, in 1951, we had a beautiful spring and summer. We had a hundred straight days without any rain. In any event, I had for about the last two years, planned to move back to Saskatoon and resume my relationship with my school days sweetheart, Mary. We had continued to carry on a casual romance by letter, although she had mentioned that she had recently been seeing a young man who worked for the railway.

In June, 1951, I took a free train trip to Saskatoon to visit my friends and, while there, I visited the local radio station, CFQC, and applied for a job in their news room. Back in Vancouver, one Sunday morning in September at work, I received a phone call from Godfrey Hudson, the newsroom director of CFQC, offering me a job as newscast editor and reporter. The job paid $215 per month, far more than the $35 per week that I was now making. I accepted and a week later, I was on my way.

I moved into a bedroom in the basement of Mirelda and Francis's house and arranged for board and room. It was like living at home and nothing had changed in the three years I had been away – still the same bunch of boarders and kids making the same noise and commotion.

My job consisted of going to the police station and the city and fire halls in the morning to see if there were items of interest. However, there was very seldom anything newsworthy and I couldn't bring myself to write about the small events such as a chimney fire, arrest of some drunk, or the letting of a contract for building maintenance, etc. Hudson got frustrated and told me so, and finally took me off that part of my job. I didn't mind losing those duties, because that had been in addition to newscast editing and, besides, I was a lousy reporter. I kept getting mixed up in recording who said what – Mills, the mayor, or Milne, the police chief, (or was it the other way around?).

We worked either of two shifts: 5:30 a.m. to 2:00 p.m. or 2:30 p.m. to 11:30 p.m. There were four major newscasts per day, each fifteen minutes long, at 8:00 a.m., 12:00 noon, 6:00 p.m. and 10:00 p.m. There were also several five minute newscasts, usually on the hour. Hudson always entered one of our major newscasts in an annual competition in New York or Washington and our station always won first prize. This was in the days before television and people took radio much more seriously. My newscasts were chosen both times while I was there. The newscasts were introduced as "Now we present the news, edited by Elmer Benoit and read by (announcer's name)".

One of the events I covered and reported on, successfully, was the Royal Visit, when King George and the queen spent a weekend in Saskatoon, accompanied by Princess Elizabeth and her new husband, Phillip. At one occasion I stood a few feet from them as they were introduced to some veterans from the local hospital. I recalled many years later how much Elizabeth resembled my dearest wife, Phyllis.

My time off work was spent with my school day friends, Homer Hearne, "Silent" Moore, Gerry Munroe, and Bill Cook, drinking beer, playing pool, and partying. Homer was still speed skating, competitively, and I attended his local meets if I could. Mary had started going steady with the guy who worked at the railroad, so I usually went stag to dances.

One Saturday afternoon in October, a couple weeks after my arrival, I was sitting in the King George beer parlor after work, with a bunch of my friends and acquaintances, and having a good time, when somebody came in and said "Hey, everybody, it's snowing". I went to look, and found I could hardly see across the street. I was only wearing a light gabardine top coat, certainly not suitable for a long, freezing, prairie winter. There was a men's wear store in the lobby so I went in and asked the manager if he had a good overcoat. He showed me a beautiful black Elysian wool coat that fit perfectly and I promised to pay for it over the winter. With that, I went back and had another beer with my friends and announced I was moving back to the coast as soon I could. It was nearly three years before I managed to leave.

Around Christmas, 1951, I got a blind date with Rosemarie Verekovsky, the sister of the girlfriend of one of Mirelda's borders, Al Boot. She was blond, attractive, lived with her sister and worked as a cashier at a super-market. We hit it off and started going steady, got engaged and planned to get married in early October. Homer started dating a girl, named June, and eventually married her.

I got whooping cough during the springtime, and, when the cough persisted, the doctor gave me a skin test in case it was tuberculosis. It was very positive, I was put on sick leave at the station, and there followed weeks of resting and X-rays while the doctors debated whether I needed to go to the sanitarium. After a couple months it was determined that the TB was not getting worse and I could go back to work. I had been practicing announcing and had read short newscasts on the air before I got sick. Due to the tuberculosis, I no longer had the lung strength to read fluently on the air and was restricted to editing newscasts from then onwards.

As the time for my wedding neared, I started getting cold feet as I real-ized I was being manipulated by Rose, and she controlled everything that I did. I pondered whether to break off the engagement a few days before the wedding but didn't have the guts.

We were married on October 6, 1952, at the Cathedral, and had a small reception of about twenty guests at Rose's parents' home. Her parents had moved into Saskatoon from Wilkie, a small town about 100 miles west, during the summer. Rose' father, Joe, was a carpenter and worked as a project manager for a large local builder. He was Ukrainian, but was born and lived in Poland before immigrating to Canada. Joe and his wife, Mary, had eight children: Alban, Wilma, Marge, Rosemarie, Maynard, Georgina, Dennis and Jimmy. Mirelda's two sons, Marty and Louis, were the altar boys for our wedding and they got into the booze during the afternoon and ended up sick in the yard.

On our honeymoon, Rose and I took the train to New Westminster to visit Mom and Dad. During that time, we went with Lou and Marge, up the Fraser Canyon to Kamloops and Kelowna. It was a beautiful time, Indian Summer, with wonderful weather and scenery. Rose didn't appreciate Lou's teasing, particularly when he accused her of stinking up the bathroom and it actually was him that had done it. There were many instances during that five day trip that she was the butt of his jokes and she became more and more angry with him, and then with me for laughing.

Lou had recently bought a new Morris Minor car, which had a very small motor and he had to gear down for the smallest hill. He cussed it the entire trip and swore he was going to get a bigger car as soon as he had some more money.

After the honeymoon we returned to Saskatoon and settled into our suite. It was on the third floor of an old house close to downtown, about five blocks from work, and a block from Mirelda. The suite had three rooms and a bath. The kitchen had only a three burner hot plate/rangette and when using more than two burners at a time, it caused the fuse to blow. There was only one outlet in each room, so we had extension cords running all over the place. There were three or four rooms on the second floor rented to old couples who were trying to get by on their pensions of $40 per month. There was only one bathroom on that floor and there was a rule that no one could flush the toilet after 11 o'clock so as to not disturb the sleep of others. When I left for work at 5:00 a.m., the stink as I went past that bathroom almost made me throw up. The landlady kept the wooden stairs waxed so I often slipped on them and slid down to the next landing, waking everybody in the house.

My boss, Hudson, was a supreme egotist and a verbal bully. One day in the spring, he said he wanted me to go golfing with him so I had to walk to his apartment and he drove me to the municipal course. He mentioned more than once that he was a pretty good golfer and had been taking lessons from a pro all winter and also regularly went to the driving range. I had golfed with Homer and Silent about five times during high school, so I had low expectations for myself. I teed off, hitting my ball straight down the fairway, about forty yards. Hudson shanked his ball about two hundred yards to the right, took another ball and shanked it about the same distance to the left. His game went downhill from there. Finally, at the fifteenth hole, I was looking at a dogleg fairway, and being afraid of losing my ball, I selected an old ball that had a big slice in it. I could hear a whistling sound as the wind caught the gash in the ball and it made a wide curve around the dogleg. Hudson decided to shoot his ball over the trees bordering the dogleg to the green. Unfortunately, he landed in the trees, and lost another ball. My ball was on the edge of the green and I holed out with about three putts. Hudson chipped back and forth several times between sand traps on either side of the green and finally gave up. I beat him by several strokes, even though he only counted a fraction of his. He was furious, cancelled the rest of the holes. He drove me back to his apartment building in silence and as I got out of his car, he asked me to go again, but I declined. I quit while I was ahead.

After my wedding, I guess that Hudson assumed that now that I was married, I wouldn't be able to quit my job, because he started giving me shit every day for the least excuse. He would look over my newscasts and go on and on about spelling mistakes, content, choice of news items, etc. The announcers never had a problem with any of my newscasts or ever complained. One day in November, 1952, he picked on one word in my newscast that was misspelled and went off the deep end at me for about ten minutes.

I left the office and walked down to the Canada Manpower office and asked to see the manager. I knew him quite well because I had been coming in to get news items about jobless rates and farm labor, etc. When I told him I wanted a job, he laughed and said he had been expecting me for some time. I was the twenty-seventh person to quit the news room in two years, and the staff only totalled eight. He took me to one of the placement officers and found two jobs that would be suitable for me.

One of the jobs was at the Federal Treasury office administrating the Veterans' Land Act. The salary was only a bit less than I was making at CFQC, and I would be working for my cousin, Maurice Beaulac. I hurried to see Maurice and he hired me as a ledger keeper.

After the war, the government set up a program to help the veterans re-integrate in civilian society. They had a choice of money to further their education, start a business or money plus a loan to buy a farm or build a house. The houses were required to be small holdings, a quarter or half-acre of land with a house, of which the department inspectors supervised the construction. It was a good deal, with the veterans ending up with a nice house and enough land to grow vegetables and fruit trees, all on a loan of under $10,000.

We had a staff of about six, all war veterans except me. Maurice was well liked and highly respected. He eventually rose to be the Treasury Officer for Western Canada, based in Vancouver. He had boarded at Mirelda's when she and Frank first moved to Saskatoon, and Mirelda had introduced Maurice to Margaret, whom he married a couple years later. They were a lovely couple and had a lovely family. In later years, Maurice told everyone that theirs was an arranged marriage – Margaret's mother had advertised, and his mother had answered. Maurice was the son of Napoleon, who played such tricks on Uncle Harvey, so Maurice obviously inherited a talent for teasing.

I had only worked at VLA for nine months when Maurice called me into his office and said he had been talking to a friend who was the supervisor of the Provincial Public Welfare Office. Over coffee in the bus station across the street, the person, named Van Slyck, mentioned that he had an opening for a public assistance assessor. Maurice thought it would be a good opportunity for me and an interview was arranged.

I was hired and received a good raise from what I was making. My new section included a supervisor, whose job was to check our work but usually trusted us, me and another assessor and a clerk. The clerk, a man in his thirties named "Timmy" Tymoshenko had been dropped as an infant and was badly deformed (he was about 4' tall and had a huge hump on his back) became one of my dearest friends. We had coffee and lunch together daily, and often went for a few beers after work. He talked occasionally about his childhood, and it had been a pretty sad and lonely time for him. With me, he was happy, and occasionally joked about lying on the ground and getting flattened out by a steam roller.

My duties included administering various forms of provincial assistance, mainly proving the age of applicants for provincial old age allowance which had to be 65 -70 years old, and, in all forms of assistance, assessing their incomes, called a "means test", which determined their entitlement. The proof of age was often a problem if the applicant didn't have a birth or baptismal certificate, because many had immigrated as children and their parents may have lied about the ages in order to obtain lower priced passage on the shipping lines, and then overstated their ages on census forms when the child was approaching marriage age. Other documents that were useful were immigration records, the 1940 National Registration records (when people were required to be listed in order to get ration cards), as well as notations in family bibles.

Often we found only two proofs that agreed out of five or six searches. That meant referring the file to head office in Regina for a decision. I believed that these people were in real need of the money, so, as soon as I got two proofs that agreed, I shredded the others and sent the file for approval. The old folks would be transferred to the Old Age Security (Federal) program at age 70 any way. Also, if we didn't give them Old Age Assistance they would have to go on welfare. Same difference!!!

The case load was divided pretty evenly with the other assessor who had been on the job for many years, but she wasn't very efficient. We each had about 45 pending cases and I dropped my pending to about 25 after a couple months, while hers grew.

One day, Van Slyck asked her to go to the Prince Albert office for a couple weeks to cover for a sick employee. I said I could cover her desk as well as mine and, while she was away, I cleared all of her old cases, shredding some stuff and removing other stuff while I sent the files to Head Office for approval and then replaced it when the files were returned. She was pretty pissed off with me when she came back and found she now only had about 20 pending cases, all recent.

We also handled Blind Persons' Allowance and Mothers' Allowance for widows with young children and those who had husbands who were incapacitated. In the cases of incapacitated husbands we required a doctor's certificate as proof which we forwarded with the file to Head Office for review and approval. Our office serviced about 24 municipalities as well as several towns and cities, and about half of our total cases were in three small municipalities, just north of Saskatoon which were of mostly one religious sect and included their own doctors and lawyers as members. The allowance was limited to a maximum of twelve children and some families always had another child to add when one child turned sixteen and became too old to qualify. Such reasons given for incapacity included back aches, headaches, and even obesity. In one case, the incapacity of the husband was listed with a medical condition which I didn't understand. When the file came back it was marked "Refused" and the reason the department doctor gave was that the medical term meant sleeping sickness , and the fact the husband in question had sired eighteen children was proof he wasn't sleeping much of the time.

In May, after I'd been on the job for about eight months, Van Slyck called me into his office and told me he was very pleased with my work and that I seemed to grasp the whole reason for our department, i.e., to help people that were in need. Therefore, the department was offering me a living allowance plus a year's leave of absence and free tuition to attend the University of Saskatchewan to take courses in social work and then I would have to return to the office for two more years as a Social Worker. I was tempted, but I said I was going to be quitting in June and moving to B.C. I left that job with real regret. Timmy cried when I finally left the office.

During that spring, I received a call from the news director at Radio Station CFQM, the other station in Saskatoon, offering me a job in his station, doing much the same work as I had been doing at CFQC. I worked for about three or four evenings just to see if I would enjoy it, but it was too much the same, both the work and the boss, he was an egoist, same as Hudson. I turned the job down.

Meanwhile, things were not going well for me at home. Rose was soon revealed to be schizophrenic, manifested in having a persecution complex. She went through periods when I couldn't even visit Mirelda and her family, so I had to sneak over for a few minutes when I went to the store. At night, she kept me awake for hours complaining that no one, particularly me, liked her. She believed that people were gossiping about her behind her back. All through our marriage, she went through periods of about a month when she would like a person, or a couple, and we would visit back and forth and then she would suddenly say to me as we went to bed: "did you hear what so and so said to me? He (or she) insulted me." Then followed an hour of debating what the person actually meant and why the person didn't really like her, and we wouldn't see them for a long while. Then, in the following week, we'd start visiting somebody else and repeat the whole routine. She was the same with all of our families and friends. She went to a clinical psychiatrist for several months and he gave her several electric shock treatments, but without any benefit. We no longer had friends with which to socialize.

At the time, Rose was having interpersonal trouble at the store where she was working, and I suggested she quit, so she did. To make some extra money, we rented a big house near downtown and started a boarding house. We had about eight boarders and they shared, two per room. We only charged $12 per week and fed them three meals a day, six days per week. The house was not insulated and that winter was terribly cold: 40 below through all of January. The furnace had been converted from coal to oil and the oil tank was located outside. The line from the tank to the furnace in the basement had a filter, which filled with condensation and that froze, necessitating me getting up several times each night to pour boiling water over it to get the oil flowing again and then re-light it.

I made arrangements with a little corner store nearby to supply us with case lots of canned fruit and vegetables as well as other, highly discounted, bulk foods and supplies. One of our boarders was a personal friend of mine and he arranged with his father, who owned a farm east of town, to butcher a steer and a pig to sell me at a good price. My friend and I had to cut the meat up into steaks, chops, roasts, stewing meat, etc. but we managed it all in one weekend. The rent for the house was high, but we made a good profit on the boarding house and at the end, we were debt free and with a small savings account.

In June, 1954, we packed up and moved to the West Coast.

Chapter 17

NURSING

Rose and I arrived in New Westminster in early June, 1954, and moved into the garage at the rear of Mom and Dad's home on Sixth St at 3rd Ave. They had hired somebody to make the garage habitable, installed flooring, plaster panelling, windows, wiring, and had it painted, inside and out. It was suitable to live in, rent-free, during the summer while I looked for a job.

I was looking forward to a couple weeks of holiday but Rose got onto me, after just a couple days, to find work. Marge and Lou came over to visit and Lou suggested I take the psychiatric nursing training. He said the nurses had formed a union and were expecting to get a big contract with significant raises. So, the next morning, I went out to Essondale to apply and was accepted for the classes which would begin in early September. I needed a job for the interim and Andy Bowes, Margie's dad who was head cook at Woodlands School, arranged for me to be hired as a nurse's aide at the school.

Woodlands School was a branch of the Essondale Provincial Mental Hospital and housed patients, mainly children, who suffered mental disabilities. Probably more than half suffered from Down's syndrome, while many others suffered from such conditions as cerebral palsy. There were probably eight or ten wards, each with about thirty patients. Male and female patients were in separate wards staffed by same sex staff.

My instructions, when I started my job on the ward, were to assist another aide in supervising the day room where the patients played or sat on benches around the perimeter of the room. Organized games were not planned or even encouraged, so the children were expected to just sit quietly all day. Of course kids act like kids and got antsy often, in which case the aide would caution them and, if it persisted, the other aide would sometimes spank them. A couple of the aides that I worked with were quite sadistic and would use the leather straps attached to their keys to lash the kids on their backs or legs. The sight of such abuse sickened me but it seemed to be condoned by the senior staff or, at least, overlooked.

I had only been working there for a few weeks when I was asked to take a tray into one of the bedrooms to feed a patient who had contracted Hepatitis "A". A sign outside the room said "ISOLATION" but no one told me what that meant, so I just walked in, wearing my regular clothes, chatted with the boy while I fed him, then left. My two days off followed and when I went back to work, I asked one of the nurses why my skin had turned yellow, just like the kid in isolation, and I felt sick. He told me that I had obviously contracted the same disease and I better see the charge nurse and go home before I spread it to more people. He also explained to me the actual meaning of the word "ISOLATION". I went to my parents' doctor and he told me to stay home and rest for two weeks. He didn't explain what the side effects of the disease were, like alcohol can seriously damage the liver of anyone suffering hepatitis, so on my way home, I picked up a case of beer to help me pass the time. After I had begun the nursing course two weeks later, I was later able to study the disease and realized why my side hurt and my pee was bright yellow every time I had a beer. The condition passed after a couple years. I have never been able to donate blood.

Anyways, I was determined to start my training on time, so I showed up for nursing classes in early September, 1954, after my two weeks rest. On the first day, our class of about twenty five students, about ten men and fifteen women, were taken on a tour of the hospital. When we arrived on the Coma-Insulin ward in Crease Clinic (a treatment facility in which patients were admitted for a maximum of four months), I was feeling quite weak. In this particular ward, patients who commonly suffered from bi-polar syndrome were given an overdose of insulin. The insulin caused the patient to become unconscious and he was left in that state for an hour or so, then he would be revived by pouring a pitcher of sugar-syrup down his throat. On this occasion, a patient didn't have the proper reaction and instead went into convulsions. A nurse attending him tried to insert a catheter through his nostril into his stomach. The darn catheter, instead of going into his stomach, kept coming back out of his mouth. After repeating the process a couple times, the catheter became bloody and looked absolutely gross. Watching the process proved to be too much for me and I fainted. Fortunately, I was standing next to an empty bed and landed on it. I came to minutes later with all my classmates standing around me laughing. Any ways, the patient was given a large syringe full of sugar-syrup, injected directly into his artery and he immediately was revived. I and my classmates then continued the tour.

The total nursing course consisted of six weeks of classes with exams, followed by six months of working on the wards, then repeated with another six weeks of classes and six months on the wards and then a final six weeks of classes followed by the balance of our second year. That meant eighteen weeks of classes during the two years. The male graduate nurses were earning about $265 while the female nurses were getting considerably less. In 1955, the nurses got their first contract and the wages, for both male and female grads, were to start at $247 and rise over about five years to about $270. This was called "equal pay for equal work", although the wards with female nurses had twice as many staff as similar wards with male staff. The reason was that a female patient requiring to be moved required two female staff while a male patient was picked up and moved by one male nurse. I know that to be a fact, because most male wards I worked on were adjacent to female wards with similar patients, as in admitting, treatment, old age, or chronic psychosis treatment wards. The vote on accepting the contract was split about two to one in favor, which approximated the ratio of female to male staff. By that time, I only had a few months until graduation, and I thought I should wait and get my nursing ticket so I would have something to fall back on in case I ever needed another job. If I stayed on as a grad, I would have received a raise of $22 per month.

The class work was interesting and I enjoyed my fellow students. There was a separate classroom for the female students, depending on the subject matter. Each class room had a bed containing a dummy on which we could practise nursing skills, such as bed-making, washing, and giving injections, enemas, etc. The girls often came into our classroom when it was vacant and tied ribbons on the penis of our male dummy.

The female students were required to live in the girls' dormitory, while the married men were allowed to live at home. Several of the girls were expelled after the first set of lectures, when nightly room checks noted absences past curfew. The evidence was explained as "footprints on the window sill".

A couple of the students were terribly uncoordinated but they hung in and eventually graduated. One fellow, when he was required to practice giving an injection into a foam rubber insert in the arm of the dummy, stuck the needle about a half inch into his thumb. When the time came for us to practise giving injections to each other, he found it difficult to get a partner.

Working on the wards was mostly interesting, although it was also frustrating. We were taught the symptoms and treatment for the various types of mental illness, but when we were actually in contact with the patients on day shift, we were so short staffed that we only had time to deal with their physical needs. On afternoon shift, I often had an hour to spare after dinner in which to work with a patient. For example, I was assigned for two months to the communicable diseases (mainly tuberculosis) ward, and, I started working with two patients who were catatonic schizophrenics. Both men were so withdrawn that they were totally immobile unless someone physically moved them. Every evening, I would get them out of bed and lead them to the shower room, push them into stalls, and turn the hot shower on them, talking all the time. After twenty minutes, I would turn off the water and toss each a towel. At first, the towels would fall to the floor and I would pick them up and dry them off. Then I'd lead them back to bed. After a week, they were catching the towels and drying themselves and walking back to their beds without prodding. I was congratulating myself on actually helping sick patients, but then I was transferred to another ward. I came back to relieve one day a couple months later and when I checked the two patients, I found they were as withdrawn as much as ever.

I was equally frustrated on other wards and realized that, to affect permanent cures, the hospital would need three or four times as many trained staff. The veteran nurses no longer tried to improve the mental states of chronic patients; they just had time enough to tend to physical needs. In one chronic ward in West Lawn Building, there was one nurse, one student, and one aide looking after 125 patients. Tuesdays and Fridays were hectic when we had to shave all the patients. The least of the problems on those occasions was that we had to it all with only two safety razor blades.

Working in Crease Clinic was different. The patients were mostly suffering breakdowns and responded to treatment within the four months permitted for them; those who didn't respond to treatment were transferred to the chronic wards, first to the admitting ward in Center Lawn Building, then to a treatment ward or a chronic ward in East or West Lawn Buildings. Besides the coma insulin treatment ward, Crease Clinic also had an electric shock treatment ward, where an electric shock was administered using electrodes held against the patient's temples. The patient was placed on a table and held firmly while the shock was administered, causing the patient to convulse before becoming unconscious. There were two more wards in the clinic, one for occupational therapy (woodworking, rug hooking, weaving, etc.), and another for recovery after the series of treatments, in which patients rested and talked to staff. The wards in Crease Clinic were duplicated on every floor for male and female patients. The treatments were performed on day shift, while on afternoon shift, the nurses had a couple hours to talk to the patients, but there were only a couple nurses and a student available on that shift. I spent two months on the coma insulin ward, one month on each shift. I found the afternoon shift a bit troubling; in talking to the patients I found myself to have many of the same basic concerns and the only difference between us was that I had the keys to leave when the shift was over. There were about forty patients on each of the three wards. There were about sixty suicides per year among the patients that were released, not a great record for permanent recovery.

I also spent two months on the admitting ward in the Center Lawn Building and would like to mention a couple incidents that occurred there.

One of the patients was a young man from Kelowna, named Bobby, who had a nervous breakdown. He played hockey for the semi-pro team, and had trouble dealing with an uncertain future after hockey, providing for a lovely wife and a beautiful little daughter that I met when they came to visit him. The man was coming around nicely and after a couple weeks he was asked to help out on the ward. On day shift, a student from my class, Frank, asked him to carry some bags of garbage to the incinerator at the rear of the building. As they turned to go back to the ward, Bobby looked up the hillside to the forest, and took a few steps in that direction. Frank said "stop" and Bobby turned and returned to the ward. Frank should have let it be, but chose to make a big deal of it and reported that Bobby had tried to escape. By the time I came in for the afternoon shift, Bobby had been transferred to a chronic ward and, believing he would never get out, he went berserk. With just a little common sense on Frank's part, Bobby could have recovered and been out in a matter of weeks.

Another incident involved a logger who had snapped while working at a logging camp in northern Vancouver Island. He was brought in wearing a straightjacket (a jacket that is laced up to the neck at the back, and the arms of the jacket end in long straps which are wrapped around the person's body and tied), escorted by two Mounties. They just untied him and left him in a side room, which was totally empty of furniture. He arrived about 2:30 p.m., so the day staff decided to just leave him for us to deal with when our shift started at 3:00. When I arrived, I looked through the little window in the door and saw that the patient had been stripped except for his jockey shorts. He had managed to pull an 8-foot length of oak quarter-round trim off the door frame, had broken it into two pieces, and was poking out the glass panes of the window, through the heavy wire screen covering it. He was a really tough looking fellow and I wasn't looking forward to being asked to go in. However, one of the psychiatrists arrived and a table was set up in the corridor and the electric shock equipment was made ready. Two nurses holding a long leather sofa seat cushion before them, and I, with a smaller leather cushion, prepared to enter the room. When the door was unlocked, the patient backed into a corner with his sticks raised, prepared to battle. The two nurses with the long cushion jammed him against the wall and I came in low and pulled his legs off the floor. Within seconds we had disarmed him carried him out on to the table in the hall, and held him while the doctor administered the electric shock. I happened to have chosen the wrong position and was lying across his knees and holding the far edge of the table, because when he received the shock, he went into convulsions and his knees just hammered my chest repeatedly. The convulsions soon ended and the unconscious patient was placed on a bed in another side room. An hour later he woke and calmly asked where the heck he was and where was the logging crew. He was discharged after about a week, at which time my ribs were still sore.

I'll tell another story about that ward. On afternoon shift, we hosted a dance party for our ward on Friday evenings, to which we invited the patients from the female admitting ward across the hall. We got the recreation department to arrange for a phonograph, records and snacks.

One of our male patients was a boy of about twelve years, named Lenny, who was diagnosed as suffering from "simple schizophrenia", which is characterized by a partial withdrawal from reality, and was very difficult to treat, at least at that time. Lenny insisted on coming to the party, even though we didn't think he was a candidate. The party was going really well and I was dancing with a female patient, when I noticed that patients were snickering at something at the other side of the room. I steered my partner over that way and saw Lenny. He was busy masturbating, but with his other hand he was covering his eyes so that, he thought, nobody was able to see him. I called Frank, the other student nurse, and we hustled Lenny out of the room and into his bed. When we took him out of the room, his hand was pulled from his eyes so everyone was then able to see him and he had quite a noisy reaction.

Okay, one last story about that ward. One of the patients had been on the ward for a year and was under observation for a crime he was assumed to have committed while he was momentarily insane. He had been working in a logging camp and had come home to visit his mother. I guess she nagged him too much, because he killed her with a kitchen knife. I was rather surprised to learn that fact, because he worked in the little ward kitchen and one of his jobs was to count the knives after each meal. He seemed to be totally normal, and so his lawyer arranged for a court hearing to determine if he was recovered from his mental illness and could be released. As the date of his hearing neared, he became increasingly anxious, and two days before the hearing, he snapped and so he was transferred to a chronic ward.

I also spent two months each at the Home for the Aged and at Woodlands School and at one of the chronic wards looking after patients' physical and medical needs – there was no time for psychiatric nursing. One event sticks in my memory of my stint at the Home for the Aged. I was working on HA6, which had some fifty-five patients, mostly bed patients who were suffering from dementia. The death rate on the ward was high, with at least one or two patients passing on each month, in spite of excellent nursing. The nursing students seemed to always be the ones who were picked to prepare the bodies for the morgue.

It was a job that had to be done and I didn't really mind it, although most of the students detested it. The process consisted of washing the body with Detyl or some other antiseptic, stuffing the cheeks and other cavities with cotton and tying the penis with gauze to prevent leaking, then wrapping the body in a clean sheet and labelling it. One afternoon as I started my shift, I was asked to give a particular patient his regular injection of medicine in his arm. When I prepared to give the injection, I found the patient had already died some hours earlier, and his noon-time injection was still visible just under the skin. I looked at the patient's chart and found that he was reported to be alert when he received his injection and had eaten his lunch. The entry was not signed by the morning shift student. I told the charge nurse and he only chuckled and said it looked like I was stuck with the job of stuffing another body.

While I was taking the nursing course, and later when I was working at the paper box companies, Rose had a succession of jobs which she left because she felt the other girls were talking about her, behind her back. She would be off work for a month or two and then would try something else. I think her first job was as a switchboard operator for the telephone company before automatic switching equipment was available. For example, if you wanted to call someone in the Hastings Area from your phone in the Granville area, you dialed "0" and the operator would connect you to the number that you asked for.

At the hospital, I received nine statutory holidays which I could combine with my five days off (we worked five days, got 2 days off, worked five days and then got 1 day off, etc.) which was taken in October – April period. Our two weeks of annual vacation was scheduled for us in the summer.

It was impossible for us to get the summer vacations together, and as a result of my low wages, I thought I might work during the summer time off.

My first job was in peat field, south of Marine Drive in the New Westminster – Burnaby area. My only knowledge of my job was that I would be "turning peat". I arrived at the job site to find a pit that was about 50 yards long by 10 yards wide and 5 feet deep. The material that had been removed with a flat spade in pieces of about 18"X15" and 4"or 5" thick. It was laid out in the area adjacent to the pit and the upper portion had already started to dry. My job was to stand two pieces on end touching at the top in the shape of an inverted "V" in long rows so that they could dry more thoroughly. On the following day, I was to stack all of them in stooks, i.e., piles about five feet high so that they could dry thoroughly over the next few days before they were put through a threshing machine which reduced the material to a powder and was baled for marketing. At the start I could only touch my knees when I bent over. By noon I could put both hands flat on the ground and by quitting time, I couldn't straighten up. The back pain was almost unbearable. I struggled out of bed on the following morning determined it was good for me. I managed to stook the pieces of peat that I had stood on end on the previous day and I don't remember going home that day or going to bed, but I did go back to the peat field on the third day to quit and get my pay. The boss told me that most of my stooks had fallen over, and so he gave me a bit over half of the piece rate for what I had done. It was certainly good experience for later years.

During my next year's summer vacation, my friend Bernie suggested that I pick pole beans for his company, and he assured me that lots of people made good money at it. I went to Surrey and took the little ferry to Barnston Island and the farm. I was given a large burlap sack, a bucket and assigned a long row of beans to pick. A school girl of about twelve was assigned to pick beans on the other side of my row and I asked her about herself. I learned that she was one of several children and was trying to earn some money to give to her mother. It was a really hot day and just after we had stopped for lunch, an ice cream truck arrived at the job site. The girl said she couldn't afford the cost of the treat, so I bought her a sundae and a soft drink. I brought my bag of beans to the scaler at the end of my shift and had them weighed, was given a ticket showing the amount, and dragged my aching body home. The following day my back was so sore I couldn't get out of bed. A couple weeks later, Bernie and Mary came to visit and he asked how I had made out in the bean field. I explained that I had had to give up the job and he insisted that I give him the ticket and he got my pay for me. After allowing for the ice cream and pop, I made less than five dollars for the day. That was about the same as the previous year in the peat field, but with a net improvement in the pain that I had to endure.

Those were the only attempts I ever made to supplement my income with manual labor, and I was now satisfied to yield to my father's wisdom that if you get your high school education you don't ever have to work outside; although I did get some extra schooling before and after the nursing.

When I had completed my first six months and got my raise from $150 to $195 per month, I went out and bought my first car, a used 1954 Chevrolet. In April, 1955, Rose and I drove back to Saskatoon for a holiday. I worked from 7:00 a.m. until 3:00 p.m., came home, packed the car and we were on our way at 5.00 p.m. The Trans-Canada highway was blocked by snow in the Fraser Canyon, so we headed for the Stevens Pass in Washington. When we arrived there, we found it was also blocked, necessitating a further detour onto the Snoqualmie Pass on Highway Ten. We drove through the night, stopping only to buy gas and junk food and crossed back into Canada near Bonners Ferry, Idaho, in the morning. I drove all day and most of the next night, arriving in Saskatoon about 5:00 a.m. after some 36 hours of steady driving. I had been awake for 48 hours. The last night on the road was scary, and I began having hallucinations.

First was the appearance on the highway of mountains (on the bald prairie), visible in the bright moonlight, which fell away as I drove over them. This was followed by a series of giant seagulls standing in the middle of the roadway, which also faded away as I drove over them. Finally, the weirdest sight of all, a dragon which was wearing a toque, turtle neck sweater and mittens, flew beside the car, looking at me and smiling at me with the jolliest look on his face, for about a half hour. I finally pulled over and rested for about a half hour, then drove on. I only saw one other car between Regina and Saskatoon.

The Lord was certainly watching over us, because we arrived safely and fell into bed exhausted at Rose's parent's house. A few hours after our arrival, a blizzard struck and lasted for two days. On the day after the storm, it was reported that two cars had been caught in the blizzard, and one of the drivers nearly died. He had left Regina for Saskatoon, wearing light clothing and without any food, water, or emergency gear. He became stuck on the road, the snow banked around and over his car, he ran out of gas keeping the car heater going, and his windows and doors froze tight. He was rescued two or three days later by a snow plow driver who stopped his rig to take a picture of the car and heard shouts from the driver. The other motorist who became stranded in his car was okay because he had packed food, water, sleeping bag, and extra, warm, clothing.

In the summer of 1956, I attended the convocation exercises for the two classes of 1954-1956, (fall and spring), about 50 students, and I was awarded the Medical Director's Medal for General Proficiency, the top student award, combining class marks and ward ratings. I completed my student training in August, and resigned.

Chapter 18

ACCOUNTING STUDIES - AND GOODBYE ROSE

My friend, Bernie Martineau, was back in my life after I returned from Saskatoon in 1954 and I had started the Psychiatric Nursing program. Bernie had married Mary and they had a little girl. When he finished his business course, he got a job at Royal City Foods which operated a cannery in New Westminster, as well as a frozen foods processing plant called Delnor. He was given the job of Cost Accountant and was encouraged to enroll in the Cost Accounting course offered by the Society of Industrial and Cost Accountants of B.C. Bernie did so, and he was progressing well in his job.

When I was in my second year of nursing, Bernie learned how little I was earning as a student and what my prospects were as a graduate nurse, he insisted that I follow his lead and get into industrial accounting. I was hesitant because Bernie had started having trouble in his studies, (he flunked his advanced cost accounting course and never did get his degree), but when I won the top award in my nursing course, I decided to give it a try.

I applied for membership as a student in the Society of Industrial and Cost Accountants of B.C. and started my studies in September, 1956, attending evening classes at U.B.C., and taking two classes per week. The total program involved seven courses followed by submission of a 12,000 word thesis. I intended to take two courses per year for three years, and one course in the fourth year while writing my thesis, thereby getting my degree in four years. I thought I'd be clever and take the difficult, technical, courses in the first three years and take the easier, management practices course, in the fourth year when I could write my thesis at the same time. I passed the first six courses but flunked the easy course and had to repeat it.

I spent two nights per week at the university taking two courses, two nights doing assignments, and two nights preparing for the next lectures. I often needed to spend part of the weekend also. It was wearisome, sitting in our tiny bedroom from just after helping with the dinner and cleaning up until nearly midnight every night. The upside was that I had two nights out of the suite and four nights in seclusion, away from Rose's bitching and complaining. She didn't let me off that lightly, just compressed the nagging from bedtime until one or two a.m.

When I enrolled in the accounting course, I had to quit my nursing job because that involved shift work and I needed to work steady day shift. I got a job at Industrial Engineering Ltd., packing chain saws at the end of the conveyor chain in the shipping department. It was backbreaking work, but the other men were young and easy going and I found it a pleasant work-place. I worked there for six months, until one of my classmates arranged an interview for me with his boss at Vancouver Paper Box Ltd, as estimator and junior accountant. The manager was Frank Weiler, a really fine man who remained my close friend until his death at Christmas of 2014.

The plant was located just off East Hastings, in a fairly seedy part of town. The company produced rigid boxes, as used for gifts or jewelry, and were covered with a decorative paper, very attractive and expensive. A major customer was Birks Jewellers. The company also manufactured relatively small orders of folding boxes, as in suit boxes and frozen food packaging. We were able to compete because we had low overhead costs - a small plant, old equipment that was well maintained, and a small, versa-tile, work force and low building maintenance.

As mentioned, the plant was located in a rough part of Vancouver, and it was broken into often. The petty cash and other valuables were kept over-night in a small safe in the office and never was broken into because it was in a well-lit area and visible from the street. However, inventory records of raw materials and finished goods were stored in a huge, extremely heavy, metal safe in the plant for protection in case of fire. There was a large sign on it saying it contained only inventory records and was not locked. Invariably, we found that the burglars had not even checked to see it was actually not locked, and instead beat on it with a sledge hammer before finally giving up on it, once even leaving behind their sledge hammer. Like I said, it was a seedy part of town and we didn't attract the smartest of the losers.

Our parent company was National Paper Box, which produced large volume orders, such as Pur Pak milk cartons. A sister company was Burton Brothers Lithograph, which produced canned food labels, magazines, and lithographed paperboard which was used to manufacture folding boxes. I worked at Vancouver Paper Box for a couple years and then moved to the National Paper Box location when the three offices were combined. It was sad to see that the elderly general manager of Burton's was being frozen out. He moved to the new location and was given a nice, big office and then was not given anything to do. He came in at 8:00 a.m., sat at an empty desk, was not even invited to management meetings, and left at 4:00 p.m., not having done a bit of work. He finally retired after about six months.

About this time, Rose and I applied to adopt a child. Thankfully, we were refused.

It was while I was at National Paper Box that I almost caused Helen, one of my clerks, to have a nasty accident. Her desk was just in front of mine and she turned to me and said that when she was pulling the plug of her adding machine out of the floor socket, the prongs had broken off in the socket, and asked what she should do to get them out. I said "use a bobby pin", thinking she would realize I was joking. A minute later I noticed her on her knees, prepared to use a bobby pin to dig into the socket. I yelled "stop" just in time. My sense of humor occasionally gets me into serious trouble.

While working at the box companies, it was much easier to go directly from work to my classes at U.B.C. rather than rush home to New Westminster for dinner and then back to the university. It also allowed for additional study while having a meal in a small restaurant near the campus.

It was while I was working at National Paper Box that I first asked Rose for a divorce. It seemed that I couldn't please her and she felt that everyone was against her. We were still socializing with only one couple and that would be only for a month or so at a time before Rose would perceive an insult to her by the other couple. I would explain that there had been no ill-meaning by what was said, but she was determined to interpret otherwise. It was weird to listen to her and her sister, Marge, talk about their mental problems and who was sicker. It sounded like a contest to determine who was the nuttiest. I always felt like I should throw my full support onto Rose, but both Jack (Marge's husband) and I kept our mouths shut, and carried on private discussions about something else. Anyways, Rose threatened to take me to the cleaners if I ever tried to leave her. I guess I was pretty dumb because it was about three years before I finally realized I didn't have anything for her to take.

While I was nursing, Rose applied for a job at Sears' catalogue department in the new Kingsway Mall and she met a lady, named Helen Dryer, who lived in the fourplex next door to us just up the hill from the Royal Columbian Hospital in New Westminster. Helen had just moved from Winnipeg with her husband and two teen aged daughters. Helen's husband, Frank, had been a prisoner of war of the Japanese when they invaded Hong Kong, and had suffered beatings and starvation in the camp, and was now an alcoholic. Rose and Helen became good friends and remained so for several years. Frank and Helen also struck up an even stronger friendship with Helen's hairdresser and her husband. The hairdresser was also an alcoholic, so they partied several times a week, with Frank and the hairdresser passing out during the evening, facilitating the start of an affair between Helen and the hairdresser's husband, who was also named "Frank" (Thompson). Frank Dryer was in poor health and passed away, and following the funeral there was a big party with lots of rum and it turned out to be a rather sordid event. Soon after, Frank Thompson divorced his wife and he married Helen.

Although Bernie continued to be my best friend, we didn't see each other very often because Rose didn't seem to like seeing me enjoying myself. Or maybe Rose and Mary didn't have much in common. Mary and Bernie had a little boy, named Jamey, who was a happy little guy and I really became attached to him. When he became old enough to talk, I taught him his first words: "Quack Grass", which his parents didn't appreciate because they were each hoping for the usual "mama" or "daddy". Bernie and Mary brought the kids to visit one day and the little ones were getting restless so I asked them if they wanted to watch TV in the kitchen. I turned on the light in the oven and sat them in front of the stove. They seemed to be quite enjoying it but when Mary saw what they were watching, she was a bit annoyed that I would play such a trick on them. Bernie was diagnosed with cancer in his neck and had a series of radiation treatments, and was clear for a couple years.

Frank Weiler quit his job at National Paper Box, because there were too many accountants after the offices were combined. He was hired by Tide Bay Construction on Annacis Island in New Westminster as office manager/accountant. Soon after that I decided that I needed to get a job which would provide me with more advanced accounting duties in order to prepare myself for a job as an accountant. I answered an ad for a job with Crown Zellerbach, a large forest products company. I was called and asked to take a bunch of aptitude tests. After the tests, I was told a couple days later I would be offered a job but they first wanted to check my references. I gave them Frank's name. The next evening I got a call from Frank asking if I was seriously looking for another job. I said yes, and he then asked if I would be interested in working for him as his assistant. He hired me right then.

Between the time I gave my notice at National Paper Box and when I started my new job, I had all my teeth pulled and an upper denture fitted. When I started work at Tide Bay, my mouth was not yet fully healed, and for the next six months I brought a thermos of beef consommé for lunch every day and spoke with difficulty; I still do, but that's because of all my strokes. (I also go into too much detail, but that's not because of the strokes.) It was a happy day when I finally was fitted with my bottom dentures and celebrated with a big steak.

The company was involved in heavy construction, installing mechanical, electrical systems, building pulp mills, bridges, sewer systems, tunnels (the Deas Island tunnel on the Fraser River was a major project), and highways and fire sprinkler systems. My job was to check invoices against purchase orders and approve them for payment, prepare monthly invoices to charge for work completed on each project, and then prepare monthly estimated cost and profit statements on each project. I occasionally had difficulty getting estimates from the engineers as to the stage of completion on the projects so that I could invoice properly. I remember one particular tiff when I ended up in a shouting match as to who was the most incompetent.

The head of the electrical engineering department, Fred, was a person that I really disliked. He made a habit of cheating the company, like filling his wife's car with gas and charging it to his company credit card. In those days, the filling stations always wrote the licence plate number down on the charge slip, so I was able to identify the scams. He also used to hire a sub-contractor who had a backhoe and other equipment to lay underground wiring, etc. The sub-contractor and his crew and equipment were diverted to work about five days on Fred's creek-side property during a storm, and it was all charged to an electrical project. I took delight in finding such fiddles and every month I prepared an invoice for Fred's personal charges. He always protested his innocence but when I suggested that I would speak to Herb Fritz, the president, he suddenly had a recollection and paid the charges.

I often helped out the hourly paymaster, Gordy, with the weekly payroll. He was a young, deeply religious man who was fully trusted by Frank and the other staff. One July 1st holiday weekend, we returned to work on the Tuesday to find the fireproof vault had been smashed open with a sledge hammer, and all of the records and ledgers had been removed, including all of the employee records, cancelled payroll and other cheques, etc. The police were called to investigate, and the auditor company was hired to provide a bunch of staff to rebuild the records. No clues were found, until a few days later when bundles of cancelled checks and ledgers were found washed up on the banks of the Fraser River, and sea shores as far away as West Vancouver. It became obvious that whoever had cleaned out our vault had dumped everything off the Queensborough Bridge, into the Fraser River. The police were stumped until Frank insisted that they investigate Gordy and his property. While Gordy was out one afternoon, the RCMP checked his property. In a barrel used to burn waste in the back yard, they found three metal tags from Unemployment Insurance books in the ashes. They found that the three names had been on the payroll for about three years, were getting regular journeymen wages, took regular vacations, and paid union dues. The manager of the bank on Annacis Island said Gordy always came in on paydays with a handful of checks to cash for the "employees" who were busy at work. When confronted, Gordy readily admitted putting the "horses" on the payroll, and that he always included several casuals, who were not required to have UI numbers. His justification of the thefts was that it somehow was punishment for the company allowing Fred to steal. Gordy was sentenced to a couple years in prison and I understand he enrolled in an accounting course; I guess he felt he needed better skills to steal. (He should have studied to be a lawyer or politician.)

While working at Tide Bay, I lived much closer to work, and, because there was no bus service for the staff, I used to pick up the girls at their homes and bring them to work and then take them home in the afternoon. All of them were unique. For example, the woman who replaced Gordy on payroll was just out of the army. Every morning she complained that she had just snagged her new stocking and had a large run, which was visible on alternate legs each day. Beryl worked full time on accounts payable, with my help a couple days each week. She sang Christmas songs all day, (I saw Mommy Kissing Santa Claus Last Night was repeated about five times a day, all year). When I was in the same office with her she talked or sang almost incessantly, and usually came over to my desk while she talked. At the same time, she caressed her bum, hips and stomach, while I tried to keep my eyes on my work. One morning she was late and told me she had had a small car accident in which she had fallen out of her car and ended up on her head with her legs up in the air and her skirt had fallen up around her neck. I commented that it sounded like a big crack-up. Instead of being insulted, she thought it was the funniest thing ever and took off for a half hour telling everyone what I had said. A new young woman started work in the office, named Lea Derkach, who I was quite impressed with. Her husband, Omar, played guitar and sang in a Western Band, and one evening she invited Rose and me to go to one of his concerts at an Army and Navy Club. Omar and I hit it off at once but, because Lea was very attractive, vivacious, and sexy, Rose perceived her to be a threat and didn't want the friendship to go any further.

It was early in 1962 that my mother was diagnosed as having leukemia and was admitted to Royal Columbia hospital, just a few blocks down the hill from where we lived in the Sapperton district. The doctor said her condition was so far advanced that she probably wouldn't live more than a month. There wasn't any treatment at that time for leukemia. Mom thought she was just anemic and would be home in a few weeks, and no one ever told her otherwise. I often visited her after work, playing her favorite songs, (Yellow Bird was her most favorite) on my portable tape recorder, before I picked up Rose from her job at 6:00 pm. Mom was in a private room, so the nurses didn't mind that there would be at least six visitors in the room every evening. Mom really enjoyed the visits.

Somehow, Mom's condition didn't seem to get worse and the weeks just went by and became months and she was still with us. In July, I was scheduled to go on vacation and, thinking Mom would be around for another month or two, Rose and I went camping with Helen and Frank at Wood Lake in the Okanagan for two weeks. Rose was particularly mean to me whenever the two of us were alone and I decided that I would leave her when we got home. On our return, I told her I was going to leave because it was obvious she would never be happy with me and I certainly was not happy living with her. I said I would take only the car and my personal stuff and would continue paying her rent until we divorced, which I believed might take as much as a year.

I remember packing the car with my clothes and tool kit and the few cheap tools I had accumulated, and driving to Mom's house to be greeted warmly by Aunt Edme, who had been living with Mom since my Dad passed away. While driving across town, I looked at the back seat and at my pitiful assets that I had accumulated in ten years. The car was about half paid for and was worth about what I still owed. Nevertheless, I was now FREE!!!

I went to a lawyer and had a separation agreement prepared, which Rose agreed to after some consultation with her. I agreed to continue paying her rent of $75 per month until such time as we divorced, which she assured me would be soon.

Rose harassed me for several months, phoning me and then just not speaking for several minutes until I hung up, then at other times asking me to come over to talk and resolve our problems. She threatened to commit suicide and once told me that she had taken a bunch of sleeping pills, so I rushed over and told her I was calling an ambulance, at which time she admitted she had lied. She once talked me into going to a marriage counselor with her. The counsellor listened to her list of complaints about me, then he asked what my complaints were and I told him it was the constant nagging. I gave him a couple examples, to which she lashed out at me for forcing her to nag. The counsellor finally said he couldn't see any reason why we should continue the marriage and that we should get a divorce. One of his comments was that it seemed that Rose expected me to get her permission to breath. On the way home, Rose said "see, he said it's entirely your fault". I just shook my head. (I could have mentioned to him that Rose always closed her eyes when we were making love because she couldn't stand the sight of me enjoying myself. But I didn't.)

Soon after this, Bernie passed away from the cancer which had spread to his lymph nodes and then through all of his vital organs. I knew that his condition had become more serious but I couldn't bring myself to visit him in the hospital. At first it was Rose's not wanting me to spend time with him, and then, after I had left her, I couldn't cope with losing him and Mom at nearly the same time.

Mom passed away in September, 1962.

My life began changing immensely in so many ways and at such a rapid pace. Omar became a close friend and remains so. I went to most of his shows, which were held at Army and Navy Clubs, Legions, and occasionally at dances and at private parties. I carried Omar's amp or guitar and therefore was able get in without paying or having a membership. There was always a table reserved for the band and there was usually free beer for the band (and me). The band often did a week-long gig at the Kublai Khan, an after-hours club in China Town, and Omar got to know Tommy, the manager, so we would often go there after doing a show at one of the clubs, and Tommy let us in free. On the way, we would stop at a liquor store on Skid Road to pick up a mickey of rye whiskey. There was always good entertainment at the Kublai Khan, both on stage and by the crowd.

The band included the leader, George Poburn, who played guitar and sang, Omar, who did the same as George only better, a lead guitar player who was really talented, a fiddle player who was fantastic, and a pert female drummer who was always a crowd pleaser. When the band wasn't playing, I hung out with Omar, playing pool, or listening to him play on his guitar and sing by himself while Lea and I played cards.

After Mom's passing, I started repeating my final accounting course. I didn't have to pay the full cost because I only enrolled to audit the course and was not required to submit assignments weekly. With my extra time off, I started my thesis, titled "An Accounting System for a Medium Sized Construction Company", a 13,000 word description in which I was able to describe several improvements that I had made in our company's system. After completing the first draft, I went to visit Lam Milne, the past president of the B.C. Society, who was also assisting any candidate living in the area with their submissions. He suggested a few changes in my thesis and after I had made them, he presented it to the Thesis Review Committee which accepted it.

Lam Milne was head of the Society's Publicity and Public Relations Committee and when he learned I had been a radio news writer and editor, he asked me to join his group and I was invited to the Society's monthly Board of Directors meetings. This was the start of a close association with the Society which has lasted for over fifty years. I will talk more about this part of my life later.

In the spring of 1963 I got the urge to treat myself to a brand new car. Not just any car, but a new 1963 Pontiac Parisienne convertible. I went into the local dealership in New Westminster, and looked at a floor model. It was not quite what I had in mind, but the salesman was very helpful when I was trying to pick a number for the trade-in value of my 1958 Chevrolet Bel Aire. He suggested that I pick a fairly high number, about two thousand, on the basis that the floor model was loaded with more extras than I wanted. We were sitting in a small cubicle discussing the deal while we waited for the sales manager to come in and finalize the deal. I learned later that all the cubicles were wired and the sales manager was listening to our conversation. He finally appeared and we discussed the price and I told him what I wanted for my trade in. He protested but I insisted and finally he agreed with my demand. Then I told him I didn't want the floor model. It had a 350 HP motor and I wanted only 250 HP. Also it had bucket seats and I wanted a bench seat. He said that I couldn't have as much for my Chevy but I said I was sure I could get a better deal if I went to a dealer in Chilliwack. He finally agreed and so I ordered one from the factory to my wishes. When I was notified that my car had arrived, I looked for the salesman that had been so helpful but he had left the company. There was a story in the newspaper that the cubicles at the dealership were bugged, so I assumed he had been fired.

A month or so later, I finally took possession of my new car, a 2000 pound beauty with an additional 1000 pounds of big fins and chrome over everything. It was white with red leather upholstery; a fun car and I totally enjoyed myself, even if it was a gas guzzler. I was now 32 years old and young enough to date whoever I wanted, assuming the girl was willing to go out with me. The convertible helped my image.

I received my RIA degree in 1963 at the convocation exercises in Vancouver.

Elmer with new convertible, 1963

Chapter 19

1963 - 1971:
PAT, CHILDREN
AND FINAL JOB

With my freedom from Rose in 1963, and with an enhanced image made possible by the new convertible, I dated several girls over the next several months but no one steady. I renewed my friendship with Art Burrows, who I had chummed with during my first job at Lou's fish and chip shop in New Westminster in 1948, and he had a steady girl-friend but no car. It was in their best interests to keep me supplied with blind dates so that Art would have a ride to Nancy's in Vancouver, then to a club and back home. I was still having a great time with Omar and the weekly band shows. In the following spring Nancy arranged a blind date for me with a girl she had met at her exercise gym, named Patricia Higgins.

Pat was the second youngest of 11 children born to Bill and May Higgins; seven girls and four boys: Joan, Margie, Irene, Tony, Peter, Chris, Sheila, Anne, Danny, Patricia, and Brenda. An uncle, Henry Higgins, was a character name in the musical production, "My Fair Lady", and was said to be a frequenter of a pub in the area also attended by the composer, George Bernard Shaw.

Pat was quite vivacious and had a good sense of humor. She was about nine years younger than me, but we hit it off really well. She was from Birmingham, England, and emigrated to be with her two sisters, Sheila and Anne, who had come to Vancouver a few years earlier. Sheila was married to a Dutchman, named Bert Steunenberg and they had a little girl named Lucy. Pat shared an apartment in the Kitsilano area with Anne, who was dating an ambulance driver named Ken Barr.

We spent a lot of time driving in my convertible in the lower mainland, to the beach at White Rock, and to various parks like White Cliff at Horseshoe Bay, Ambleside and other beaches, as well as in the Fraser Valley. Often, we would stop to eat at a drive-in like the White Spot. (Drive-in restaurants were a new type of diner at that time and were becoming extremely popular, as were drive-in theaters.) We often would stop at a particular dairy outlet in Vancouver to buy ice cream cones and sit in the car to eat them. Pat always seemed to finish her cone a few minutes before me and would fix her big eyes on me in expectation until I would offer the last inch of my cone to her which she would accept always with a look of triumph. After this had happened at least six times I got annoyed and the next time we bought ice cream cones, I quickly ate my entire cone. Shortly after, Pat finished hers and turned to claim her final bit of my cone, only to find that there was no more. She proceeded to give me the dickens and then wouldn't talk to me for the next half hour.

We were returning from a day on the beach in White Rock one afternoon and while driving along the new freeway across the Delta mud flats, Pat looked at the speedometer and asked if I had ever put the needle at the maximum speed of 120 mph. (This was before the switch to metric and kilometers.) I said yes, just once I had reached 120 mph. She said "I want to see how it feels". The traffic wasn't heavy, so I floored it and when we had reached 120 mph, I glanced at her and she was exhilarated, smiling and simply beaming. I quickly dropped the speed to 60 mph, which was the speed limit at that time. About five minutes later, my left front tire blew. Thank the Lord I had got power steering and brakes on my convertible, new features just becoming popular, so I was able to safely stop on the shoulder and change the tire. I have never been quite that stupid at the wheel while driving since then, although there have been several incidents that bordered on it, the "stupid" part, I mean.

In July, 1963, I drove to Prince Albert and spent a couple weeks with Lawrence and his family at their cottage at Emma Lake. I packed some clothes and a case of beer and left home after dinner on Friday, arriving in Kamloops about eleven pm and stopped at a restaurant for a snack. Soon after, four young local ranch hands came in and sat in the next booth, obviously after leaving a beer parlor. They all ordered steaks and the waitress asked how they liked them cooked. Three said "rare" and the fourth said "really rare". When she asked "how rare is that?" he replied "just knock the horns off, wipe its ass and lead it in." The entire restaurant appeared to have gone quiet, and then erupted in laughter.

It was a beautiful night and I pulled off the highway near the outskirts of town and slept under the stars for a few hours.

While driving along in the morning just east of Banff, I picked up a hitchhiker and we were enjoying a beer as we drove along. I got pulled over for speeding and had to follow the cop back to Banff where there was a magistrate waiting to issue justice to a steady stream of tourists that were being hauled in for any number of infractions. The cop asked me before we went into the court room, how much I could afford. I told him fifteen dollars and that was what the fine turned out to be. There was no mention of the hitchhiker that I had picked up earlier, or that we were drinking beer when I was pulled over, so I guess I got off lucky.

While driving into P.A. a few days later I got caught in a violent storm with thunder and lightning. The rain came down in such a torrent that I had to pull into a vacant farm yard and wait until it eased. The storm included large hail stones that I feared would damage the cloth top of my convertible, but it cleared shortly and I resumed my trip unscathed. A few days later I drove to P.A. with Larry to buy more beer. He stopped at the Pontiac dealer that serviced his car and we saw a car that had just been towed in from a town about thirty miles west of P.A., which really had experienced much worse hail during the same storm. Every bit of glass on the car was smashed and the body surface was totally covered with dents about a quarter inch deep from hail the size of golf balls. I don't know if the guy wanted to get the damage repaired or a new body or a whole new car.

On the Saturday, Larry took me fishing at a lake about 30 miles to the northwest, and it was a perfect day. The lake was only about two miles in diameter and was located just inside the boundary of the Waskesew National Park, had mainly pickerel fish. No one lived nearby. The lake bed was sandy and the water so clear that we could see the fish swimming below us. We caught several fish and then ate our lunch that Doreen had packed for us, with a couple beers that we were dragging in the water to keep cold, and then resumed fishing. We couldn't understand why the fish had suddenly stopped biting even though we could see the lures just inches from their mouths. Minutes later, the sky got dark and we witnessed a total solar eclipse. We then understood that there would be no more fishing for a few hours because of the eclipse, so we packed up and went home. I can still picture that little lake, surrounded by aspen trees and the pristine water. So beautiful!!

Back in BC, and while returning from an afternoon at the beach, I stopped at the house with Pat and suggested we make dinner there. Pat said okay but wasn't hungry and so I could cook whatever I wanted. When dinner of spareribs and mashed potatoes and veggies was ready, she refused to eat and seemed quite annoyed. I tucked in and ate as much as I could, so as to not waste. Months later, she confessed she had refused to eat because she hadn't helped in the preparation, and that was because she was too embarrassed to admit she couldn't cook. In fact, she said her and Anne usually ate cereal for breakfast and then sandwiches the rest of the day or bought something already prepared. On one occasion, the two girls had roasted a duck, but they couldn't eat it, picturing the poor thing with feathers, alive and swimming in Lost Lagoon, and they tossed it into the garbage.

Pat decided she would like to learn how to drive, and what better way, than by using my car with me to instruct her. We started in the Oakridge Mall parking lot to learn the basics and then ventured onto the streets, first in residential areas and then downtown. It was while driving along Georgia Street, and we had just passed Thurlow, that I said to her that she should get into the right lane and turn right onto Burrard Street. She sped through the intersection on an amber light, then got into the little space between the cars in the right lane and the row of parked cars, and hit the gas. We squeezed through with about two inches to spare on both sides and turned onto Burrard before I could take another breath. She looked at me as though she expected to be congratulated. I should have put a stop to the lessons, but I didn't. She passed her driver's road test, (the examiner was very nice and let her parallel park between two cars about thirty yards apart), and she got her licence.

That fall, I talked to Pat about me getting another job that required greater use of my accounting knowledge than I was using at Tide Bay. Pat was working in the Human Resources Department of MacMillan Bloedel in their head office in Vancouver and knew quite a few department managers who would often come by on business. When Alan Humphries, manager of Internal Audit Department, stopped in one day, she asked him if he needed a good accountant who had recently received his R.I.A., and he said he would need someone in a few months and asked that I phone for an interview. I got the job and started at MB on February 1, 1964, as junior auditor/relief accountant which meant I would be relieving accountants who were on vacation or sick leave, and when not doing that, I would do internal auditing. (Only Chartered Accountants were able to work as senior auditors in that department at that time. So I could only assist.)

The first month was mainly spent in various year-end activities. My first audit was in March at Port Hardy Division at the northern tip of Vancouver Island. Just getting there had me scared out of my wits. The plane was very old (pre-war), and carried about twenty passengers. The wings tended to flap as we flew along, which someone told me was good because it reduced stress on the plane. (I still think that was b---s---) The senior auditor, named Al Misener, had been in his job with MB for about twenty years, and I had no clue of what I was supposed to watch for. He had me add columns of numbers in ledgers and journals, and trace journal entries and check payroll records for the two weeks, and I found no irregularities. This was prior to personal computers, so every transaction was recorded by hand and therefore easier to manipulate.

We stayed in the guest rooms at the logging camp and had our meals in the cook house. The chefs were Greek immigrants and produced the greatest food using a couple huge wood-burning ranges in the kitchen. About five a.m. a cook would place dozens of eggs in the oven and bake them for the crew to have at breakfast and to pack in their lunch pails. There were hotcakes the size of dinner plates, hot and cold cereals, ham and bacon, cheeses, and pastries as well as a full assortment of fruit and drinks. The crew made their own lunches to take with them to their job sites in the woods.

I over-ate and then started work at eight o'clock. At ten, we went to the cook house for coffee and fresh pastries, hot out of the oven, and again over-ate. Lunch was do-it-yourself sandwiches with more pastries. Three o'clock saw us stuff more pastries and coffee down. At five o'clock, the whole crew came in for dinner – a big meal even by their standards. Some of the men loaded their food directly onto their trays, not bothering with plates. Bed time snacks were available, but I was still too stuffed. In the morning, I didn't care if I had breakfast, but, of course, I did. After I got home, I found I had gained ten pounds in the ten days I had been in camp. Misener decided we would go back to Vancouver for the first weekend and that was okay with me. I know that Alan Humphries was not pleased when he reviewed our expense claims after the audit was complete, thinking it was a waste of money.

One particular event stands out in my memory to this day. During the second week of the audit, Humphries arrived at the camp to check how we were doing. He decided that I should take a trip to the Wakeman Sound logging operation, which was part of the Port Hardy Division, but was located on the mainland about 75 miles east of Port Hardy, and situated at the head of Wakeman Sound and off Kingcome Inlet. Stan Herman, the Divisional Accountant, was asked to charter a very small float plane to fly Stan and me and the payroll cheques to the camp. Stan reported back that the pilot said there were gale force winds over Georgia Strait and the inlet, so there would be no flying until conditions improved. After lunch, Stan was asked to call the pilot again. The pilot said the winds had only slightly improved, but that he would take us only if it was absolutely essential, and Humphries decided it was essential and the pilot should prepare to leave. Stan drove me and the cheques down to the harbor and we all climbed aboard the little plane, but only after the pilot made one last plea to cancel the flight.

We took off on a flight that should have taken a half hour but, fighting head winds all the way, actually took us an hour. As we flew up Kingcome Inlet the plane was really pitching and bucking and, as we turned up Wakeman Sound, we flew close to the mountain side. Suddenly, the plane hit a down-draft and dropped toward the mountainside with such a rate that my head hit the ceiling of the cockpit. My heart was in my throat and I saw my imminent departure for a place not of this world. I was sitting next to the pilot, while Stan was sitting on a canvas bench just behind. Stan was killing himself laughing as he watched me, while I failed to see any humor at all in the situation. The fall ceased while we were still about fifty feet above the trees and then we continued on a few miles until we landed at the camp.

There were about 75 men working in the camp, which consisted of bunk houses and a cookhouse and shops. A few had brought their wives, and one of them told me over coffee that she didn't know how long she would be staying there, because her trip in was so terrifying that she was too scared to make the trip back to Vancouver. Word reached us that a larger plane (similar to the one we flew in from Vancouver to Port Hardy) had gone down that morning in the area of Kingcome Inlet and Georgia Strait, where we had passed a couple hours earlier, with the loss of two lives. It was decided that we would spend the night at that camp, and return to Port Hardy in the morning.

The payroll distribution was uneventful and pointless as far as I was concerned, because the same person could have come by three times during the afternoon and picked up a cheque because many of the men looked much the same in their work clothes, beards and hard hats.

During dinner, a couple of men from the fish and wildlife department, were guests and told of a scare they had that day. They had travelled up a logging road on their motorcycle and had stopped to check the fish in a stream. While fishing they were the target of a grizzly bear which apparently had already claimed that particular spot as its favorite fishing hole. The government men took to their heels and, because the bear was between them and their motorbike, they had to circle around and retrieve their machine later. Such was life in the boondocks!!!

On the following morning, we were able to fly back to Port Hardy and, with the help of a tail wind we made the journey in twenty minutes. I was really upset with Humphries for placing such little value on my life for the sake of a useless (in my estimation) audit procedure. Of course, Humphries had already departed for his flight back to Head Office, and I cooled down before I next saw him.

In June, there was an earthquake off the coast of Alaska which resulted in a tidal wave that caused terrible damage in Port Alberni, particularly to the pulp and paper mill, located at the end of the Alberni Inlet. The wave was less than a foot high in the open ocean, but when it entered Barkley Sound it was funneled into the Inlet and, as it travelled up the waterway, the narrowing of the inlet increased the depth of the wave to some thirty feet. The wave totally submerged the basement of the mill as well as the lower part of the machines. All of the huge motors for the ground wood mill (each about 4,000 HP) had to be rewired, as well other large and small motors. I was asked to go over a few days later and help with the huge insurance claims for direct damage as well as for lost sales and production. The claims involved millions of dollars. I was there for weeks and met all of the management and staff and was impressed with their aggressiveness and dedication to get back to business.

In late September, I went with a senior auditor, named Dale Carlson, on an extended audit to the prairies which lasted about a month. We audited a building materials distribution center, a paper sales office, and a corrugated container manufacturing plant in Winnipeg, and then, while Dale went to Regina, I went to Saskatoon to audit a building materials distribution center. I then went on to Regina and rejoined Dale to audit a corrugated container plant. All I recall of Winnipeg is that it was bloody windy and freezing cold. Also, there were a million little flies in the office, buzzing around our faces and fingers as we worked. During coffee breaks, Dale and I used rubber bands stretched over our rulers to see who could kill the most flies in a day.

While in Saskatoon for the weekend plus two days of auditing, I stayed at Mirelda's house and had a great time. Marty and Louise who had just returned from Germany where Marty had been stationed in the RCAF, and the rest of the Sader kids were there, as well as Marlene Benoit, most of whom were going to University. We had some great parties.

During the summer I had moved to Vancouver to be closer to work and rented an apartment on Barkley Street in the West End. Soon after, Pat moved out of her unit that she shared with Anne and into my apartment while I moved into another unit in the same building and shared it with a young English immigrant that had just started work in my department.

It worked out fine for a while because we both were seldom home at the same time. One day while I was out of town, Pat left her door open while she went next door to check on her laundry and returned to find a guy in her apartment. He left without incident, but the event left her unnerved. Pat then moved to another apartment on Nelson Street and I moved to a sleeping room nearby, on Denman Street.

In the summer, I returned to Alpulp for a couple months to help in the Cost Accounting Department while the office workers were out on strike for over two months. They had formed a union in order to get better wages. The way that the system had worked was that, in the spring, Head Office would allocate a certain percentage of the payroll for raises for all the salaried employees and the division managers would then allocate their amount to all of their non-union staffs. The manager of Alpulp, Jim Petrie, had pet departments and pet staff. Being a paper machine manager in his earlier days, Petrie favored the supervisors of that department, then the Kraft Mill, then the Groundwood Mill, etc. When it came to the clerical employees, who were at the bottom of the list, there would be only five or ten dollars per month for raises for each individual worker, and they ended up far below the going rate for similar jobs outside.

The Office and Technical Workers Union were unsuccessful in reaching a first contract and finally called a strike, shutting down the entire mill for weeks. The Company finally agreed to a fair settlement, placed Petrie on early retirement, and made several changes in the Human Resources Department and in the way that employee relations were to be handled in future.

In August, I was entitled to one week of vacation, so Pat and I decided to go to a dude ranch in the Cariboo area, west of Williams Lake. It was a small working ranch with a lodge and about three log cabins. We rented one of the cabins and spent our days riding good horses surrounded by the most beautiful scenery. We were each assigned a horse for the entire week; Pat's was quite docile, while mine was smaller but full of life. We rode for about 2 ½ hours in the morning and again in the afternoon on the many trails. There were many meadows, each connected to the next by short trails through the trees. I would hold my horse while the others galloped across a meadow, then let my pony race as fast as he could to catch up. Once we caught up to the others he didn't want to stop. I spied a trail leading off and turned onto it, still racing madly. About fifty yards farther, I saw a deadfall across the trail, about four feet off the ground. My pony didn't slow a bit and we just sailed over it, the only time I had ever jumped over anything on a horse. What an exhilarating experience that was.

Pat fell off her horse once when it was startled and shied at something, and as I helped her up, it seemed she only bruised her ego.

Each morning during the first three days, I rolled out bed onto my knees and pulled myself up with the aid of the bedpost to a standing position with the most painful backache. But after climbing onto my horse I would immediately find my aches gone. After the third day I woke pain free. The meals were delicious and I returned to the office totally rejuvenated.

That fall, I was asked to relieve the accountant at the pole division in New Westminster for about three months while he was off work, on sick leave. The assignment was noteworthy only because the division manager was fired a couple years later for embezzling what I believe amounted to well over a hundred thousand dollars, through crooked sales contracts with an American customer.

I finally contacted Rose to arrange for a divorce and agreed to give evidence of adultery (the only basis accepted in court at that time). I was contacted by a private investigator and the evidence was arranged: he knocked on the door and when he entered, he saw me lying on a day bed in the living room, fully clothed, in Pat's apartment. The investigator told me he had already been following me for a couple weeks but kept losing me in the traffic. (He did mention my speed and going through amber lights was a factor.) Rose never mentioned that part (sneaky!!!), and I never asked her about it.

I assumed that now that she had the evidence, she would proceed with the divorce. But, because she was receiving a cheque from me every month, she changed her mind and just let it hang for another year, and I couldn't get evidence to sue her because her boyfriend's mother was living in the same house.

Rose had entered into a relationship with a man named Jim, and eventually moved into his house which he shared with his mother. After work on the last day before Christmas, Jim and a bunch of work mates went to a beer parlor for a few drinks. When Jim arrived home, Rose lit into him with a typical tirade. She shouldn't have done that, because Jim wasn't understanding, like Elmer. He beat her severely and threw her out of the house, and told her to never come back. She visited Lou and Marge a couple weeks later, and they said her face was still badly swollen and a mass of bruises. I still think my solution of running away from home was better.

One day, someone walked up to the reception desk in Pat's office and asked for Pat. Because there were two Pats in the office, the receptionist wanted to find out which, so she asked "which do you mean, the fat one or the skinny one". Pat was mortified when she heard the question and realized that she was the one referred to as being the fat one. She was full-bodied with nice curves, about 120 pounds, but certainly not fat. That started years of depression and fasting for Pat.

When our next audit program started in early April, 1965, our first job was at Harmac and then Chemainus Divisions, on Vancouver Island. We stayed in the newly built Tally Ho Motel, in Nanaimo, for the first week, and I remember sitting on my bed that first evening and saying: "Lord, not another year of being away from home for six months", and feeling quite down because I realized that working at a different location every couple weeks was not my cup of tea. I had developed a mindset that when I went to a division to audit, I spent the first week wishing I could find a major irregularity in the books, in order to relieve the boredom, and the second week hoping we wouldn't find anything, just so I could get the heck out of there.

The next week, we moved to the Yellow Point Lodge, an ocean-front resort, located southeast of Nanaimo and in between Harmac and Chemainus. The place was lovely and the owner had cold beer waiting for us every day after work. About a week later, I got a call from Bob MacDonald, the office manager of Alberni Pulp and Paper Division, asking me to come for an interview. I was there in a flash and I accepted the job of Cost Accountant. It was the division that had impressed me most of all the ones I had worked at during the previous year.

I talked to Pat when I got home and we decided to make long term commitments to each other and she would move to the Island with me and we would live together until my divorce from Rose came through, and then we would get married. She was able to get a transfer to the sales documents section at Somass Sawmill Division, about a mile from Alpulp.

Also, because we were living together while not married, (it mattered at that time), we rented an apartment in Parksville, about 50 kilometers away) and tried to adjust to life in a small town. People in both offices soon found out we were living together.

During the first month, a local real estate agent, named Arnie, asked if I would be willing to drive a beauty pageant contestant representing the local Credit Union during the local Canada Day Parade. The girl was beautiful and we figured that with my beautiful convertible, winning would be a cinch. The day was fun, and everyone seemed to know everyone on the floats and all the contestants. The girl I drove actually won first prize. I was asked to escort the girl during all the festivities and to the banquet that evening plus the big dance, but Pat said no, that I was hers (Pat's), and I was contributing quite enough just by driving. I was later asked to drive and escort the girl, now "Miss Parksville", in the parade and competition for Miss PNE in Vancouver, but Pat (selfishly again!!!) said "no way".

We had two weeks of vacation in September and drove down to San Francisco and stayed with my niece, Muriel Benoit, across the Bay in Oakland. We drove down on Rte. I-5 and every day, for lunch, I ordered a Crab Louie. In Bellingham, the plate was piled with lettuce with a small scoop of crab meat. The next place had half as much lettuce with two scoops of crab. The next day, I got a small bed of lettuce and more crab. On the trip back we took Hwy. 101, the coast route and stopped for lunch at a tavern in a small fishing village, just north of San Francisco. The plate contained one wilted lettuce leaf, piled high with crab, at least eight ounces.

While in San Francisco, we visited Fisherman's Wharf, Chinatown, rode the cog wheel streetcars, and had dinner at a nice restaurant on Nob Hill. The twisting drive down from Nob Hill was exciting. On Saturday, the three of us drove to Lake Tahoe for a bit of gambling and to take in some of the free entertainment. The stage shows were in the bar and consisted of four groups which alternated as in Numbers one, two, one, two, three, two, three, four. I was most interested in No. Four, which was Harry James, the trumpet playing band leader whose records I had listened to and danced to while I was a teen and still enjoyed. After waiting for five hours in the bar, he finally appeared at about midnight. What a disappointment. I guess it was the result of all the years of playing in clubs and drinking and smoking, but he looked like a bum and the talent just wasn't there anymore. We left right after his show, arriving back at Muriel's after sunrise.

My parents' house in New Westminster was finally sold and the estate was distributed. My share was $5,000. I asked Arnie to keep an eye out for a house for us, preferably close to the water, which we could purchase with a down payment of that amount.

In the meantime, I was learning my new job, which required a good understanding of the manufacturing process so that I would be able to identify causes of higher or lower costs which affect the productivity and profitability. I would quickly eat my lunch and then visit different departments each day, asking questions of the supervisors and observing each process until I fully understood it. Some of the processes were complicated, particularly the Kraft Mill and the Recovery System/Steam Plant. However, the effort was worthwhile because in later years I was able to create long range plans that were accurate and which top management had confidence in, basing decisions that involved hundreds of millions of dollars in investments.

I was directly supervising a staff of six, and developed a good rapport with them, although I did have a couple of problems resulting from the union contract which stipulated that the senior applicant for any job vacancy had to be given the job, and that any employee could retain his/her job if he/she could meet the least, minimum, requirements. One of the clerk/typists resigned on my first day due to family issues, so I ended up with a lady who had very limited typing skills and even less general office abilities. However, as she explained to me during the interview, "I'm the senior applicant and I want the job, so let's quit talking". Unfortunately for her, she started on the job at month-end, on the day when we had to complete and type the three product summary statements and get them out by courier to Head Office by five p.m. that same day. She was given the easiest statement only, while the other clerk typed the other two. Oh, yes!! This was before photocopying was available at the mill, so the statements were produced using a Gestetner machine. The forms were two parts and the second page had a dark purple gel on it and when they were typed, the mirror images would be transferred to the back of the form. The form was then put on a drum on the machine and the statements were produced by turning the drum and feeding in blank sheets. The major problem was that if you made a typing mistake, you had to stop, roll the form back to where you could get at the mistake, scrape off the incorrect number, return the form to the appropriate spot, and then type in the correct number. The new clerk was making so many mistakes that she ended up with purple dye all over her hands, which she then transferred to her nose as well as her sweaty brow. At three o'clock, I was concerned about meeting the deadline and asked her if she was really capable of the job, and she pushed her chair back and said "I'm going back to my old job". I asked her about the statement that she hadn't yet finished, and she replied "Do it yourself", and stomped off. The next clerk that I hired was very capable and both clerks and their husbands became good friends with Pat and me.

The person that I replaced as Cost Accountant had remained at Alpulp in a new job as Budget Coordinator, in an effort to better control costs and explain variances to plan. After about a year, he was transferred to another division and I assumed his duties, while still keeping my regular job. It meant a higher position rating as well as another raise so I didn't complain.

Early in the following spring, 1966, I learned that my marriage was finally over and, as soon as the waiting period was over, Pat and I got married. It was a very small affair, just Bert and Sheila and Anne and, from my side, Lou/Margie and Emile/Julia. The ceremony took place in the United Church in the west end of Vancouver, followed by dinner at a nice restaurant in the downtown area.

Soon after the wedding, Arnie contacted me about a couple of properties. The first was nine acres at French Creek with a broken down house on it and 450 feet of water frontage, that was going for $15,000. However, before I could arrange financing, somebody from Calgary snapped it up with all cash. (It was later sub-divided and the lots were each sold for thousands.) The next week, Arnie came back with another property, about a half-acre lot with a summer home on it at Beachcomber sub-division on Northwest Bay, between Parksville and Nanoose, which had 410 feet of beachfront. It was also available for $15,000, and although the house would need major work, it certainly had great possibilities. We bought it and proceeded to renovate it.

The house had been built with rough lumber produced from trees on the property, using a little sawmill that was located a block away, up our road. Over the years, the lumber had fully seasoned and was so hard that nails bent when being pounded into the boards. The chimney was huge, about 18 inches thick around the flue, and was built of cement with stones and shale rock from the beach. The rough fireplace was also huge, had a heatalator insert with an opening of at least 40 inches, and was able to handle 36-inch pieces of wood. (You could feel the blast of heat standing eight feet from the grill.) The windows were large and afforded a beautiful 360 degree view of the bay and the forest beyond, with Mount Arrowsmith in the center, flanked by other smaller mountains. The foundation followed the contour of the rock base, so the crawl space varied in height from 18 inches to 8 feet, and included one area of about 12' by 8' where a person could stand erect, and included a work bench. A smaller area had room for the hot water tank and garbage containers.

I arranged bank financing and then proceeded to hire a carpenter. I found one in Parksville who was semi-retired and had recently relocated from Edmonton with his wife. He came out to look at the house and we discussed what he could do to transform it into a comfortable home, incorporating some of the features that were important to me, like indirect lighting, walnut panelling and a built-in music center in the living room. I said that I would arrange with the lumber yard in Parksville to supply whatever materials he needed and deliver them and I would pay for them every week or two; also, he should keep track of his hours worked, and they could be flexible, and I would pay him every week or two.

I learned the name of an Italian artisan in Nanaimo who could finish the fireplace and he came out to look over the job. He suggested using "Old Dutch" bricks that resembled reclaimed varied-colored bricks that looked to be dusty and re-cycled. When he was finished the fireplace, and the carpenter topped it with a walnut mantle of 18" x 8', and the walnut panelling and indirect lighting above, it was amazing and beautiful.

I ordered an oil-fired furnace from a shop in Parksville and agreed it was not urgent that it be installed immediately, only that it be done soon. About two weeks later, I phoned to find when I could expect the installation. He said he had planned to do it during the previous week but the weather was so nice, he went fishing instead, but would be there on Monday. On Tuesday, he said he had needed to postpone it because a relative had popped in and they went fishing, but would be there on Wednesday. On the weekend he said he had had to postpone it again because someone else had wanted to go fishing. It went on like that for another month. I guess he was living on fish every day, because he sure wasn't making any money. When he finally installed the furnace, the only suitable position for it was lying on its side on top of the rocks in the crawl space. It worked well and remained there as long as we lived there.

The previous owner was quite a plant person, because she had built an addition of rough lumber onto the side of the house and used it as a greenhouse. The walls were mostly glass which consisted of small panes salvaged from a commercial greenhouse. The carpenter replaced them with Pearson Sashless Windows which gave an unobstructed view of the bay, forest and mountains. This room, about 12' x 18', became a rec room and we furnished it with a bar and stools with cane furniture.

The carpenter covered the rough flooring throughout the house with plywood and we covered that with carpet in the living, dining and bed rooms and the rest with lino. We had the house painted inside and out.

The carpenter said it was the best job he'd ever had. He worked hours that suited him, his wife came out to the house most days and brought lunch, often she made soup for them, and they would eat while looking at the beautiful scenery and watching the little teal ducks bobbing around in the water which was only about 15' from the house. Also, the fact that I trusted him and never questioned his hours or the rate of progress on the job seemed to please him. Pat and I used to drive out on the weekends and see how it was progressing and were always happy, especially considering that nothing had actually measured to be really square or really straight or really level, before he started.

We moved in that summer and were totally satisfied. Every day, when I arrived home from work, I put my swim suit on and dove off the rocks, directly in front of the house, into eight feet of crystal clear water. The rock outcropping was about four feet above the water when the tide was in. Storms were even more exciting, especially those from the northwest which followed the coastline of the Island, and slammed directly onto the point of land where our house was situated. The waves would crash onto the rocks in front of the house and send splashes of water against the windows as they rattled in the wind. I would put on warm clothing and go out onto the rocks, and crouch down beside the higher rocks to have some shelter from the wind, and watch the water boiling below me. I felt like I was living in the greatest place on earth, and maybe I was. It was certainly a spiritual experience, and I also had a feeling of intense gratitude for being put in that spot. I celebrated by taking my wedding ring from my marriage to Rose and threw it as far as I could into the bay.

We were to have many visitors over the following five years as friends and family came yearly to enjoy the holiday atmosphere. There was a small cove across the point and about a quarter mile away, where there was an oyster bed which few people knew of or took oysters from. I picked a couple pails of oysters which I planted in the bay, right in front of the house. In the first few years, I went to the cove and got a pail of oysters to cook on the barbeque along with steaks whenever we had company. While the steaks were cooking, we'd have fresh oysters off the grill with a bit of sauce, and beer. Life was good!!!

Pat once asked what was happening to all of our money that we earned and when the heck would we ever go out for dinner? I said I was using it to pay all the bills, and that she was welcome to take over the family finances at any time. She felt she could do at least as good a job as me, so I showed her how to keep proper records and gave her the cheque book. We didn't eat quite as good, and we still didn't go out for meals, but she didn't complain any more about where the money was going.

Pat was still watching her weight and would be quite depressed if she gained even one pound, resulting in a diet of only green apples with tea for days until she had lost the extra weight.

That fall, I was contacted by the Accounting Society and asked if I would be willing to take over as chairman of the Society's Victoria Chapter and expand it to include the rest of Vancouver Island. When I moved to Port Alberni, I was the only R.I.A. graduate north of Victoria, except for one member in Duncan. The Victoria Chapter was the only chapter in BC except for Vancouver. At that time, the chapter consisted of about twenty or thirty members, and their functions consisted of about four or five members meeting in a bar for drinks. I agreed, a meeting was called, and I was elected unanimously along with representatives from Victoria, Duncan, Ladysmith, and Nanaimo. I was promised some support from the Provincial Office in the way of funds to host various events and speakers.

With my urging, the company made it mandatory that any employee had to be enrolled and progressing in a course of studies in a recognized accounting organization, in order to be promoted to a management position. Within a year, there were more members of our society in the Alberni Valley than in Victoria. The membership showed similar growth in all other areas on the island as other forest product companies quickly adopted similar requirements.

The first Chapter event I put on was a dinner meeting in Nanaimo and I arranged with the Mayor of Nanaimo, Frank Ney, to be the guest speaker. Mrs. Ney was invited also and I spoke to her while waiting for members to arrive; she mentioned that her and Frank had twelve children and their family sedan was actually a bus. I was very surprised because she had a gorgeous figure and looked to be still in her early thirties. (Several years later, she and Frank divorced and she married Ron MacIsaac, a local lawyer and long-time friend of her and Frank. Ron was also divorced from his wife who had given birth to their eight children. Ron then went around telling everyone he had eighteen kids.) Meanwhile, there were still only about ten people for the meeting, and Mrs. Ney very sweetly asked me if we always got this large a crowd. Ha Ha!!! Anyhow, we went ahead and had the dinner and speech.

During that winter, Pat and I discussed starting a family and adopting kids, how many, and the order, and agreed it would be two boys and then two girls. In March, we called the Child Welfare Department and a case worker came to the house to check us out and fill out an application. She seemed pleased with us as applicants and told us we would be notified in about a month or two if we were approved and then we would be placed on a list and could expect to get a child in another six months or a year. Pat gave notice at work to leave her job at the end of May so that she would have ample time to relax and get ready for the new baby.

I received a call at work on Friday morning, May 25, barely four weeks later, to tell me that there was a suitable baby available at Grace Hospital in Vancouver, and we could pick him up on Monday, if we wanted him. She cautioned me that the baby had a large bump on the side of his head caused by instruments used in the birth, plus a bad infection in one eye that caused it to remain shut and was oozing a discharge, and that, after looking at him, we could refuse him and go onto the waiting list. I said we'd be there on Monday, unless Pat objected. I phoned Pat and told her I was coming over to pick her up for lunch. On hearing the good news, she told her boss, Mary, she was finished work as of right now. We hadn't started buying anything for the baby yet, so Mary offered to come along and help with shopping. We bought a crib, diapers, bottles and everything else we could think we would need. We spent Saturday putting the crib together and getting his room ready. Sunday, we drove to the mainland and were all ready to meet our new son.

On Monday morning we arrived at the hospital and were met by a Child Welfare worker. She cautioned us that we could refuse to accept the baby because he did have the bump on his head and he had an eye infection, but that both would clear up. We said we'd have a look at him. She took us to the maternity ward and the nurse brought the baby to us. He had a lump on the side of head, the size of half a boiled egg, both of his eyes were closed and oozing matter, and just then he threw up his last feeding of formula. The worker said "Oh my God", and both of us said "He's beautiful, we'll take him".

Back home, it took a lot of adjusting to parenting but we did our best. First item was selecting a name and Pat soon solved that when she phoned her mother, May, in Birmingham, to tell the family the good news and told them his name was Daniel, after her brother. His middle name would be Lawrence after her mother's maiden name and my brother. I was a bit surprised, but what could I do?

In the evening, I would hold Danny in my arms and sit under the stairs where the light was very dim, and he would be able to open his eyes. The infection cleared in a couple weeks and the lump gradually disappeared in about a month. Danny was not a good sleeper and always fell back to sleep after drinking about one ounce of formula and then waking soon after, wanting to be fed again. The public health nurse who came by the house had the correct solution. We took off his sleepers and laid him bare on the cold kitchen table and that kept him awake until he finished the bottle. I took my turn at night time feeding at 2:00 am.

When Danny was about two months old, we enrolled him in a Scholarship Trust Fund, depositing his monthly Family Allowance Cheque of five dollars, with the expectation that Danny would receive about $1200 per year for four years when he went to university. If he chose to not attend university, then I would be refunded the amount I had paid in, without any interest earned while it was in the fund. I did the same for Matthew and Holly.

The following year seemed to fly by as Danny grew quickly. We bought a dog without very much thought about who would look after it, or even how much time we could devote to it. The pup was a Keeshond (a Dutch breed used as a guard dog on barges in the canals) and was supposed to be good with children. Pat named him "Nitty" and when taking Danny for a walk in his stroller, she would put the dog on the seat next to him. It was cute to see them, each looking in different directions, totally ignoring each other.

Bert gave me a backpack that he had modified for Lucy, and in it he had fastened a wooden seat and cut holes for the child's legs to hang down. I would pack Danny around for several hours every weekend while Pat was able to have time to relax, and I was able to see beautiful scenery in the forests and along the shore.

Pat's brother, Chris, came for a holiday. He worked for Iberia Airlines (Spanish), as a ticket agent and it was his job to balance their planes before takeoff, in order to assist in their stability and fuel economy. He was able to travel on standby (free) on any airline. His first leg was to New York City. While making his way to the United Airlines desk there to arrange a flight to Seattle, he was a few feet behind an airport employee who was carrying a large armful of papers, when someone coming by bumped into the guy, causing him to drop all of his papers. Being a perfect gentleman, Chris immediately stopped and helped pick up the papers for the very surprised and grateful airline employee. When Chris found the United Airlines counter, he asked the clerk bending over his desk if he could be placed on standby to Seattle. When the clerk looked up, Chris found himself facing the man he had just helped. Chris soon found himself on the next flight, sitting in a first class seat next to the president of US Steel Corporation. The flight was most pleasant and interesting with complimentary food and cocktails.

In September, 1968, we decided it was time to plan for another son, and called the Child Welfare worker. She stopped by and took our application, saying she would let us know within a few months, when a suitable baby was available. A week later she called to say a boy was available and we could come to Vancouver in a couple days to pick him up. The next day, the worker called and said the mother had decided to keep the child, but that there would be others. Pat cried and was sure we wouldn't get another one, ever. Then, the next day, we were told that, in Kamloops, an adopting couple decided they didn't want a baby that was offered, and, now a month old, he was available if we wanted to go and get him. We said sure, we'd be right there.

That afternoon, we packed Danny into our little Volkswagen Beetle and spent the night with Lou and Marge. The next morning, leaving Danny at Lou's, we took off for Kamloops, which took us about six hours (top speed of the Beetle was 60 mph). We arrived there at lunch time and promptly went with the CW worker to the house where the baby was being cared for by foster parents. The lady met us on the porch with everything already packed. The chubby little baby looked so happy, smiling, with lots of dark hair, and we instantly fell in love with him. On the trip back to New Westminster, we fought strong cross winds in the Fraser Canyon which sometimes made it hard to keep the little car on the road. On the way, I claimed it was my turn to name this baby and I was choosing to call him Mathew Joseph.

Matthew was the most placid, happy baby and all he wanted was to be fed regularly and given a bit of attention. Whereas Danny had been fed a diet of Enfelac formula and baby food that was pure lean meat and pure vegetables and pure fruit, etc., Matt seemed to be happy with regular milk and mixtures of meat and pasta or vegetables, and was soon eating the food from the table along with the rest of us. After a few months, Danny was forced to walk on his own, while Matt took over the seat in the back pack.

As soon as Danny was able to start talking, I started teaching him to count and to learn the alphabet, using two posters that Pat's family had sent us from England. He was a quick learner and I was proud of his progress. We bought a large cowbell with a clapper attached by a leather strap and hung it from the eaves near the back door, which we used to call the kids, much better than yelling. We also kept the bell near the back door in North Vancouver and in Port Alberni. The neighbors never complained.

In the meantime, I was very involved with the Accounting Society as Chapter Chairman. I hosted monthly dinner meetings with guest speakers at various locations on Vancouver Island for members and students. I arranged a full day professional development seminar in Parksville for our members and invited a number of engineers from the mill. I booked a hotel meeting room, arranged for catering, and printed and sold the tickets and then emceed the event. The Provincial Office in Vancouver supplied four speakers, including Jack Moore, president of the International Woodworkers Union, Conrad Lamont, a prominent industrial psychologist, and a provincial cabinet minister and a business leader, both names I can't recall. I put on another one-day seminar during the next year.

I was also asked to attend the monthly meetings of the Provincial Council, and then later I entered the flow of elected council members, progressing to the position of President of the BC Society. The Vancouver meetings entailed taking the ferry and staying overnight. A newly arrived accountant at Harmac, named Graham Alce, also became a member of the provincial council, and we were able to travel together. Graham and I became friends over the next number of years.

My convertible started to leak and the rear floor mats were constantly soaked from the rain during that winter so I traded it in on a used, white Nash Rambler. It was only slightly better on gas mileage. I then bought a used Volkswagen Beetle from Omar. It had an air-cooled engine, and a gas fired interior heater and it was much better on gas mileage, thus making it more suitable to commute the seventy-eight miles round trip to Port Alberni each day. The top speed was about 60 mph and I was seldom able to get enough speed to enable me to pass another car that was going below the speed limit, especially during the busy tourist season and on the winding road. I never regretted the long commute because the scenery was so varied and beautiful. Cameron Lake never seemed to look the same, and, occasionally, there would be an eerie mist about three feet above the water and I would picture a hunch-backed villain rowing a small boat out to deep water in order to dispose of a body.

Pat was now able to have a car in which to do her shopping and go to the library. When she visited the library, she and Danny were always warmly greeted by the librarian, Mrs. Mitchell, who would take Danny to a table where she would have already placed a stack of books for him, about planes, astronauts, trucks, and dinosaurs, etc. She would spend time with him reading and telling him stories and pack a number of his books for him, while Pat selected a stack of six to ten books, enough to last her another week. Everyone in Parksville treated us kindly and as good neighbors.

My job was going well. One day, during my annual performance review, MacDonald asked why I had never suggested that we alter the format of the division's cost statements. I replied that the statements had just been revised by head office staff a couple years after I arrived and I assumed they were fixed for all time. He said the statements were bulky and otherwise lousy and if I could improve them we would make the change. I gave the matter a lot of thought during my commute and a couple days later came up with a brilliant solution: combine all of the hundred and some cost centers' data into one statement for each department. I prepared mock-up statements and gave them to him. He just put them aside, saying he'd look them over later. A month went by with no word, and then we were called to a joint meeting of the accounting supervisors of the four pulp and paper mills in the group. Just before the end of the meeting on the second day, MacDonald had me present my revised statements and discuss them with those present. They were accepted and became the new standard cost statements for our Group.

In my fourth year at Alpulp, I was promoted to Assistant Office Manager, and was now supervising the cost and financial accounting, payroll, and sales documents departments. As well, I was responsible for hiring all clerical staff and for office union administration. When hiring to fill any vacancy, I always was filling an entry level job, because other vacancies were filled by promotion from within the union ranks. I was occasionally required to hire a beautiful, mature woman to fill the mail clerk/messenger (Group 2) position because she was the most promising applicant that I had on file and could be a candidate, eventually, for a senior clerical position (Group 6 or 7). I remained in that job until I transferred back to Head Office in 1971.

Besides being chairman of the Victoria/Vancouver Island Chapter of the Accounting Society, I was now an elected member of the Provincial Council and chairman of the Education Committee. That meant more meetings in Vancouver and attending National Board of Directors meetings in Toronto and Hamilton, Ont.

In 1970, I was approached by Malaspina College in Nanaimo to teach the Principles of Accounting course to a class of about 30 students enrolled in the night-school program. The pay was $750 for 20 lectures in the eight-month period. I took the job and found it to provide mixed results; although I liked the extra money and I was helping most of them, I felt that many of the students just didn't want to be there but they needed to earn the credits.

Things were sailing along smoothly at home, as I was at home for weekends and three or four nights per week and more often in the spring and summer, so I assumed that Pat should be happy and contented. On most evenings that I went out to teach or to meetings, it was almost time for the children to go to bed. I helped with the housework on weekends and evenings when I was home. I also took the boys out for the day every Saturday in order to give Pat the day for herself. However, living at Beachcomber was quite isolated and her only outside contacts were with the librarian and the store clerks and occasional visits with friends who lived either in Nanaimo or Port Alberni. Thinking back, Pat did have good reason to feel depressed as I look inward and at our relationship.

I became good friends with a couple of guys from the data center, which adjoined our office building, Bruce Corneliuson and Brian Johnston. Every day, we went to the Canadian Legion club at lunch time and played snooker, taking turns putting a dime in the slot to turn on the lights over the table for 30 minutes. We became quite proficient at the game, and, when one of us would be absent, other players often challenged the two that were present, with the stakes being the price of a beer, 35 cents. It was rare that any of us lost, although Brian didn't play well and didn't enjoy it if there was money to be won or lost. Brian was the best player of our threesome, but if Brian was left with an easy, dead-on shot, Bruce would put a dime on the rail and say, "Ten cents you can't make that shot"; Brian invariably would miscue and miss it.

It was our anniversary in June, and Bruce and his wife, Gail, Brian and his wife, Cathy, Pat and I went to Victoria for a weekend to celebrate, staying overnight. We had dinner at the Oak Bay Marina, a new restaurant that had good food and a combo that played dance music. During the evening, I excused myself to go to the bathroom. While in the john, I heard the announcer say the Benoit's were celebrating their anniversary and the next song was for us. When I returned to the table a few minutes later, they were still laughing, because Brian had acted as my proxy and danced with Pat.

I should mention that Brian was notoriously cheap when it came to treating Cathy and would only spend a minimum for their entertainment. For dinner, Bruce, Gail, Pat and I all ordered T-bone steaks while Brian ordered the cheapest steaks for him and Cathy. The same thing happened when we ordered desserts. When the bill came, it totalled about $80. Bruce was sitting nearest the bill. He picked it up, said to me, "the total is eighty dollars; if we add ten for the tip it'll come to ninety, split three ways it comes to thirty dollars each. Is that okay Elmer?" I said yes. Bruce then asked "okay, Brian?" Brian gulped and said "You buggers". Cathy was killing herself with laughter and said to Brian, "Serves you right for being cheap". The same thing happened the following morning when the six of us went for breakfast. Bruce, Gail, Pat and I ordered nice big meals while Brian ordered small and cheap. When the bill came, Bruce picked it up and told me the amount, added a tip, said that, split three ways, it would be so much for each, "Okay, Elmer?" I said "fine". When Bruce asked, is that "Okay Brian?" Brian just got red in the face and said, "You buggers did it to me again". Everyone had another good laugh, especially Cathy.

Our family finances were improving all the time, there were fewer bills and we were now able, often, to get a baby sitter for the kids and we went out for a nice dinner. Pat suggested we save up and take a trip to England in order to visit the family, and I readily agreed.

We joined the Credit Union in Nanaimo and were able to get tickets on a charter flight to England in May/June, 1970, at a very reasonable cost, through the Credit Union. We took a chartered bus to Vancouver and then the plane to London. We were able to get three seats next to the forward bulkhead, so the boys slept on the floor near our feet during the night. We arrived at about one pm, and were met by Pat's brothers, Chris and Tony, who drove us to the family home in Birmingham. We were welcomed by Pat's mom, May, and the rest of the family. After dinner, while May and Pat's sister, Joan, looked after the boys, the rest of us walked to the Ex-Servicemen's Club a few blocks away, and met about ten family friends. There was a comedian to entertain during the evening, followed by cribbage games and lots of pints of ale. We finally left the club when it closed, stopped at the fish and chips shop across the road to buy papers of chips, and went home. We repeated that routine many times during the following month, varying it only by going to different clubs which were putting on a show. The comedy was often quite risqué and usually contained racist jokes. During the first evening, everyone in the club was smoking and one of the Pat's brothers asked if I really didn't smoke. I had quit smoking about five years before but had started to buy a nice cigar after dinner when I attended Accounting Society dinners, so I mentioned it to him. A few minutes later, I was given a package of three Panatellas. They were good cigars and I smoked them all. The next night, I received another pack of three. When I found out they were quite expensive, I decided to buy my own. I bought a package of seven cigars every day until we went home to Canada, then switched to big White Owls, and smoked five of them a day for nearly a year, inhaling every puff. I finally switched back to cigarettes, but couldn't kick that habit until 1985.

The boys, Danny had just turned three and Matthew was nearly two, were also well entertained and the aunts and uncles were always supplying treats. On most afternoons, they were taken by their Uncle Danny to the pub at The Beggars' Bush, a shopping area nearby, where he would sit them at a table in a patio area at the rear and buy them potato crisps and "black pop", which was actually Dandelion and Burdock pop. They made quite a mess, but Uncle Danny just said to the manager, "they're just wee lads and there's no harm".

Chris and Tony rented a car for our month-long stay, and we were able to visit various places like the Darby Dales, a beautiful area of hills, fields and villages. We went to Oxford one day, and after wandering about the colleges and squares, we went into a very old and quaint restaurant. We sat at a table and while waiting for our orders, we talked about what we had seen. A couple stopped by our table and told us they had never seen such well-behaved children, and since the boys obviously were not from England, where were we from. We were proud to say "Canada", as though all Canadian kids were of the same high standard.

With Chris, Pat and I went on a week-long trip through the south-west area of England, travelling only on secondary highways and country lanes, using a Michelin Road Atlas. The road maps each covered only a very small area, and connected to other maps on other pages, which made it possible to identify the smallest road, often one lane, but took us to the smallest, but most quaint and picturesque villages. We headed west from Birmingham to Wales and then proceeded south to the Severn estuary, over a very long bridge to the Weston-Super Mare area. We thoroughly enjoyed driving through the Cottswold Hills which rise from the Thames.

I recall a few unusual and interesting places such as the Jamaican Inn. It was very old and was located on Bodmin Moor in Cornwall. Outlaws had congregated there and then went across the moor to the coast and lit fires on the shore to direct ships onto the rocks where they were wrecked. The bad guys then looted the ships and escaped back to the Inn. It had been renovated and was now a tourist attraction, but still operated as an inn. Another place we visited was Clovelly, a town built on a mountain-side, with the very narrow main street leading down to the ocean about a half mile away at an angle of about 25 degrees. All of the buildings were adorned with hanging flower baskets.

We spent a night on the Channel coast in a town called West Loo, from which we could have seen France on a clear day. While we were walking down the street, I spied a very old model ship in a shop window and went in to enquire about it. It was a model of the Golden Hind which was Drake's flag ship during the sea battle against the Spanish Armada. It was available for ten pounds and I bought it.

We had dinner that night in a pub which was built a couple hundred years before of timbers salvaged from wrecks in the area. There was a panel in the wall which contained steps down to a cave where pirates would board their boats and go out to attack merchant ships, returning to the tavern with their loot.

We then visited an old aunt of Pat, who lived in Portsmouth with another old lady. Their passion was making home- made wine of all sorts of fruit and berries that they grew, and with dandelions that they picked in the nearby park. They insisted that we sample it and found it tasted okay, but it was potent.

Our last stop of interest was at the Forest Inn on Dartmoor, where we could hear the wild ponies on the moor during the night. Spooky!!! I should mention that it was customary in the morning for a girl to come to the room, wherever we were staying, bringing each of us a cup of tea. That morning, Chris got up early, washed, shaved, and carefully brushed his hair in anticipation of the particular attractive girl whose job was to "knock us up" as it was called. She entered a few minutes early and found Chris in bed, holding my model ship, and burst out laughing. Chris, whose bed was in a little alcove in our room was quite embarrassed and couldn't see anything funny in the situation.

Back in Birmingham, Joan treated Pat and me to a weekend in London, where we all stayed in a nice hotel near the Marble Arch and Hyde Park. Joan got us tickets for a play in the theatre district and we had dinner with some of Joan's friends in a nice restaurant on Saturday evening. The play was quite good and had been running for quite a few months already. On Sunday morning, we spent a couple hours in Petticoat Lane, a huge outdoor market, where they sold almost everything you could carry. From there, we walked along the Strand to Trafalgar Square, past 10 Downing Street where the Prime Minister lives, and on to Buckingham Palace. On the way, we watched as they were holding a rehearsal for the celebration of the Queen's birthday, complete with all of the carriages and marching bands, etc. We then walked through the adjoining Green Park, and then on through Hyde Park. In Hyde Park, we stopped at Speakers' Corner, where anyone that wanted to, could stand on his soap box and rant about whatever injustice or other message that he cared about; some were talking about conditions in their home countries in Africa, Asia or the Caribbean. No speaker had an audience of more than twenty or thirty people, includ-ing hecklers, while a few had no one at all listening. There were about fifteen speakers in all. Outside the wrought iron fence nearby, were dozens of artists who had hung their paintings for sale on the fence, and many had set up their easels on the sidewalk and were busy painting, some doing quick portraits of people that stopped to order them. The painters extended about four blocks around the park and the sidewalk was crowded with pedestrians that were looking at the pictures. I didn't see any Rembrandts.

While we were in Birmingham, I bought a lot of clothes as I had intended to do, and had brought an extra, empty suitcase to bring them home. Chris took me to his tailor and I was able to buy two lovely wool serge suits, a sport coat and slacks, shirts, and a raincoat, plus two pairs of good shoes. One pair was brogues and they instantly felt like they were made just for my feet and I bought them at a cost of ten guineas (eleven pounds). When I arrived at the Club that evening, news had already preceded me, and one of the Higgins' friends said, when he greeted me, "I hear you bought a pair of ten guinea shoes, I've never even seen shoes that expensive ". The shoes lasted about fifteen years and were re-soled several times.

The rain coat also had a story. It was long, black gabardine, had a wide yoke over the shoulders, a wide collar, and a belt. When I first wore it to the office, Brian Johnston was most impressed with it and called it my "spy coat". Years later, when he was working for H.A. Symonds, a consulting engineering company in Vancouver, he travelled to foreign countries to study proposed manufacturing installations such as pulp and paper mills. He and an engineer that he worked with each bought similar "spy" coats and would pretend they were spies in the various airports and hotels during their trips. That included turning the collars up to their ears, wearing black hats, dark glasses, holding a magazine and surreptitiously looking around, and exchanging hand signals, all the while still appearing obvious enough to fellow travellers to draw curious stares. They were both in their late thirties, and acted like kids. Brian was always a character.

Arriving back in Vancouver we passed quickly through customs, declaring just under the limit of $200, and boarded our chartered bus. We had to wait nearly an hour for a couple who said when they boarded the bus, that their entire luggage was dumped out and thoroughly searched by customs agents. Nothing was found and they were actually under the limit. We were lucky!!!

Our family had thoroughly enjoyed the trip and everyone had treated us so kindly and was very generous to us. For some time after our return, I considered moving over there, but enquiries indicated a reluctance to admit any more immigrants, since millions were already coming there from Pakistan and the Caribbean Islands.

The Nash Rambler was giving us trouble and Pat drove it into the ditch on her way to town, so we traded it in and bought a Toyota. The Japanese cars were quite new in Canada, and were getting mixed reviews. Ours was one of the not-so-good types, and we had constant trouble with the transmission.

That summer was particularly happy, the weather was great and the water was warm in the bay. The boys wore swim suits every day, plus rubber boots when playing on the rocks. Matthew seemed to always have large scrapes on his tummy from crawling over the rocks. Guys from the mill used to come by on their way back from fishing in their boats and wave to me if I was in the yard. I would hold up my beer and they often would come over after they had docked and give me a salmon in return for a cold beer.

During the summer, Pats brothers, Tony and Peter and Peter's wife, Beryl, came over to stay with us for a couple weeks and really enjoyed their visit.

That fall, 1970, we decided it was time to adopt a little girl and we called Child Welfare. A worker came to the house to check us out, and to fill out an application form, with the usual result: "we'll let you know in a couple months if your application is approved, and as soon as a suitable baby is available, we'll call you". A week later, we received a call to say a baby girl that was born October 2nd, was available, and we could pick her up in a few days when she was ten days old. We were there early that day with the boys and were so very happy to see how beautiful she was and we hurried home with her. We pondered over what to name her and I mentioned it to my secretary, Zoe, at the office. She said she had a very beautiful friend who was sweet and intelligent, called Holly. I told Pat when I got home and she liked the name, so we called her Holly Rachel, and she grew to be a beautiful, intelligent and sweet woman.

It was fortunate that we adopted Holly when we did, because that was the year that birth control pills became available in Canada, with the result that very few babies were put up for adoption after that.

That winter was particularly difficult for Pat, having three children under the age of four and not having frequent contact with friends. We did entertain often, but bad weather that winter meant it was not enough. I helped out as much as I could after work and on weekends. I was out several evenings each month, teaching night school in Nanaimo, and, in the New Year, one night per week at Toastmasters Club, where I was trying to improve my public speaking skills, plus attending Accounting Society meetings. Pat had more frequent spells of depression and spent more time in assessing our relationship, as well as feeling more isolated in our lovely home at Beachcomber.

As a Vice President, I had a four day trip to a meeting of the Board of Directors of the Society in Toronto during February, 1971. On one of my trips to Vancouver for a Council meeting, my Volkswagen Beetle died on the road, stabbed through the block by a broken rod, and I had to abandon it on the highway about eight miles from the ferry. The next day, I stopped by an auto wrecker who gave me fifty dollars for it. I bought a used Pontiac for Pat to drive for shopping and drove the Toyota to work.

In the late winter, Pat asked me if I could tell my boss that I wanted a transfer back to Head Office in Vancouver, because she was having too much trouble coping with everything, especially the isolation. I agreed and discussed the matter with my boss. He talked to his boss, Bob MacDonald, who was now working in the Pulp and Paper Group Control Office in Head Office, who checked with the other product group departments. In the spring time, a new position became available in our group as Budget Coordinator, and I accepted it. We put the house on the market but we were not able to sell it quickly. The Company had three appraisals done on the basis of quick re-sales and I was offered the average. I accepted $45,000, which gave me a profit, but now makes me wish I had been able to keep it till the market price had reached closer to the present value of a few million dollars. However, just having been able to live there for five years was priceless.

Chapter 20

BACK IN THE VANCOUVER AREA

The move to Vancouver in April, 1971, went well. We rented an apartment in North Vancouver on the way to Deep Cove and settled in. Pat's brother, Danny, immigrated soon after and lived with us for quite a few months. He was easy to get along with, although Pat wouldn't pick up after him the way his mother had.

During the first couple weeks, I commuted to Nanaimo to complete my last lecture and administer the final exam. I also quit attending the Toastmasters Club meetings.

I commuted to work on a little passenger ferry that operated between a terminal on the North Shore, near where the Iron Workers Memorial Bridge is now located, to a downtown dock near the CPR station. The profit forecasts were rather silly, in that the industry was in a recession and we were still forecasting full sales at unrealistic prices. The monthly forecasts had been deemed necessary because the same system was used when the group forecasted big profits on a quarterly basis during a previous period, and a regular dividend was declared. A loss was incurred, but the dividend still had to be paid to shareholders, causing great angst among the board of directors, to put it kindly.

I asked to take a year off from serving on the Provincial Council of the Accounting Society, in order to facilitate the move and get the family settled.

A couple months after moving to North Vancouver, Pat went out on her own with a realtor to look at houses. When I came home from work one day, she told me she had found the perfect house on Everglade Place, in the Delbrook area of North Vancouver and asked me to look at it. It was a lovely Tudor-style, four bedrooms and two baths upstairs, a rec room and a separate dining room and bathroom on the main floor, as well as a 10 x 10 office that the kids could use as a play room. It was on a cul-de-sac and backed onto Braemar Elementary School. There was a nice grove of trees at the rear and on one side where no one lived. The house needed quite a bit of work, inside and out, but altogether it was great. We bought it for $50,000 and made arrangements to move in.

Pat was undergoing considerable stress at the time, and finally had a mental breakdown and was admitted to the psychiatric ward in Lions Gate Hospital, just before moving day. I took Holly to Sheila and Bert's home and arranged with the welfare department to provide a housekeeper to look after the boys while I was at work. A couple days later, I was called at the office by the police and told my boys had been turned in to their office by a lady who found them wandering on the street and they didn't know where they lived but did know that their mother was in the hospital. Pat told the police how to contact me. I hurried home to find the kids had already been returned and that Pat was furious with worry and I was too. It seems the housekeeper had taken a nap on the sofa and left the boys playing outside and they wandered off and became lost. I called the welfare department and they sent a new lady the next day.

I went to see Pat every evening and she seemed to be acting normal. Then, one night at about midnight, I awoke to find Pat crawling into bed with me. I asked her how the heck she had got out of the ward, and she said she squeezed through the little hinged window in her room that opens about eight inches high. That's how thin she was, still fasting and being depressed if she gained a pound, which resulted in her living on only green apples and tea until she had lost the pound. She then weighed only ninety pounds. The hospital phoned at about one a.m., to tell me that Pat had disappeared and they were calling the police to search for her. I said that she was with me and that she wouldn't be returning, as it was more stressful for her being in the hospital than at home. She seemed to be back to normal, certainly not irrational, and thereafter only had the usual monthly short spells of depression.

During the summer, Brian and Cathy Johnson put on a weekend house party at their home on Sproat Lake at Port Alberni, and Pat and I took the kids over and spent the weekend there, along with Bruce and Gail and Ted and Shareen Williams. In the afternoon, Ted and I were sitting on the shore while Holly was playing in the water nearby with the Johnson's kid, who they referred to as "Precious", but was a three-year old monster. Ted suddenly said "Elmer, grab your kid". I looked at Holly whose head was being held on the bottom of the lake, in about 18 inches of water. "Precious" just held her under the water, watching me until I had nearly reached them, at which time he released her and stepped back. I pulled Holly out of the water and held her till she stopped crying, but wondered later what I would have done to "Precious" if he had stayed within my reach.

In the fall, we enrolled both boys in playschool in the Edgemont Village area and we were fortunate that we had chosen that facility because the owner/teacher was very skilled and both boys developed well.

We decided to redecorate the interior of our home, painting and wall papering, etc. Danny had done a lot of interior decorating in England, moonlighting while working for a life insurance company. He offered to redo the family room to resemble an English Pub and I said, please do. He applied a rough coating of white stucco on the ceiling and walls. Then, he used rough lumber to make fake beams and posts and braces, and stained the wood dark brown. On one end of the room, I hung a dark stained 2 x 6 shelf on chains from the ceiling. With the leaded glass windows, and the bar and stools, it looked realistic and we were happy with it. Danny moved soon after to his own apartment in the West End of Vancouver, not far from Anne and Ken.

My job went okay, but I certainly didn't enjoy working in Head Office nearly as much as at Alpulp Division. I took the transit bus to work and brown bagged my lunch. I tried eating lunch in restaurants for a while but found it too expensive and I was still only eating sandwiches, so I made my own.

It was nice to be closer to family and we often visited with Lou and Marge, Emile and Julia, Bert and Sheila, and Anne, as well as Omar and his new wife, Merle. (Omar's first wife, Lea, who I had worked with, had divorced him and moved with their daughter to the United States, remarried, and died soon after of natural causes.) We also had three fantastic neighbors, Bruce Partrick, a pilot with Canadian Pacific Airlines, and his wife and two children were next door; Dr. Reid, a dentist, and his family were across the street; and Mr. and Mrs. Crawford and their daughter Jennifer, were next door to them. Leslie Reid, a teenager, babysat for us a few times but then stopped. We then used Jennifer Crawford whenever we needed a sitter and although she was a bit slow, she was very gentle and dependable and we came to trust her. She often came to visit when we were home.

In the following spring, I was again elected to the Provincial Council of the Society of Management Accountants of BC and was selected to serve as President of the BC Society for the year 1972-73. In July, Pat and I, along with about a half dozen members and staff of the Society office, attended the national conference and Board of Directors meeting in Halifax. The conference was attended by about 250 members and guests, and lasted three days. There was a separate program for the wives who were not interested in the serious stuff, and Pat joined the other ladies for tours and parties. The evening entertainment programs for the entire group included happy hour(s), dinner, and dancing.

On the first evening, when we arrived in the ball room, I went to one of four bars set up around the room to get drinks for Pat and me. I noticed that three of the bars had no line ups, but the fourth was crowded, with all the men gawking at someone in the corner. I asked a guy what everyone was looking at, and he said, "Oh! It's just Denise, from Montreal. I wandered past and found the object of such interest was a lady who resembled Marylyn Monroe in every important category, except her face. The next day, I heard that when she was coming down the steps in front of the hotel, she was wearing a skin tight and low cut outfit. Two cars passing by rear-ended a third car which had stopped, all of the drivers looking at Denise. A cop was standing nearby and he demanded Denise to go back to her room and put on something else, because Nova Scotia drivers couldn't handle that kind of distraction.

The second afternoon was clear of conference sessions and we were taken by bus to Peggy's Cove, a very scenic spot, and then to a little fishing village for dinner. We had happy hour first, standing on the big lawn just above the shore, and were entertained by a musical group, while a large steel barrel full of water was heating over a wood fire. When the water came to a boil, the cooks dumped basket after basket of live lobsters into it. That was the first time we had attended such a cook-out, and hearing the lobsters squeak when they hit the boiling water was rather unnerving. A few minutes later, the pitiful cries of the lobsters were forgotten, when we lined up and were each given a paper plate with a large lobster on it. We were directed into the dining room which seemed to have once been a warehouse. The room had rows of wooden picnic tables and we sat wherever there was space. We were each given little bowls of melted butter and lemon juice to dip the lobster into, plus slices of fresh bread and butter, a fork and a wooden pick. There was no sign of potatoes or vegetables and no mention was made of their lack. It was certainly the best lobster feed I had ever had.

On the third day, everyone left for home except for Pat and me. We rented a car and spent a few days touring Nova Scotia, including a drive around Cape Breton on the Cabot Trail. It was a very pretty area and we really enjoyed ourselves.

Back home, paper prices had risen and my job was eliminated in 1972, and I needed to find something else to do. Just then, a Corporate Controller's Section, called Accounting Development, got permission to review and document the accounting procedures and record keeping for the Pulp and Paper Group. The manager of that section, Larry Fournier, asked our Group manager to assign someone from our office to work with him. They not only assigned me to work with him, but I was transferred to that section, something I later regretted.

Larry was a Chartered Accountant and I guess he was a thinker because he certainly wasn't a "doer". Larry was a really laid-back person and in fact he spent several hours every day sleeping at his desk. It wasn't unusual to see him fall asleep during meetings, surrounded by people who simply ignored him or rolled their eyes. Larry told me that on one occasion he had fallen asleep while he was attending a lecture as a student in university.

The professor, who later served as Education Minister in the BC cabinet, wakened Larry and made a sarcastic comment to Larry, who replied, "I've fallen asleep during a lot more interesting lectures than this". On one occasion, I gave Larry a memo I had drafted to send to one of the group controllers, and while I was sitting across from him as he read it, he fell asleep; so, I just sat waiting for him to wake up about ten minutes later at which time he just smiled and shrugged his shoulders. When he was awake, he was okay and we got along well. I just did my job and he seldom interfered. I was nevertheless somewhat tainted by Larry's reputation.

We visited all of the Pulp and Paper Mills in the group and Larry would leave after a few hours when he was sure he was redundant, and I spent whatever time was necessary, reviewing procedures and writing manuals for each. Our company also owned and operated a paper mill in St. John, New Brunswick, and we spent about three weeks there, which was quite interesting.

One day, we went on a tour of their logging operation in New Brunswick and that was a laugh. We went with two of the accountants from the mill, and travelled about three hours to get to the operation, and found the camp had a new bunkhouse and a new cookhouse. The crew were contractors from Quebec and the manager was a jovial little Frenchman who was happy to show us around. He took us into the little commissary where they sold pop, cigarettes, etc., to the crew. He reached behind a cabinet and brought out a mickey of Alcool, and offered drinks to everyone. The others all took about a half-cup of it and added seven-up. When it came to be my turn, I looked at the bottle, saw it was 98% alcohol, and took only about a quarter–inch in my cup, filled it with mix and took a drink. Boy, it still packed a heck of a punch!! The manager said it was time for lunch, so we walked to the cookhouse and on the way a couple of the men were quite unsteady and even stumbled off the boardwalk.

Lunch consisted of boiled ham, cabbage and potatoes, with apple pie for dessert, which I thoroughly enjoyed because it reminded me of one of my mother's meals on the farm. After lunch, we drove to an active logging location and were amused to watch as a faller/bucker walked among the trees, all about six inches or less in diameter, falling them with a small chain saw, then trimming off the branches and cutting them into eight foot lengths. A young fellow followed, picking up the small logs and putting them in little piles. Then a little tractor with a "cherry picker" mounted on the back, picked up the little piles and placed them a tray in the front, took them to big stack of logs to wait for transport by truck to the mill where one 2 x 4 was cut from each log and the remainder went into a chipper. We were accustomed in BC to see trees of four feet in diameter, felled with a mighty crash that shook the ground, and then were yarded and loaded by huge equipment.

We also visited a kraft paper mill at Pine Hill, Alabama, and spent about three weeks there. There was no accommodation near the mill, so we had to stay in a hotel in Selma, about seventy miles away. It was generally a pleasant time, except I never did acquire a taste for grits, which was a staple in their diet.

Selma was where Martin Luther King, leading a large group of activists, started their march to Montgomery, Ala., in 1965, only to be stopped on their way by the National Guard on orders of the governor. King was assassinated in April, 1968, and the Civil Rights Act was signed into law a week later by John F. Kennedy. All of these incidents and other related events were still quite fresh in the minds of the white folks that we dealt with during our stay, although they avoided discussing the matter with us Canadians. The only time that the topic of segregation came up, was when we were out for lunch with the controller who said that the blacks would be worse off after desegregation, because the whites would no longer give them handouts. He described the blacks as being like children who would never be able to hold jobs that involved deep thinking. We didn't say anything about how the few blacks in Western Canada seemed to us to be quite capable of understanding complex concepts.

Most of the idle talk during lunch and coffee breaks revolved around sports, such as football, mainly college, (the only team that seemed to matter was the Alabama Crimson Tide, located in Tuscaloosa and coached by Bear Bryant), dove hunting, referred to as "doov huntin", and turkey "huntin". There was never a dirty joke or mention of girls or sex. Weird!!!

One of the computer systems workers that Larry knew had been transferred to Pine Hill from Head Office a few months earlier and he invited us to visit him in his suite that he had rented in a nearby village. It was actually just a kitchenette and living room/bedroom in a very old plantation house. His bed was a four poster and the top of the mattress was about 40 inches off the floor. In the kitchen we saw a cock roach, at least as big as my full thumb, scrambling along a shelf. In the huge yard were large oak and pecan trees and I picked a shopping bag, over half full, of pecans that I brought home in my luggage. Fortunately, I didn't have to open my luggage for customs inspection at the Vancouver airport.

By the time I had written up manuals for all six Divisions, a year had passed and I now had to scratch to find something useful to do during my work day. Mostly, I just spent a good portion of most days in reading Business Week, Fortune, and other business magazines.

We eventually were asked to review the accounting systems and procedures for the Packaging Group, which meant visiting all of the MB Corrugated Carton plants across western Canada, plus the folded paper board plant which had been purchased from National Paper Box and which I had once worked at. The Group Controller had designed the cost accounting statements when he first joined the company and thought they could not possibly be improved on, even though I thought they were quite useless in measuring the efficiency of the various manufacturing departments. I designed new statements and discussed them with the manager and accountant at one of the divisions and they agreed they would be a vast improvement. However, back at Head Office my boss's boss wouldn't even consider discussing the matter with the Packaging Controller, so that meant that about six months of work was shelved. Head Office politics was brutal and very frustrating and I began watching out for another transfer.

My year as President of the Registered Industrial Accountants Society of BC was interesting. We were involved with the Institute of Chartered Accountants in discussions about unifying and creating one body. However, the Certified General Accountants Association joined in the discussions and then screwed up the whole process, as they had planned from the start. There was also an issue with our members being barred from public practice unless they took additional courses of study, which was resolved in our favor in the following year. Also, our BC Society was preparing to host the national conference in 1973, so the planning for that was of primary importance. During my lunch breaks, I walked to the Society offices and dealt with whatever matters had come up, signed cheques, etc. and discussed business with Bert Sommerville, the executive director. Apart from two two-day meetings of the National Board of Directors and one meeting of the National Education Board, all held in the Toronto area, I was home every night. I did have the great pleasure as president, of signing the graduation diplomas of my friends from Alpulp, Ted Williams and Brian Johnston.

When we moved to the house on Everglade, I again let Pat have all day every Saturday and most Sundays for herself. After making their breakfast on Saturday morning, I took the kids to a park, usually Stanley Park, where we visited the zoo and aquarium and then, after a lunch of fish and chips, we hiked around the park on the sea-wall or on one of the many trails. We would return home in the late afternoon and I would make French crêpes for dinner. In the evening, Pat and I would often hire a baby sitter while we went out to visit family and friends or to a movie. On Sundays, we often went for a drive or some other family thing. On days when the weather kept us at home, Pat spent most of her time reading while I was with the children.

We joined the Capilano Winter Club and signed up for the activities that were offered: Peanut Hockey league for the boys and curling for Pat and me. We bought tiny skates for Holly and the five of us often took part in family skating in the evenings.

The boys were very enthused and excited when they received their uniforms and I purchased their skates. The age limit for Pee Wee hockey was five to eight years, and Matt was made an exception at age four. Matt was so short that his hockey pants were only about three inches above his skates, and he couldn't skate properly, just sort of walked or ran on his skates. The rules for the house league were that each team was comprised of eighteen players and the best six players were put on the first line and played against the other team's best six; the worst six were on the third line, and the remaining six were on the second line. Our team was mainly new kids and players that were not committed to teams from the previous year. Of course, some of the coaches cheated and put one or two eight-year-olds on each line and they dominated the play.

Matthew, when he was on the ice, mainly played between the two blue lines, chasing after the puck as it passed him, going towards one goal or the other. When the other team had the puck, Matt headed directly for it and would throw himself at the puck carrier, no matter if it was an eight-year old that was twice his size. On one occasion, when he was heading back to his end where the puck already was, someone shot it back up the ice and Matt had only crossed the red line. He turned and rushed toward the puck which was now lying just over the blue line and just waiting for Matt to have a clear breakaway shot to score his first ever goal. Unfortunately, an opposing eight-year-old raced back and reached the puck when Matt was still about three feet away and cleared it. There was a groan from all the parents of both teams who were all hoping to see the little guy score. On the way home, Matt said, "Dad, did you see me when I almost scored. I really would have, except that big guy surrounded me". I had to agree with him.

We withdrew the boys from the hockey program in 1974, because they were getting body checked too often by the big players who were playing on the third line and were dominating the game. The matter was discussed and complaints and warnings given, but nothing changed for the few coaches that were responsible.

Pat joined the women's curling league and quite enjoyed it, both the curling and the socializing afterwards in the lounge.

I joined the men's curling league as a spare, because the teams were already set for the winter. However, in the second week of the season a man on one of the teams decided he didn't want to curl anymore, so I took his spot for the rest of the season. At the end of the season, our team won a little trophy, but the other guy received it, because I was still considered to be only the sub. Anyways, I quite enjoyed being on that team. The skip was about seventy-five years old and wasn't very agile, but the third and second were quite skilled and made up for what was lacking from the skip and the lead (me). We got along well and we enjoyed having a drink together in the lounge after each game.

After Christmas, the Figure Skating group put on a big pageant that ran two or three nights and was open to the public. The boys from the Pee Wee hockey league were volunteered to fill in the "chorus line", and Pat was asked to make costumes for Danny and Matt. They were very intricate cat costumes, black velvet with silver trim and had hoods attached.

The pageant went over very well and Matt was most noticeable because he was the smallest and fell down a few times. The costumes came in handy and were used for many years at Halloween, until even Holly grew out of Danny's.

The first Halloween at Everglade Place, the boys visited the houses in the immediate neighborhood and were overjoyed when they visited the Reid's home across the street. There, Dr. Reid gave each of them a toothbrush and a tube of toothpaste. Their daughter, Leslie, apologised to the boys on the side and said it was embarrassing that my kids were the only ones that came to their house for treats. The boys couldn't understand why not every kid in the neighborhood didn't want such a great treat. At every house they went to that evening, they stopped and showed the person giving out treats the wonderful treats that Dr. Reid had given them. Needless to say, they didn't get to very many houses. In succeeding years, the highlight of their Halloween treats was the toothbrush and toothpaste that they invariably received from Dr. Reid. And Leslie continued to be embarrassed by her father's largesse.

We used the Club often during the summer as there was a large swimming pool and tennis courts with a tennis pro who gave Pat lessons. The children received swimming lessons. Pat took up tennis quite seriously and believed that she must be a better player than me so she challenged me to a serious match. I had played a bit at boarding school and while I was with Rose, so I accepted. I just lobbed the ball all over the court, from the back line to the front and from one side to the other. After the match, she said I hadn't play fair, hitting the ball all over the court, and even though I had won, she was still the better player. We both laughed over that.

We bought the boys each a two wheel scooter, and in no time they were tearing around our cul-de-sac and up and down our sloping driveway. Fortunately, there were few cars on our little street, and the neighbors were always very careful of the kids. A couple that we met at the winter club had a son that was Danny's age, and they had bought him a two wheel bicycle with training wheels. After weeks of practice, the father took the training wheels off and they brought the boy and his bike to ride in our back yard. The boy had no luck and was quite discouraged. Danny asked if he could try riding it, because he had never ridden a two wheeler. He got on the bike and immediately rode it all around the yard like he was an experienced rider, because riding the scooter had taught him proper balance.

In 1973, I enrolled the boys in the Cubs section of the Boy Scouts of Canada Association, and volunteered to serve on the Group Committee. We had a few fund raising events. Before Christmas, we were able to go to a holly farm in the Fraser Valley to cut and package holly which the Scouts and Cubs sold, door to door, and we raised quite a bit of money. A less lucrative project was a manure sale in the spring, although it helped to pay expenses. In February, the Cubs were each given a kit containing a block of wood, four little wheels and four little nails, with which they were required to build racing cars for a big rally. A track was brought from the storage area, which was about 40 inches high at one end and quickly ramping down to ground level and extending for another twelve feet. Two cars raced against each other in each heat. The rules allowed for the parents to give minimal assistance to the Cubs and prizes were awarded for design as well as for the racing competition. Matt and Danny designed and shaped their cars with my hand saw, attached the wheels and painted them. The finished products were pretty crude by some standards, but just fine by ours.

Race day came and we arrived with our entries, not exactly Ferraris by any means, but able to roll until they stopped and we had no idea how far that would be. We saw one car that looked like it had been designed by an aeronautical engineer and built for Andretti or Greg Moore. It was sleek, like a bullet, and gleamed with the shine of five coats of shellac. It had the exact weight of the original block of wood, because the kid (?) embedded lead slugs on the underside of the car to compensate for the weight that had been shaved off. The kid wasn't even allowed to touch his car until his race was called and then his father handed it to him within a couple feet of the track. The winning car was one that still had the original square shape but had two holes bored into the front seat and wooden figures, Bert and Ernie, from a Fisher Price set of toys, inserted. The car was painted a vivid green and it was the cutest sight to see it zoom down the track. Matt and Danny didn't win any prizes but they were proud to know they had lost, honestly, to a bunch of grown men.

There was also a Cub camp during the winter, held in a local school gymnasium, which I attended with the boys. It was the first of many that

I attended during the following several years, although it was the only one held indoors.

I was asked to go back to MacMillan Rothesay Division in St. John, New Brunswick, during the winter to relieve the accountant/office manager who was going be away for two months on sick leave. I stayed in a nice hotel downtown and formed a friendship with the young assistant accountant and his girlfriend. We all went out together to a club for drinks several nights per week. When I first arrived there, I started growing a full beard, which was pretty scrawny at the start, but had filled in pretty well by the time I returned home. When I was back at Head Office, I used to go downstairs to a barbershop every few weeks for a haircut and have my beard trimmed. The barber was a beautiful Swedish girl who would recline the chair totally and then hover over me while she trimmed my beard and told me about Sweden, I think, although I could never remember what she said. I kept the beard until 1985.

In July, 1973, the BC Accounting Society hosted the National Conference at the Hotel Vancouver, a three-day event. As Past President of the BC Society, it was my job to host the guest speakers, who were internationally renowned experts in their fields. The only Canadian speakers were a professor from Simon Fraser University, and someone from Toronto; all of the others were Americans.

Pat and I were assigned a large, beautiful suite, complete with a very comfortable meeting room which contained a fireplace, bar, and leather sofas and chairs. The remainder of the suite was for the private use of Pat and me, and included a large bedroom with an ensuite bathroom, a sitting area, kitchenette and dining area.

My job was to greet all of the speakers in the morning in the meeting room of our suite with a full breakfast and a casual discussion about the day's program. The speakers were invited to attend as much of the conference as they wished and they were able to bring their wives. Only two brought their wives, and one of the couples and one of the single men stayed for the entire conference. Pat and I became good friends with the three and we spent a good deal of time together, lunches and evenings. The single man was head of the Adult Education Department at the Los Angeles Times, and the married man was the dean of the linguistics department at the University of Oregon. They were an older couple, but both were very interesting and gracious people. On the second evening, delegates had a free evening, so we went up Burnaby Mountain to the relatively new Simon Fraser University for a look at the campus and the view of the city. From there, we went to Gas Town for an Italian dinner. The man from LA was quite suave and impressed the two ladies by presenting each of them with a long stem rose. Cute!!

Each day, all of the speakers came to our suite for happy hour. The hotel supplied the bartender, and we supplied the booze. We all went together to the dining/ball room for dinner on the first and third evenings. Our table was naturally always in a favored spot and we were treated with great attention. We loved it. The third evening was the National President's Banquet and Ball and it turned out to be a very memorable event. Each course was preceded by some sort of circus spectacle wending its way through the room, between the tables, followed by a line of waiters, bearing their trays of food. One was four men in costume bearing a wooden cage containing a full grown tiger. Another was a cowboy riding his prancing horse. Another was a man in an alpine costume carrying an eagle on his arm. It had its 6-foot span wings outspread. I can't recall the fourth parade, but it was equally impressive.

I was allowed to bring two guests to that evening's event, so I invited Lou and Marge, who came for happy hour and stayed for the banquet and dance. The guest speakers were very pleasant to them and included them in the conversation. Lou said, later, that he was pretty proud of his kid brother from Meadow Lake.

The rest of that year was very interesting but not really exciting. Pat seemed to be mostly happy with a few short spells of depression each month. Pat learned that if she gained a pound of body weight, she could quickly get rid of it by taking a diuretic (water pills) which she was able to get prescriptions for from her doctor. As a result, she was able to keep her weight down to 90 – 95 pounds, but, because she was not drinking enough water, she started developing bladder and kidney problems.

For our vacation that year, we went to Osoyoos in the Okanagan and stayed in a motel that backed onto the lake. The kids had fun in the lake, swimming and going out in paddle boats, as well as eating cherries and seeing how far we could spit the pits. The owner asked us to sweep them up as the parking lot was starting to look like a garbage dump.

At home, we hired someone to paint the outside of the house and replace the long flower box that spanned the living room windows. The house had never been painted since it was built, and, because the painting took place during the hottest week of the summer, it needed four coats on the stucco and trim. The painter complained that he lost money on the job, but I didn't quite believe him. He just didn't make as much. Pat decided that we were due for another trip to Jolly Old England in the following year, so, being in charge of the purse strings, she put us on another strict budget.

In late May, 1974, we flew to London, except that this time we needed to pay for four seats, not three, and we went for five weeks, not four. Again, we were met at Heathrow Airport by Chris and Tony in a car they had rented for a month. Life hadn't skipped a beat since our last visit. The club was full of "old" friends when we entered that evening, and a steady flow of pints came to our big table. We again were taken on scenic rides and to old castles and manor houses.

Chris took us on another week-long tour of England, this time to the Lake District, mainly Lake Windemere. It was a beautiful area and we enjoyed ourselves totally. On one night when it was my turn to choose the accommodation, I picked a village called Hawkeshead. We found it down a little lane and checked into a large bedroom upstairs in a pub. The window overlooked a Church and its graveyard, with sheep grazing in it. The floor slanted from one wall to the opposite wall by at least two inches, and a large wardrobe that was about three inches from the wall at its base, was touching the wall at its top. While we wandered around the village, we passed a cottage about three doors over that had belonged to Wordsworth when he was writing his beautiful poetry. Anne Hathaway's cottage was down the street. When we visited the church, we found their records started in about the eighth century. The dates on the gravestones corroborated that, although many of the grave markers were crumbling. When we went into the pub for a pint before dinner, we found the locals in a heated discussion about the price of wool. It seemed that these people spoke an English dialect that made it impossible for Pat and me to understand them. Chris eventually was able to grasp some of their conversation, and said it was mainly caused by a different cadence as well as the pronunciation.

Back in Birmingham we prepared for a trip to Benidorm, Spain, with Pat's oldest sister, Joan, who was accustomed to spending three or four months there every summer. Joan had been studying Spanish for many years at night school at the University and was thoroughly fluent in the language both speaking and writing. Joan was accompanied by a girlfriend, a cute cockney woman, named Vera, who left her husband at home in London and went to Spain for fun. Joan had arranged for us to take a charter flight to Benidorm that included three-star hotel accommodation, including meals and sangria. The room was okay but the food and sangria wasn't. We went out for all of the dinners and most lunches.

When we arrived in Spain the chartered bus left the airport without us as we waited for our luggage, necessitating a 45-minute taxi drive to our hotel. We were able to get reimbursed for it later.

The week was lovely, with perfect weather. Every day, after breakfast, we walked to the little bakery where Joan was staying with the owner, who was a very long-time friend. In fact, Joan normally worked at the bakery every summer and would again after we left. After lunch at the bakery, we would spend an hour on the beach and then go home for siesta. At five p.m., we would shower and get dressed for the evening.

Our first stop was at a hotel down the street and met Joan and Vera in the outdoor bar where an excellent mariachi band was playing. The vocalist was a beautiful girl who had an equally beautiful voice. We would spend an hour or more, drinking gin and tonic, and just enjoying the entire scene. I was with three ladies and therefore a bit of an object of curiousity. The vocalist wore a tight dress that buttoned in the back, and the buttons kept popping open, making it necessary for her to reach back to redo them, often standing and singing near our table and was often smiling at me. Meanwhile, Vera who sat across the table from me always wore a tight dress that buttoned in the front and her buttons were also popping open. I didn't really know which way to look, mostly I watched Pat out of the corner of my eye to see if she was noticing. It became quite a source of amusement for the girls and one of discomfort for me.

From that hotel, we went for dinner, and then to a nightclub. Our favorite club was very large, very crowded and very noisy with a good band that played a lot of modern music as well as Latin. During the evening, there was a stage show, often featuring Flamenco dancers, and the rest of the time there was dancing.

I knew the drinks were strong, but not exactly how strong. One evening, I went to the washroom and on my way back to the table, I stopped at the bar and ordered a gin and tonic. The bartender took a large tumbler, tossed in a little slice of lime, and, while facing another bartender that he was talking to, he started pouring gin into the glass. When the glass was nearly full, he glanced down, took the mixer hose, squirted a tablespoon of tonic into the glass and handed it to me and I paid him the price of less than fifty cents. I then realized why I had been coming home pissed every night since I arrived in Spain. From then on, I limited myself to one drink at the first hotel (the site of the defective buttons), and two in the nightclub. Well, okay, maybe I would have another in a cantina that we passed while walking home.

I think the Spanish men there took male chauvinism to a whole new level. Every evening the nightclubs were full of local men who chatted up, danced with, and romanced the unaccompanied tourist ladies who were mainly English and who paid for all the drinks. The exception was on Sunday night when the restaurants were crowded with the same men, but were now accompanied by their wives and children.

When we arrived back in Birmingham, Chris met us at the airport and he remarked that good weather always seemed to follow us around by the minute. It had been raining, almost non-stop for weeks prior to our visit but had stopped an hour before our arrival in May, and we had enjoyed sunny days until we left for Spain. He said it had started raining again before he reached home the previous week after dropping us at the airport and it poured until just before he arrived back at the airport to pick us up a half hour earlier. We recalled that we had also enjoyed beautiful weather for the entire month on our previous visit in 1970.

Pat seemed to be especially reluctant to return to Canada and our home in North Vancouver at the end of June. Anyways, we did come back to our usual routines, although she seemed to be looking for something more interesting in her life. We talked about arranging for child care for the kids, and her going to work. In fact, she was offered a job at a fitness center that she regularly attended about two blocks from home. However, she wasn't interested in that idea, and I got a premonition that she was secretly planning on leaving me.

In early September she phoned me at the office and said I should come home immediately. I caught the bus and walked in a half hour later. She proceeded to tell me that she had decided to leave me and it was just a matter of where she would go. She said that my choices were that we would sell the house and she would take the three children and move to an apartment and I would pay support for them and have weekly visits, or I could stay in the house with a house keeper to look after the boys, and she would move back to England with Holly. If I chose the latter, I must agree to bring the boys to England every summer to visit her and Holly, and I must pay her a small amount for her share of the house. It wasn't much of a deal – either I lost all three children or just one. I opted for choice number 2. She said that she wouldn't leave until I had arranged for a housekeeper, so I got busy. I advertised for a live-in housekeeper and received two phone calls, one didn't want to look after two boys and the other, an older lady, seemed to be quite eager when I interviewed her and I hired her.

The lady brought her sister who was visiting from England and they proceeded to spend the next two days at the PNE and sightseeing but not working. After the two days, I told the new housekeeper that I needed to get her personal information to arrange for employee insurance and income tax remittances. When I insisted that she tell me her birth date, she got agitated and when I asked why she didn't want to tell me her age, she said that I was much younger than her and it might affect our relationship after Pat left. I said I was definitely not attracted to her and there was absolutely no way that there would ever be a relationship other than as employer/employee. She said well, in that case she might as well go back to her apartment. As I was driving them back to Vancouver, the sister said to me, "You must pay her wages for the two days, and that would be twenty pounds".

I then checked the newspaper ads and saw a notice that a company was offering to bring in domestic servants from the Caribbean. I phoned the next day and found that it was true and I put my order in for a lady whose picture I was shown along with meager personal information. She did have a pleasant face and a lovely smile. She would arrive in the middle of October.

Meanwhile, Pat and I maintained a friendly relationship while she made final arrangements and packed. When I was speaking to a friend in the shipping department at Alpulp, I mentioned that Pat was going back to England, and he asked if she would be taking many belongings with her and how she would be shipping it. I said she was only taking a small trunk and suit cases and I assumed we would call a shipping company for the trunk. He said, nonsense, just deliver it to him through the company's mail system and he would give it to the captain of our company's newsprint carrier. I did so, and the trunk was delivered to the Higgins' door in Birmingham a couple weeks later, free of charge.

During this period, Pat and I talked about what had gone wrong with our marriage, and I told her I felt that one important contributor was her frequent analyses of our marriage. I compared our marriage to a beautiful, healthy rose, growing in the garden. If you pull it out of the ground to check the roots, find them to be fine, and replant it, it will still flower. But if you keep pulling it out of the ground often to check the roots and replant it, it will eventually die. She agreed that it made sense, but it was too late to start over and she was now looking forward to being back in England.

Edith Millar of St. Vincent Island, the largest island of the country St. Vincent and the Grenadines, in the Caribbean, arrived on schedule and was delivered to our home by the agency. She was shy, and a little scared of what she might be getting into, but she relaxed as we talked about our situation and what her duties would be. I explained that besides the housework and making our meals, she would have to take a taxi to a supermarket in Edgemont Village once a week to shop and I would give her a signed blank cheque to pay for the groceries and she would then bring them home in the cab. Also, I would pay her wages by cheque which she could cash at the bank across from the street from the store, and she would be able to transfer money to her family. She seemed to be pleased with the arrangement.

Edith had three children with her boyfriend, Elwin, who worked for the local phone company in St. Vincent. She sent money each month and bought clothes for her kids, who lived with Edith's mother, and shipped the parcels home by air freight. The oldest daughter was fifteen and the youngest was a five year-old boy. Within a few weeks of her departure from St. Vincent, Elwin got a new girlfriend who moved into Edith's house. Edith's comment when she heard the news was, "Elwin's a Tom cat, that's why I never married him". Edith came to love my kids and they really appreciated all that she did for them. She was a good cook and her chocolate cakes were to die for, always moist and with an unusual taste, which she later admitted was the result of substituting a cup of red wine from my liquor cabinet for the regular liquid called for in the recipe. Edith had Saturdays off and would spend the day downtown hooking up with some of her countrywomen. She would return home before five and I would make dinner for all of us, always French crepes, which she seemed to enjoy. On Sundays, Edith always prepared a lovely roast beef dinner which she served in the dining room. Edith always dined with us and was treated as one of the family.

Pat was satisfied that we were now in good hands and left for England with Holly on a Saturday in mid- October, while I took the boys to a lake near Pemberton for the weekend. It was a pretty difficult weekend for all of us, and we discussed how things would be without Holly, and when we would be able to visit her next summer. I assured the boys I would be close by as long as they needed me and I wasn't going to rush into another marriage unless I was absolutely positive she was the right woman to be my wife and their mother.

Danny later remarked, "That's two mothers that didn't want me". I assured him it was never his fault or the fault of the other children. In short, Pat just no longer wanted to be a wife or mother, and definitely not in Canada.

Chapter 21

EXIT PAT – ENTER PHYLLIS

Once Pat and Holly had departed to England in late October, 1974, I started trying to adapt to a new life while retaining as many of the daily routines for the boys as I could. Edith, the new housekeeper, co-operated and did what she could to reassure the children that she would be as kind and caring as she could, and that helped.

I checked with an organization that was designed for single parents called "Parents Without Partners" which was currently inactive in North Vancouver, but that Chapter was intending to start up again in mid-November. Its aim was to provide support for members and activities for the parents and children, and, less importantly, social events for the parents.

In the meantime, with someone at home to take care of the boys, I was free to look after my own social needs and I started dating. My first date was with Matthew's Grade One teacher, Mrs. Ossenchuk, a gorgeous divorcee who had a ten year old son. During the evening she asked me about Matthew, who had told her in class that his home town was Kamloops, and his parents had gone there in a jet plane to get him. I laughed and confessed that, although we had gone to Kamloops to pick him up, it was in a Volkswagen Beetle. When we said goodnight, she thanked me for a nice evening but said she wasn't interested in getting involved with somebody who had two young sons, and please not ask her out again. My hair was already quite grey all over (thanks to Rose and Pat), but particularly at the temples.

On the following Tuesday evening, November 11, I went to the start-up meeting of PWP (Parents Without Partners) along with about 20 – 25 other people. The speaker was a child psychologist who spoke on dealing with common childhood problems facing single parents in modern society. After the speech, we had coffee and held a meeting to organize ongoing activities. We elected members to fill various positions and I volunteered for something. A wine-and-cheese party was planned for the following Saturday, with the men bringing the wine and the ladies bringing the snacks.

It was suggested that we all go to the Coach House Hotel for a nightcap and I went, along with most of the group, and we sat around several tables that were pulled together. We had just got our drinks when one of the ladies said she had to phone her baby sitter. She returned and told her friend that she had to leave right away because her sitter was already late to go home. Her friend said she just couldn't drink her scotch quickly, so I piped up, "I'll give you a ride, where do you live?" I had been noticing this particular "friend" throughout the evening and seized the opportunity to make my move. She was a classy lady, with the most beautiful eyes and smile. I joined her at her table and asked her to dance to the little combo.

She said her name was Phyllis Ellis and that she had only come for the one event which was of particular interest to her, namely the child psychologist's speech, and wasn't planning to attend any further functions. After a couple drinks, I drove her to her home on Ridgewood Drive, in Edgemont Village. I suggested to her that I could pick her up on Friday evening and go to Park Royal to shop for wine and snacks for the party on Saturday night. She said she definitely was not going to the party, but she did tell me that she worked at the Royal Bank in Edgemont as the manager's secretary. I phoned her a couple times every day, pleading to change her mind about the party, and finally, on Friday afternoon, she relented.

In the evening, we went shopping at Park Royal and we bought a half-gallon of wine as well as some sliced meats and cheese. It was still early, so we went to the pub in the Park Royal Hotel for a drink. That pub was particularly popular because it featured a piano player and an enthusiastic singer who conducted a sing-along with the patrons. The entire crowd sang and it was a fun evening. Phyllis and I each drank a few bottles of cider and were feeling quite happy when we left. Arriving at her home, she invited me in and told me some of her life story, and the rest of the story I'm adding from later talks over the years.

Phyllis was born on April 30, 1925, in Johannesburg, South Africa, to William Patrick and Marie (Mimi) Glendon, the youngest of four girls. Apparently, her father was so disappointed when another daughter was born and still no sons, he refused to even hold her. A few days later, when he was told that he must register the child, he refused and sent his friend, Denis, to the registry office to do it. Denis asked what names should he give, and Mr. Glendon said he didn't care, "just as long as she has my initials". Thus, she ended up with the names Phyllis and Winifred. Denis thought it would be nice if his own name was included, and that's why she received another middle name, "Denise". She later became her father's pet because she always supported him in family arguments, when the three older sisters (Sylvia, Zena, and Maureen) always sided with their mother. Her father had emigrated from Edinburgh, Scotland, after serving as an officer in the British Army in India. He was now a stock investor/promoter. Mimi had come from Alsace Loraine, France, with her family.

Phyllis was a bright girl, always on the honor roll at school. She attended a private boarding school and only came home for weekends. Her teachers were all English schoolmarms who were sticklers for proper diction and spelling, as well as decorum. Her education was in both official languages, English and Afrikaans, so she seemed to be more than twice as smart as me, since I was still having trouble with English.

When Phyllis was just a toddler, she had a bad accident at home when she crawled to a table on the porch and pulled on the tablecloth causing an urn of boiling tea to spill on her. Her nanny picked her up and cuddled her and that caused a large patch of skin on her side to be chafed and resulted in severe scarring.

Phyllis obviously had a happy childhood among a close and loving family because of the way that she spoke of them. She had a little pet monkey that was kept in the yard on a long chain tied to a post that was about eight or ten feet high and it had a little platform on the top, which the monkey would sit on and chatter at anyone that came by. Apparently it didn't like the garbage men that would come by each week, and would screech at them.

Mr. Glendon was not at all racially intolerant. In fact, he was a close friend and shared the belief of Jan Smuts, who was a national political leader, and who was convinced that all that the blacks needed to succeed was education and training. Smuts was a frequent visitor to the Glendon home. Unfortunately for South Africa, Smuts lost the election, Botha won and his party instituted an apartheid policy.

When the Second World War broke out, the three older girls saw their husbands go off to war. One did not return; I believe it was Sylvia's husband, who died at sea, the victim of a German U-boat attack. Mr. Glendon's comment was that he was now grateful that he had only daughters, because the loss of a son-in-law was almost unbearable, and the loss of a son would be even worse.

The Glendons' large house was open to servicemen, and every weekend saw every spare room occupied by men in uniform. There was always a group crowded around the piano singing all the popular songs and dancing. One of Mr. Glendon's friends usually had a bit too much to drink and would wander upstairs during the evening and come down wearing a ceramic chamber pot on his head. Phyllis was a teenager until the last year of the war, and she spent a good deal of her time at the Servicemen's Club as well as at home entertaining the men.

As I mentioned previously, Phyllis was her daddy's pet and had free use of his credit account. She would regularly go shopping and would simply say to the clerk to "Put it on my father's account". He indulged her always, with the result that she had about fifty pairs of shoes in her overstuffed closet.

It was during this period that she met Leo Ellis, a sailor in the New Zealand Navy. After the war, he was demobilized in New Zealand, and returned to South Africa and married Phyllis. They had two daughters born in Johannesburg, Barbara Marion, on June 12, 1952, and Monica Eileen, on July 18, 1954. Leo worked as an insurance adjuster.

The Glendon family were Christians and staunch members of, and active in, the Methodist Church. Phyllis had taught a children's Sunday

School Class for many years. Her very close school friend was a Jewish girl, and Phyllis was a very frequent visitor to their home, and was included in many of their Jewish rituals and at one point, when she was dating a Jewish man who was serving in the air force, she actually thought of converting to Judaism. Their romance ended when he was shipped back to Britain.

Phyllis's curiosity about religion didn't end and she was encouraged to study various beliefs. She came to the conclusion that Roman Catholicism was the true religion and converted to that religion, which was, coincidentally, the same as Leo.

In 1954, they were spending an evening visiting with their extended family when Phyllis commented about the black singer, Nat King Cole, whose song was being played on the radio, "Oh, I just love him!", to which a little niece piped up with a racial slur. Phyllis looked over to Leo and said "I think it's time we moved".

Leo applied for, and received, a transfer to England and they set sail, minus most of her shoes as well as a large portion of the wedding gifts they had received, Leo being of the opinion that they were superfluous and too expensive to ship. Phyllis was also very pregnant when they arrived in London, where they were met by her friends, Mary and "Uncle" Bob. He wasn't really an uncle, just a good friend who was kind and generous to the family. Soon, Leo was posted to the company's Liverpool office and that's where Stephen was born on January 6, 1955. Life was still pretty grim in England, just ten years after the war ended. The flat that they were able to rent was cold, damp, and drafty.

After a few months, Leo decided it was time to move on, first to Canada for a couple years, and then, finally, to New Zealand. He quit his job and sailed to Canada, leaving Phyllis and the kids to follow when he got a job in Toronto. On the first day of job hunting, he was offered two jobs, and he summoned Phyllis to join him. She soon was able to sail, and was treated kindly by the crew and other passengers on the ship, arriving in St. John, New Brunswick, in early October, 1955. A group of ladies in St. John met the passengers and had gifts for all of the war brides on their arrival in Canada. Phyllis was especially pleased to receive gifts for her and the children, considering she was not joining a Canadian husband/veteran. Leo met them at the boat and drove them to Toronto. They settled into an apartment where they lived until they were able to buy a house in the Don Mills area of Toronto.

They quite enjoyed Toronto and did quite a bit of travelling and camping. They went to Cape Cod, Mass., several times and made friends there. They also went for holidays in the cottage country of Ontario, visiting various lakes.

Annemarie was born in Toronto on March 25, 1963. A short time after being discharged from the hospital, Phyllis suffered a serious haemorrhage and was rushed to the hospital. They couldn't stop the bleeding in time and she was pronounced dead. The priest had been summoned and she was given the Last Rites. Phyllis recalled that when she died, her spirit left her body and entered a column of light that was ascending. As she was moving up the light beam, an image that she assumed was the Virgin Mary and mother of Jesus Christ appeared and faced her, holding up her hand and shaking her head. Phyllis' spirit then returned to her body. The doctor, priest and Leo were already leaving the ward when a nurse again checked Phyllis' body and called out that she had felt a pulse. Everyone rushed back to her bedside and got her condition stabilized and she recovered. She didn't speak of her out-of-body experience to other people, but I believe it was a miracle, and that she was returned by God for His purpose.

While they were still in Toronto, Phyllis took Annie back to Johannesburg to visit her family. While they were there, her father noticed her Canadian passport and inquired if she had given up her South African citizenship and she said, yes, her and Leo had both become naturalized citizens of Canada. Her dad was very disappointed and disinherited her. When he passed away soon after, she was not mentioned in his will.

They moved to Vancouver in about 1965 and bought the house on Ridgewood Drive. The three older children left home while still in their teens, and Phyllis separated from Leo in 1973 or 1974, and that's when she entered my life, never to leave it.

Getting back to the original story, I picked up Phyllis on the Saturday evening and took her to the party at Bette's home a few blocks away. It was a fun evening and everyone seemed to have a good time, although I have to admit I had a bit more than my share of the half-gallon jug of wine I had brought. Everyone did get to know each other, and we started to bond as a group.

We were able to use the North Vancouver City Neighborhood House for family activities and they helped our group immensely. We tried to plan for a family or kids' event every week as well as a social for the adults. We put on a dance that was open to other PWP chapters and that was a successful fund raiser for our group. We had a couple camping trips for families to Birch Bay, where we shared cabins and enjoyed a bon fire with hot dogs and roasted marshmallows.

Phyllis and I became a steady couple right from our first date. Neither of us conceded there was anything really permanent though, as Phyllis vowed she was through with marriage, and I wasn't about to let go of my freedom, made possible by having Edith to look after the kids and keep house. Nevertheless, I had the feeling deep down, that I was falling in love again, in spite of my resistance.

At Christmas, I invited Phyllis and Annemarie, Bert and Sheila and their children and Anne and Ken, and Danny for turkey dinner. At a recent PWP meeting, I had also invited any single parent to bring their children to my home if they were going to otherwise be alone for Christmas, and one lady came with her young son. It was a very pleasant affair and my sons still felt part of a familiar family. For Annemarie, eleven years old, and Phyllis, it was also their first Christmas without Leo. Phyllis mentioned that for the previous Christmas, Leo's gift to her was a pair of slippers, both for the left foot.

The winter and spring passed with weekly events for the single parent group, afternoon events for the children and parties for the adults. We formed some close friendships with several members, particularly Ray Harris, Lani Ghiske, Nan Pemberton, Bette, and Bill Amos, who was an amateur photographer. We were good friends with several others but never kept in touch with them after we got married.

In January, 1975, I suffered a slipped disc and had to go into Lion's Gate Hospital for a few days. I had just got home when, a few days later, I received a phone call from Pat telling me that Holly missed her brothers so much that she was making everybody's life miserable, and asked if I wanted her back. I said yes, definitely, but I couldn't travel to go and get her because of my back. Pat said that the airline refused to allow Holly to fly alone, so I offered to pay her fare and expenses if she would bring Holly back and she reluctantly agreed. On the following Saturday, I took the boys to the airport and when they saw her, they rushed to hug her. I was so happy to have my little girl back, I couldn't stop crying. Holly was clutching a stuffed "Paddington Bear" that the family had given her and which she treasured for years. I dropped Pat at Sheila's and hurried home, but first stopped by Phyllis's home to introduce Holly to her.

On Saturdays I still took the kids to Stanley Park to the zoo, followed by lunch at a concession stand, and then for a long walk around the seawall or on one of the many paths, except that Phyllis now often accompanied us. In the late afternoon, we would return home and I would make a dinner of French Crepes for everyone, including Phyllis and Edith. The first time that Phyllis joined us for this particular dinner, she offered to spread the crepes with butter and brown sugar as I did, and serve the kids. A few minutes after the kids started eating their first crepes they all called out, "Dad, these are better than yours". I tasted a bite and had to agree, so I asked what she had added, and she said she had sprinkled lemon juice over the brown sugar and butter, followed by cinnamon, before rolling up the crepes. I had to agree that they were better than mine. Annemarie normally spent weekends with her father at his apartment in West Vancouver.

On Friday evenings during that winter, I drove Phyllis and Annie and my kids up Mount Seymour to the base of the ski lift where the children would toboggan on the snowy slopes near the parking lot. Phyllis and I would sit in the warm car, which was parked close by, so we could keep watch over them. When the kids were sufficiently tired, cold, and damp, they would climb into the back seat and have hot chocolate from a thermos bottle and a snack. On the way home, Annie would sing some of her summer camp songs. One evening, Holly asked if she could sing a song that she had composed on her own. We said, please do, and she chanted "Far, far away from the ocean", several times, and then awaited our applause. We have never forgotten that song, much to her embarrassment.

Phyllis and I joined the Vancouver Symphony Society and signed up for the winter season series of concerts at the Queen Elizabeth Theater and I quite enjoyed receiving a bit of culture. We also went to several concerts featuring Neil Diamond, Nana Mouskouri, Marie Mathieu, and Burl Ives, among others. The only annoyance in attending concerts with Phyllis was that she could never be ready early enough that I wouldn't have to speed more than normal, with the result that I was always expecting a speeding ticket on the way. On one occasion, we arrived too late, the concert had already started, and we had to sit in the lobby listening to the music on the speakers, until intermission. It was about the only thing about her that I could ever complain about, and I'm sure she could have listed many more faults that I had, but she seldom ever did.

Our PWP group attended dances put on by other affiliated clubs as well as holding our private house parties. I noticed that everyone got up to dance when the song "Please Release Me" was played and it became a little joke for me. One of our members, Nan Pemberton, had a beautiful big house in the Lynn Valley area and it was the site for several parties. Bette's, Claire's and my house were other frequent sites for parties.

Nan's husband had left her for a divorcee that lived across the street and a couple doors along and he moved in with her. They were able to watch Nan and her daughter, Jill, from their window. Nan and Jill stayed on in their house which was not finished. Nan applied to the court to have the house's value assessed and that half of that amount would be her husband's share when it was eventually sold. That was written into the divorce agreement. Nan was a very capable and energetic person, and she pretty well finished the interior in the next year. One night, as Phyllis and I were coming home over the Iron Workers' Memorial Bridge, we saw the glow of a house fire in Nan's area, and, on the following day, we learned that it was Nan's house that had been torched while she was out. Although everyone had their suspicions about the arsonist, there was not sufficient proof to lay charges.

Several of the PWP members were struggling financially, and we helped each whenever we could. One man was a marine architect who insisted on being an independent designer and manufacturer. I offered to do his accounting for him at a ridiculously low rate and to advise him on his bidding process. Trevor was a brilliant designer from England who had pictures of himself and Prince Phillip on a small yacht that Trevor had designed and built for the prince. Also a modular scow that you could add as many units as you wished and was meant for transporting freight on the rivers of Africa. Unfortunately, Trevor wouldn't take advice and was almost starving. He won a contract to design and build a fiberglass conning tower for a miniature submarine and almost lost money, even though he had only included about ten dollars per hour for his labor. The contract to build fiberglass seats for the new Sea Bus for Burrard Inlet had similar results. I couldn't bring myself to even charge him for the accounting service. After I was transferred I asked my friend, Frank Weiler, who was now a professional management consultant, to give Trevor a hand but after a year of frustrating attempts to help him, Frank gave up.

In July, I took my three children camping for two weeks at Osoyoos, in the Okanagan, and pitched our tent in a nice open area in the provincial camp ground that was on the spit that ran far out into Lake Osoyoos. Actually, we left home about three a.m. and arrived at the campground just before eight o'clock so that I could be waiting when the first campers were ready to leave their spot. I asked a young couple who were having their breakfast, if they were leaving that day and the lady said, yes, right after they were finished eating.

I had just bought a used tent and we were pretty well set with all the necessities. The tent was 10' x 14', with two rooms and the walls were about forty inches high. It weighed a ton, certainly all I could manage to erect by myself. The following two weeks were really fun, although Matthew was required to spend two hours every afternoon completing the two-thirds of his math work book that he hadn't finished during the school year. His teacher, Mrs. Ossenchuk, had assured me that although he was having some minor difficulties, he was just a slow learner, and, because he was such a sweet boy, he would be fine. I was surprised to learn how far behind he had lagged.

One day, we went to a nearby apiary and bought a big can of honey that had been produced right there. I was then able to introduce the kids to the awesome taste of fresh bread covered by butter and honey mixed together. We were down at the edge of the lake, one evening, when a young woman asked me if I was a single parent with my kids. When I said, yes, she then asked me how I was making out with cooking, "probably hot dogs twice a day?" When I said, no, she wanted to know what kind of meals I was making, so I told her we had steak and baked potatoes the previous night and that night I had made French crepes. She said she was very impressed and that she wouldn't even attempt crepes on her electric range at home, let alone using a camp stove.

One night, we experienced a severe storm, high winds and a heavy downpour. Our tent was in about the center of the spit, higher than most of the campsites, and quite exposed. I awoke to find the tent was flapping and a couple of the short aluminum posts holding up the side walls were bending and the walls were sagging, Also, the wind was blowing under the tent and lifting the floor. I hurried out to attach more cords to all of the poles and then used firewood all around the base to keep the wind from getting under the floor. It made for a largely sleepless night, and the children, especially Holly, were scared being in a bedroom that was not at all solid.

The park had a couple university students working that summer, doing talks about nature. One evening, the student was talking about how you learn a lot about animals and their diet just by examining their scat. She brought out a bag of bear scat as well as a necklace that she had made out of dried elk scats which she had varnished and threaded on a leather thong. One of the boys asked me what it was and I whispered "it's pooh". The kids got quite excited and began talking in loud whispers, 'That's pooh"; "Dad, is that really pooh?"; "boy, I wouldn't wear pooh around my neck", and it went for some time until the young naturalist got annoyed with me and my noisy kids.

I also taught the kids how to annoy bats. On our way back from the naturalist's talk, I noticed a lot of bats swooping between the trees, feeding on mosquitoes. I picked up a bit of gravel on the path and tossed it into the air and we could hear the clicking sound of their teeth as the bats caught the gravel in mid-air. They have such amazing radar!!

While we were camping, Phyllis took Annemarie to Victoria for a few days. It was during this period that I was missing Phyllis a lot and I realized that I was already madly in love with her, although I was still not willing to make any long-term commitment. I felt that two failed marriages were already too many.

Phyllis had grown to love me too, but she had more to fear in a permanent relationship with me. The fact was that she was fifty years old, had three grown children and two grandchildren, plus a twelve year old daughter who wanted her parents to reconcile instead of divorce and did what she could to stop our relationship from going further. All this time, Leo was reassuring Annie that he would be coming home, as soon as he was ready.

Besides, she realized that marrying me meant taking on three young children, the youngest of whom wouldn't graduate from high school until Phyllis was sixty three years old, and how would the kids feel when they brought friends home and saw the mother was old enough to be their grandmother. Phyllis's friends at the bank all cautioned her to not get too involved with me, because they were sure that I only wanted a mother for my kids. Lots of different currents were swirling around.

I felt that I should try dating somebody else to find out if I was only seeking companionship. I discussed the matter with Phyllis, and, because we were both getting tired of my inability to decide what I wanted to do, she agreed that I should go out with someone. I dated Yvonne, a new member of PWP, and had what should have been a lovely evening but wasn't, because I kept thinking of Phyllis. I took the lady home and dropped her off at her door, then drove home passed Phyllis's house. It was only about ten o'clock and, seeing the light still on, I dropped in. When I told her the experiment had failed miserably, she laughed and suggested we have a drink.

About Christmastime, Phyllis' daughter, Monica, broke up with her husband in Ontario, and came home to live with Phyllis temporarily. She brought her daughter from a previous marriage, Angeline.

One evening when I called on Phyllis, I found Leo in the kitchen with Monica. I was told that Phyllis was in her bedroom so I went to her and found her crying because Leo had come in and, when he looked in the freezer section of her fridge, he saw two little lamb chops that she had bought for her and Annie. He proceeded to give her heck for buying such expensive meat, and she retreated to the bedroom in tears. I went back to the kitchen and told Leo he had no right to barge into her home, or look in the fridge or even talk to her that way. I was quite a bit bigger than Leo, and as I glared down at him, I thumped him on the chest with my finger for emphasis. Monica told me later that Leo was really scared that I would hit him. I warned him not to come back unless he phoned Phyllis first and got permission.

Phyllis introduced me to long-time friends from Portland, Joy and Noel Edwards, who came to Vancouver to buy tea and to meet her new boyfriend. They had met Phyllis and Leo during a holiday in Penticton where they were staying in the same motel, when Barbara and Monica were just into their teens as was the Edwards' daughter, Noeline. Annie had remarked to Noel in the yard that he talked just like her daddy. Noel soon came knocking on their door and asking, "I hear there's a Pig Islander here, bring him out". There followed a lengthy friendship, particularly with Phyllis. They didn't care much for Leo.

That Christmas season, Phyllis and I went to San Diego on Boxing Day for a week and stayed in the Mission Bay area, and had a great time. We took the city transit bus to Balboa Park several times and thoroughly enjoyed the Zoo. On another occasion at the park, we attended a meeting of the local chapter of Parents Without Partners, and again, when we were just wandering around the many buildings in the park, we stumbled on the Art Museum and later, a building that contained a huge model train display. A large section of the building housed the many train lines which were built up the side of a fake mountain and featured several tunnels as well as miniature towns and country scenes. There were a large number of old men operating the trains, dressed in railway clothing, such as conductors and engineers. Cute!!

On New Year's Eve, we went to a night club in La Holla, just to the north and on the waterfront. On another day, we spent a few hours downtown and I bought my first ever pair of blue jeans. We had lunch at a counter in the store. We were served by a cute blonde who was from Texas and who was chatty, speaking with a drawl and saying things like "Y'all" and "I wouldn't lead you wrong". Over the succeeding years, we made "I wouldn't lead you wrong" a part of our vocabulary and it always brought a smile to our faces.

All of this time at home, I had been waiting every evening till the kids went to bed and then I would go to spend a few hours with Phyllis at her home, and then returning to my bed. On weekends, Phyllis and I were together with my kids while Annemarie went to Leo's apartment.

In about February, I gave up my fight for my independence and asked Phyllis to marry me. As I said to her, "I'm tired of going over to your house for a several hours every weeknight and then going home to my bed; I need more sleep". We set the date for Saturday, June 19, 1976.

It was to be a real family event. A few months before the wedding, Matthew came into the room where Phyllis was sitting and, perching himself opposite, saying to her: "I have to ask you, when we get married, will I be able to call you Mom, instead of Phyllis?"

From the time that I first met Phyllis, the children and I often accompanied her to a Catholic Church on Sunday mornings. Having been excommunicated when I divorced Rose, I was able to attend the services, but was not able to take the sacrament of Communion. Now that Phyllis was divorced, we were both excommunicated, and we decided to get married in the United Church which seemed to allow pretty much anything, as long as you believed in Jesus Christ as your Savior. The church was located two doors from Phyllis's house on Ridgewood Drive.

On the Thursday evening before the wedding, Joy and Noel Edwards had already arrived and we were all sitting in the family room waiting for Edith to serve dinner, when we saw Lou and Marge pass the window on their way to the door, and Lou was carrying a bottle of wine. We had invited them to come for dinner on Friday and they were one day early. Joy had never met any of my family, but that didn't stop her from playing a joke. She said, "Let me go to the door". She hurried and as Lou rang the bell, Joy opened the door, said "You're a day early, but I'll take the wine", grabbed the bottle, and shut the door on them. She watched through the curtain on the little window beside the door, as they looked at each other, and Lou said "What the hell!! Who was that?" A couple seconds later, she opened the door, killing herself with laughter, and said to come in. As was common, Edith had prepared a big meal, enough for everyone, and we had a great evening.

The wedding day was sunny and everything went off without a hitch. We were married at the United Church in Edgemont Village and, because there were only 37 guests, the guests sat in the choir section at the front of the church, very close to where we took our vows. Phyllis wore a long gown in a dusty rose colour that she had had made for her, and she looked beautiful, with that smile that was her constant trademark. Phyllis had as her matron of honor, a long-time girlfriend, named Bernice Meakin, a lovely and very devoted confidante. My brother, Lou, was my best man. At the end of the ceremony, as Reverend Slocum turned us to the guests and said "I'd like to introduce you to Mr. & Mrs. Benoit." Little four year old Teena, Barbara and Hans's daughter who was sitting in the front row, turned and said in a loud voice, "That's my Grandma", to which everyone applauded.

As we were going out the door, Danny stepped in front of Phyllis and said "Hi, Mom". The afternoon was spent taking pictures and drinking. The family photographs included my three children, three step children (Annie was away at camp and missed the wedding), and two grandchildren. Barbara's husband was also there. We had arranged for caterers to deliver a buffet dinner and everyone seemed to enjoy it. One of our wedding gifts was a pair of silver wine goblets that I used to drink from as well as blessing everyone in Latin. The evening was spent, dancing in the living room. At one point, as we were dancing, I asked Phyllis if I should ask Omer, who was there, if he would get his guitar and sing "Please Release Me" so more people would get up to dance. She wasn't too shocked and only said no, there's not enough room for everyone to dance.

At the reception, Lou warned me that three was the limit, and that he was not buying me any more wedding presents. I assured him that this would be my final marriage. He said he had a good feeling about Phyllis and he was sure that she would be around for a long time.

During the evening, while everyone was drinking and dancing, Teena went around the room taking a sip from all the unattended glasses and ended up very tipsy, and guests wondered why she was acting so silly. Edith had been watching her and ratted on her.

We left for a short weekend honeymoon and spent the first night in downtown Vancouver at the Four Seasons Hotel, where I had booked a bridal suite, complete with champagne, and bowl of fresh fruit. As the bellhop showed us into the room, thinking we were from out of town, he opened the drapes with a flourish and asked, "How's this for a view?" and I replied, "Great, I think I can see our house from here." We went down to the lounge for an unnecessary drink and listened to the pianist sing a few songs while we calmed down. We then went to Victoria for a couple days of sightseeing.

Back in the office on Tuesday, my back went into spasm and I had to go home. It was getting worse that evening so Phyllis and I took a cab to the Lions' Gate Hospital. When I mentioned that I had just got married last Saturday, the doctor and nurses had several jokes to tell, much to the embarrassment of my bride.

Leo and Phyllis sold the house on Ridgewood Street and, with part of her share of the proceeds Phyllis purchased a small condo on Comox Street in the West End of Vancouver. It was done on the recommendation of our good friend, Frank Weiler, and it turned out to be an excellent investment. We rented it to a single man who worked downtown, for a modest amount. The rent covered the mortgage payment but not the monthly maintenance fees. It was Phyllis' decision based on her feeling that at least there wouldn't be a constant turnover of tenants. We also traded the Dodge Dart on a used Buick Cutlass station wagon.

In September, Phyllis and I went on a honeymoon to Hawaii. For the first week, we rented a penthouse suite in a hotel right across the street from the beach in Waikiki. Bernice and John rented the other penthouse suite and we all had a really pleasant time. A major problem though was that John was an alcoholic and he would come to our suite at about eight a.m. with tall glasses of orange juice and vodka. Another, older, couple who were friends of John were staying at a nearby hotel, would come by for another drink and breakfast and then we would spend a couple hours on the beach. The afternoon was spent sightseeing. Happy hour was when John wanted to start serious drinking at some bar which had live music. It was sometimes difficult to get John to have meals. However, one evening all of us went to a seafood restaurant which was particularly elegant, Nick's Seafood Restaurant. A waiter was stationed near our table just to light our cigarettes and bring our drinks. John ordered a fresh seafood platter. When it came, it was a tall three tiered tray with prawns, raw oysters on the half-shell, and several other items. For my entree, I had roast tortoise. It was nice but won't replace beef on my list of favorite meats.

All the booze we were consuming was definitely not good for our relationship and once had words. Phyllis and I then spent a week alone at the

Beach Boy Hotel on Maui, and it was so much nicer. We cut back on our booze intake, which made a big difference. Our second floor room was only about twenty feet from the water's edge. The food was excellent and the garden salads with fresh pineapple slices were delicious. We took a boat about two miles up the river to a fern grotto and there, in the forest and on the hillside, was the grotto, a large natural amphitheater. We all stood as a group in it while some Hawaiian ladies sang several songs, including the Hawaiian Wedding Song. I'll never forget the moment, holding Phyllis and listening to the words; it was so romantic, and it became our favorite song forever. We rented a car for a day and explored the beautiful island. On the west side, the area next to the shore was a desert, while the mountain top a few miles away, was the wettest place in the world, where it rains constantly.

A couple months later, I had another session of back problems and the doctor told me that, because I was dragging my heels when I walked, it was time for a permanent repair. I had the disc removed and after three weeks of recovery, I went back to work. The doctor recommended that I start swimming regularly to strengthen my back. The YWCA about two blocks from my office, had a men's keep-fit program that provided swimming daily from 12:00 to 1:00, so I enrolled and went every weekday for about six or eight months. My swimming style was anything but graceful at the start. I was able to dog paddle and do my version of a side stroke for about two lengths of the pool and have a shower in the 45 minutes I allowed myself. However, within a month or so, I learned to swim more or less properly, and was able to do a mile within that time frame. My stamina increased greatly, despite my still being a heavy smoker.

Back home, we lived a very comfortable life style. We had season tickets for the symphony concerts, and went to many pop concerts of the big name performers of the time. We continued to attend the PWP parties because some of the members were now our best friends, but we didn't attend the meetings. Annie came to live with us but didn't like sharing a bedroom with Holly, so she went to live with her father.

Edith continued to do the excellent cooking, baking, cleaning, and shopping, and looking after the children, taking them to dentist appointments, etc. She went home to St. Vincent's, to visit her children and

Elwin. She found that Elwin still had a girlfriend living with him in her house, but, as Edith put it, he was still a tom cat and would never change. Edith said she quite liked his girlfriend. The children were still living with her mother.

Phyllis continued working at the bank and after I got home I went to pick her up. On Fridays, after the bank closed, all of the staff would gather in the back room for drinks. I was invited along with any other spouse that happened along. The Royal Bank purchased a lot of season tickets for the Canucks games which were then offered to customers at a discount. Because the team wasn't doing very well, the branch often had some of their allotted tickets still available, and Pearl Williams, the manager, would offer them to Phyllis for us to take the boys to the games.

We went camping a few times on weekends. I recall one trip to Alice Lake and Annie came with us. In the afternoon, she and Danny swam out to a floating platform some distance from shore. When they came back and told me, I was surprised that Danny was able to swim that far, but he had already proved that he could, so there was no need to caution him.

One evening at dinner, Holly asked Phyllis, "Mom, when you die, can I have your ring?" and Phyllis said yes. Danny then asked, "Dad, when you die, can I have your ring?", and I said yes. There was silence for a moment and then Matthew piped up, "Dad, when you die, can I have Edith?" We all laughed, especially Edith, who fell off her chair and slapped the floor as she roared. Matthew was seven years old and he had already learned that a good cook was very important.

On another occasion at dinner, Danny told about an encounter he had had that afternoon on the stairway which led from the schoolyard up the hill to the street above. He and his friend Murray-Driver were just standing on the stairs and talking, when an older child came up the stairs and said to Murray-Driver, who was a bit obese, "f--- off, fat boy, and I stuck up for him." I asked "what did you do". Danny replied, "I told the big kid that that wasn't a very nice thing to say". I asked, "What did the big kid say?" Danny replied, "he told me to f--- off too; and so I told him that wasn't a very nice thing to say either". Thankfully, no blows were exchanged.

One evening at the table I was giving the kids some advice about the importance of family members supporting each other. Matthew eagerly reported that just a couple days previously, he had stuck up for Danny against a big kid that was bullying Danny. Again, it occurred on the stairs at the schoolyard. As Matthew recalled, the big kid pushed Danny and told him to f--- off. There were some words exchanged and a bit more pushing. I asked Matt what he did to stick up for his brother, and he replied "Well, I told him he couldn't pick on my brother, and then I hit him right where, Dad, you know, where it hurts the most". I asked, what happened then. He replied, "We both ran like hell, 'cause Dad, he was really big and really mad".

Spurred on by the continuing boredom of not having meaningful work to do, I had been applying for every position that was circulated at Head Office which I thought I would like to work at, but without success. A recession was now starting and, being in a corporate position considered by most people as "dead weight", I felt it was only a matter of months before my job would be eliminated, so I started looking at jobs out of town. I talked to Phyllis about relocating and she felt it would be a good idea, and, since I would be staying with MB, I could transfer back to Vancouver in a few years when things got better.

I saw that a position was available at Taylor Division in Port Alberni as Accountant/Office Manager and I applied for it and got it. It was a lateral move, but they gave me a raise anyway.

Elmer & Phyllis

Elmer & Phyllis - Wedding, 1976

Elmer & Edith, 1976

Wedding – 1976

Danny, Matthew & Holly – 1975

Danny, Matthew & Holly – 1978

Danny, Matthew & Holly – 1980

Reunion in Penticton 1982 - Emile, Laurence, Lou, Elmer, Mirelda

Lou & Marge 1984

Danny, Matthew & Holly – 1987

Chapter 22

RETURN TO PORT ALBERNI

We sold our lovely house in North Vancouver and went to Port Alberni to see what housing we could find, not with any great expectations. After looking at several, the agent asked if we would be interested in an older home, and we said we would at least look at it, expecting it would be a post war style, probably split level.

The house he took us to see was more than 3,000 sq. ft., two-story with a finished basement, situated on a half-acre of property on the top of the hill, three blocks above Woodward's store, and overlooking the downtown area, the Alberni Inlet, and the western side of Vancouver Island mountains. From the other side of the house, there was a clear view of Mount Arrowsmith and other mountains to the east side of the Island.

This charming house had been built by the Victoria Lumber Co. in 1916 for their mill manager. That sawmill, was now the Somass Sawmill Division of MacMillan Bloedel Co. The house was originally on one acre or more of land, with a barn and other outbuildings. It was intended to be the finest house in town and was for many years. As various mill managers made it their home, they added to and modified the house, mainly to please their wives. The yard contained a few fruit trees, such as apple, cherry and plum, as well as some more unusual and uncommon trees like a walnut, a Ginkgo

Biloba, and a Mayberry tree. A large two-car garage was built about forty yards from the house and everything was connected by a long paved driveway. At some point, probably during or soon after the war, the barn and outbuildings were removed, the property was sub-divided and four houses were built on the southern lots. During one of the many downturns in the economy during succeeding years, the main house was sold.

Inside, there were three bedrooms and a full bathroom upstairs. The largest, which we used for guests, had a sitting area with large windows that had a view of Mount Arrowsmith. Next was a small bedroom for Holly which she loved. The third bedroom was very large, and was shared by the two boys. It had a walk-in closet and a view of the Alberni Inlet and downtown area.

Downstairs, the front door opened into a hallway with stairs on one side leading to the second floor and to the basement as well as a door leading into the master bedroom and the living room, separate dining room, kitchen and utility room. The master bedroom was huge, with a fireplace and large windows looking out to Mount Arrowsmith, and an area to sit on rockers at a round coffee table. A full ensuite bathroom was in one corner, and extended to the porch. The last owner of the house had owned a store which sold and installed carpets, and he had installed wall-to-wall carpeting throughout the living area and bedrooms. It was a rich, green shag rug made of a mixture of British and Australian wools and said to be the finest you could get. The plumbing fixtures appeared to be those installed originally and seemed to add to a feeling of elegance. The basement had a bedroom with ensuite bathroom, as well as a large rec room that included a big fireplace. The furnace provided oil-fired hot-water heating and was quite an efficient system. There was a good sized wood bin downstairs too, as well as a workshop. The roof had cedar shingles and although it wasn't leaking, it would have to be replaced in a couple years.

Phyllis loved the house and so we bought it. It became the favorite of all of the houses she and the children had ever had.

We arrived in Port Alberni in late August to start my new job with great enthusiasm and eagerness to again contribute some meaningful work.

When the van delivered our furnishings, we were kept busy for a few days unpacking and finding places for everything. The company had a generous allowance for relocating and we ordered new curtains and drapes for all the windows, and linoleum for the rec room. We had to replace the appliances, fridge, range, and dishwasher with new ones at our expense.

We enrolled the three Benoit children at Eighth Avenue Elementary School, just a block from our house. Holly was in Grade Two, Mathew in Fourth and Danny in Fifth grade. Annie had been living with Leo in his apartment in the West End of Vancouver and going to school there. When we moved to Port Alberni, she chose to go to Cranbrook to stay with Barb and Hans and take her Grade 9 there.

Taylor Logging Division had been created a couple years previously and was the result of splitting the large Sproat Lake Division into two smaller ones: Coos (Creek) which was mainly the area around Great Central Lake, and Taylor (Arm) which included the area around Sproat Lake and the forests to the west and southwest. The two divisions shared common shops and booming grounds, but each had a separate administration building for forestry and accounting and management offices. The Taylor Division's administration building had been the sales office building for Lindal Cedar Homes on the Lower Mainland and when it had recently become surplus, MacMillan Bloedel bought it and moved it by barge to its new location. The new site was on the shore at the end of the Alberni Inlet, opposite the Alpulp mill, and was nestled in the trees overlooking the water.

My office was the ultimate of any I had ever had or ever would have. It was on the second floor and had a balcony with a picnic table and deck chairs on it, and had a picture window overlooking the secluded cove and inlet. The little cove was the winter nesting place for a flock of trumpeter swans, and was also the home for a small bird sanctuary. There were also many eagles nesting in nearby trees and it was not unusual to see one swoop down before soaring off with a salmon clutched in its talons.

About once a month, all of the division staff would gather on a Friday afternoon to say farewell to or welcome to one of the staff members, and there would be a table set with finger food and various bottles of liquor and mix to make the occasion more amiable. The leftover booze was stored in the bottom drawer of a file cabinet in my office for safe (?) keeping. So, after our month-end accounting reports and statements were complete, the accounting and payroll staff would gather on my balcony to relax and enjoy the scenery, while taking advantage of the contents of my file cabinet. It did wonders for morale. The office bus collected all of the staff for both Coos and Taylor Divisions so it wasn't long before the word spread to the Coos office manager that we Taylor office staff were "boozing it up" on my balcony after every month-end. However, my manager never mentioned it to me.

Phyllis asked me if we could keep Edith with us for six months to let her, Phyllis, have a break from work and give her a chance to decide whether she wanted to go back to work or stay home with the kids. I agreed. However, about four months later, when one of the kids came in after school and got permission from Phyllis to go to a friend's to play, she heard Edith say, "I don't care what your mother says, you have to stay home until after dinner. When I got home, Phyllis told me she had made up her mind to not go back to work, and would be staying home to be a full time mom.

When we broke the news to the kids, there was a mixed reaction. Joy for Danny and Holly, shock for Matthew who demanded, "But, who's going to do the cooking?" He relaxed somewhat when Phyllis assured him that she really could cook. I agreed that Phyllis could have a cleaning lady come in for four hours, once a week. The lady that Phyllis hired had more problems than you could imagine and spent at least an hour after she ate her lunch, sitting over coffee with Phyllis, every week, just updating her. I was paying her for four hours in return for two hours work.

I gave Edith the sad news and assured her that I would help her find another job. We found her a job in a home in the South Grandville area of Vancouver, working for a single parent with two small children. It proved to be unsuitable and she moved on to the home of Joe Segal and his wife, of furniture manufacturing fame. That proved to be of mixed blessings for her because, although Joe treated her nicely, his wife treated her as an inferior. After Edith served them breakfast, Mrs. Segal would hand Edith two slices of bread and tell her to go make toast and take it to her room to eat her breakfast. She had to eat all of her meals alone in her bedroom. Also, she paid Edith her wages in cash instead of by cheque, a sign of disrespect in Edith's eyes. I had always paid her by cheque, not realizing how important it was for her self-respect.

A few months after our arrival in Port Alberni, Phyllis learned that her sister, Sylvia, had suffered a heart attack in the office where she worked and had passed away. Phyllis quickly arranged for a flight to Johannesburg for herself and Holly, arriving in time for the funeral. During an overnight stop in London, Phyllis took Holly on a tour of the city by taxi. The taxi driver asked if there was any particular place that she would like to visit. Holly's reply was that she would like to see the building in the picture on the bottle of HP sauce. The surprised driver said he knew it well and he proceeded to take her there.

After the funeral, Phyllis's nephew, Roddy and his wife and two children took Phyllis and Holly to spend a few days in the Krueger National Game where they able to drive about with wild animals roaming free around them. I'll go into much greater detail about the park in a later chapter dealing with our trip in 1991.

One of the perks for my job was the use of a pickup truck with fuel for getting to work and home. Because I was never required to go out into the woods, except occasionally on fire patrol during high danger periods of the fire season, the truck was not brand new, usually a one- or two-year-old hand me down from the Division Manager who also didn't put much mileage on it.

One day at work, the head engineer of the division asked me if I'd like to go for a helicopter ride to the top of Mount Klitsa to install a new radio repeater station. I said I'd love to go, so we went out to the Mars Water Bomber station at Sproat Lake where we boarded the helicopter and took off. We flew about half way down the lake and climbed to the top of the mountain and landed on a small flat area on the peak and four of us dismounted. The helicopter took off again, back to the base to get the repeater station. Mount Klitsa was the tallest peak in the area and was already home to two other repeater stations, one of which was owned by the RCMP and another, I think, by the taxi association. They were located there because it provided the clearest signals to receivers in logging trucks or patrol cars and taxis in the central part of the Island. The four of us waited for over an hour, not talking, just soaking in the silence and the grandeur of the surrounding mountain peaks and the lakes and rivers below. Finally, the helicopter returned with the radio repeater station suspended by cables and it was lowered onto the cement base that had been prepared in advance, and the four of us on the ground guided it to fit onto screwed anchors and then bolted it in place. Our job completed, we boarded the helicopter and flew back to the base. That time on the mountain peak, and the silence and the beauty, has stayed in my memory ever since as a time that God was present and close to me.

The job went fairly well at the start. But as I had feared would occur in Head Office as a result of the recession, we were also required at the division level, to do a complete review and justify the cost of our continued existence. The Alberni Region Logging Group management decided to re-merge the Coos and Taylor Divisions into the original Sproat Lake Division, leaving me and several other staff members as surplus.

Fortunately for me, Frank Reynolds, the Accountant/Office Manager at Cameron Logging Division, just south of Port Alberni, resigned to go to work for a family business on the mainland, and so I was transferred to his job. I was now even closer to work and maintained the same status, although I was now also responsible for the financial side of the shops and warehouse, as well as the record keeping for production and shipments at the Dry Land Sorting grounds.

The office building and the shops were located in a clearing in the forest and were quite comfortable. There was a bit of lawn around the office building and it seemed to be a favorite place for deer to graze.

Stephen moved to Port Alberni and I arranged for him to get a job on the forestry crew. He got a suite near the downtown area and once, when I stopped in, I noticed a young hippy girl there, although I don't know if she was just visiting or if she was living there. A few months later he was let go and he left town alone.

That fall, we drove down to southern California over our Thanksgiving Day holiday, keeping the kids out of school for an extra week. We stopped for one overnight with Joy and Noel in Lake Oswego. We also had one overnight at Red Bluff, in northern California. I asked the room clerk if there was a good restaurant nearby, and she recommended a tavern called the Red Barn, so we went there for dinner. We ordered steaks and when they came, we couldn't believe the size of them. They were on oversized plates and hung over the ends. They were as tender and juicy as I've ever had. Danny said he felt like he'd died and gone to heaven. Even Matthew was impressed. Matthew normally ordered a hamburger for both lunch and dinner every day on the trip. I was surprised, though, that months after we got home, he could recall, and describe, particular hamburgers he had eaten somewhere on the trip.

During the drive, I often pointed out something of interest, but Matthew barely looked up from his matchbox cars that he played with on the back seat while he knelt on the floor. Holly and Danny were much more interested in the scenery. On one occasion I said, "Look at the eucalyptus trees, that's something we don't have at home". I watched Matt in the rear view mirror and he slightly bobbed his head and said, "I see them", without actually looking up from his cars.

We stopped at a motel in Anaheim for three days. On the first day, we visited Disneyland and went on all the feature rides and shows. Phyllis and I enjoyed "It's A Small World" and went on it again, and again and again --. The next day, we went to Universal Movie Studios and saw several movie sets that were familiar, like Jaws, and the parting of the Red Sea from Exodus. We also watched on a screen as Matthew appeared to leap over a 747 jet plane, and the boys took turns lifting a full sized car up on end with one hand (assisted by hidden hydraulics). On the third day we went to Knotts Berry Farm, where the kids had a fantastic day on all sorts of rides. Holly and I went up in a basket to a considerable height and then floated down on a parachute. Not long before we left the Farm, a goat came up to Matt and, before he knew it, the goat grabbed his ride pass and ate it. (Was the goat trained to do that?)

On one evening we visited my cousins, Leonard and Margo Benoit, who were living there. Leonard owned and operated a garbage collection and disposal business in Anaheim. His two sons were also working in the business which was very successful. Leonard was a double cousin, from Leask.

From there we drove down to San Diego for a couple days and took the children to Balboa Park and the Zoo. Among the animals was a giant panda. On the second day, we visited Sea World and quite enjoyed the trained dolphins and other sea life.

We left for home and stopped in San Francisco where we visited Fishermen's Wharf for lunch, then rode the cable car downtown and the boys were able to hang over the roadway while holding onto the posts.

On the drive home, we took the scenic coast route, Highway 101, and stopped to see the caves on the southern Oregon coast. We took an elevator down to the caves and were able to see hundreds of sea lions on the rocks, swimming around and doing sea lion things, mostly just grunting.

One night, we stopped overnight at a motel on the Oregon coast, in the Cannon Beach area, and while Phyllis was cooking dinner, I took the children to the indoor pool. Matthew was still not able to swim, and as we were the only people in the pool, I finally got him to jump into the pool from the pool apron and I was able to grab him and then encouraged him to swim back to the side. Holly was so excited, she ran back to our unit and got Mom to come and see Matt swim.

When we first moved to Port Alberni, we became quite involved in the community. We joined the First United Church, and the kids were enrolled in their version of Sunday School. It was held after school on a weekday, but it was a similar program. Phyllis joined the United Church Women and became involved in their activities. Once a month, they put on a party for all the seniors that cared to attend. They came by car, taxi, bus and ambulance for the event and were treated to entertainment and dancing as well as a nice lunch, including a birthday cake for everyone that had a birthday that month or any month. Phyllis served two years as president of the United Church Women.

The elderly minister, who had moved to Port Alberni from the east a couple years previously to get his moving expenses paid for by the church, retired less than a year after we arrived. His replacement was Ted Fenske, who arrived with his lovely wife and two teenaged sons. The younger boy, Paul, was Danny's age and they became good friends. Ted was from a German family and he had been ordained as a Lutheran minister; his preaching was very definite – no gray areas. He was just retired from the Royal Canadian Navy where had been a senior chaplain, and had attained the rank of commander. Ted once, in his sermon, referred to pseudo Christians as, "those people who don't really act like Christians all week, and then come to church and sit in the third row, looking pious". Everyone roared with laughter as I and my family sat blushing in our seats in the third row. Ted finally realized the cause of the laughter and apologized to us.

The boys were enrolled in the Cubs as soon as we arrived, and then moved up to Scouts as they got older. Holly joined Brownies and then moved up to Girl Guides. I volunteered for the Group Committee and, a year later, I took a training course and became a Scout Leader. I found that, during the meetings, the only Scouts that paid attention to me were my kids, so I moved to Cubs where I became Aquela, and stayed in that position until my serious stroke in 1985.

I enjoyed working with the Cubs and tried to be a positive influence. I once had the chief of the local First Nations band come to a meeting and tell us about his childhood in Port Alberni. He told about when he was small, his grandfather would take him out in a canoe to catch fish with a spear. They would use a small curved piece of peeled willow, carved in an arc and with a hollow in one end, as a lure. They would fit it over one end of a thin pole and push it deeply into the water and withdraw the pole, letting the small lure rise slowly spinning to the surface. A fish would be attracted by the lure and follow it to the surface where the grandfather would spear it. The Cubs were nearly in as much awe as me at the skill that was required.

Another evening, I arranged with a Sikh friend for the Cubs and leaders to visit a Sikh temple in Port Alberni. There, we took off our shoes and were taken into the main room, examined the Koran, and a Sikh leader explained their religion and practices and some of the history of their religion. They served a nice snack with special treats for the boys. It was very much enjoyed and the kids and leaders were able to ask questions.

Phyllis was the only one not fully occupied, but not for long. The District Commissioner of the Girl Guides in Port Alberni, Angie Blake, had been named the Regional Commissioner and she asked Phyllis to take over her old job. Phyllis agreed and so our whole family was now in uniform.

Phyllis was often asked to be present at the meeting of a Brownie or Girl Guide group, and when I went to pick her up, I would be invited to join them for cookies and hot chocolate. When the little girls served Phyllis, they addressed her as "Madam Commissioner". Then when they came to me they would invariably ask me "Would you like a cookie, Mr. Commissioner?"

I needed something else for the boys to occupy more of their time and so, about a month after our arrival, I enrolled them in soccer. On the day of registration, I was told that all of the teams from last year were set and wouldn't be taking any new players. The only solution was that a new team would be formed, providing coaches could be found, and my kids would be on that team. "Do you want to be the coach?" There was only one other father out of all the parents of our team, and he said he would coach and I could be his assistant. None of the kids had played organized soccer, and I didn't even know how many players were supposed to be on the field during the game. The coach came to the first practice and that's the last I ever saw of him, because he didn't even come to see his son play. I became the head (and only) coach. I went to the head of the youth soccer association and he told me a bit of the basics, but I was left on my own. I only had two extra players, not four like I should have had, and I was usually short at least two players every game. Matt played as an underaged player on our team because we needed him to fill out the undermanned roster.

Fortunately, our team had a sponsor which paid for the players' uniforms, the Port Alberni Credit Union. For everything else, we were on our own. Our team had a great group of players, character-wise. Even if we had been at full strength, we would have lost because our opponents had all been playing together as a team for at least three or four years. Before each game, the opposing coach would come over and ask me if I wanted to borrow a couple players to fill out my roster. My team always had the same answer, "if we're way behind at half time, we'll concede and borrow the extra players for the second half". Every game ended the same lop-sided way, until the last one of the season, when by some miracle, our full team showed up and we won the game. If anything, the total experience was good for the boys, as well as me, as we certainly learned humility.

That was the end of my career in soccer to everyone's relief. In the following season, the Youth Soccer Association decided to form rep teams for all the age levels, starting with eleven year olds, playing against teams from all other centers north of Duncan. Both Matt and Dano (as he was now called by his friends) were considered to be good enough to play on their respective rep teams. Both played rep soccer until they finished senior high school, and both became very good players.

When we first arrived in Port Alberni, and the boys registered for soccer, Holly joined the Alberni Gymnastics Club, which practiced in a vacant supermarket on the corner of 10th Ave. and China Creek Road, just two blocks from home. She was very good and was well coached at the start. It was cute to watch her walking down the street with her friends and all the time she would be doing a series of cartwheels, summersaults, and walkovers, while carrying on a constant conversation. In her second or third year, the Club decided to concentrate more on the competitive side of the business. Some of the kids were putting in more than twenty hours of practice per week and they received constant supervision from the few instructors, which left Holly to practice the same basic moves over and over for weeks. The Club raised the dues for everyone in order to cover the expenses of going to competitions in other cities, which Holly didn't take part in, so she quit.

A couple years after our arrival in Port Alberni, a man who lived a few blocks away, stopped by and asked if we would be interested in selling our house. He offered us $125,000, and I would have jumped at the chance to make $50,000 profit in two years, and avoid some very expensive upgrades. The house had most of the original fixtures and they needed to be replaced. Mainly it needed a new roof, a new wood burning furnace and insulation for all of the walls and attic, plus vinyl siding. Phyllis agreed to the sale, but when the man came back to finalize the deal, she changed her mind. The chap understood my position and said if we ever decided to sell, to let him know. The original oil burner for the hot water heating system was so expensive to operate after the price of furnace oil jumped to about four times the normal cost. Of course, not having proper insulation in the house didn't help.

A few months later, the mortgage on the condo in Vancouver came due. The country was in a recession and bank interest rates had shot up from five percent to eighteen percent. The company that sold the condo to Phyllis had given her a mortgage in her name at bank rates plus two percent. Now, because she was unemployed, they insisted on twenty four percent. She tried the Royal Bank, her old employer, and they refused to consider a mortgage in her name. Rather than lose the condo, I got a mortgage in my name for enough to pay off the condo, plus upgrade the house. The rate was 18%.

The upgrade was complicated in certain aspects. The new wood-fired boiler for the hot water heating system was set up next to the old oil burner and was wired in such a way that the wood fired system would be the primary heater. However, if the wood burner was not functioning, the oil burner would kick in. The concern then became getting a steady supply of dry firewood, and that was a major problem. I would order a load of firewood from someone who offered good, dry fir and maple, and what I got was usually 95% wet, yellow cedar. The problem with yellow cedar was that it smelled terrible and also released so much oily soot, which blocked the boiler tubes. My sons were now required to help me with the additional chores of storing wood in the garage and then hauling it to the house every Saturday by wheelbarrow, where they tossed it down a slide to the basement where I piled it near the furnace. On Saturday, they were also required to help me to take the top off the furnace and clean the heating tubes and the stove pipe. We all grew to hate that furnace with a passion and dreaded the coming of every winter.

Phyllis insisted on keeping the rent on the condo at the same amount for about eight years, in spite of me having to pay about a quarter of the cost of the mortgage applicable to the condo, plus the maintenance fees out of my salary.

Our house was a favorite destination for all of the family, and the Ellis children came to visit often. Christmas time was especially popular and they all came home for the holidays. One year, we had eighteen children, spouses, and grandchildren who stayed for a week. All of the children slept on the floor in the basement rec room, by the fireplace. Phyllis was so happy that she could have everyone there at such a family time. Except for Christmas dinner, she was not allowed in the kitchen as the adult children took over.

We always went to church on Christmas Eve for the candlelight service and Danny and Matt were allowed to bring a friend. Afterwards, we all went to a Chinese restaurant for a big feed. Phyllis made sure that there was a present under the tree for everyone whether they were expected or not. One Christmas Day, Matt brought in a very large young friend, Joe, who was feeling depressed as he had no place to go. We invited him to stay and have dinner with us. Phyllis found a present for him with his name on it, and, with a beer in his hand, he soon felt quite comfortable, but continued to wonder how his name was on a present under our tree when he hadn't even known he would be invited, not realizing that Phyllis was a speed writer as well as a quick thinker. Joe mentioned during the evening that his family were Jehovah Witnesses and never celebrated Christmas the way that most Canadians do, so this was something entirely new for him.

On a previous Christmas, Danny's friend, Curtis, looking quite dejected, dropped in during the afternoon and said his dad had cancelled Christmas. Apparently, on Christmas Eve, Curtis's fifteen year old sister had come home at about three a.m. and was pretty drunk. His dad, who was normally the designated family drunk, flew into a rage, threw the decorated tree out the front door onto the sidewalk as well as all of the presents, and cancelled dinner and all the rest of their plans for the day. Early in the morning, his dad called him to go with him into the forest and get a pickup truck load of firewood. By the time they got home it was lunch time. Curtis made himself a sandwich and then came over to our place. We asked him to have dinner with us and found a present under tree for him with his name on it, and he went home that evening quite happy about how his day had turned out.

In about 1979, I took the boys backpacking in Manning Park for a week. We invited Paul Fenske, Ted's younger son, to join us. We went to Vancouver and bought backpacks, foam mattress pads and sleeping bags, a one burner stove, some pots and pans and food. The food was mainly freeze-dried, but I did include bags of trail mix and nuts and a big slab of cheese. Phyllis and Holly took the bus to Cranbrook to stay with Barb and Hans and Teena.

We drove to Manning Park and then up a mountain road to the top where we left the car in the parking lot and took off on the Heather Trail. The 18-mile trail followed meadows and ridges and would have been a snap, if not for the heavy packs which killed us. Because Matt was so small for his age, his pack only consisted of the dried food and his sleeping bag, a total of seventeen pounds. Dano and Paul each carried twenty eight pounds, while I carried the rest, which amounted to fifty four pounds. We started hiking and made it about a hundred yards before I had to stop to rest. I realized then that maybe I should have practised a bit to get in shape before starting on the venture. Not to worry, we carried on until it was time to pitch camp for the night. The following day, it went a bit easier after my cramped muscles got into it. The scenery was absolutely beautiful as we hiked through alpine meadows of flowers, with mountain peaks surrounding us. On the second night, while having our dinner, we had to constantly shoo the whiskey jacks from the sheet we had set our plates on. The darn birds would try to take food off our plates while we were trying to pick it up with our forks. They were back again for breakfast. There were also many other species of birds and we also saw a wolverine nearby. On the third day we arrived at a small lake, some distance below the ridge we were on, and camped next to the lake for two nights.

The three boys spent the day building a raft and took it a few yards off shore. I really needed the day of rest and I took full advantage of the chance to rest my weary muscles.

On the way back, I thought I would have a mutiny on my hands. Paul thought that my pack was getting a lot lighter while theirs were staying relatively the same. His thought was that every time I lit the camp stove, I was consuming fuel which was heavy; also, we had eaten over half the cheese as well as the trail mix, and other things, all of which combined to reduce the weight of my load. However, they got over it when I told them that they could quit and go home, but they had to first get their packs back to the car. We got back to the car safely and dropped Paul at the Lodge where he caught a bus back to Port Alberni.

The boys and I then drove to Cranbrook and picked up Phyllis and Holly and returned home.

In August, 1979, Lou and Marge came to spend a few days with us and accompanied us to celebrate the 60th wedding anniversary of Aunt Loretta (Lala) and Uncle Sam in Duncan, on Vancouver Island. In 1947, after the war, Sam and Lala moved to Duncan, where he got a job with a forest company as a "Whistle Punk" on a yarding and loading crew in the woods. His job was to signal when the choker men had securely attached their chokers to the logs, and to the long yarding lines and had moved to a safe position. He would then blow a whistle and the yarding machine would drag the logs to the loading pile where they would then be loaded onto trucks for transport to the booming grounds. Sam was always the oldest man on the crew and looked at his fellow workers as family. He arrived early and lit a bonfire to make fresh coffee for the crew when they arrived and otherwise mothered them. Later, when the job was automated, he was put on a one-man road crew. He was given a wheelbarrow and a shovel and he looked after the half mile of gravel road between the office/shops complex and the main road, filling in pot holes and ruts.

The Diamond Wedding celebration was a riot. First was the bride and groom in their finest wedding garments and the occasion included a Mass in the Catholic Church and a repeat of the wedding, complete with repeating their marriage vows. I should mention that Uncle Sam was brought from the local Care Center where he was living, suffering from deafness and bit of dementia. The priest was a brother of Sam and had travelled from Quebec where he was now in retirement. The best man was another of Sam's brothers, Oscar, the original best man from sixty years ago, and who was now suffering from dementia.

During the mass and ceremony, Oscar would drop off to sleep, so that when the congregation was required to stand, Oscar would remain seated. My cousin, Raymond, was sitting nearby and he would give Oscar a tug and Oscar would immediately stand, smile to everyone, and bow a few times. When the congregation was required to sit, the same thing was repeated in reverse. The congregation found the reaction of bowing and smiling rather amusing as it continued throughout the ceremony.

When the vows had been exchanged, the priest told Sam that he could kiss the bride Sam couldn't hear him, so he just stood there. Lala gently tugged at his arm and held her puckered lips up to him, whereupon he bent over and held his ear to listen to what she was trying to say to him. When she didn't say anything, he straightened up and looked down at her with a puzzled look. She again tugged his arm and held her lips up to him, and again he bent over with his ear to her lips. Again he heard nothing and straightened up with an annoyed look on his face. With that, she reached up with both hands around his neck and pulling his head down she gave him a long, loving, kiss. There was a loud burst of applause from the congregation.

During the following summer, the two boys went camping with a friend at Nahmint Lake, about half way to Bamfield. The friend's dad drove them to the end of the road and they hiked in to the lake. They stayed for several days and really enjoyed themselves. They didn't see another person during their camping stay. People asked me if I was worried that they might encounter serious problems and I said, no! , I had complete trust in their ability as Boy Scouts to handle anything that came up. They came home safely.

When Matt was in about Grade Four, I came home from work and Phyllis stopped me in the kitchen and said I should talk to Matt because there seemed to be something bothering him. I found him in the den and asked him what it was. He confessed that he was being bullied at school; that some of the other kids were picking on him because of his small size. They were calling him "shrimp" and other names. I said to him, "Matt, they won't ever stop unless you fight back. The next time some kid calls you one of those names, you have to warn him that if he calls you that name again, you are going to hit him. The big kid is sure to call you that name again. Then you have to make the hardest fist you can, and hit him on the nose, where it really hurts. It doesn't matter if the other kid hits you back; he won't to do it again because it might result in another punch in his snot box." Matt thought about it and decided it was worth it if it would stop the bullying.

The next day when I came in, Phyllis said to me, "whatever you said to Matt must have worked".

When I saw him, he was all smiles and said, "Dad, what you told me to do, it really worked". I sat down and he gave me the details, which went something like this:

"This big fat girl called me 'shrimp' and I told her if she called me that again, I'd hit her. Like you said, she called me that again and I made a tight fist and I hit her. Well, I know you said to hit the kid in the face, but you also said, before, not to hit girls, so I hit her right in her big fat belly. My fist went in about this far", he held up his fist and marked off about an inch. I was getting ready to grab the phone and call a good defence lawyer, but I asked Matt, "What did she do?" He smiled as he replied, "Oh! She started bawling and went over and told the teacher that I hit her. The teacher (who had witnessed the entire episode) just told her 'serves you right'. After that, nobody picked on me the whole day."

There was a covered area at Eighth Avenue School where the neighborhood children gathered in the evenings and weekends to play ball hockey, and other things. Although I had to pay for a broken window in the school, I felt it was better that it happen there than at home. I'm not sure how it happened, but Matt broke his arm one day at school. I think he fell off the roof. He had to go to the hospital and have a cast put on his arm from below the shoulder to his knuckles. He was so happy with all the attention, he had all of his friends and classmates autograph it. By the time it was ready to come off, it was so dirty you could hardly read any of the names.

When we arrived in Port Alberni, Holly met a nice girl, named Carmen, who lived just a half block from our house, was the same age, and they became fast friends and have remained so ever since. The family went to our church. Holly and Carmen were always at the top of their class at school and they spent nearly every moment of their spare time together or talking to each other on the phone. Carmen spent so much time at our home that we considered her to be almost one of our kids.

Before he left Cameron Division, Frank Reynolds had for a few years been teaching first year accounting at night school at North Island College in Port Alberni. Frank asked me if I would like the job and so it was arranged that I would take over from him. It was the same course I had taught at Malaspina College about eight or nine years before, so I slid in easily.

About three months into it, I had a heart attack at the start of the lecture. It was my first heart attack, but I knew instinctively what it was. I assigned homework for the following week, dismissed the class, and asked one of the students to drive me to the hospital. I asked a nurse to phone Phyllis and explain why I wouldn't be home that night, and she took a cab to be with me.

I was kept in the intensive care unit for a couple weeks and that proved to be very boring. I found, though, that to occasionally create a bit of excitement, if I held my breath for ten or fifteen seconds, the nurse would leave the monitoring station and coming running in to see if I was okay. Of course, by the time she arrived at my bedside, my monitor would indicate everything was normal.

Ted Fenske came in to visit me most evenings, and we became good friends as we talked about his years in the navy and I asked him questions about the bible and the church. Ted would drive Phyllis home and stop in for a "rum-and-anything" before going home.

One night while I was in the hospital, and Phyllis was in bed at home reading, the three children came into her room and climbed onto her bed. Danny, as spokesman, asked Phyllis, "If Dad dies, could Pat come and take us back to England?" Phyllis assured them that their Dad wasn't about to die, but that yes, Pat could legally come and take them away to England. The boys said that they didn't want to live in England and would run away first. Holly, not being quite as brave, just said she just wanted to stay with Phyllis. Phyllis assured them that I was no longer in any danger, but she would discuss it with me when I came home.

When I was discharged, Phyllis explained to me the concern that the kids had in case I should die. We discussed it and Phyllis agreed that the best solution was for her to adopt the kids and that she really wanted that to happen. When we talked it over with the children, they were all for it.

I called my friend, Griffin Layne, a lawyer in Vancouver. Pat and I had met Griff and his wife, Laurie, through Bruce and Gayle. Griff had started his own practice soon after his graduation from law school and passed his bar exams. Griff agreed to take the case on and assigned it to his legal assistant, a man who had flunked his exams, and was willing to take low wages for the sake of any job. The assistant wrote a letter to Pat, asking her to approve the adoption, and she refused. About two years went by with no progress by a succession of inept and disinterested assistants, and I finally called Griff and told him if he didn't proceed soon, I would get another lawyer. A couple months later Griff called to say he had a court date and we would proceed without Pat's approval. Years wasted!!!

On the date for the hearing, we arrived at the Vancouver Courthouse with time to spare. The boys were anticipating a Perry Mason thriller, with everyone behind the bar wearing full robes and white dusted wigs. They had also rehearsed what they would say to the judge under tense cross examination. ALAS!!!! It didn't happen.

The judge appeared, a trim, attractive lady wearing a smartly tailored business suit and with a stylish hairdo, and everyone stood for a moment until she took her seat. Our case was the second on the docket, and was presented by the clerk. The judge asked if Pat was present and the clerk said no, but that Pat had written that the children should be given the choice of who they wished to live with at such time as I actually died. The judge said, in that case, the adoption by Phyllis was approved. All this took place over the space of about three or four minutes, and we were on our way. So much for drama!!!!

From the courthouse, we walked across the street to the Hotel Vancouver and celebrated with a lovely, expensive lunch. The boys were still moaning about their missed opportunity to take their places in the witness stand and declare how much they wanted to live in Canada and being sure of having Phyllis as their mother. Phyllis felt pretty good about the love that she had lavished on the children and was now being returned.

While I was off on sick leave due to the heart attack, the Company Management decided not to take a chance on me having another one, and so they brought in another Accountant/Office Manager. When I returned to work, I was transferred and demoted to Assistant Accountant at Sproat Division, and worked in the building which was used by Coos Division when I first returned to Port Alberni in 1977. I no longer had my own pickup truck, and instead rode in the little staff bus with the other office employees. My salary remained the same, but was red circled until the regular wage rate exceeded my present salary.

The bus driver was a young man named Rick Lewicki who worked as a clerk in the office and, in the evenings, operated a taxi in town. We became good friends and were usually partners in the daily cribbage games during lunch and coffee breaks, playing against two of the girls. I once had a hand of 29 points.

I found the work boring and my only challenge was in seeing how quickly I could finish the month-end statements and reports. The Accountant/Office Manager, my boss, was an egotist. When I handed over any statements or reports he would remark that it was average, but if he had done the work it would have been done faster or better, only because he was not the average man. His wife was an alcoholic – I wonder why!!

One noon, one of the workers from the booming ground, Charlie Watts, came into the office lunch room where we were eating and playing cribbage. He asked if he could have a cheque for his vacation pay because he was going down to Seattle for a week to see his girlfriend who worked as a prostitute in a cat house. He sat down in the lunch room while the paymaster went to make up a cheque. One of the girls said to him that if he wanted a cup of coffee, to pour a cup. Charlie's comment was "If I have to pour it myself, I won't bother. I'm kind of lazy. I'm an Indian, you know." There was stunned silence and then we all laughed because he was trying so hard to shock us.

Leonard and Margo, of Anaheim, organised a joint family reunion for all the Benoits as well as Margo's side, to be held at Spirit Lake in Idaho. Most of the Joe Benoit family of Meadow Lake and a few of the Ovila Benoit family (Leonard's side) of Leask were there. We took Monica's oldest daughter, Angeline, with us. It was a fun time for all of us. One afternoon, I went to a little tavern nearby with the kids to buy treats. There was a young guy who called me "pop" and challenged me to a game of snooker. I hadn't played for several years, but I took him on. The guy kept calling me "pop" to rattle me, but I beat him and then my sons were so proud of me for showing the young guy that I hadn't "lost" it.

One evening at Spirit Lake, we had a pot luck dinner around a campfire in the yard. Afterwards, there was pretty much an empty silence. I stood up and announced that the boys were going to entertain everyone for a while. One of the distant cousins from Saskatchewan was a Boy Scout and he, along with Matt and Danny, performed a series of skits that they had done at various scout camps. They would do a skit and then I would tell a joke or two while the boys prepared another skit. A group of singers, accompanied by humming on paper and combs, also took turns. We entertained for a couple hours and finally the party broke up, everyone still laughing at some of the things that had happened.

On the way home from Spirit Lake, we drove though miles of wheat fields and I once stopped the car and took Angeline, who was about ten years old, into the edge of the field. I showed her how to pluck a few heads of wheat off the stalks, and rub them between her hands to release the grain, blow away the chaff, and then chew it to make a sort of gum. She was quite impressed as I explained the vastness of the prairies that extended over thousands of square miles in the United States and Canada. We stopped for an overnight in Seattle and saw the Space Needle.

I was still driving the Buick station wagon and it was starting to give me trouble, and when I remarked in the lunch room that I was looking for another car, Rick offered to get me a good used car at an auction he was going to in Vancouver on the following Saturday. It was an auction of used police cars and were usually well maintained and in good shape. I agreed and the following week he delivered a year-old black Mercury Marquis. It had no door handles in the rear compartment, so I had to go to the local auto wreckers and buy some and install them. The auction lot had rented the car to a movie production company which had it painted black for use as a prop for a movie. I took it to a local body shop and had it painted medium and dark metallic blue. It was a comfortable and powerful car and we enjoyed it.

In about 1981 or 1982, I received a call from Ted Williams who had worked for me in the Cost Accounting Department at Alpulp in the late nineteen sixties, and was now the head of Administration at Alpulp. When I told him I was feeling fantastic (even then I was always "fantastic"), he asked if I would like to go back to Alpulp as Accounting Supervisor and straighten out a mess they had. I agreed and went back to where I had always felt the most comfortable.

When I got there I found that the accountants were not very well organized or trained. When I checked the total cost of manufacturing on the statement against the general ledger account, there was a discrepancy of about $500,000. When I asked Colin, the Cost Accountant, he said, seriously, it was due to "rounding off". I nearly choked and told him I could accept that rounding off could result in up to five dollars of the difference, and I wanted him to account for the rest by Monday, or else. I don't know how long he spent at the office that weekend but he did find several mistakes that accounted for the discrepancy. Colin was required, according to his job description, to be progressing to a recognized accounting designation. He was stuck at the third level and had failed one course twice already. That spring he failed again, was dropped from the program, and he was let go by the company.

The cost analyst was a jolly sort. Not ambitious or eager or serious about his work, but he was jolly. He always had a joke to tell. He also came in fifteen minutes or half hour late every morning and again after lunch and then, to make up for it, he left that much early at quitting time. His job was to do cost studies and financial justifications to support submissions to Head Office for capital projects. He went into such trivial and needless detail and took so much time to do each financial justification that the engineers were trying to do their own, instead of sending them to accounting. Whenever I spoke to him about it, he just laughed it off. I finally got him to apply for a transfer to another division and he moved on. There was no one else in the office trained to do the work that I could promote to the job. That left me to do all of the cost studies, financial justifications and long range planning as well as supervise the accounting department. Because I was enjoying the job so much, I didn't complain.

About the same time that we moved to Port Alberni, Monica and Angeline moved to the Victoria area. There, she met David Mitchell who had recently arrived from Newfoundland. They developed a relationship and on September 18, 1981, they were married in Port Alberni. They had a small reception in our home. We invited my husband-in-law, Leo, to come. It was the first time we had had direct contact since the incident in Phyllis's kitchen soon after we met. During the evening, I went across the room to talk to Leo, and I noticed that he became quite nervous, fearing I might thump him on the chest with my finger again, but he relaxed when I made no threatening gestures. We talked for a few minutes, mending fences. A few months later, on February 13, 1982, Monica gave birth to Kyle.

Soon after my arrival in Port Alberni, I was asked to serve on council at our church and, when Ted Fenske became our minister he asked me to also become an elder. About 1983, Ted's wife developed cancer and passed away. About a year later, Ted was remarried to a widow that he had counselled at the time of her husband's death. Not long after, they moved to Mill Bay, north of Victoria, and then to Whiterock, BC.

A new minister was found in Ontario and he took over at First United. He had been working in a tech company before going back to Theology College and becoming a minister. He claimed that he was vitally committed to ministering to youth and seniors and hospital visits, and that's what got him the job. He did have a physical problem, a "wandering eye", which resulted in the eye wandering about the room while he looked at you with the other. He could see with both eyes, but both were seldom focussed on the same object. This, he said, caused him to stumble often when he was mounting the steps to the pulpit.

In July, 1982, the family had a reunion in Penticton, B.C., where Mirelda and Francis and Emile and Julia were living. Lou and Margie, Lawrence and Doreen, and Phyllis and I, came with our children. It was a great time, with lots of fun and food and a good deal of beer. One evening, an arm wrestling contest started with Lawrence's son-in-law, Don Klassen, challenging anyone. Someone pushed me forward and I took my seat. Lawrence had taught me a technique many years before and I used it, just pulling his arm toward me until, after about five minutes, he tired and I won, to everyone's amazement. Imagine, a middle aged accountant beating a young mill worker!! My sons were very impressed.

Hans, who was there with Barb, had a heart attack at the end of the reunion and went into the hospital in Penticton. Barb, who was very pregnant with Johanna, stayed with Mirelda and Francis until Hans was able to drive them back to Cranbrook where he went back into hospital and died soon after. Two weeks after his death, Johanna was born in Cranbrook.

One Saturday in the summer of 1984, while I was sitting in the breakfast nook and having lunch with the family, I suddenly found myself unable to speak or move properly. Phyllis immediately realized I was in trouble and called the ambulance. By the time I arrived at the hospital, I had mostly recovered but was still admitted, and then spent a month or so recuperating. I had an excellent doctor, John Wilson, and he gave me all the tests and treatments available at that time.

In the fall, my brother, Lou, passed away from heart failure. He and Margie were holidaying with friends near Punashee, west of Williams Lake, at their fishing lodge. Lou was sitting in a boat as it was being towed over some rapids, when he suddenly collapsed and died. Margie was on shore and saw him topple over in his seat. Phyllis and I went to the funeral in New Westminster. Lou was only sixty two years old, just two years into his retirement.

Doc Wilson decided that I needed an operation on my carotid artery to clear the blockage and prevent another stroke. On New Year's Day, 1985, Phyllis and I both quit smoking. Since moving to Port Alberni, we had been smoking three cartons of cigarettes (total 600 coffin nails) per week, which proved to be a major problem for our arteries and lungs. I had tried to quit a hundred times over the years, but was never able to last more than a month or so before starting again, except for a five year stretch from 1965-70.

I went into Victoria General Hospital for surgery. It was scheduled for Friday, April 13th, 1985. Could it be an unlucky date? Phyllis came along and stayed with Monica and David. Just after dinner, an aide came to prep me for my surgery and he shaved off my full beard, but left my moustache. When Phyllis arrived a few minutes later, I asked her, "I guess you're going to proceed to divorce me?" She looked alarmed and asked me, "Whatever for?" I reminded her that when we first were married, I had asked her if she would like me to shave off my beard, and she had said if I ever got rid of it, she would divorce me. That was when she finally noticed that it was gone, and she laughed, saying that she could still tolerate me without the facial hair. She asked if I still had all of the hair on my chest, and I had to admit that the aide had shaved off all eight hairs that I was so proud of. We prayed especially hard that night that the operation would go well.

On Friday morning I was wheeled into the operating room and was soon under anaesthetic. Several hours later, I awoke in the recovery room with two nurses standing over me, talking. They said they were just waiting for a bed to be made ready for me in the Intensive Care Unit. Then, the three of us talked about my surgery and how we all were pleased at how well the operation had gone. One of the nurses was from Montreal and spoke with a strong French Canadian accent, very soothing and calming.

Suddenly, I realized that I couldn't speak or even move a muscle. Panic gripped me when I realized I was unable to even attract the attention of the nurses who were now talking to each other above me. Pictures of Phyllis and my children flashed through my mind and I started praying. My three children were still in high school. One nurse glanced down at me a few moments later and realized I was in big trouble. She picked up my arm and watched it drop limply back onto the bed. They immediately raised an alarm and called for a doctor. The French Canadian nurse kept speaking my name and reassuring me, and I still recall how she spoke with such a sweet voice, sort of purring, and I regained a certain degree of calmness.

My surgeon had already left the hospital and was on his way home, twenty miles away. However, there was a surgeon in the hospital who just washing up after an operation, who heard the call for help and rushed into the room. He happened to be one of the best surgeons in Victoria. When he looked at me, he recognized that, as a result of the blood transfusions I had received during my operation, a clot had formed at the site and part of it had broken away and had lodged in my brain, shutting off the flow of oxygen to the brain. He needed permission to open it up and clear the blockage, and he came to the door of the recovery room where Phyllis was watching the whole scene through the window. She had no way of knowing what was actually happening, but feared it wasn't good. He explained the situation quickly and got her permission.

This second procedure took from early evening until about two a.m. David returned in the evening to pick up Phyllis and found her in terrible distress with worry. She asked David for a cigarette and then bought a pack. She kept smoking for another two years or more before she was able to finally break the habit for good.

When I returned to my ward later on Saturday, I was still unable to speak or move my right side. However, I was alive and resolved that I would, with God's help, recover fully. I proceeded to concentrate on regaining the use of my limbs. I found that, soon, I could speak a bit and was able to move my leg and arm. I then concentrated on my fingers and on Sunday, I was able to move my little finger. The next day I could move my ring finger. It improved that way, regaining movement of one finger every one or two days. On the following Sunday, it was only my thumb that wasn't responding. I remember lying in my bed, staring at my thumb and willing it to move. After several hours, it moved about a millimeter, and I told myself, "I've got it licked, I'll recover." I continued to steadily improve.

Three weeks after the surgery, I was transferred to Gorge Road Hospital in Victoria for rehab. The hospital was located on beautiful grounds next to the Gorge waterway and I loved to be able to walk about outside. I soon found out that most of the patients were in worse condition than me and I counted my blessings. Some had given up hope of recovering and were only there at the insistence of their family. Most were stroke victims, but a few were young people who had sustained head injuries in car accidents and were now confined to motorized wheel chairs and were accustomed to occasional violent behavior.

I was placed in a ward of eight or ten patients, most in worse condition than me. One patient did resent that I seemed to be not having as many problems as him and told me so. In the dining room, I was given sponge tubes to fit over the handles of my fork and spoon. None of the food needed to be cut with a knife. They didn't serve steak or pork chops, for sure.

After breakfast each morning, I bought a Victoria Times newspaper and after reading it I went to see a speech therapist who would ask me to discuss some article that I had read. It was difficult to pronounce many of the words and I often became frustrated. I remember once that, when the therapist made me repeat something about four times, I said in a very loud voice, "I can't say the f---ing word." Margie and her sister, Bev, came to visit a few days later, and they got quite a kick out of my story. The speech therapist did help a lot, as I had to really concentrate on the pronunciation. I continued to have a lot of difficulty after I got home. Words like "probably", which I pronounced as "prolly", and which Phyllis always just smiled at, but never corrected me.

During the afternoon, I had physical therapy and occupational therapy sessions to help with my physical problems. In the evenings we had a group speech therapy session. One of the ladies had suffered a stroke and was only able to make a chirping sound. I thought she was not likely to ever be able to speak properly again, but I learned that one of the other patients there had been in a similar condition two years before, and was now able to carry on a normal conversation, although not fluently. More hope for me!!

It was difficult for Phyllis, wanting to be with me, but still required to be at home, looking after the children. She was able to get a ride to Victoria on several Friday afternoons with Bob Hunter, the paymaster at Alpulp, who also was a friend from the church. She was able to stay with Monica and David in Victoria and David drove her to the hospital to visit me. While she was in Victoria, she arranged with Dolores, the cleaning lady, to stay with the kids.

I learned that on the day of my surgery and through the entire period of time I was recovering, a group of ladies from our church, as well as friends and relatives all over the world were praying for me. I give God full credit for my successful recovery.

I returned home and Doctor Wilson arranged for me to have some therapy at West Coast General Hospital in Port Alberni as well as at Nanaimo General. I was also having trouble sleeping, so he arranged for me to take Bio-Feedback training at the local hospital. It involved deep breathing, and listening to calming music while a soothing voice instructed me on how to relax. It was helpful with all facets of my recovery.

Barbara and Johanna, who was just a toddler, came to stay with us for a couple weeks while I was at home that summer.

Ted Williams came to see me and offered me a chance to go on long term disability benefits. I would receive a monthly pension of about 65% of my salary, which would continue until I was 65 years old, at which time I would start receiving a reduced company pension. There was a chance that after a few years, the insurance company could consider me fit to return to work and would just cut me off the pension and I wouldn't have a job. I assured Ted that I intended to be back at work when my three-months of sick leave ran out. He was skeptical, but agreed that I could try to return to my job.

When I went back to work at about the end of August, my job had been split. The daily accounting routines and supervision were now assigned to a new Accounting Supervisor and I was left with all the interesting stuff - cost studies, financial justifications for capital projects, and long range planning - at the same salary. What a plum job!!!!

I had done many studies which involved the effect of making new products while deleting or modifying existing ones and I knew that each set of calculations required about four days of work with a paper and pencil with the help of a calculator. Every variation took about the same amount of time. When I started back at the office, I was unable to even pick up a pencil in my right hand, let alone write anything legibly. A sponge rubber tube slipped over my pencil allowed me to at least pick it up and hold it. I found that, instead of trying to write unsuccessfully, I could print legibly.

Thanks to my nursing training when everything had to be printed, I could still print nearly as fast as I could previously write.

This was at a time when personal computers had just come onto the market, and one of the first Apple PC's had been purchased for our department while I was on sick leave. I started to experiment with the computer and soon the company bought me my own, and arranged for several training courses. Most helpful was a course on using the Lotus 1-2-3 system program. It involved a spread sheet, with several basic commands such as "at if" which allowed the computer to do certain alternative calculations depending on whether certain conditions existed. I could use all of the fingers of my left hand to key punch, but could only use the first or second finger of my right hand. Over the years it has come to feel natural to use just the one finger on my right hand plus my left hand.

I had a good ally in Gary Dillon, who was the assistant division manager in charge of engineering. He arranged for me to have a new, faster, and more powerful computer every year, whatever was the latest. By the time I retired in 1991, I was using a Compac 360. Neither the computer nor the Lotus 1-2-3 system is available anymore because they are so obsolete. However, I worked closely with Gary for several years which resulted in installation of several major projects that materially changed the mill and the products that were produced.

First was installation of a CTMP plant (chemo thermal mechanical pulp) which replaced a major portion of the ground wood mill with a superior, but cheaper, pulp for use in the manufacture of newsprint and fine papers. The cost of the project was well over a million dollars.

I developed a program, using Lotus 1-2-3, to do a complete set of calculations based on a menu that contained various standard production or requirement volumes of raw materials, chemicals, etc., costs and selling prices, equipment requirements, plus return on investment calculations. After a half hour or so for inserting key data, I could push the "calculate" key and about fifteen minutes later provide a typed 12-page summary, ready for submission to head office in order to support a request for capital expenditure. The program was versatile and could be used for various products and modifications. Ted sent a copy of my program to head office to check its accuracy, and corporate analysts were very impressed with it and congratulated me on it. Ted was promoted to General Manager of Alpulp, and he deserved it, moving up from mail clerk/messenger to the top job in the division in less than twenty years. Ted and his wife, Shareen, had been good friends with Pat and me, but they were much younger than Phyllis and me, and, although we were still friends, we didn't socialize much.

Although I had plenty of cost studies and smaller capital projects to work on, I was primarily concerned with two major projects which would determine the future direction of the mill. One involved a major expenditure for the Kraft Mill and the other was everyone's favorite, conversion of our largest newsprint machine to lightweight coated paper. With the use of my program, I was able to frequently do many variations.

The problem was that the company was reluctant to spend hundreds of millions for a new product and then not be able to sell all of the production. As a result, I was kept studying the proposal for a couple more years until I retired. A short time later they proceeded with the conversion. They made some high profits for a while but the market dried up, and soon the machine only operated part time.

Meanwhile, at First United Church, we were having trouble with Max, the minister who had replaced Ted Fenske. Attendance and membership had been dropping steadily. Visiting our church members and working with the youth group, which he had claimed to be the strong points of his ministry, were non-existent. His sermons were not very inspiring because, on Sunday morning, he only read the sermons that were issued from the United Church head office in Toronto, and he stumbled over the words, as if it was the first time he had read them. The church council decided that we must do something to turn things around quickly. I, as chairman of the council, was delegated to speak to him. He claimed that he was doing a fine job and didn't have to change anything. We got somebody from the presbytery in Victoria to help us in our discussions for a couple months without any improvement in Max's performance, and we finally received his resignation. Max was then hired as minister in a church in the Kootenay area, but he only lasted there for a couple months until they learned he was actually an alcoholic. It finally became clear as to why he always stumbled whenever he stepped up to the pulpit, and never did any work.

Another minister was brought in, but I was no longer involved in the church administration. A few months later, we started attending the Presbyterian Church and have never left.

The minster in the Presbyterian Church in Port Alberni was named Paul Vera, who was a Portuguese man, divorced, and a very talented minister. We had been attending that church for about a year, when he married the mother of one of Holly's best friends, Lorinda.

Holly collected a group of about six girlfriends in high school. They were all very bright, intelligent girls who maintained honor roll standings in school and were from good families. I would have been happy if all of them were my daughters. I was very proud of Holly for surrounding herself with such good friends. Holly always volunteered me to drive them to all of their dances and then drive them home afterwards and I was always pleased to do it.

The boys also had good friends who spent a lot of time at our house. While they were in high school, I once asked Danny if he was ever picked on. He said, "A long time ago, I made friends with Alphonse, and if anybody ever gives me a hard time, Alphonse just asks, 'Do you have a problem with Dano', and they back off." Alphonse was about six feet tall and weighed about 175 pounds, looked fierce but was actually sensitive and gentle, and used to come over to our house occasionally. I knew what Danny meant.

The children had been enrolled in a University Scholarship Trust program since birth. About a month after Matt started his Grade Nine or Ten, he said to his Mom and me that he would like to drop out of French class. He felt that, because he could hardly do English, he sure as heck couldn't be expected to do French. He suggested that he be allowed to switch that course for Home Economics. That way, learning to cook would ensure that he would never starve. He said that it would mean that he wouldn't be able to go to university after he finished high school, so I might as well cancel his University Scholarship Trust membership and get my money back. Danny then said that we might as well cancel his too because his marks were not good enough to get him into university. I agreed and told them that it would be a wasted effort if they went to university without the desire or expectation to succeed, and that at any time in the future that they wanted to take courses to get a better job, they could do the same as me, go to night school.

On May 18th, 1983, the family was planning to travel to Victoria, to visit Monica and her family. A couple days earlier, Danny got sick with mumps, but he assured us that we should go without him and he'd be fine for the day. It happened to be his birthday so we arranged for Mount St. Helens to erupt, or so he told everyone. There was a lot of the ash that drifted up to Port Alberni in the next couple days.

The children were also into music, starting in about Grade 6, with learning to play the recorder. At EJ Dunn Junior High, the boys took band classes and joined the stage band, Danny choosing to play tenor saxophone and Matt, when he reached that school, played alto saxophone. I recall that when Danny was in Grade 10, we went to a concert featuring the stage band. Danny played a full solo of Harlem Nocturne which brought the house down, girls screaming, the whole bit.

Matt started taking private guitar lessons when he reached junior high school. He then was playing alto sax in the stage band and guitar in the regular band. He still plays his guitar, of which he has he has several, and he has composed some songs although he has never published any. He was always a very deep thinker and quite artistic. He did some beautiful artwork in class and composed some poetry that I was very impressed with.

Holly, when she reached junior high school joined band and chose the trumpet, with only moderate results. She also enrolled in Home Economics and I bought her a sewing machine. She made some items of clothing that the teacher considered sufficiently impressive that they were displayed in the school.

In about 1985, Danny finished high school. In late May, the grad class held the traditional drunk party at the Gravel Pit outside the town. They had a big bon fire and most of the kids were pretty drunk. One of the boys had got a new car from his parents for a grad present and had driven some friends to the party in it. Just for laughs, a group of class mates pushed his new car into the bon fire and they watched as it burned. There was too much money and too many stupid people in the town in those days, when Port Alberni had the highest average wage of any city in Canada!

After high school, Danny went to Ucluelet, where he got a job at the Wickaninnish Inn, a very good restaurant, and he was very good at his job. He told me of an incident when a rich American landed his small private plane on the beach near the restaurant and came in for dinner. Danny served him and I guess the man was impressed, because a month later the guy returned in his plane and carrying a group of friends. Danny showed them to a table overlooking the shore and ocean, and the man said to him the "usual". Danny thought for a few seconds and then repeated what the guy had ordered on his previous visit and asked if he wanted the same wine, by name. The man was so impressed, particularly by the fact that his friends were impressed with their host, that he left Danny the biggest tip he ever received.

In about 1986, we sold the big house on Seventh Avenue. It was quite an emotional event and the entire family, including the Ellis children, were sorry to leave it.

We rented a house on Fifteenth Avenue. It didn't have much character, but it did have a lovely vegetable garden. The owners had created a huge garden, complete with a frame for pole beans and the soil was black and rich. I planted the whole thing and worked my ass off, tending it and then trying to give away the production. I had never planted a garden in all my years of owning houses that had such good soil or yielded a fraction of this one. I planted four mounds of zucchinis and they looked like a jungle, leaves as high as my chest and fruits that grew to be about fifteen inches long and six inches in diameter. The pole beans were in two fifteen foot rows on either side of the frame and climbed ten feet on strings to the top and over. When I shopped for tomato plants I decided I would like to have three varieties. The plants came in flats of six plants, so I ended up with eighteen plants and I replanted all of them. I put wire cages around each of them, but they grew in such profusion that I had to put a bunch of wooden stakes among the plants and tie the branches to them to support the weight of the fruit. In the rest of the garden I planted carrots, lettuce, onions, etc. By early July, I had so many vegetables that I was carrying shopping bags to the office and to church every week to give away. As I drove past the Alberni Soup Kitchen daily on my way to work, I stopped and asked if they could use some vegetables. Thereafter, I delivered three or four bags of zucchinis, pole beans and tomatoes to them each week, although I was asked to quit bringing so many zucchinis, because the poor folks were threatening to stay away if they had to eat very many more.

Phyllis and I drove to Cranbrook to visit Barb and her two little girls. We went for lunch at a restaurant, called the Kootenay Cattle Company. When the waiter came to take our orders, four-year-old Johanna asked him, "Do you have snails?" When he answered, yes, she said "Okay, I'll have snails". He asked if she would like anything else, so she ordered fries. When the plate was put in front of her, she tucked in like it was her normal lunch. Barb reached over and took one the escargot and Johanna looked sternly at her mother and warned not to take any more, because she had only got six. Joey finished off with a huge dish of ice cream (the waiter thought she was so cute!!). I thought Joey had ordered a pretty well balanced meal, although her mother wasn't quite so sure.

Matt finished high school in 1987 and followed Dano to Ucluelet where he got a job in the kitchen at the Wickeninish Inn. He moved into an old house on the main street that was being rented by Dano and a couple other friends. It was pretty shabby but it was cheap. The few pieces of furniture were from the dump, I think. Matt found an old stuffed chair that had been tossed into the bushes about a half mile away and he carried it home on his back. It took quite a while because he often had to stop and rest, sitting on the chair on the sidewalk. When he arrived back at the house, he announced that it was his chair, and that when he entered the room, anyone sitting in it would have to move to a seat on the floor.

It was only about a year after we had moved into the house on Fifteenth Avenue that the owners notified us that they were leaving the Queen Charlottes and wanted to move back to their home, so we had to find somewhere else to live.

We were fortunate to find the penthouse in the high rise on Tenth Avenue was available, and we moved in. It was the top floor of the tallest building in Port Alberni, the twelfth floor, I believe, and provided a fantastic view of the town and the valley, and the mountains including Forbidden Plateau and Mount Arrowsmith and Mount Klitsa. There were three private balconies on the roof outside of our unit. Inside, were three bedrooms, a kitchen and a very large living room and dining area.

Holly was still with us until she graduated from high school. There was a swimming pool in an adjoining building. We were again blessed with a nice home.

Holly graduated from high school in 1988. She had a week off school before her final exam and went to Vancouver to stay with Annemarie, for a few days to look for a job. On the first day, she was offered two jobs and chose one with a firm of chartered accountants. After finishing school, she lived with Anni until she was joined by her boyfriend, Doug, who she had dated through high school. They moved into an apartment in Richmond and then to a house in Surrey. They married in 1990 and moved to Surrey in the same year.

I was required to attend frequent meetings in Head Office or at either Harmac or Powell River Divisions in connection with the long range planning process for the company. I was part of a team that also attended Board of Director meetings to present our proposals. The team included the Division Manager as well as Gary Dillon and one other of the assistant managers and me. We travelled by helicopter which took off from a pad near the office and flew over our apartment. Phyllis always came out onto the deck as we flew over and waved to me. The pilot was amused the first time and commented that the woman down there was acting like she had never seen a helicopter before, and I told him it was my wife waving to me. After that, we all waved back to her.

One afternoon, on our return trip from Vancouver, just after passing over Stanley Park, we flew through the center of a rainbow. It was the strangest sight, seeing the rainbow in about a three-quarter circle, extending from above us and all around to below and beyond.

While we were in the high rise, Johanna came to spend a week or so with us, while Barb went to France with Leo, her dad, for a holiday. It was a lovely time and Joey charmed us with her wit and enthusiasm.

While Danny was working at the Wickaninnish Inn, he met a girl from England, Kelly, who was about to be deported because her visitor's visa had expired and she needed to get married in order to be allowed to stay in Canada. Dano was still being a good Scout and ready to help anyone in distress, and despite my warning that he would regret it, he married her on December 31, 1986. Within a few months, she was pregnant and, in due course, she gave birth to John Joseph, who was called JJ, and that was shortened further a few years later to Jay.

One weekend, Matt's chum, Lindsey Lowe, got married in Port Alberni and Matt was to be an usher at the wedding. The evening before the wedding, all of Lindsey's friends gathered for a stag party. Matt and Lindsey came to spend a few hours in the afternoon in our apartment before the party, and on one of their trips to our unit, they began jumping up and down in the elevator finally put it off its rails, and causing it to stop between floors. They were able to contact the building manager who called the elevator repairman in Nanaimo to come and release the boys and repair the elevator. That took about two hours for the travel time and repair. The boys assured the manager that it was an accident, and they were certainly not jumping in the elevator. It's lucky that they, or even worse, me, weren't charged for the service call.

I believe that Matt only worked the one season at the Wickaninnish Inn and, when he was laid off after Thanksgiving, he got a job as a sous chef at a fine dining restaurant in Vancouver, so he moved to the mainland. The job necessitated that he work evenings and weekends, so his days off were on week days when none of his friends wanted, or were able, to go out. He phoned me and asked if we could help with the cost of his tuition and living expenses while he took a meat cutting course at BCIT. We were happy to help him and Matt excelled in the course, earning top marks in the final test, which consisted in receiving a side of beef at a certain cost and then cutting it into final saleable products, such as steaks, roasts, etc., and then finally weigh and price it all at specific selling prices and calculate the gross profit which had to be at least 25%. Matt ended up making about 34% and received his diploma. His first job was in Victoria, but he soon was drawn back to Ucluelet where he got a job in the meat department at the Co-Op store in 1990.

While he was at that store, he was encouraged to take up surfing by a fellow worker and soon became one of the top surfers at Long Beach, between Ucluelet and Tofino. He often went surfing before work in the morning, then after work in the afternoon, and again in the evening. His body developed dramatically, with shoulders and torso expanding and becoming powerful. His thighs and legs also became really strong. I marvelled at the way that he had changed in just a couple years from a boy of 5' 7", to a man of such large proportions. Matt continued to be witty and easy to get along with.

In 1988 or 1989, I went as part of a team which included the president of the company and several analysts and engineers that were involved in the long range plan, to Maastricht, Netherlands, to visit a mill which produced only lightweight papers. Our company, MacMillan Bloedel, was a major owner of the company in Holland, which had considerable expertise in lightweight papers and we were able to get a lot of information. The city was probably fifteen hundred years old, and was the most picturesque place I had ever visited. The hotel we stayed at was very old and also elegant. A couple years earlier, while they were doing some excavating to install certain amenities in the basement, they found the remains of an ancient building dating back to Roman times, and that became one of the hotel's advertised features.

One evening, our hosts took us by bus to a village about thirty kilometers away to have dinner at a very elegant restaurant. The restaurant backed onto a large hill, which contained miles and miles of tunnels which ran all through the hill. The hill was composed of chalk and was now used to store the restaurant's wines. During World War Two, the national art treasures as well fine wines, etc., were stored in the tunnels. The tunnels were unlit and unmarked, and it was reported that some of the German troops who were checking the tunnels, became lost and perished. The valuables and art were saved.

On one April First, I asked one of the accountants during coffee break to phone Phyllis and tell her that he was a telephone repairman, and ask her to please cover her telephones with towels or other cloths, because BC Tel was doing the annual cleaning, blowing the dust out of the telephone lines, and he didn't want to get dust all over her apartment. About five minutes later, my phone rang and it was Phyllis asking if I knew anything about the phone company cleaning the lines, and I, of course, denied it. At home I confessed, and she admitted that she hadn't realized it was an April Fools' prank until she was about to place a towel over the phone.

At the office, in about 1986, I spoke to Ted about all of the overtime I was working and he was firm that, because I was classed as a manager, I couldn't collect overtime pay. However, he agreed that I could record my overtime and take half of it as time off when it wasn't busy. I was working ten or twelve hours per day, plus one day on the weekends, whenever we were preparing to make a presentation to the company Board of Directors. As a result, every January, Phyllis and I would go to Yuma, Arizona, for four or five weeks and then again somewhere else for two or three weeks in the summer, all of it on overtime leave. I banked all of my vacations as well as my supplemental vacations. When I retired, I received nine months of vacation pay.

In the summer of 1990, we decided it was time for us to go to places on the island that we had always wanted to visit, but had put off for later. We were already starting to consider taking early retirement in in 1991.

I took a trip to Bamfield, at the mouth of the Alberni Inlet, on the Lady Rose, a tiny freighter that carried a few passengers and made frequent trips down the inlet and to Tofino. The day was lovely, and the scenery was spectacular, with sightings of bears and eagles. Phyllis had previously made the trip several times with friends and relatives who were visiting us and I had always been at work on those occasions, so I went by myself.

On a long weekend, we went to Saltspring Island. The hotel was full, so we went to the Chamber of Commerce or Visitors' Bureau to check if any B and B's were available. All were booked, but the agent said she could call a lady that used to take guests. Sure enough, she had a vacancy and we hurried there. The old house was unpainted and in pretty bad shape, but we knocked on the door and were greeted by a lady that I could only describe as a 50'ish hippy. She said that she had two rooms available, the larger one being the "primrose room". We climbed a flight of stairs that was about two feet wide, making it necessary to go up sideways. The room was painted an ugly blue with bare floors and contained two items – the bed, which had an old fashioned coiled spring and a thin mattress. The other item was a picture of a primrose, about 6" x 8". The bathroom was tiny, and was squeezed under the slanted roof, necessitating having to bend over and back up to the toilet and to bend over to use the wash basin. It was good for a laugh and we managed to get a few hours of sleep that night. The next morning, we went downstairs for breakfast, wondering what sort of meal we would be served and not having great expectations.

What a surprise lay in store for us. The lady took us to a rustic table on the rustic porch overlooking the meadows and the bay, and sat us on some very rustic chairs. She brought us orange juice and cereal, then bacon and eggs, then a delicious freshly baked scone with homemade preserves. We were stuffed. She then asked if we would like a bit of Cointreau with our coffee and brought mugs of really good coffee with about four ounces of Cointreau in a pitcher. I think that was the best breakfast I ever ate. We always looked back at that weekend as a special experience.

On other weekends that summer, we visited Port Hardy and Port McNeil, Tahsis, and Gold River, all in northern Vancouver Island. We also visited the boys in Ucluelet and Monica in Campbell River.

In January, 1991, I took stock of my situation and it was time for a final decision. Although I felt fine and I still enjoyed my work immensely, I was now sixty years old and didn't feel confident that, if I continued to work as much overtime, I would last until I hit sixty five. Besides, Phyllis would soon be sixty-six years old and she deserved to retire and to start doing the things we had planned to do during our retirement, mainly travel to other countries. I inquired about my pension and we decided that, what the heck, if I retired now and we lived on our combined pensions, we would still have the same amount in the bank at the end of month, i.e., nothing. Paper prices were again dropping and the company was offering early retirement packages to various middle managers, consisting of full pensions if you left before the age of 65. I spoke to Ted Williams, the mill manager, about the possibility of me getting such an offer. He just laughed and said I had a job for as long as I was willing to work.

I gave notice that I would be retiring March 31st, 1991.

Chapter 23

RETIREMENT AND OUR VISIT TO SOUTH AFRICA

We had been thinking for some time of what we would do if I took early retirement. Certainly, we would do some travelling overseas as well as in North America before we settled down to a routine. I couldn't see myself spending twenty years of travel, parties and/or watching TV, so I thought I would eventually volunteer for some sort of service in developing countries. However, our first priority was to take a long trip somewhere.

Phyllis received an invitation to attend the Fiftieth Wedding Anniversary of her sister, Maureen, and her husband, Edwin Rooke, to be held in May in the Krueger Game Reserve in South Africa. I had never met Maureen in person but we had talked frequently on the phone over the years and so we eagerly accepted and started making travel plans.

I thought it would make sense to stop off in Europe to see some of the sights there on the way back from South Africa and so our trip just grew from there.

My cousin, Leslie Colleaux, and his gracious wife, Grace, had retired from his job in Nanaimo and built a lovely little home in Fanny Bay, just south of Courtenay. His mother was my Aunt Edme, who I lived with, in my parent's house, after I ran away from Rose. Aunt Edme now lived with Les and Grace in their home for a few years until she needed to go into a care home where she passed away a short time later. Phyllis and I used to visit them regularly until we left the Island.

Les and Grace, after their retirement, had taken a trip to Europe and told about buying an old van in London and driving around Europe. They described a camp ground in Salou, Tarragona, on the Costa Dorado, in Spain. They said it was their favorite place to stay in Spain.

I then learned that we could buy a brand new Volkswagen camper van in Vancouver, pick it up at the factory in Wiedenbruck, Germany, tour Europe for months and then ship it back to Canada, and save on the cost of transportation, food, accommodation and taxes.

To test our ability to live in a small camper van, we decided to rent one and drive up to the interior of BC and visit some out of the way towns and lakes as well as bigger resorts. I arranged to take a week of overtime leave during the summer of 1990 and we rented a VW Westfalia camper in Victoria. We drove up to the Cariboo area and camped at Green Lake and as far as 100 Mile house before taking a back road to Little Fort and down to Kamloops and the Okanagan, before returning to Victoria and then home. I found the camper easy to drive and to manoeuver and it was cozy but not claustrophobic.

Upon our decision to get on with early retirement, we went to a Volkswagen dealer in North Vancouver and ordered a Westfalia Camper, with a date to pick it up at the factory of June 5, 1991.

In January, Margie phoned and asked us to come to White Rock to celebrate our birthdays (hers was just a couple days from mine) and we readily agreed. We arrived to be greeted by a room full of people wishing us a happy retirement. Besides many old friends that we had partied and visited with over the years, we were happy to see Holly, Barbara and Annie, as well as my old pal Omar Derkach and his wife. During the evening, Omar entertained with his guitar and singing.

We phoned my husband-in-law, Leo, and asked him if he would be interested in making all of the travel arrangements for our big trip, from April 15th to Oct. 15th. He agreed, and came to Port Alberni, to discuss the details. I thought it would be a lovely start to our trip if we stopped for a couple days in Buenos Aires or Rio de Janeiro at the start of our trip to South Africa. However, a few days later, Leo phoned to tell us the large extra cost of doing that, versus a stopover at London, so we scrubbed that idea and decided to visit South America on a separate trip in some future year. Leo did a fantastic job and found significant savings for us. In fact, just a week before we left, he cancelled our return flight from London to Halifax in October and re-booked it a saving of a couple hundred dollars.

Our itinerary ended up as a bus ride from the Sandman Hotel in Vancouver to Seattle on April 15th, flight on the 16th to San Francisco, a three-hour wait, followed by an flight to London, an overnight stop there, and a flight on the 18th to Johannesburg, a three-hour wait, and then a flight to Cape Town. We would fly back to London on June 4th for an overnight and then on to Frankfurt on June 5th and make our way by train to Weidenbruch. Our final plane flights would be from Amsterdam to London and Halifax on October 2nd where we could retrieve our van for the long drive back to Vancouver.

Back at the office, I continued with my usual work. I was asked what I would like for a retirement gift and it was suggested I could take my computer. I said absolutely not, I had had my fill of computers and never wanted to see one again. The alternative was anything up to a value of $500. I phoned Noel Edwards in Portland and asked him to price a good zoom Pentax camera and a pair of compact binoculars. He found both items on sale in Portland and bought them for me and I submitted the receipts and received repayment; they would have cost much more in Port Alberni or in Nanaimo.

On my last day at work, there was a large party for me in the main office, with all of the managers, as well as department superintendents and the office staff present, for food and refreshments. I received several gifts including a framed montage showing all of the major projects I had assisted in obtaining approvals for, designed by Gary Dillon.

In the evening, Phyllis and I were guests for a retirement dinner, attended by the mill managers and their wives. The mill manager, Ted Williams, and his wife, Shareen, had been close friends of Pat and I, back in the sixties and until Pat ran away. I was about nine years older than them and Phyllis was another six years older than me, so we didn't have much in common anymore, so our friendship slipped. Noel and Joy had come up from Portland for a visit and were invited to the dinner.

During the next two weeks, we were busy sorting out the items we would take with us to our little apartment in Vancouver. Monica and David rented a cube truck and took a lot of the stuff we wouldn't need back to their home in Campbell River. They were in need of a dining room suite and we loaned them ours which wouldn't fit into our unit in Vancouver, but we would need later when we expected to move to a bigger place. When the boys were still in school, I promised the dining suite to Danny and the liquor cabinet to Matt when they eventually would get their own homes. Matt stopped by and asked how much I wanted for our barbeque; I said make me an offer, and I accepted $100. He also bought our Ford Taurus and Anni bought my old Ricoh camera. That was the extent of our garage sale. About April 13th, Johnston Movers came by and packed everything that was left and put it into storage for the summer.

As we drove out of town, we had to chuckle as we passed the home-made sign at the side of the road which read, "Last person leaving Port Alberni, please turn off the lights."

In Vancouver, we checked into the Sandman Hotel, and had dinner with Barbara and Johanna. Joey, who was about the same age as she sometimes acts today, five, asked me during dinner if I would take my dentures out so she could see what I looked like without them. We were seated in a lovely boutique dining room, and I still shudder at the thought of me doing such a thing, even to hear the laughter of my precious granddaughter.

On the following day, we caught our bus to Seattle for an overnight. On the next morning we flew to San Francisco, waited three hours for our connecting flight to London and arrived there at about noon on the following day. We did not have a hotel booked, so went to a kiosk in the concourse where we were able to get a special rate at a new, very posh, boutique hotel nearby. I hadn't slept a wink for the past 24 hours, so we had a nap before going to dinner. When we went to the dining room for dinner, we found that the cheapest item on the menu displayed in the window was a hamburger for C$25.00, so we turned around and found a very nice restaurant a few blocks way where we had a lovely full three course roast lamb dinner with wine for under C$10.00 each.

On the next day, we flew to Johannesburg, a 17-hour flight and there we waited three hours in the airport lounge for our final leg, a flight of two or three hours to Cape Town.

While sitting in the lounge, I watched an airport employee standing behind a large sign on the mezzanine floor and only visible to people near me on the main floor. He just stood motionless, gazing into space for the entire time we were there. It was my first sight of such a display of a lack of productivity, but not my last.

Maureen and Edwin met us at the airport in Cape Town and drove us to the home of their son, Roddy and his wife, Felicity, in the north eastern part of the city. Maureen and Edwin had a studio apartment in Roddy's home and they let us use their beds while they went to a friend's home to sleep. Roddy and Filly had two teenaged children, Jonte and Maureen (Junior), plus a pet pit bull terrier, named Griffin, which served as a guard dog.

Their home had a very small back yard, about ten feet of cement patio which ended at a ten-foot high cement wall which was covered with flowering vines, purple and red bougainvillea and yellow jasmine and golden shower. The front yard was wide but not too deep, enclosed by a low wall, and included a small swimming pool, lawn, bushes, and beds of colorful flowers.

Other homes were similar in size but were enclosed by walls about five feet in height, and all had guard dogs. It was interesting that, when a black person walked down the street, all the dogs in the block barked until the person was past the next corner; yet, when I, a complete stranger, walked to the store a few blocks away, only a few dogs barked at me and soon stopped. It seemed to me that even the dogs were trained to be prejudiced.

After our arrival, we needed an early night because I had been, again, without sleep for about thirty hours. Each day, we ate breakfast and lunch with Maureen and Edwin in their studio suite and we all ate dinner with Roddy and his family. On the first evening, the barbequed meat consisted of lamb chops with a side of boerwors, (also called boerverst), a coiled sausage that was made of various kinds of meat, from beef to many species of wild game. I found that boerwors was served along with the main course at most meals, and enough was cooked at dinner to serve, warmed up, at lunch on the following day. All of the boerwors had a particular spice(s), was most delicious and I loved it. I have tried to buy it back in Canada, but even the product made by South African immigrants doesn't have the exact same flavor.

Our first sightseeing event was to Cape of Good Hope, the most southern point of South Africa. The most southerly point is called Cape Pointe and, although it is not accessible by road, it is clearly visible from the higher viewpoints of the park, and we could see both the Atlantic and Indian Oceans. While driving slowly on a narrow road, we had to stop for a troop of baboons that were sitting in the road. The baboons slowly, and casually, climbed all over the car, looking in at us from the roof and hood and tried to rip the windshield wipers out of their sockets, all the while waiting for us to feed them. After about ten minutes the baboons got tired of waiting for these cheap tourists to give them food handouts and gradually dropped off the car, letting us drive off while they took up their previous positions in the middle of the road, in the hope that the next car would have a bunch of bananas for them.

On another outing, we travelled by cable car to the top of Table Mountain which is in the eastern outskirts of Cape Town. From the top we had a clear view of the city, the ocean and shoreline, as well as Robben Island, the prison that held Nelson Mandela for so many years until his release just during the previous year. That event marked the end of apartheid, which Botha's government had installed many years ago. The mountain top was the home of a large colony of dassies (rock hyroxes) that were about the size of our bush rabbits. By 1999, these little rodents all but disappeared for unknown causes, and for that reason, a particular species of eagles that preyed on the dassies, also became exceedingly rare, and in 2014, numbered only a single pair.

Cape Town is the legislative capital of South Africa. An interesting fact is that the city council of Cape Town is comprised of 221 members. Nevertheless, they are quite advanced in their city planning.

During the next two weeks, Phyllis and I took a trip by ourselves on the Garden Route along the east coast to Port Elizabeth, and thoroughly enjoyed the beautiful scenery.

One Saturday morning, we went with Roddy and Filly to the Stellenbosch Valley to visit a number of wineries, tasting at each, and found the wines to be excellent. At noon we had a lovely lunch at one of the wineries which included a bottle of their wine for each couple. By regulation, both of the bottles had to be opened. We agreed to share one bottle and take the other home. We retrieved a cork and put it back in the bottle. While driving home, Fillie was holding the bottle between her thighs and I guess the vibration built up pressure in the bottle. Suddenly, there was a loud bang as the cork popped and ricocheted around the interior of the car. Roddy, who had served in the army for a couple years under the country's compulsory military training program, thought it was a rifle shot and that we were under attack. He hit the brakes, ducked, and yelled "Take cover". When Fillie said it was only the cork, we all relaxed and had a good laugh. Fillie received considerable teasing about the excitement that her thighs could cause.

After church one Sunday at the end of April, we all went to a restaurant for dinner to celebrate Phyllis's 66th birthday.

On another day, we were taken to the Kirstenbusch National Botanical Gardens in Cape Town, where we were able to see a vast collection of South African plants and flowers. Such beauty!! Pity that so many of them are becoming rare and even extinct.

Finally, it was time for us to make our way up to the Krueger National Game Reserve. With Maureen and Edwin, we drove north, through the Transvaal, to Bloemfontein, the judicial capital of South Africa, where we stopped to spend a few days with Edwin's sister, Margaret, and her husband, Pat Kay.

Margaret was a serious collector of a variety of items, notably Hummel figures, although there were also large collections of silver spoons, shells, and Wedgewood China. One end of her living room contained Hummel figures on the shelves of what looked like four tall book cases. There were hundreds of such figures, worth a fortune. On every available bit of wall space as high as the ceiling, were paintings. I'm not familiar with art, so I couldn't say if it was valuable.

In the long hallway was a collection of native weapons, spears, shields, knives, masks and other wooden carvings, hides, etc. Margaret and Edwin's father had been a magistrate for many years, and these were items that had been seized at the scenes of serious crimes, murders and massacres.

The items were hanging in front of colorful woven blankets, together with many items of beautiful bead work and other hand crafts.

Margaret also had a large collection of pigs: knitted, carved, ceramic and pottery. In the house, she wore a pair of knitted slippers that were in the shape of pigs, similar to bunny slippers that kids wear in Canada.

Margaret and her husband have a son, Peter, who is a chiropractor in Tucson, Arizona. He had already arranged a year previously for green cards for his folks to emigrate to join him. The only problem was that Margaret couldn't bring herself to part with any of her stuff, and she certainly couldn't take all of it with her. So she just kept putting off the decision, saying they still had another year before the green cards would expire.

Their home was on just one floor level, they had no guard dog and no surrounding high wall, and their only protection was steel bars on the inside of every window and door. I did not feel safe that night, thinking that if the house caught fire near the front door, there would be no way out and we would all perish. I didn't express my concern to the others, thinking I might cause undue alarm.

One day, Pat drove Edwin, Phyllis and me to Kimberley to visit the very famous Kimberley diamond mine. The mine was still operating, although at a lower production level. A bit of the history of the mine follows:

In 1866, a man named Erasmus Jacobs picked up a shiny pebble on the banks of the Orange River. It turned out to be a diamond, weighing 21.25 carats and was sold to various people, at some point getting the name "Eureka". A couple years later, a larger diamond was discovered in the same general area and was named "The Star of South Africa". In 1869, a diamond weighing 83.5 carats was found on the farm of the DeBeers Brothers on the slopes of Colesberg Kopje by the cook from the Fleetwood Rawstone's "Red Cap Party" of prospectors where he had been sent to dig as punishment. Rawstone took the news of the find to nearby diggings of the DeBeers Brothers and the rush was on. Within a month, 800 claims had been cut into the hillock and two to three thousand men were at work digging on the small hill. More men came. The small hill disappeared and was replaced by "The Big Hole", which became The Kimberley Mine. Smaller, various, mining companies became amalgamated by Cecil Rhodes into DeBeers, and others by Barney Barnato into the Kimberley Mine.

The two companies merged in 1888, to become the DeBeers Consolidated Mines which still retains the monopoly over the world's diamond market. The main mine closed in 1914 and the last three holes nearby closed in 2005. A total of 2722 kg of diamonds were taken out of the mines. The Big Hole has an area of 42 acres and is 463 meters wide. It was dug with picks and shovels to a depth of 240 meters. It was partially filled in with 25 meters of debris and then 40 meters of water. Below the surface, it was mined to a depth of 1097 meters.

When Phyllis and I visited, the mine was mostly just a tourist attraction. Upon paying for our admission, we were each given a pail of tailings with the assurance that their "might be" a diamond in it if we wished to sort through the dirt on a sorting table. If we found a "diamond" it would be plastic, but we could take it to the office and exchange it for a real, smaller, diamond. All we ended up with was dirty hands.

The museum proved to be more interesting. Besides the history of the mine, there was a lot of information about Cecil Rhodes, the great benefactor. Rhodes and his partner, Charles Rudd, put together the DeBeers diamond empire and Rhodes was named Chairman of the Board in 1888. Rhodes also had considerable investments in agriculture and vast holdings of farm acreage and crops. A staunch British loyalist, he worked to expand the influence of the British throne through the dominions and colonies. One of his priorities was to award university scholarships to all worthy students of the British Empire, as well as to students in the United States and even Germany, where he hoped to attract influence.

The museum contained artifacts of Rhodes at the time of his mining days. One magnificent artifact was the mounted head, including the horns, of one of his team of oxen. Mounted on the museum wall, they measured a span of at least ten feet. There was also a photo of the team that was most impressive. There were many other items on display as well.

Our visit to Bloemfontein complete, we then continued on to Pretoria, the executive or administrative capital of South Africa, where Maureen and Edwin's younger daughter, Patsy, lived with her husband, Nando, and their two children.

Patsy is the sweetest, kindest person you could ever meet, while Nando was a husky, happy man who was always ready to help. He was the general manager of the large Nissan assembly plant in Pretoria. Unfortunately, the plant closed a couple years after we left and Nando was unable to get a decent paying job again. Their son was doing his military service, and their daughter, Lisa, was working for a company which assisted in planning and organizing conferences.

We had only a couple days to visit going on to the Krueger Park. One day was spent touring Pretoria and its beautiful parks, buildings and artworks.

We finally left for the Krueger Game Reserve, which was at that time 7580 square miles, about two-thirds of the size of Vancouver Island, and measured about five hundred kilometers between the northern and southern boundaries. It was totally enclosed by a high fence and bounded on the north by Zimbabwe, and on the east, partially, by Mozambique. Since our visit, several other parks in that area and in Zimbabwe have been added to make an even much larger Krueger Park. Entry to the Park was through one of nine gates. There were a number of main paved roads with many connecting secondary, dirt, roads, all well sign-posted to direct tourists to the various best views of game and to ten main camps. The camps were fenced enclosures to keep the wild animals out, while inside were the commissaries and lodges and rondovels to house tourists, individuals and families. The gates were closed at six p.m., so it was important to be inside before they were locked.

On our way to the park, we stopped at a roadside stand that sold fresh fruit and vegetables. I wandered into the little market to see what unusual products they might have. At the door were three young men who smiled broadly at me and one of them asked if I was Gary Player, the famous South African professional golfer. I wondered what brought that on, and Maureen suggested it might be the white cap that I was wearing which was similar to one that Gary wore during some of his matches.

Maureen and Edwin's children arrived with their spouses in separate cars and through various gates, depending on the direction they were coming from. Billy and Berdine entered via the south gate and were fortunate to see a cheetah on the side of the road, a very rare spotting. We all gathered at the Olifants Camp and each couple had their individual rondovel.

The hut is built in a round shape, but the wall is indented at the door, so that the roof extends over the door and patio; it also covers the eating area, and shelters the fridge. The floors in most modern rondovels, such as ours, are cement, whereas the common native floor consists of a compacted mixture of cow dung, clay, anthill soil, sand and soil. The roof is made of thatch, which is cool in the summer.

We gathered for dinner at Maureen and Edwin's unit where a "cook boy" came by and lit the barbeque and then cooked the meat. The fuel was a few small pieces of wood which resembled petrified or fossil wood. It threw off such heat that our meat was cooked in no time, including the boerwors for that evening and enough for lunch the next day.

The camp generator was turned off at about ten p.m., so we had an early night. Soon after the lights were turned off, the sound of rustling was heard from the roof. I asked Phyllis if she thought that there might be snakes in the grass roof, but she just laughed and said, "It's only mice, get used to it".

During the night, I awakened to hear lions, elephants and hyenas, and other animals, in the distance. One night, an elephant came to the camp and caused minor damage to the gate, trying to enter, but soon gave up and left quietly. On another evening, just before the lights went out, a bat flew into our unit. I had no idea what it was, except that it was darting all over the room, and I was immediately on the attack. I finally caught it with a blanket and disposed of it outside. Phyllis was killing herself with laughter and after everything had quieted down, she gave her hero a hearty applause. I assured her I would there to protect her from bats, lions and bears forever.

On the following day, Phyllis and I went with Maureen and Edwin to the Olifants River. We saw quite a number of wild game species, including elephants, giraffes, zebras, warthogs, African buffalo, hippos, and various deer and antelope species, (impala, elands, wildebeests (gnus), kudus, waterbucks, etc.). On the sandy river bank we could see seven crocodiles basking in the sun. What made the scene so memorable was that the crocs seemed to have been parked there by a valet – all were perfectly aligned, the same distance apart and at exactly the same angle.

We went out daily, taking a picnic lunch, usually with a different niece or nephew, so I'm not sure who we were with when we encountered various animals, but that's not important. At one watering hole, we counted seventeen giraffes, while waiting nearby for their turn to drink was a herd of bucks.

The elephants seemed to be the most dangerous and we saw several each day. We often met one, or more, walking down a road and it always seemed to have the same reaction. We would both stop at a distance of about a hundred yards and look at each other. After a few seconds, the elephant would walk forward a few paces and we would back up ten feet and both would stop. After a minute, we would repeat the movements. The next thing that happened was that, after the elephant stopped for a half minute, he would start to flap his ears and swing his head from side to side. A minute later, he would start walking toward us again, except that this time he obviously had no intention of stopping again, and it was time for us to turn around and get the heck out of his road.

On one occasion, we met an elephant at a curve without time to turn around. Fortunately, there was a small side road that passed behind a small grove of trees before rejoining the main road. It formed a little island of about a hundred feet long and fifteen feet wide, so we were able to wait for the animal to pass by. The sneaky elephant just waited on the far side for us to emerge. We could make out his form through the trees, so we just waited for a few minutes more until it became apparent that we were the ones having to make the first move. We suddenly hit the gas and raced back onto the main road and looked back to see the elephant racing after us with his head down and trunk reaching for us. He never got closer to us than about thirty feet. It seemed kind of funny to us later, when we were safely on our way.

The elephants seemed to be very sensitive to making eye contact with people and even more so if people in cars were aiming a camcorder or camera at them. At the camp that evening we spoke to a nephew of Edwin who was working as a game warden in the park, and told him of the incident. He said that recently a couple of German tourists had stopped to film an approaching elephant. Ignoring the warning signs, they were surprised when the elephant put his tusks through their car door. Fortunately, they were not injured. Phyllis and I were lucky to have drivers who were experienced in park safety.

Edwin's nephew also told of a recent incident that involved some travellers from Mozambique. Apparently an elderly man was leading his three young nephews and nieces on foot from their country to a better life in South Africa, and they were taking a short cut through the game reserve, a trip of several days. One night, they were attacked by lions and one family member was killed.

While driving one day, we came upon two lions that were lying in the shade of some brush, while they digested a kill they had made during the previous night. The lions were somewhat obscured from a clear view by the brush and so one of the several cars that had stopped, drove off the road to get closer. There were two young men in the car, and the one in the passenger seat opened his window and leaned out, sitting on the window sill with his camera. We left at that point, as the whole scene was so stupid.

We had many sightings of game each day that were so serene and beautiful, giraffes and various deer and antelope at watering holes, each waiting their turn to drink, depending on their position in the hierarchy in the power chain. We were fortunate to see, on a ridge, a klipspringer deer, one of the smallest species of antelope, which stand about 22 inches tall at the shoulder and can stand with all four feet balanced on a rock projection the size of one of our loonie coins. We were also treated to views of many species of birds, including huge buzzards and storks.

On the evening of Maureen and Edwin's fiftieth anniversary, May 17, we all gathered in the dining room of the lodge for a lovely meal and a family get together. I don't recall the main entrée, but do remember that it included elephant boerwors, prepared from an animal culled from one of the herds in the park. Our gift to them was a carving of an orca in BC jade, made by a First Nations man in Port Alberni. It was greatly appreciated by Maureen and Edwin.

On the following day, the children left for their homes and the remaining four of us moved on to another camp, Letaba, for a change of scenery and different animals, same species. On the next day, we moved on to a third camp, Shingwedzi, for the final day of our visit to the park and more sightings of wild game. As we left the park, just outside the gate, was a large bush of red double poinsettias. Beautiful!!

So ended our visit to the Krueger National Game Reserve!! What a spectacular experience for this boy from Meadow Lake. As a child, I never dreamed I would ever see such a different world and I gave thanks to God for such a blessing.

We returned to Pretoria for another couple days. One day, we were picked up by Phyllis's nephew, Neil Johnston, who was the only son of her sister, Sylvia. He lived in Johannesburg and so he drove us around that city, including the neighborhood where Phyllis and Leo had lived until they moved to England. In the afternoon, we went to Neil's home and met his wife, Sue. Neil's two daughters, Cynthia and Gillian, came to visit during the evening and enjoyed meeting them.

Neil was a chartered accountant and lived in a very nice home. It was enclosed by a ten-foot high cement wall, with broken glass embedded in the top. An equally tall locked steel gate opened to the driveway and garage. The front porch was also behind a steel lattice and gate that was kept locked at all times. Behind a locked, heavy wooden, door was a lovely home that we entered after disconnecting the burglar alarm. In the back courtyard was a swimming pool and small garden, all within the high wall. The bedrooms were on the second floor, accessed by a stairway that was blocked off half way up by another locked steel gate. All of the windows in the house had steel bars on the inside. Before bedtime, Neil warned us to not move about during the night because the burglar alarm would be activated when the lights went out.

I asked Neil if he had ever had a break-in and he said, "Yes, just a couple months ago." He was wakened by a noise downstairs. The burglars came up the stairs as far as the steel gate but couldn't get past. Neil was holding a revolver just inside their bedroom and was prepared to use it if necessary. Neil said if the burglars had gained full entry, he was sure they would have both been murdered if Neil was unarmed. The burglars took his computer, television, and stereo system and left. Neil was sure that it was their maid's husband that was one of the burglars, but he just claimed the loss on his insurance and nobody got hurt. I didn't get a really good sleep and after the second night, we were happy to get back to Patsy and Nando's, where they didn't take such precautions or at least make such a big deal of it.

The next day, we flew to Durban, in Natal. Natal was discovered during the Christmas season in 1497 by Vasco da Gama while he was searching for a route to China. He named it Natal, which is the Portuguese word for Christmas. A group of 25 British troops arrived in 1824 to establish a base and make friends with the Zulu king. The King of the Zulus, Shaka, had recently been badly wounded in battle and he was helped to recover by an adventurer, named Henry Francis Fynn, who was accompanying the British. In gratitude, King Shaka granted the British a 30-mile strip of land on the coast and extending 100 miles deep.

The purpose of our trip to Durban was to visit Phyllis's brother-in-law, Gus, who was the husband of Zena, as well as Phyllis's cousin, Lovell and his wife, Pat. We stayed with Lovell for two nights and were able to visit Gus for lunch and met his daughter, Carol. Gus was a pleasant, gregarious gentleman who still carried a torch for Zena, who had passed away many years ago. Gus was an accomplished pianist. Phyllis recalled the many weekends during the war, when Gus was courting Zena and they gathered around the piano, along with servicemen that would drop in for the weekend. Lovell was also there often.

Something interesting about Durban was that it was so humid in that area that all the chrome and other metal surfaces in Gus's home had become badly corroded into weird shapes.

We returned to Pretoria and on the following day, along with Maureen and Edwin, we left to spend a few days at the Blydepoort Resort in the Drakensburg Mountains. The scenery was very beautiful, with some of the lookouts being absolutely breathtaking.

We drove one day to a lookout very high up in a park. We parked the car in the lot and walked to the lookout point. It was a ledge thousands of feet above the wooded valley far below. The river below was barely visible. Edwin calmly walked out to within a foot of the edge and stood looking down into the distance for several minutes, taking in the view, while the rest of us turned away, praying that he didn't fall. The closest I could get to the edge was by almost crawling on my hands and knees to a point about fifteen feet from the edge, and even at that distance, my knees were weak. What really impressed me with Edwin's display of guts was that he only had one eye. Maureen just shook her head at him. From the parking lot we could see Mozambique and, if I remember correctly, in the distance the faint sight of the island of Madagascar.

In the same area, we came upon three small round mountains, each about a kilometer in diameter and with sheer vertical sides and conical tops, named The Three Rondovels, because of their resemblance to the native huts. They were very unique, because I have never seen even one mountain of that shape and here there were three, resembling almost a native village.

Not far away, we came upon Bourke's Potholes. The interesting rock formations were pools in a riverbed that had formed over the centuries in the rock by erosion and were quite far down from the surrounding surface. They were named after a British prospector who managed to climb down and found that the water was crystal clear and the weird sparkle was from gold particles that had collected in the bottoms of the pools. Needless to say, he cleaned out the bottoms of the pools and became rich.

That was nearly the end of our exciting visit to South Africa, as we returned to Cape Town for a few more days of quiet visiting with Maureen and Edwin. We were very impressed with South Africa and planned to return to spend our winters there in future, renting a secure apartment in Cape Town at very low cost, buy a used car for five months, and, after paying airfare, still be money ahead. The thought of an annual visit to the Krueger Game Reserve was mouth-watering. Unfortunately, the next year Maureen wrote to say that it was no longer safe for visitors, unless you came as part of a tour group.

On June 4th, we said goodbye to our very generous and hospitable relatives and flew back to London. We were sorry to leave such lovely and loving people.

Chapter 24

TOURING EUROPE

We arrived in London on June 5th, and caught a cab to the same boutique hotel, The Edwardian Inn, that we had stayed at in April. On arrival, we were surprised to learn that the regular room rate was actually about four times the amount that we paid on our first visit, and that, in April we had received a promotional rate. We thought we would have to go somewhere else, but the manager said we could have it again at the same rate.

Our flight to Hanover on the 6th was uneventful as was the train trip to Gutersloh and then by taxi on to Wiedenbruck. The train ride was a bit unusual because we shared a compartment with a romantic German working man who was a bit drunk. He was being a bit too charming to Phyllis and he kept offering her one of his hard boiled eggs of which he carried about six in his coat pocket. She kept refusing, so he ate several by himself, and they stunk up the compartment.

It was too late to pick up the camper that day, so we went to a hotel where we later had dinner in the dining room. I ordered schnitzel and was disappointed to find it was made of pork, not veal. I kept ordering schnitzel as long as we were in Europe and it was always pork. I'm a slow learner, because I just kept hoping that, just once, I would get veal; but it was always pork. In the evening, we took a stroll around the 1000 year town and were impressed with the condition of the buildings. Two churches dated back to 1721. Also, there was a McDonalds. Surprise,

Surprise!! People were very friendly and when we said we were Canadians, they always asked if they could help us with anything. People were well dressed, from teenagers to seniors. There was a very well kept park with a small lake near the downtown area.

The next day we picked up our Westfalia camper at the factory which had a small campground in a grove of trees next to the office that we were able to stay at for a few days, rent free, while we got used to the camper. There were about five campsites and it had a clean washroom with two sinks and toilets. Except for one day, we were the only campers during our stay. We spent the next two days at the local dealership, having various things done to the camper, including installation of a porta-potty and learning how to care for it. Unfortunately, the dealer did not have a padded box for the pottie or an awning, so we decided to wait till we found a dealer that did have these items. We purchased a Michelin Road Atlas and Camping Guide for Europe, both proved to be excellent. We drove to Gutersloh, where there was a department store, and purchased the things we needed to equip our home – sleeping bags, pillows, dishes, pots and pans, cutlery, cleaning supplies, groceries and wine. Our first night in the camper, we slept like a couple of decadent old people, waking at 9:30 a.m.

Finally, on Monday, June 10th, we took off on our tour of Europe, with only one set "first destination", Maastricht, Holland, and no timetable, except we were booked to fly back to Canada in October. Taking a second-ary highway, we travelled through small forests, passed by market gardens, small farms and pastures, towns and villages, all looking neat and prosper-ous. We also saw several manor houses and chateaux. In late afternoon, we decided to stop for the night under the trees near a small lake just off the road. After dinner, we watched two fellows, looking like landed gentry and wearing plus-fours, high leather boots and caps, training a couple retrievers to flush out duck decoys from the reeds. It started to rain so we snuggled in our bed and went to sleep.

On the following day, we arrived in Holland and drove through similar landscape and we were amused to see a woman on her knees, scrubbing her front steps and, down the street, another washing her mailbox, in the rain. Phyllis commented that this was giving new meaning to the expres-sion "Dutch Clean". We arrived at Maastricht and found an excellent campground. During the next couple days we spent our time looking at the many sights that I recalled from my business trip before I retired, visiting beautiful churches and public buildings, dating back to the year 1100. The churches were where I found myself particularly drawn, the stained glass windows and ceilings that were so beautifully and intricately designed, and still retaining their original vibrance. We came upon a huge outdoor market in a large square, which was not at all tacky, being well stocked with good quality garments, fabrics, lace curtains and drapes, as well as fruit and vegetables, meat and fish and flowers. By the Maas River we viewed gray stone fortifications and casements and ancient cannons facing the river. We spent a few days in Maastricht, hoping that the weather would improve. It was not pouring rain, just a light drizzle or frequent showers, but always cloudy and chilly, so we decided to head to where we could be certain to find sunny skies and warm weather, that is, on the Mediterranean Sea. We had no specific route in mind, just south and generally along the Rhine River.

On June 13th, we left after breakfast in Holland, had lunch in Belgium, and arrived in time for dinner in Luxembourg. For lunch, we purchased meat pies and apple strudel at a patisserie. The campground in Luxembourg was at the rear of a restaurant and pub. The pub owner and his wife were very friendly and invited us to come in to play bridge that evening. They gave us some advice that proved to be helpful wherever we went in Europe: be sure to let people know that we are Canadian, and we wouldn't want to be mistaken for Americans, because Americans were often naturally disliked outside of North America; and we wouldn't want to be mistaken for Germans due to our German license plates because of the lingering feelings of resentment all over Europe due to the German occupation during the Second World War. Therefore, in addition to having two decals showing the maple leaf flag in the rear windows of the van, I always greeted someone as soon as we pulled into a campsite, in a loud voice, "Hi, we're from Canada." The response was usually very positive, and we often made new friends within a few minutes.

From that campground, we drove south to Diekirch, Luxembourg, on the Sure, at the entrance to the Ardennes. The history of Diekirch goes back to the Stone Age, and here, archaeologists have located the "Devil's

Altar", an altar built of stones. The museum houses remnants and beautiful mosaics of the Roman epoch, and there are wonderfully restored sculptures in the 5th Century Church of St. Laurent. There was also a newer museum devoted to World War Two and the Battle of the Bulge.

Continuing south on our travel to the city of Luxembourg, we encountered the old town of Clervoux, which was built all around the Castle with its adjoining church and school. We were so impressed with its picturesque beauty that we drove out of our way some four months later to spend a night there in the hotel.

We were not much impressed with Luxembourg City. It was such a mixture of the palace of the ruling Grand Duke, mansions, and the steel and black glass high rises housing Giorgio of California, Abercrombie and Fitch, and MacDonald's. The traffic at two p.m. resembled rush hour in Vancouver, so we left after a couple hours.

From there, we drove into France and later crossed the Rhone near Strassbourg, and back into Germany arriving in Kiel, where we found a lovely campground on the banks of the Rhine.

When we entered the campground we were surprised to find a Westfalia camper identical to ours and sporting Canadian licence plates, then we spotted two more. After making camp, I went over to their camp and found that the people were servicemen and women from the RCAF bases in Baden-Baden and Lahr, both near Kiel. We were invited to join them after dinner around their big bon-fire. One couple, Cliff and Barbara Dunham of Pembroke, Ont., were particularly friendly and invited us to go with them to the base at Lahr for the big Father's Day lunch on Sunday. Cliff was the sergeant major in charge of the All Ranks Mess at the base, while Barbara was a nurse at the base and as a lieutenant, she outranked Cliff.

On Saturday, we strolled around a nearby park on the Rhine and were entertained by members of the Stuttgart Flying Club who were free fall parachuting in their wet suits into the river. We also met a nice couple from Leicestershire who were camping there. We decided to do a load of laundry after dinner, with not good results. We couldn't read the instructions printed in German and were surprised at nine o'clock when the power went off and we had to wait until morning to finish it. The manager was quite annoyed and scolded me, I think, but I couldn't understand her anyway, especially the word "dummkorpf" or something like that.

On Sunday morning, Barbara's brother, who was also based at Lahr, picked us up and drove us to the base for lunch. What a spread!! After lunch they took us to the PX and we were able to buy a few bottles of duty-free liquor and several English novels, crossword books, Canadian coffee, and several other items common to Canada but not available in Europe.

As a sideline, Cliff arranged for servicemen on the base to buy Westfalia Campers and ship them back to Canada when they completed their stint overseas, saving the shipping costs and also getting duty and tax refunds, and he received a commission from Volkswagen. He gave me the location of a Volkswagen dealer nearby which would provide and install a box for our porta-pottie and an awning, which we had done as soon as we left the campground on Monday.

We had planned to go directly south, into Switzerland, but the weather was the pits again, so we went back into France and followed the Rhone, hoping to reach sunnier skies sooner. We continued to travel slowly and only on secondary highways, but always were blessed by beautiful country sides of low mountains, terraced slopes of vineyards, charming homes with lovely flower gardens (geraniums and roses, roses, roses!!) and on the roadsides, masses of red poppies, purple, pink and blue lupins, daisies and broom. We stopped in a village at a patisserie for coffee and pastry and the waitress, when we mentioned that we were from Canada, she asked many questions about our country. When we asked her about the local area, she advised us to not stay there, but to go on to Tournon. What a delight that turned out to be, an old picturesque town with gray stone houses, buildings, churches, schools, narrow cobblestone streets, with boutiques and stores of every kind. Our campground was in a park near the center of town, on the bank of the Rhone, with a river cruise boat tied up just yards away. That night, we left the drapes open on the side facing the river, with a view, across the river, of Mt. Penay, covered with vineyards; and on the top, flood lit all night, was a tiny chapel with a cross on top.

The next day was Wednesday, June 19th, our wedding anniversary, and we decided to do something special to mark the occasion, so we headed for tiny Andorra, perched on the border of France and Spain. It did sound romantic in the tour book. I found a sign directing us to the road to Andorra and spent an hour driving around, trying to locate the road, always ending up back in the same spot, so we gave up and continued on towards Spain, finally stopping for the night in a little campground, which was almost totally vacant but, at least, it was on the shores of the Mediterranean. It was late and the only place to eat in the area was a little concession stand which we made do and postponed our anniversary dinner. Phyllis assured me that it would cost me extra for every day that she had to wait (her joke).

The next day we arrived at Salou, on the Costa Dorado, and checked into a beautiful, large campground, two blocks from the beach. The beachfront had a wide boulevard, lined with palm trees, statues, and fountains, summer home mansions, shops and restaurants, including a McDonald's. The weather was sunny and hot. Yeah!! We said we would book in for a week, and we ended up staying for two weeks.

The campground had great amenities, including a large swimming pool as well as a paddling pool for little kids, a small supermarket that was well stocked with food and other goods, a restaurant and bar, and clean toilets including some English type toilets, similar to ours, i.e., bowls with seats and flushing systems. There was also a separate outside section at one side of the washroom building that contained about ten or more stainless steel sinks in two long counters just for cleaning and preparing fresh vegetables.

We had dinner in the resort's restaurant, paella with various fresh seafood – prawns, scallops, mussels, clams, etc. – and chunks of chicken, on a bed of saffron rice, with peas and pimiento, and accompanied by a bottle of local white wine. I commented to Phyllis, "I wonder what the folks are doing right now in Meadow Lake." I felt that I had been truly blessed by God – to be here on the Mediterranean and with the woman I loved so dearly. I had, without doubt, already far surpassed any of my boyhood dreams. After dinner, we strolled along the promenade, together with entire families who had their little ones with them at 10:30 p.m. Other children, not yet in their teens were skipping along with their ice cream cones and seeming to feel quite safe. We sat on a bench on the boulevard for an hour, listening to a band concert – Beatles to Beethoven.

On the following day, after lunch, while Phyllis was tidying the camper, I grabbed the beach towels and headed for the pool to hold a pair of chaise lounges for us. I arrived on the large deck and looked for two chaises next to each other, among the hundreds. I found a pair and spread my towel on one and lay back and took a look at nearby sunbathers. To my surprise, the lady on the next chaise was topless. Thinking that Phyllis would never believe that I had chosen that particular spot innocently, I gathered our stuff and moved to another spot with the same result. I found a third pair of vacant chaises, but before spreading out our towels, I took a close look around me. I then realized that about half of all the women there were topless, and Phyllis (and I) must just get used to it. When Phyllis arrived, I tried my best to explain all of the trouble I had experienced, but I finally couldn't avoid snickering, and then we both burst out in laughter. Through the afternoon, we both were busy reading our novels, but every time I looked up at Phylllis, I found her to be checking if I was actually reading, or if I was gawking at the boobs in the area.

After dinner, we went over to the bar at poolside for a coffee and a liqueur. We were seated at an outdoor table and when we were served our drinks, we received little demi-tasses of espresso which I found to be very bitter. I found that getting a good cup of coffee in Europe was almost impossible.

A few minutes later, we saw a mariachi band setting up their equipment at the edge of the deck. We were soon entertained for about two hours of lively Spanish singing and beautiful girls performing flamenco dancing. Again, I asked, "I wonder what the folks are doing in Meadow Lake." I continued to ask that question every day for the next four months. I seemed to be living in a dream world. There was a band and entertainment every night at that campground.

It was the first day of summer and school was out, so the place was noisy until late that night, fireworks being set off and loud music and people were celebrating as they started their vacations. The next two weeks passed in a joyful blur. People camping near us were kind and gracious. One young couple, in their late twenties arrived on a little mo-ped, their tiny dog riding on the little platform between their feet, packing a tent, cooler, cooking gear, sleeping bags etc., and were enjoying themselves as much as anyone. One day, they presented us with a delicacy for our dinner, a little squid. Phyllis had never prepared a squid and when the ink poured out of it in the pan, it was just too much, and she had to toss it. We thanked the couple profusely, but never mentioned the sad fate of the squid.

During the next couple weeks, we either spent our days near the pool and our campsite or walking on the beach or on the promenade or in the shopping areas. We spent one afternoon at the beach and it was jammed with bodies a couple feet apart. Again, at least half of the ladies were topless. Being so far from the water, we got bored and went back to the camp.

One morning, we were awakened when the van began to rock. I was out like a shot, only to find it was a twelve-year-old boy from the trailer next door, who was trying to retrieve his soccer ball from the tree overhead that our van was touching. While speaking to the boy, he said he had been studying about Western Canada in school, and he and his dad asked us about where we lived, and we were also able to show them photos and postcards that we had brought with us.

Every evening, we went to the bar next to the pool and had a liqueur and espresso and I kept trying for a coffee. I thought I had hit it lucky one evening when, using my Spanish-English dictionary, I asked for an Americano, and the bartender pointed to a couple large coffee mugs on a top shelf. I said "si, si" and so he poured the demi-tasse of espresso into the big mug and handed it to me. I pointed to hot water tap and asked for "agua, caliente". He added about an ounce of hot water and gave it back to me. When I asked for more hot water, he just said "no, too much agua" and turned away. I had to take Tums in order to put out the fire in my stomach. Three months of retirement and my ulcer was not yet healed.

Phyllis reminded me that we had not yet had our Anniversary Dinner, so one night we went to a nice restaurant, a block from the campground, but unfortunately, it didn't measure up to her standard and so, the inflation continued to pile onto the cost of the meal, whenever that might happen. I suggested that if we waited until we got to Switzerland, we would be certain to find a restaurant that would compare to the William Tell in Vancouver which was our favorite. She agreed and we were able to carry on for the next month.

We intended to proceed slowly along the coast toward Portugal, stopping at nice campgrounds each night. We followed a secondary highway which more or less paralleled the shore line, through Castellon and Valencia, an area that was quite arid, except for a few vineyards and orchards that were the source of the delicious Valencia oranges. Most of the homes in the villages were quite shabby and the people looked unhappy and belligerent. While driving slowly through the small towns, pedestrians often shouted to us that our head lights were on. Our van had been manufactured to Canadian standards, so the lights came on automatically when I turned on the ignition. My explanations in English were ignored. That proved to be an annoyance all summer.

Finally, we rounded a bend in the road and, in the distance, we saw Benidorm, a resort city that I had visited in 1974 with Pat. The suburbs were a mass of beautiful houses on terraced hillsides and cliffs, down to the beautiful aquamarine Mediterranean Sea.

The city itself was a massive traffic jam, with wall-to-wall people on the streets and beaches. It was impossible to find a parking spot, and with car horns constantly tooting in a fruitless gesture of urging other vehicles and people to get out of their way faster.

We continued out of town and soon found a campground at Villa Joyosa, right on the beach. It was very nice and well equipped, but without the nightly entertainment that we had enjoyed at Salou. Two nice couples from Germany were camped nearby and we visited with the older couple each day. The man spoke quite good English, and he explained that he had been a prisoner-of-war of the American army, captured in France, and had been put to work in a paper box factory. When we mentioned that we were headed for Portugal, they warned us that it was not safe to go farther, because they had had a scary experience on their trip.

As they were driving along the autobahn in Spain, not far away, a car pulled up beside them and three men inside shouted that there was something wrong with the caravan that they were towing and to pull over. Knowing there was nothing wrong with their little trailer, and aware that this was a familiar tactic of highway bandits, they speeded up until they were directly behind another car with the bandits next to them. Finally a fourth car caught up at high speed and flashed his lights to signal that he wished to overtake. The bandits had to speed up and pull over into the right lane, directly in front of the car the Germans were tailing. As soon as the overtaking car had passed, the Germans pulled over into the passing lane and got into a position alongside the car that had been immediately in front. A few minutes later, the bandits turned off the autobahn.

The younger Germans were honeymooners from Saarbruchen, and had brought their small boat with their caravan, and had already been to Portugal. They said that most of the campgrounds on the Portuguese coast in the Algarve region were quite far from the water or often on cliff tops, with steep steps down to the water.

The Germans also told of another recent incident involving bandits, this time occurring on a night train from Paris to Madrid. During the night, bandits injected gas under the doors of the sleeping compartments and robbed all of the occupants while they were unconscious, before leaving the train. It sounded a lot like a scene from "The Oriental Express" by Agatha Christie, except nobody was killed.

With that in mind, we decided to defer our visit to the Algarve to later years, and that we would, later in the summer, travel down from the Bay of Biscay in France, through Spain and into northern Portugal. We did decide though that we might return in the fall to rent an apartment in Benidorm for the winter, and defer our return to Canada to the following April.

After a week in the Benidorm area, on July 9th, we headed east, back along the coast, staying one night again at Salou, and then drove into Barcelona. What a fabulous city, a mixture of old and new buildings, beautiful stores, and magnificently sculptured statues of heroes, dating way back in history. The huge downtown area has streets so wide they are divided into three sets of lanes with two medians, planted with tall palms and brightly colored bushes and shrubs in full bloom, and flowers everywhere.

We got lost a few times before we got out of town. Our great street maps proved to be quite useless, because the city was preparing to host the Olympic Games in 1992, and the entire city seemed to be a mass of streets that were closed or detoured, plus they were busy with construction of the Olympic Village.

As we re-entered France, the countryside changed – green vineyards and fields replacing the dry and mostly barren stark land. We left the coast road and drove north along lovely tree-lined country roads to visit Avignon, the area that spawned most of France's most notable artists: Cezanne, Chagall, Monet and Lautrec. The countryside with its old farm-houses and the villages were so beautiful that we could understand where their inspirational paintings originated. There were many roadside stands which sold the usual fruit and vegetables, but also local wines, crafts, soaps, fresh and dried herbs, honey, and floral sachets. We bought some wine and some other food items and a bag of homemade nougat with almonds and pistachios. Yum yum!!! We drove past some impressive wineries that Phyllis recalled seeing the names of on bottles on dining tables in fine restaurants and homes all over the world that she had visited.

In late afternoon, we found a campground in a pine forest near Petius. We soon learned that we had made a bad choice, because suddenly a million cicadas started the damnedest racket. The male insects have a pair of resonating organs that produce a high pitched droning sound. During the mating season they start and stop in unison and the noise goes on in three or four minute bursts from dawn to night. We would have moved on but another camper assured us the noise would stop at night and I was really tired.

On the following day, July 11, we reached the French Riviera on the Ligurian Sea, starting at the very attractive city of Hyeres, with its luxury villas, and fancy boutiques, etc. We found a beautiful campground at Le Lavandu, right on the beach and settled in for three days in the sun serenaded by another chorus of cicadas, although not quite so close, and a great number fewer and thus not as loud.

The couple camped next to us were a retired doctor and his wife from Bristol. They had arrived a day early for their two week vacation and they moved the following day to a site right on the beach. They explained that they had been coming to this campground for over twenty years, and after moving closer to the water each year, had finally reached the first row of campsites, next to the water. They had towed their caravan through the Loire Valley and as usual they had purchased quite a few cases of wine which they were accustomed to take home each year. Their names were Dr. Peter Archer and his delightful wife, Jean.

The following day, Sunday, was Bastille Day, and it was a national holiday equivalent to our Canada Day in terms of excitement. Peter and

Jean invited us to join them that evening for the fireworks display in the small bay, directly in front of their campsite. The fireworks show was the first one we had seen, with accompanying synchronized music, similar to the ones which started in Vancouver's English Bay a year or two later. At the end of the show, Peter commented that the fireworks would have been so much more beautiful to watch in color, and then confessed that he was totally colorblind and thus could only witness them in various shades of gray.

While we were in Le Lavandu, we heard the news that Gromeko had been arrested in Russia and the borders to Eastern Europe were again closed, in effect a return to the cold war status that had been in effect since 1946. This meant a serious change had to be made to our loosely formed planned itinerary. We had planned to drive down through the Italian Riviera, over to Rome, and on to Bari, where we would catch a ferry to Dubrovnik, Yugoslavia (now Croatia), and on to Prague, and then to somewhere. Now, we must cut off our visit at Rome, and then head north from there.

We left Le Lavandu for a side trip inland to Grasse, where France's perfume industry is concentrated. On the way, we stopped in a small village called Roquefort to mail a birthday card to one of the children. Then on to Grasse where we visited some perfume museums and admired the old buildings and other scenery, stopping to take pictures. We were on our way back to the coast when I realized my wallet was missing. We returned to the post office at Roquefort, where a kind British ex-patriate was kind enough to act as an interpreter. He went back to Grasse with us to file a loss report with the police, and a couple hours later, we were notified that the wallet had been found with my driver's licence, credit cards, etc., intact, but without the US$60.00 or so that it had contained. When I picked up the wallet, I was asked if I would like to give a reward, but I said that I had no more cash, and besides, the missing $60.00 was ample enough reward.

We camped a few nights inland, in the Massif des Moures, one night at Bormes-les Mimosas, a fascinating little hillside town, gorgeous homes and beautiful gardens, and an old church on the hilltop and fantastic views. Unfortunately, the heat was oppressive and Phyllis was up most of the night, throwing up and on the porta-pottie. In the morning, I turned on the engine to operate the air conditioner while I broke camp and packed up our gear. A French woman came over and started giving me the dickens for making such a noise. I apologised profusely and explained that my wife was sick and I must operate the air conditioner for her or she would have to go to the hospital. She refused to accept my explanation and insisted that I turn off the ignition. I then politely asked her to shove it, and I completed packing up our stuff. It was one of only two run-ins I had in Europe.

When we left the camp we stopped a few blocks away, while we both cooled down, and decided on our next destination. While sitting there at the curb, with the motor idling, we saw a fat Frenchman walking up the hill and carrying three unwrapped baguettes, one under each armpit and another in his right hand while he tore pieces off it and was eating them as he walked. Above his waist, which hung far over his belt, he was wearing only a sleeveless undershirt, soaked with sweat. Phyllis and I watched him walk past us and shook our heads, wondering what the guy's wife would think when he presented her with two baguettes which were soaked through with sweat. We had a good laugh and then proceeded on our way.

We then spent a couple days at Saurieres, had dinner in the camp restaurant — salad, tough steak with nice herbs, and wine — and spent the evening playing cards in the camper. Not much sleep the first night because of a busload of noisy Irish tourists. They must have enjoyed themselves because they left a broken window in the restaurant-bar where they had a sing-along. They left the next day, so we caught up on our sleep and made the acquaintance of our next door neighbor, an English chap who had immigrated to Florida a number of years ago, where he now spends six months of the year and the other six months in France. He was a bit of an eccentric, but interesting, nevertheless.

We returned to the Riviera, driving along the coast, through towns and villages on the shore, such as St. Tropaz and St. Raphael. The traffic was bumper to bumper for miles, and whenever we spotted a building, statue or park that we wanted to have a close look at, we had to circle several blocks before giving up our search for a parking spot and returning to the main road and driving on.

We drove through Antibes, Cap d' Antibes, and had a look at the fabulous Eden Roc Hotel, where the world's rich and famous vacation. We went on to Nice and Monaco, amazing places oozing wealth and good living. We pulled into the curb opposite the sea in Menton, and raised the top of the camper while we prepared and ate our lunch. While eating, a handsome German fellow stopped to wish us "bon appetit" and admired our van and mentioned that he owns homes in both Germany and the Riviera. Also, to point out that it is a small world, his mother lives in Vancouver.

A few yards on, there was a pullout at the side of the road, which seemed to be unusually popular with motorists, because there was a steady constant flow of drivers who pulled over, got out of their cars, stood looking down at the beach for a few minutes, then returned to their cars and left. I was curious and went to see what was there. It turned out to be a small cove and not at all secluded, and was congregated by quite a number of nude sun bathers.

We crossed into Italy at Ventiniglia and drove in bumper-to bumper traffic along the Italian Riviera on the Ligurian Sea. What made the driving more unpleasant was that in Italy, if you left any more than one car space between you and the next car, someone would overtake and cut into the space. He might turn off within two or three blocks, making the whole situation seem totally stupid. We continued until we reached Savona, where we pulled into a small campground and spent an unpleasant night. The owner squeezed us into a tiny spot, scraping our van against a small tree that fortunately didn't cause a dent. The washroom had only Italian toilets, the kind that consist of a three foot ceramic square that has a six inch hole in the center and two raised footprints to assist in aiming and pointing. Needless to say, Italians are notoriously bad at both aiming and pointing, so we avoided the whole stinking situation by restricting ourselves to using the porta-pottie in the van. Our impression of Italy worsened when, that evening, a train passed our camp site by about ten feet. The tracks were hidden by weeds when we came in and when the train suddenly went by, it scared us out of our wits. Lucky for us, there was only one more train that night.

We carried on along the coast road until we reached the ancient city of Genoa whose history dates back, according to city graveyards, to 6,000 and 5000 B.C. It remains a busy seaport.

I could no longer tolerate the busy traffic and decided to leave the coast road with its lovely scenery, and we went inland to get on the freeway. That proved to be a mixed blessing because, although we made better time, we couldn't see any scenery while racing along mountain ridges, through an endless string of long tunnels, over bridges spanning deep ravines and watching out for crazy drivers. It was not at all relaxing.

We stopped at Carrara to take photos of the renowned marble cliffs, where mountain sides were sheared off to extract the world famous white marble. We viewed huge stockpiles of marble, waiting to be shipped to every port in the world. We saw huge flatbed trucks, each carrying a single huge slab of marble, securely lashed down, and waiting to be hauled away.

Finally, we reached Pisa and took pictures of the Leaning Tower and its adjoining cathedral. The Tower was in the process of being strengthened, (not straightened) so the whole place was overrun with workers and massive scaffolding. The ancient city is surrounded by a wall that is starting to crumble, so that was also being remedied. Nevertheless, it was a beautiful and interesting place to visit.

The thought of travelling further south was no longer among the things I really wanted to do, so we headed north towards the Italian Lake district. It was a breathtaking drive through the forests in the lower Apennines (Italian Alps), winding roads through ancient villages and towns, prosperous farms and old churches. Just past Lucca, we came onto a lovely campground down a winding road, on a riverbank. It was very peaceful and tranquil, a chance for us to relax and forget the stress of the past few days.

Next day, we carried on through forested countryside, and narrow, winding roads, past interesting places like Madera, and Mantua, near Verona, and made another fortunate wrong turn and ended up in a medieval cobblestone square, completely walled in, we noted statuary on the top of stone facade ancient houses, little cobblestone streets that were so narrow that our side mirrors were almost touching the walls. It was a delightful experience.

Later, I went into the bank in Pavullo and withdrew C$1,000.00 and returned to the van to report to Phyllis that her lifelong dream had been answered – she was to be sleeping that night with a millionaire. I showed her the 1,300,000 lire that I had received from the bank for my Canadian

1,000 dollar cheque. She didn't seem to mind that I was to be the millionaire in this case, or that my million was about the equivalent of Canadian Tire currency.

We were slightly tempted to drive eastward to Venice, but considering the narrow streets, and Italian drivers, and all that intermingled with a network of canals, we put that idea into the basket of "maybe someday" ideas, and carried on to the Lake district.

On July 19th, we arrived at Desenzano, on the southern tip of Lago de Gardo and checked into one of the nicer, newer, campgrounds that we had stayed at in Italy. The campground was well equipped, and beautifully situated in the Italian Alps. We stayed for a few days at that camp and took side trips to various scenic spots nearby.

One day we drove to Torbole, an interesting experience to say the least. The narrow road follows the western shore of the lake, and includes several miles through tunnels. The tunnels were unlit, narrow, and had frequent turns and also junctions with other tunnels that were poorly signposted. Making the drive even scarier, was the high speed travelled by most of the other travellers. We would see the reflection of an approaching car's headlights on the tunnel walls and suddenly the car would scream by, leaving Phyllis gasping for breath and me cussing the idiots. Often, other cars would overtake us and roar past on turns in the tunnel. I know that I have been known to speed, and even take the odd chance, but this was crazy.

We arrived at Torbole, at the north end of Lago de Gardo, and soon forgot the trip as we were totally enchanted by the beauty of this old city. It was visited by Goethe, the German author and poet, in 1786, and he wrote extensively about the city, describing its architecture and the scenery. We found it to be still as lovely as Goethe had described. Driving a few miles down the eastern shoreline proved to be breathtaking, with a series of villas, mansions, and castles that were all a mass of flower gardens and landscaped estates. Most of the islands in the lake, if they were large enough, contained castles or estates with manor houses. I don't think you could find as extensive an area that would be its equal in beauty anywhere else.

We had to postpone our departure from Lago de Garda because of bad weather. We were not prepared to venture onto the narrow, winding, mountain highways that lay before us, in the rain, and not be able to enjoy the scenery.

Finally, we were able to get on our way, and during the next few days, we were able to visit most of the other lakes in Northern Italy: Lago d' Iseo, Lago di Como, and Lago Maggiore. We took many photos in the area: Villa d'Este, Villa Carlatta, magnificent hotels, and fabulous antique stores.

Most of the campgrounds in Italy were dirty, with only cold water in the washrooms, filthy toilets, and were the most expensive in Europe. That was unfortunate, because it could be a trip through paradise, with all of that beautiful scenery. On balance, we were glad that we had toured much of Italy, because of the beautiful scenery, but there were so many minuses compared to other countries. We left Italy with mixed feelings.

At the border, we could have driven through a tunnel, about 17 miles through the base of the mountain and arrived in Switzerland within minutes, but instead decided to drive over the Simplon Pass, some 6,000 feet high, and thus were able to travel between mountain peaks and enjoy the sheer beauty of the countryside. It was certainly worth the time spent. The atmosphere changed as we crossed the border into Switzerland, brightening especially in our van. It was July 26th.

At the top of the pass, we stopped at a roadside restaurant and had big slices of strudel and hot chocolate. The strudel was yummy, with a filling of apples, raisins, hazelnuts, and orange rind. The hot chocolate consisted of a tall mug of a hot water and an envelope of Nestles chocolate powder and a spoon to mix it. That was a bit of a surprise and a disappointment for Phyllis, but we enjoyed it.

As we sat there looking at the mountains around us, the forests of fir, oak, and poplars, the alpine meadows blanketed by bright flowers, clouds sitting on mountain tops nearby and rocky crags and peaks surrounding us, I looked at Phyllis and could see tears in her eyes as she was so overcome by all of the beauty at that moment.

We reached the bottom of the pass at about three p.m. and after a late lunch near Martigny, we noticed that the weather was starting to threaten rain; I saw a sign pointing to the village of Ollon, so I said, "Let's give the place a look." It was a tiny village, with an ancient church, and a town square containing old trees with wide spreading branches, and across the street from it, a little three-storey boutique hotel. I went inside and found the rates were very affordable, so I said we would take a room for three days. This was the first time we had stayed at a hotel since we had picked up the camper van on June 6th. So much for my promise to Phyllis that we would go to a hotel once a week so that we could get a nice bath and relax with comfortable furniture. She had never mentioned it during the intervening seven weeks and I never noticed that summer was passing quickly.

The hotel was well equipped and had both a patisserie and a fine dining room. On the next morning, we went into the restaurant for a late breakfast and ordered from the menu, not fully understanding what it said. (There are four official languages in Switzerland: German (74%), French (21%), Italian (4%), and Rumantsch (1%).) We were stumbling along when from the kitchen a female voice called out in a clear sweet Texan drawl, "What do you all folks want?" A cute young gal came out of the kitchen and, laughing, helped us to order. The young Texas gal said she had just finished a lengthy course in French cooking in Paris and was now getting practise at this fine restaurant, and was also visiting the Alps. She recommended the dining room upstairs for dinner that evening.

I went in the afternoon to make a reservation and returned to tell Phyllis it really was a place for fine dining and was going to be the best meal we had since we started our European trip. Phyllis's reply was that we would finally be having our anniversary dinner. (Thank goodness!!) The restaurant was not large, maybe ten tables, and when we arrived at seven, was about half full. The seven course dinner menu was a la carte, and we started with poached salmon with a butterscotch or caramel sauce. The entrée was venison from a deer farm in the area, and eventually was followed by a scrumptious dessert and then topped off with a tray of assorted types of cheese, some of which were not pleasant to smell. The bill, with the tip, came to just over double what we paid for three nights of accommodation in the hotel. Phyllis seemed happy with the dinner, as was I.

The café was the haunt for about five old men, who sat around a table all of the day, from morning till dinner, drinking wine. They each ordered local wine in tiny glasses, the size of little one-ounce liqueur glasses, and slowly sipped at it for hours, while talking about local issues and the old days. If the weather was good, they moved outside to one of the tables under the trees in the park across from the hotel.

The next day we went to see a certain formation of rocks that was most unusual. I had come across a picture of it in a brochure and noted that it was quite near. We saw a sign post about a half mile away and turned toward it, thinking that this was going to be really easy to find. The road suddenly turned and we found ourselves climbing steeply up the side of a mountain. About a half mile along, there was a small cluster of houses and outbuildings, with a bench at the side of the road. There was no sign pointing to the rock formation, so I continued further, driving along the road which now consisted of a single lane and was climbing steeply between a sheer cliff on the left and a sheer drop to the bottom on the right. It was probably about five hundred yards to the next turn, when coming around a turn towards us was a farm truck. I stopped and the truck kept coming, so it soon became obvious that one of us would have to blink and back up to let the other pass, and it wasn't going to be the truck. Phyllis had already gone into panic mode when we started going up the one-lane road. As she prayed, I carefully backed down the road to where the bench was located and found a little area where there was room to let the truck pass by.

I then started out again on the single lane, when Phyllis said, sharply, "You're not going up there again with me in the van" and so I backed up to the bench, and said "Okay, get out and wait here and I'll pick you up on my way back". She was so flustered that she actually got out of the van and I left her sitting, stunned, on the bench. I drove up the mountain road and about a half mile past the turn I found myself in a farmer's yard, with no sign of the rock formation. I drove back down the mountain, and stopped to let Phyllis back into the van. There was silence for several minutes while she rolled her eyes and then looked upward to heaven while she gave thanks that I had returned safely, and then she turned to me and asked me, sweetly but coolly, "Well, I hope it was worth it." I told her that there was no rock formation to be found, but that the experience had been breathtaking - for both of us. Phyllis just rolled her eyes some more. Later and in the following few days, as we drove, I often recalled the incident and without looking at her, I smiled to myself, at which time and, without looking at me, Phyllis would remind me, "It's not that funny, so just wipe that smug grin off your face."

We then took a drive to Aigle, a fair sized town with attractive shopping, and a two hour tour of a 13th century castle which had been restored as a museum, housing artifacts and wine-making equipment in the Ollon-Aigle viticulture – old oak casks, period costumes, etc. Some other tourists seemed amused to see me, as they entered a room, and found me lying on the floor with my mouth open under the spigot of a 4,000-liter wine tun while Phyllis was snapping my photo.

We had a nice late lunch of smoked turkey, potato salad, apple strudel, and milk, in a little park on the banks of the Rhone. Then back to the hotel for a nap, followed by a good dinner of pepper steaks.

On the following day we drove up to Villars, a ski resort about ten kilometers from Ollan - three km east and seven km up - on a narrow road with hairpin bends, beautiful views of the mountain and valley scenery. Villars proved to be a prosperous resort of beautiful chalets, shops and restaurants. One restaurant, in particular, proved to be unique in that it was owned by a man from Montreal and his Swiss wife. The police station was located in the center of town and was housed in what looked like a beautiful chalet, with geraniums in the window boxes and on the wide porch.

On the following day, we travelled along the south shore of Lake Leman, through Evian and other delightful small towns and farmland to Geneva. What a marvellous city and a heaven for photographers. We visited the Palace of Nations, fronted by its long stretch of roadway lined by flags of every nation belonging to the League of Nations. Across the street was the International Headquarters and Museum of the Red Cross, a touching and meaningful reminder of man's inhumanity to man during wars and a source of international disaster relief. We drove along the lakeshore, past the gorgeous homes of members of the Diplomatic Corps, to our next camp. It was a small, private campground on the shore of Lake Geneva, on the grounds of what had been a beautiful mansion, now gone to ruins, but the terraced garden was still there.

We travelled toward Lausanne on the north shore of the lake and took a side trip to Neuchatel, and what a nice city that was, with its well-developed waterfront, landscaped promenade and office buildings. We arrived at noon, so we witnessed many of the clerical staff exit the buildings to sit on benches in the sun to eat their lunches. We ate our lunch by the lake, next to a marina, and watched lovely sailboats pass by.

That night, we spent at a campground on a farm a few kilometers away. The washrooms were located in one of the barns. In the morning, while Phyllis was having a shower, behind her a cow poked her head through an open window and mooed. It scared the dickens out of Phyllis until she was about to have a heart attack.

During dinner, the skies opened and the rain poured down and continued through the night. We were quite comfy in our van and felt sorry for the few campers that were in tents. In the morning it was still overcast and showery, so we stayed for another night. We were amused by the many storks that had built huge nests on the roofs and chimneys of barns all around us. Just outside the gate, the farmer had built large cages all along his fence-line, housing beautiful pheasants (some were scarlet red), pea cocks, quail, turkeys, mallard ducks, and other pretty birds.

The next day was August 1st, a national holiday on which we joined throngs in Zurrich to celebrate Switzerland's 700th birthday. In the park downtown, were beer gardens, oompah bands, yodellers, choirs, folk singers and dancers in traditional costumes, tables of beer and delicious, hot wurst rolls, and happy voices. We met another Canadian couple who were also enjoying the festivities.

That afternoon, we found a campground on the shore of Lake Lucerne and checked in for several days. It was our favorite, along with Salou, of our entire trip, because of the surrounding interesting places as well as its beauty. Just outside the gate was a museum of early steam locomotives and train cars. About a block from the camp ground was a train stop where we could catch a frequent train into Lucerne, about three miles away. There was a bus service in the area also.

In the evening, we strolled along the waterfront, and sat on a bench watching swans and ducks and the sunset. As the sky darkened, we were treated to a beautiful display of fireworks. On the following morning, we befriended our next door neighbors, a couple from England, Norman (a young, 70-year old retired electrician) and his wife, Rosemary (a positive thinking and vivacious 50-year old who looks and acts like she's 40). They explained the train and bus service and some of the many interesting places to visit.

We took a five-minute trolley-bus ride into town, getting off at the Chapel Bridge, a 14th century covered wooden pedestrian bridge that is world famous, with beautiful paintings on the interior ceilings and walls extending from one end on shore, to the other end on a small island in the lake. The paintings had been carefully re-freshened. Unfortunately, the bridge was destroyed by vandals who set fire to it a couple years later, but with the aid of photos, the entire bridge was restored. The original paintings were done by Heinrich Wagmann, in the 17th century. On the island, we browsed through stores of jewellery, Swiss clocks and watches, and high fashion clothes and shoes – very pricey, but of superb quality. We had a delicious lunch of chicken curry. The coffee was also delicious and not, as Phyllis described it, like the "mud" that we were served in Spain and Italy.

Nearby, we visited the Museum of Natural History, and then the Jesuit Church, built in 1666/7 and, just a block away, the slightly older Franciscan Church. The Franciscan Church was dark and gloomy, with heavily and intricately carved dark wood in a Baroque style, whereas the Jesuit Church was built using a lot of pink and pale gray marble, good lighting coming in through tall stained glass windows, and topped off with a beautiful pastel and gold ceiling and dome. Simply awesome!!!

The next day, we visited the north end of the city and checked out the Roman Wall and towers. When we returned to camp, we invited Norman and Rosemary over for happy hour and presented her with a long stemmed rose and card to mark her fiftieth birthday. She seemed to be very touched by our gesture, and was so cheerful about turning fifty that we wondered about it, considering the trauma that Phyllis had experienced on her fiftieth.

The next day, we caught a paddle-wheeler boat across the lake to a small town which was the terminus for a cog railway. During the crossing, a man blew his Alpenhorn and we heard the sound echo and re-echo again several times until the sound died in the far distance. The cog train carried us slowly up the mountain side of Mount Pilatus, to the top, a distance of some 7,000 feet up. The ride was impressive as the gradient was 48 degrees. We arrived at the top to find a small village with two hotels, several restaurants, and easy walking trails, well sign-posted to various viewpoints overlooking a small valley with farms and surrounded by the seemingly endless range of Swiss Alps, including the famous Jungfrau and others that were identified by arrows along the trails. Perched on a knoll in the little valley was an adorable little white church.

After a lunch of bratwurst and fried potatoes, we attended a concert in the square with a "flag" performer and three gentlemen blowing Alpenhorns. One of the three had a very bushy dark beard that Phyllis couldn't resist stroking as I took their photo.

As we stood looking over the low wall, Phyllis was most impressed by the small herd of cows that were grazing on the mountainside below and wondered that they didn't fall down the steep slope. I explained that the cattle had been specially bred for the area and had shorter legs on one side to compensate and keep them at a constant level. She marvelled at the cleverness of the idea. A couple minutes later, and considering the ridiculousness of the idea, she looked at me and admitted, "You got me again".

We took a second cog railway down the south side to a point half way to the bottom where we disembarked at a terraced restaurant for hot chocolate and listened to a pair of accordionists playing polka music while people danced on the flagstone patio. We went down the rest of the way in a tiny gondola, to the little town of Kriens, where we stopped to wander through a church grave yard that was beautifully kept, with ornate sculptures and lovey beds of flowers. We took a bus back to our campground, where, after dinner, we strolled along the lake shore, watching the swans and ducks peacefully swimming by. We sat on a bench and considered the day and all the beauty and events that we had experienced. Again, Phyllis was overcome as we recalled everything that had happened during this perfect day and gave thanks to our God who has created it all for us to enjoy.

A lovely young woman stopped to chat and proved to be a very interesting person. She was from Calgary, and had, since the previous fall, been touring on her bicycle through various countries. She had been to Malaysia, Thailand, Hong Kong, Britain, and now was touring Europe, staying at hostels, homes of people that she had met, and at campsites.

During the next couple days, we did more sightseeing in the area and visited the Glacier Garden and Museum. We spent time at the Lion

Monument, a large sculpture on the cliff face of a lion with tears falling down its cheeks, which Mark Twain once described as "The Saddest Rock in the World".

On the following day, August 7th, Phyllis had her hair done (shampoo and set), at a salon, the first time she had enjoyed that luxury since before we left Pretoria two months prior. It was quite a treat considering she had been going to a hairdresser every week since long before I met her in 1974. In the evening we took a dinner cruise on the lake, passing the floodlit home of Richard Wagner, now a museum, and floodlit peaks of Mt. Pilatus. We were entertained by a ladies' fashion and folklore show featuring the three main Swiss cultures – German, French and Italian – with yodelling, dancing and music. It was a very pleasant evening. It rained most of the next two days.

While spending our final day in Lucerne, we visited the Museum of Transportation with exhibits from the horse-and-buggy days to spacecraft, including many bicycles, and trains that dated back to the time they were invented. They also had a planetarium, and, although the show presented was good, it did not compare to the MacMillan Planetarium in Vancouver.

We left Lucerne on Saturday, August 10th, nine days after our arrival, sure that the rest of our trip through Europe couldn't possibly compare, but there were many wonderful sights that followed. We drove through beautiful country sides and villages to Bern, where we walked about on the cobblestoned streets and browsed through antique and other shops. I hung around until the famous animated clock was scheduled to strike the hour, at which point a procession of little figures of men would emerge from a door on the face of the clock, march around a track, strike a gong loudly for each hour, and then disappear back into the door. It was quite a production and then the clock struck once at 1:00 p.m. I was disappointed, but timing can't always be great. I wished we had arrived an hour earlier.

We continued on through the mountains, forests and farmlands, to Interlaken, where we found a super campground at Manor Farm, and we were assigned a campsite only a few meters from the shore of Lake Thunersee. The area is called Interlaken because it separates the two lakes, Thunersee and Brienzersee. It is within the skiing area, with many ski lifts and chalets etc., nearby. Campers next door were a Dutch family with two well behaved children and a dear old (16 years) Springer Spaniel. After dinner at the camp's restaurant we stayed for the entertainment of music and singing, while we finished our bottle of fine Swiss wine.

After a day of rest, we left for Austria and the drive proved to be exhilarating to say the least. From Interlaken, we climbed gently for many miles, through Brienz and Meiringen, and then a steep climb through tunnels in the mountains. One particular tunnel was at least fifteen kilometers long, and I was concentrating so closely on the road, that I wasn't noticing the engine temperature gauge. Suddenly, the motor missed a couple beats and died. Panic gripped both of us as we realized the predicament we could find ourselves in. Moments later we coasted out of the tunnel and I was able to pull over to a widened-out area as the van stopped, safely off the roadway. I had no idea what the problem was, because all the gauges had returned to zero as soon the motor died. I turned off the ignition, so we sat there thinking what I should do; the last town we had passed was about twenty kilometers back down the mountain. I got out of the camper and tried to signal cars for help but no cars coming out of the tunnel even paused as they went by. After about twenty minutes, I tried the ignition and the engine started immediately and everything seemed normal. At that point I realized that the motor had only overheated and was actually designed to shut down when that happened instead of blowing a gasket.

We carried on, at a lesser speed, through hairpin turns and tunnels, past spectacular glaciers and tarns and over the Susten Pass, at 7,100 feet, stopping often to take photos of the wonderful scenery. The glacier ice was powder blue, not white or opaque, probably due to the high altitude. We stopped in a tiny Alpine Village where the item of interest for tourists was a crystal/quartz grotto. We carried on through the lovely ski resort of Andermatt, with its classy hotels and chalets, over the Oberalp Pass, and along the Vorderrhein River.

We camped near the small town of Flims-Dorf, high in the mountains, and, before dinner, we took a walk along a trail that was bordered by bright colored flowers and flanked by a rushing stream. We came to a wooden bridge and stopped at a bench to enjoy the beautiful moment. There were many large butterflies that fluttered about, showing off their many different colorful designs. One large butterfly of orange and blue pattern came and rested for a minute on Phyllis's knee.

We drove to a lower elevation and arrived at the border of Lichtenstein. Crossing was a hoot as we drove past the gate where an armed guard stood yawning and looking totally disinterested with us and life in general. He didn't move, so we drove on.

We were driving down a quiet road when we passed a group of soldiers at a military encampment, where they were engaged in war-games exercises, and we soon found ourselves among the combatants who were firing their guns and racing between trees on both sides of the road, ignoring us completely. An artillery shot rang out close by and I yelled "N'yia, you missed me", and Phyllis had to laugh because she couldn't decide if we should turn around and get the heck out of there or continue. What a welcome to Lichtenstein!!!

We stopped in the small city of Valduz, which contains the old cathedral and museum, and is overlooked by the wonderful old schloss which is the home of Prince Stephan and Princess Marie, whose family rules the principality. The little country/tax haven consists of 62 acres, has a population of 35,000 (exceeded by the number of companies registered), has the second highest GDP per capita in the world after Qatar, and has the lowest unemployment rate in the world at 1.5%.

An hour or so later we crossed the border into Austria, the 10th country in our tour of Europe. At the border, we were refused admission unless we could produce some particular form. After we turned around and drove back a little way, I recalled that at the factory when we picked up the camper, we were given some forms and papers. I rummaged about and located them. We returned to the border crossing and presented the forms to the guard, who took a green form from the pile that I handed to him. He made a sarcastic remark to me in German, and I replied quite crudely about where he could stick the form and we drove on. We spent a few hours in Salsburg, a marvelous old city, and visited the home of Mozart.

A few days later, we arrived at Vienna, and decided it was time to splurge, so we stopped at a Tourist Services booth on the outskirts and explained we wanted to stay at a nice hotel for four nights. We were directed to a small hotel, just a couple blocks from Schonbrunn Palace. As we checked in, I asked the desk clerk if there were any events that might interest us. She mentioned a concert that evening and phoned to make reservations for us to attend. A block from the hotel, we caught the underground to downtown and emerged near the concert hall where the Wien Walzer Orchestra was playing, and soprano Judith Bosch was singing, and we watched cameo performances by four members of the Vienna State Ballet. The hall was lined with large gold framed mirrors and life-sized oil portraits of the famous Viennese composers. As we listened to the beautiful Strauss compositions, we had to almost pinch ourselves to prove it was really happening. For the second time that day, I had to ask myself, "I wonder what the folks back in Meadow Lake are doing?"

We had bought a 72-hour transit pass for the U-Bahn underground system, so we had easy, fast, access to all points in the city. There were about four or five lines that all seemed to interconnect, and we emerged within a few feet of our every destination.

Early on the following morning, a tour bus picked us up and the very knowledgeable tour guide explained the significance as well as the identity of all the buildings, churches, and statuary, etc., as we travelled about the city. We stopped at Prince Eugen's Belvedere Palace, where the Russians signed a treaty to withdraw from Austria in 1955 in return for Austria's promise to remain neutral in future, like Switzerland. Then on to the Hapsburg's magnificent Schonbrunn Palace for a one hour tour of the area which contained exquisite paintings, sculptures, chandeliers and furnishings. The beautiful ceiling art had been restored. The public area houses a large ball room which is used for symphony concerts and other state functions. On PBS Television, I have watched many concerts that are performed on the grounds of Schonbrunn Palace. Mozart performed here at the age of eight. One area of the palace is set apart for Empress Marie Theresa's family apartment.

Because the Palace was only a couple blocks from our hotel, we detoured daily from the U-Bahn station, walking through the extensive grounds, admiring the landscaped estate with its statuary, flower gardens, ornamental trees, even a small zoo, etc., on our way home from sightseeing trips in the city.

In the evening, we went to dinner at a nearby Mandarin Chinese restaurant, and found the food to be some of the best we had ever eaten.

At first, it seemed odd to listen to Chinese people speaking German to each other, whereas in the Lower Mainland of B.C., they mostly speak in Mandarin or Cantonese.

On Sunday, we took the U-Bahn into the downtown district, emerging near the steps to St. Stephen's Platz, an ancient cathedral that is as beautiful inside as it is striking in appearance outside. We spent the whole day, walking about and taking pictures of structures and sculptures that were visible as we turned each corner.

We also went to the Imperial Palace and visited the Spanish Riding School which is the home of the famous Lipizzaner Stallions which are famous for their beauty, intelligence, and agility in performing complex dressage movements, despite their large size. Their popularity in appearances in shows all over the world is understandable. Unfortunately, the stables were closed because the horses were away, vacationing in the country.

We just missed the 3:00 pm tour of the State Opera House, but we were allowed to enter and have a look around the interior. It was quite remarkable.

Just across the street was the famous Sacher Hotel. Phyllis fulfilled another of her lifelong dreams, when I took her in and we were able find a table for two on the terrace and ordered slices of the original "Sacher Torte" with coffee. The torte was originated by the hotel's chef for the Kaizer when he visited the hotel many years ago. The chocolate layer cake features a coating, by hand, of apricot jam and is covered over with chocolate icing. It is the most popular cake in the world, and although the original recipe is still a closely guarded secret of the hotel, versions are available in most patisseries elsewhere. The service was extremely slow and when we were ready to leave, I had difficulty getting a waiter to give us our bill. After forty fruitless minutes attempting to get the attention of a waiter, I said to Phyllis that we would act as if we were leaving without paying. We had only moved about five feet from our table when the head waiter was at our side and seemed happy to provide a bill and accept payment. It proved to be the most expensive cake and coffee that I ever had, but Phyllis had enjoyed it, so that made the whole exercise worthwhile.

We spent the afternoon wandering around the parks which were a mass of rose beds and lily ponds and a series of vertical beds, which were about ten feet high, made of moss etc. enclosed in a wire cage and with flowers growing out all around, similar to a very tall hanging basket. They were quite unusual, but very pretty. There was one area around Mozart's statue that contained a large patch of lawn, in the center of which was a bed of red flowers in the shape of a musical clef.

We went back to our hotel for a drink and then dinner at a nice outdoor restaurant for snitzel (pork again) and salad and beer. Phyllis's heart fluttered when our waiter appeared to be the spitting image of Mel Gibson. On the way home, we passed a store catering to large lady's sizes, and it was having a sale. That fact was duly noted.

The next morning I took Phyllis back to the store and bought her about A1200 Shiillings worth clothes at a 30% discount. The styles were new and she wore the clothes at home for some time. I kept finding items that I liked and tossing them over the partition of the change cubicle that she was in, saying "here, try this on". The clerk just smiled as she passed me more items.

We postponed our departure because there was more to be seen. We visited the Votive Church near the University and the home of Sigmund Freud, Goethe's statue, the impressive City Hall and more parks. We had a final long walk around the grounds of Schonbrunn Palace. Now, we were ready to leave Vienna!!!

We left in a very smelly van. Someone had forgotten to remove some onions and nectarines from the little fridge which was left unplugged while we parked in the underground parkade of the hotel for five days. We drove through vineyards along the Danube and camped rough that night in a forest glade, no water, electricity or other facilities, near the castle at Ottenstein. The next day we crossed into Germany at Rohrbach and camped that night at a nice site on the bank of the Danube. We visited a Dutch couple who were on their way to Hungary for three weeks' vacation.

On the following day, we arrived in Munich and spent hours, it seemed, finding the camp ground we were seeking. We followed the one-way ring road and then turned onto the street shown in the tour book, and somehow missed the campground, and eventually ended up back on the ring road. Like I once mentioned, I'm a slow learner, because three times I passed the sign to Dachau, the Nazi concentration and death camp of Second World War infamy, 10 kilometers away, before I finally found the campground on a little side street. We discussed visiting Dachau, but decided it would be too depressing. We spent an extra day in Munich, sightseeing and window-shopping. Most memorable was the lunch of good German beer and something that I don't recall.

On Saturday, August 24th, we arrived at Bodensee, (German name), but known as Lake Constance in Switzerland, and checked into a fantastic campground at Lindau. It was only a block or so from the borders of Austria and Switzerland. When we had parked the camper and raised the top and got out to hook up our electricity, I announced loudly, "Hi, we're from Canada". Immediately, a Dutch couple across the lane came over to introduce themselves as John and Anne van Haeften. We invited them to join us for happy hour as soon as we were settled. They soon rejoined us and we had drinks with pate, cheese and crackers.

We were just cleaning up after dinner, when suddenly a big "Oompah" band started playing a polka at the biergarten on the patio, outside the camp restaurant, just about fifty yards away from us. John and Anne came by and asked us to join them in the beer garden. We had just sat down at a large picnic table and ordered beer when a young English couple, Keith and Laura, joined us, and two young German men followed. Just then the skies opened, in a torrential downpour, so John and I raced back to our camps for umbrellas while the women shielded the steins so the beer wouldn't get diluted. The band played on, only retreating to the meager shelter of the eaves of the bar and restaurant, to avoid filling the tubas with rain, the musicians standing in a long single line. What a wild and crazy evening, with everyone having too much beer, particularly Keith and I, but it was the most fun we had had in a long time. Keith was in the British Army and was stationed in northwest Germany, and Laura had come to spend his leave with him in Bavaria. The music and singing and the clinking of beer steins finally ceased at about one a.m.

On Sunday we were awakened by church bells which didn't want to stop, so we got up and had breakfast. Just after that the band returned at 10:30, and played a march while they paraded around the campground; then back to the beer garden for more polkas, etc., until after 1:00 p.m., during which time we had beer and junk food. We were finally able to hit the beach and somewhat recover during the late afternoon.

On Monday, we slept in until 9:30 then had coffee and cake with John and Anne. We invited them for happy hour drinks and snacks. About 7:00 p.m., while still enjoying happy hour, we were joined by Keith and Laura and about 10:00 p.m. we decided to pool what food we had and put on a barbecue, and had another drink or two. On Thursday, John and Anne asked us to go with them to Mainu, an island in Bodensee where Count Lennant Bernadotte and his wife, Countess Sonja, lived in their elegant Schloss with its beautiful chapel. The Island had been converted to a paradise with acres of flower beds and all types of trees in a marvelous display of landscape architecture. The Chapel was breathtaking with its beautiful stained glass windows and sculpted ceilings and interiors.

Arriving home that evening, we phoned Barbara to mail the letter to the tenants of our West End condo, giving notice to vacate because we had now decided to return to Vancouver in November as originally scheduled.

The next couple days were uneventful, except that we said farewell to Keith and Laura as he returned to his army base near Dortmund, and she went back to England to continue her college studies. They were a very nice couple and seemed to enjoy being with old folks. Or maybe, they just enjoyed partying.

John had recently retired from The Netherlands Air Force and they now operated a Bed and Breakfast home at Noordwijk, a sea side resort town about an hour's drive west of Amsterdam. When the Germans invaded Holland during the Second World War, they had billeted a number of troops at John's home when he was just a toddler. The Germans supplied some of their own food and took whatever food they wanted from the family, but the family were not allowed to share the German food. When the Canadian troops arrived to liberate the Dutch, they found a country of very scrawny adults and starving kids. John said he remembered standing by the road as the Canadian troops passed by and one of the soldiers stopped to give him a chocolate bar. John couldn't even remember ever having eaten chocolate previously. (The thought came to me that the Canadian soldier could have even been my brother, Lou, although Lou had probably already arrived a couple days earlier.) I guess it was many instances like that which caused such close bonds to form between the Dutch and Canadian people. Anyhow, John and Anne had, by this time, become our very good friends. John had a great sense of humor and Anne was a sweet lady, similar to Phyllis. They were both a few years younger than us.

The four of us took short trips into Switzerland for coffee and cake and into Austria to a forest high in the mountains where there was a large game farm featuring elk, boar, and other critters. We then attended a show by a couple naturalists who had a number of falcons, eagles and owls that were confined by netting in a huge cage. It was very impressive to see them swoop in to attack and catch prey (dead rodents, mostly) Far below we could see Lake Constance/Bodensee. It was another beautiful day with our new friends.

Having come to the camp ground in Lindau for one overnight, we were finally saying farewell ten days later. John and Anne asked us what our plans were after we shipped our camper van back to Canada from Emden. We said we planned to fly to England and rent a car and tour there for a week. They insisted that we must take the train from Emdem to Amsterdam where they would meet us and take us to their home in Noordwijk. We agreed.

Leaving Lindau, we crossed into Switzerland and followed the southern shore of Lake Constance, to France. One night we camped at a small town called "NoLay", which Phyllis found to be of sufficient interest to warrant noting in her diary, with the question, "How would they know?" While we were shopping at a small roadside market, Phyllis spotted a bottle of Chambolli-Moussigny, a wine that some rich boyfriend, before me, had impressed her with on a dinner date in Vancouver. It was quite a bit more than we were accustomed to pay in Europe. I agreed to buy it as she promised that we would save it for a really special occasion. We actually carried it around for more than a month, until we got to John and Anne's. When we opened it, we found it was disgusting, sour and full of sediment. Oh well, I tried!!!

We were now driving through France's Loire Valley with its beautiful chateaux and wine estates. We camped at several castles like Chambord which we toured for several hours. Its construction was started in 1519, during the Renaissance, by King Francois the first. His son, Henri the second, added the chapel. It was completed to the present status by Louis X1V and his architect, Mansart. The huge castle contains 440 rooms,

282 fireplaces (not nearly enough), and 84 staircases, and was filled with the most beautiful furniture and tapestries. It was used by a succession of kings, including Charles X, to entertain other royalty and as a "hunting lodge". It was also a temporary residence of King Luis XVl and Marie Antoinette. I was particularly impressed with the billiard table that Charles X had installed. The legs were intricately carved, overlaid with gold and the table looked to be just waiting for me to rack the balls and break.

That evening we camped in the front garden of the pretty Chateaux le Grenouillere at Suevres, and then moved on through the Loire Valley, and either passed by or stopped for a brief visit at Chateau Ambrois and Azay-le-Rideau on the Indre River. In the afternoon, we passed some homes that were built into the rock face of a mountainside. I believe they were actually caves, no matter what the dwellers called them. I think that some of the caves were used to store wine. We took a photo of the beautiful cathedral at Chemille. We camped at Nort-sur-Erdre and met some cheerful ex-R.A.F. types that were happy to meet some Canadians, since their unit had been seconded to an R.C.A.F squadron during World War Two.

The next day, Saturday, Sept 7th, we travelled through Portchateau and lovely countryside and finally reached the coast of Brittany.

While driving through a town, I had to stop behind a farm truck at a traffic light. The driver began waving at me and pointing downward and I knew from past experience that he was telling me that my headlights were on. I just waved at him. A moment later, he jumped out of his truck and came back to give me heck in French. I couldn't reply, so I just shrugged my shoulders and spread my hands out. He said something else and turning, he got back into his truck. He looked back, saw my lights were still on and then he got out of his truck again and was on his way back to deal with this idiot in the van with German license plates. Just before he reached me, the light changed to green and I tooted my horn and pointed at the traffic light. He hesitated and then the car behind me sounded his horn and the Frenchman walked back to his truck, shaking his fist, and cussing me in French as he drove on.

We were lucky to find a campground on an estate at Penistin, complete with swimming pool, etc., and all with very friendly English tourists as neighbours. Our campsite was next to the fence which ran along the low cliff that skirted the beach. What a beautiful campsite. In the ocean, just off the beach there was a commercial mussel farm, consisting of several long rows of posts embedded in the sand and with two or three long chains running between the posts, and, attached all along the chains were mussels growing and were visible at low tide.

On the next day, Sunday, we watched as hundreds of people appeared on the beach, all with buckets, and they proceeded to collect mussels. The sand, at low tide, extended out to a little rock island about a half mile off shore, and for all of the afternoon the beach was overrun with people, especially on and around the little rock island. Even an old car drove out there with a couple inside. Before dinner time, the tide started to come in and so I expected the people would start to return. No such movement. When the water reached knee-deep, some mussel pickers started to return but not many, although the car came back, pushing a wall of water in front, and with water over the floorboards. Most people came back through water up to their waists. The last to come in was a man with two little kids, one on his shoulders and the other hanging from his raised arm; with the other he carried his pail of mussels. The children appeared to be about 18 months and two years. No one else seemed to even be concerned. I had nightmares about that scene for years.

We thought we must have a feed of the local mussels so we went to a restaurant and ordered big bowls of mussels, done in a cream, wine and herb sauce. They were delicious, but I wouldn't risk my life or my children's lives to get a free bucket of them.

A few days later, leaving Penestin, we travelled through Vannes, where we took a walk through the "old town" with its ancient stone walls. We had lunch at a walk-down creperie; supposedly Brittany crepes are "to-die for". Phyllis commented that didn't hold a candle compared to my French crepes. After dinner at a restaurant that evening, we had dessert crepes stuffed with such mixtures as chocolate and various other fillings, and all submerged under Chantilly topping, I was ready to cry "uncle".

We received a phone call from the shipping company that we would have to deliver the camper van early to the dock at Emden on September 24th, for shipment to Halifax on the following day. That only left us two weeks to complete our sightseeing.

We left Beg-Meil for St. Malo. On the way, we stopped for coffee at the beautiful little town of Gromel and looked over the ancient church, with its stained glass windows and a very moving monument in the rose garden, commemorating the children and resistance fighters who were executed by the German occupation forces during the war, in reprisal for their resistance. We could see the many machine gun bullet holes in the walls of the church; and, on the memorial, were the names and ages of those killed. When we went into the patisserie for coffee there a cold silence in the room and people obviously were not enjoying our presence. I recognized the reaction because I knew that the people believed us to be German, based on our German license plates. I immediately announced that we were Canadians and touring Europe. Immediately there were smiles and warm greetings all around, and we were served our coffee and pastries.

We continued on through beautiful country side, passing through Quimper and St. Poriec to Dinan, an interesting old walled city that had little cobble streets that went off in all directions with pretty public gardens. It was situated where the Rance River Estuary meets the Atlantic. We found a campground at Le Petit Bois. We had just made ourselves comfortable at poolside, when neighbors from the next campsite approached. It was a Welsh couple, and I invited them to join us for a drink, which led to a few more. Feeling in a generous mood I took Phyllis for a dinner at the camp restaurant and we had another delicious meal of fresh mussels with a sauce of cream, wine and herbs. When we got back to our camper, our new Welsh friends, Mick and Shirley, invited us over for a drink (actually, two bottles of wine), and cheese and olives for snacks. Phyllis mentioned that she loved listening to Welsh men's chorus music. It just happened that Mick had several such tapes, so we listened to that beautiful music while Mick, a tattooed ex-navy type, told us many interesting tales.

We lazed around the pool and, after a happy hour with Mick and Shirley, we all pooled our supplies and had a smorgasbord as a late second meal, and more wine.

On the next morning, we headed for St. Malo, a very nostalgic experience as we walked about this ancient city which had now been almost totally restored. The old walled city had been bombarded by the Germans when they seized it, and then it was nearly destroyed by the Allies who were trying to get rid of the U-Boat pens that the Germans built there, just across the channel from England. The rubble was reused in the restoration and the results appear to be authentic. We walked around the parapets and the walls and through the narrow cobblestone streets and we imagined the city when it was known more for its pirates and buccaneers. We had breakfast in a terrace restaurant overlooking the old arched gateway and watched people passing through.

From St. Malo, we followed the coast to Mont St. Michel, and spent a short time admiring the magnificent castle on Mont St. Michel. Unfortunately the weather worsened and a mist rolled in which didn't help with the view or taking photographs.

From there, we turned inland and drove through lovely farmland until we reached Versailles in the late afternoon. We found a campground just off the Avenue de Paris, a very wide boulevard that ran from Paris right to the Palace of Versailles a few miles up a slight hill. Our French neighbors were in a small caravan and were a charming elderly couple who spoke excellent English and made us feel most welcome. They lived in southern France and were here to visit a daughter who lived in a nearby apartment.

Our neighbours, thinking we would have difficulty finding parking the next day near the palace, insisted on driving us right to the gate in the morning. We spent the day touring the enormous palace and even more enormous grounds.

For background, a brochure describes it as the "Transition from the Story of France's Showpiece Seat of Power to the Museum of the History of France."

The site began as Louis XlII's hunting lodge. His son, Louis XIV, expanded it and moved the court and government to Versailles in 1692. The next three French kings who lived at Versailles until the French Revolution each added improvements to make it more grand and beautiful. Each ruled for about twenty years. The French Revolution began in 1789.

In the 1670's, Louis XIV built the Grand Apartments of the King and Queen, and Hall of Mirrors, designed by Monsart, where the king held his grandest displays of royal power to impress his guests. (Phyllis and I were also impressed). The Chapel and Opera House were added in the next century by Louis XV.

The gardens and vast estate were developed, at various stages, and included the Trianon, which was a huge palace in its own right to accommodate visiting royalty and for a time was a sanctuary for Marie Antoinette when she wanted to have a break from the stress of living in Versailles. It is located a couple kilometers from the palace. The gardens of Versailles were enormous and intricate, with statuary all about. The canal was built in such a way that it appeared to be the same width through all of its distance that we could see.

The government seat was returned to Paris before the start of the Revolution, and the Palace became the Museum of the History of France under Louis-Philippe. Many rooms were converted to house new collections in later years.

Phyllis and I toured pretty much the entire palace and we spent some time in the room in which Napoleon Bonaparte was crowned Emperor of France, and also the bed chambers of Marie Antoinette. Marie Antoinette's bed chamber included a separate room with several chairs for her many gentleman callers. We could imagine it would be like a dentist's waiting room, except without the pain, when she would call out, "next!!" We had lunch and a coffee break in the palace. The Hall of Mirrors was spectacular with all its mirrors, crystal chandeliers, statuary, paintings and white marble.

In late afternoon we headed for home. Phyllis said "Let's walk, it's not far," and I agreed. So we walked down the Avenue de Paris, which was jammed with about six rows of traffic in each direction, and there were no lines to keep cars in separate lanes. About an hour and half and three miles of walking later, we dragged ourselves into our van, where Phyllis soaked her feet and treated her blisters. At about 6:45 we walked to the business area to find a restaurant, without luck, and just at 7:00pm when everything closed for the night, we were able to find a little deli to buy fixings for a cold supper.

The next morning, we caught a train, just outside the gate of the campground, and after a short ride, we got off at the stairs leading up to the entrance to the Louvre. We spent the entire day in the museum and saw the Mona Lisa, Michael Angelo's Winged Victory, the Venus de Milo, and dozens of other masterpieces that we had only seen in art books - by

Raphael, Tintoretto, Titian, Michael Angelo, de Vinci, and Botticelli's frescoes, and many others. We were drawn to the Egyptian Antiquities Section which included mummies in reconstructed tombs brought from their actual sites in the pyramids, old papyrus scrolls, friezes, jewellery, pottery, and utensils, etc. We returned to our camp utterly exhausted again. What a remarkable and memorable experience for this boy from Meadow Lake, and not finished yet.

The next day, Sunday the 15th, we drove into Paris early in the morning, before the traffic got too heavy, and visited the Arc de Triomphe, Eiffel Tower, Bastille, Place de Concorde, Champs de Elysee, etc., taking pictures all the way, and made our exit from Paris.

I was doing my own navigating and it was a surprise for Phyllis when we pulled into the beautiful little town of Clervoux that we had visited in June, and we had said we would like to return to. This time we stayed in the little hotel and dined in the dining room – a delicious gourmet dinner of poached salmon, scampi, an entrée of venison, dessert of crème caramel with chunks of fresh fruit, a good Bordeaux wine, coffee and liqueurs. The rain bucketed down during the night but it was clear in the morning. It was the first day of school so we sat over breakfast in the glassed-in balcony, watching the mothers walking their little ones to their first day of classes.

The next few days were uneventful until we reached Holland. There, we stopped for a couple hours at Xanten to watch workers at the anthropological digs and reconstruction site of an ancient Roman town with its amphitheatre and artifacts, etc. I believe that it is now complete and is one of the largest outdoor sites in the world, and is visited by more than a million tourists each year.

We continued towards the coast and stopped to tour the Het Loo Palace at Appeldoorn, one of the oldest Dutch palaces and where Queen Wilhelmina was born and raised. Her nursery was preserved and was on display. The palace was elegant – brass and ceramic lighting fixtures, mother-of-pearl tables, tapestries on the walls, lovely upholstery on the seating and charming four poster beds. We visited the gardens and one of the guards pointed out a maple tree that was donated by Canadian soldiers in appreciation of the care they received during the war when the Palace had been converted to a hospital.

At lunch in the palace, we were drawn into a conversation with three English folks who were part of a coachload of ex-paratroopers who had taken part in the famous Battle of Arnheim and were here to participate in a Re-union and Church Parade at the nearby military cemetery. Evidently, the ceremony was to conclude with the pipers leading the march from the chapel through the rows of graves in the beautifully tended cemetery, where a child, holding a rose, would be standing behind each cross. After The Last Post was played, the children would lay the roses on the graves. Evidently these were third generation kids, whose grandparents had started the annual tradition.

From Appeldoorn, we drove on to Friesland, through farmland with canals and locks on either side of the road. It was weird to be driving along and see the tops of boats and barges moving through fields, the water not visible to us. Cattle and sheep grazed contentedly with windmills keeping watch over them. Everything was so neat, clean and restful.

In late afternoon, we checked into a spotlessly clean campground at St. Soal on the shores of IJsselmeer, a huge lake that was created by a 32 km dam that was built on the inland sea, Zuider Zee, in 1932. At 1100 sq km, it is the largest lake in Western Europe. Fed by the rivers IJssel and Vechte, it provided storage of fresh water for domestic purposes and sports. While we were there, we saw hundreds of people windsurfing just yards off shore, zooming past, carried along by the winds that blew unimpeded from the North Sea. With so many wind surfers traveling at high speed back and forth across the surface, I expected to see many collisions but the surfers always seemed to be able to jump off into the waist deep water just in time to avoid a crash. We spent four days at that camp, just relaxing, going for walks and watching the wind surfers and kite flyers, and yachtsmen passing by on the canal, which started just next to the campground. We also spent time cleaning and packing our clothes and camper in preparation for shipping the van to Canada.

On September 24th, we drove through pouring rain to Emden, just across the border in Germany and delivered the van to the VW shipping agent on the docks. We took a taxi to the bahnhof and caught a train into Holland and after two transfers we arrived in Amsterdam, where our friends that we had met at Lindau, John and Anne, met us. That night we cuddled up in a nice bed under an eiderdown duvet and slept soundly.

The next day, we all went sightseeing through the lovely little resort town of Noordwijk, including a drive past the estate of the beer baron Heinekin. It was closely guarded, with security cameras all over as a result of the previous year's kidnapping and safe release of Heinekin. Also, Dutch Queen Beatrix is a close family friend and frequent visitor.

The next day, John and Anne's son, Patrick, dropped by with his wife and beautiful little daughter. It was easy to see why she was so pretty as Patrick is a male model and very handsome. Anne later showed us several pictures of him in magazines, posing with various products. We all went to Madurodam, an acre of parkland on which is built a landscape of miniature historic places, harbors, airports, etc., an interesting experience which we quite enjoyed. John and Anne left the next morning for the weekend at a resort in Belgium, a gift from their kids for their thirtieth anniversary. It was to be a surprise for Anne who was told they were going to her uncle's birthday celebration.

On the following day, we took the bus to Leiden where we spent hours strolling around and "window shopping" at the outdoor market, browsing through stalls of flowers, vegetables, fish, jewellery, clothing and leather goods, etc. On the way home, we chatted with a lady and her two cute little daughters. The kids howled with laughter when they heard me call Phyllis, "Honey", as they had never heard that term of endearment before. A few minutes later, a couple on the bus told us they were from Chilliwack, B.C. Small world, eh?

On the following day, I went for a walk by myself on the sand dunes and around the harbor. I met an old-timer who told me about the German occupation and the many concrete bunkers that still littered the shoreline. He also explained the large fenced off area which was restricted entry because of the likely presence of unexploded landmines. I entered one of the empty bunkers and looked out through the slits that allowed for strafing the beach or cannon fire at ships off shore.

The next day was our last day in Europe and John and Ann drove us to The Hague, past the beautiful embassies and the Queen's "working" palace, admiring the architecture and many monuments. We visited the harbor and watched as two Russian freighters were busy loading "used" cars. The cars kept arriving every few minutes and were quickly loaded onto the ships, and it struck me that they must have a large crew stealing cars and taking them aboard quickly.

We drove on to Amsterdam and after a one-hour cruise on the canals we drove past the Royal Palace, and around the square with its weird characters. John and I decided that no visit to Amsterdam would be complete without a stroll with our wives through the "Red Light District". The girls sitting or posing in the windows of their shops were lovely and looked healthy. The sex trade there is totally regulated with mandatory testing for diseases, health care and, without pimps to abuse the girls there seems to be no associated drug problem either, and the girls pay their income taxes like anyone else. The "peep shows" were interesting, to say the least.

When we got back to Noordwijk, we went to a waterfront restaurant and had a last feed of fresh mussels with a bottle of good wine. While we were eating, the wind picked up to nearly gale force and the rain poured down. What wonderful friends John and Anne proved to be. We promised to keep in touch with Christmas cards and birthday greetings which we both did for several years, and they promised to visit us in Vancouver in the following year, but they couldn't.

On the next morning, October 2nd, we flew to London and arrived just in time to catch our flight to Halifax. So ended our visit to Europe!! What a wonderful experience it was, and I remarked again, as I had every day for the last four months, "I wonder what the folks are doing back in Meadow Lake."

We checked into a B&B in Halifax, called the Heritage Inn, which was a bit tacky but it was only to be for a few days, so we decided to stay until our van arrived. On the 3rd, we spent a few hours arranging for insurance on the van for a month and got maps and info for our trip back to Vancouver. We went to the Heritage Properties Area (Halifax's equivalent of Vancouver's Gas Town), for a glass of Moose Head beer. Later, when we checked with the shipping agent, we were told that the car ferry carrying our van had been delayed a week and wouldn't arrive until Oct. 10th. Rats!!!

On Friday, the 4th, we wandered about, past the Lt. Governor's stately residence , churches, and heritage buildings, then the waterfront, getting a feel for the interesting port city and the citizens, who seemed to be a mixture of old-world Acadian, solid Scottish and modern sophisticated.

We then picked up a Chevy Corsica and took a drive through lovely fall foliage to Peggy's Cove. We walked out over the rocks and past the old Lighthouse as far as we dared. It was a beautiful and exhilarating experience. From there we drove south to Lunenberg, a port city that has a rich history. The sailing ships, Bluenose l and ll were built here, and the port has been the main fishing harbor on the east coast for the last hundred years. The area was originally settled by Germans and Acadians. In fact, on the day that we visited, they were celebrating Oktoberfest, and, in the restaurant that was recommended to us, the special was a German cuisine buffet. A few folks were dressed in traditional costume and there was a fireworks display at dusk. We enjoyed the dinner.

The next morning we checked out of our B&B and left for a three day trip to Cape Breton Island the Cabot Trail, past fishing villages, and well-kept homes and farms of the Mic-Mac First nation. We stayed overnight in a motel with a beautiful view of the Gulf of St. Lawrence.

We continued on the Cabot Trail from Cheticamp, through forest and mountains, all a mass of autumn colours, to Ingonish, then south past St. Ann, the Gaelic College, where in addition to academic subjects, the students are taught to become fluent in the Gaelic language as well as the step dancing and the fiddle and pipe music brought to Nova Scotia in the 1800's by their Scots ancestors. I took many pictures of the fall foliage and was amused when I got my prints back, one of the pictures was of a hillside and the entire picture was a mass of various colours with no visible sky or road or individual trees. It could have been a picture of a carpet.

We stopped for the night at Truro, and I stayed up past midnight so that I could witness the phenomenal Tidal Bore. When the tide starts to flow into the Bay of Fundy, the incoming flow meets the outflow of the river and the turbulence results in a roaring noise like none other, and the water seems to be boiling. It was raining and the wind was blowing through the entire time I was out there, and I came back into our room cold and wet and looking for a warm body to cuddle.

We got back to Halifax and checked into the famous Halliburton Inn and were shown to a room that Phyllis loved. It had drapes and bedspread of English Sanderson fabric, antique furniture and two "butterfly" chairs and good lighting from brass wall and table lamps. We returned the car, had lunch downtown and went back to our room for a relaxing afternoon before getting dressed for dinner in the Inn's elegant dining room. We enjoyed a gourmet dinner including a fine local Jost white wine. The hotel was originally the mansion of Brenton Halliburton, the Chief Justice of The Supreme Court of Nova Scotia. It and two adjoining buildings later comprised the Law Faculty of the University and, together, now, after further renovations, is the Inn.

We spent Tuesday to Thursday just killing time, visiting local attractions, etc., and on Friday we checked out for a few hours and then had to check back in when we learned the car ferry was in but our van wasn't unloaded; and, because it was the Thanksgiving weekend, the Health Inspectors wouldn't be working to clear the van when it was unloaded. We were stuck until Tuesday. What a mess this has turned into, and now we're not enjoying Halifax nearly as much.

We finally got away and travelled through New Brunswick into Maine and the northeastern states and came back into Ontario to visit the Niagara Falls, the first time I saw it, and I was quite impressed with it. It was too cold for camping and the campgrounds were closed for the winter. The scenic autumn colours were still prevalent but would soon cease as we travelled west. We went back down to Michigan and across to Montana where we crossed back into Canada and stopped to visit my niece, Diane and Gene Koopman, at their little ranch at Fort McLeod for a couple days.

Back in Vancouver, we stayed with Barbara and Joey in their apartment on campus at S.F.U. and arranged for our condo to be painted by David and had our furniture delivered. We visited the kids on the Island and had Christmas at Danny's.

Our camper - camped on the Rhine River

Spain - near Barcelona

Salou

Pool at Salou campground

Carrara Marble storage, Italy

Police station, Villars, Switzerland

Luzern

Cog railway up Mt. Pilatus

Phyllis with Alpen horn player

Mournful lion sculpture, Luzern

Furka Pass, Switzerland

Schonbrun Palace, Vienna

Schonbrun Palace, Vienna

Impatiens Planter

J. Elmer Benoit

River barge, Danube

Lindau, Germany

Mussel farm, Penestin, Brittany, France

Palace of Verseilles

J. Elmer Benoit

Palace of Verseilles

Hall of Mirrors, Palace of Verseilles

Cannon bunkers, Noordwijk, Holland

Chapter 25

COSTA RICA

The year 1992 was not as exciting as my first year of retirement, but it was nevertheless very interesting.

In May, I was honored by The Society of Management Accountants of B.C. by being awarded Life Membership, in recognition of my many years of service.

When J.J. was two years old, Danny and his wife, Kelly, separated and Danny kept J.J., placing him with Kelly's mother for day care, while Danny worked and then collected him for the evening and overnight.

We started the year with a three month visit to Yuma, Arizona, to spend time with family in the sunshine. On the way down, we spent New Year's with our good friends Joy and Noel Edwards in Portland, and were invited to a party with The Tea Cozy group of ex-patriate British ladies and their husbands, organized by Joy back in the 1950's. Many of the ladies were war brides, who married U.S. servicemen during World War Two and immigrated after the war.

When we arrived in Yuma, we wanted to rent a park model in a trailer court, and be close to my relatives, of which there were several in Yuma – brothers Emile and Lawrence, sister Mirelda, and cousins, Maurice Beaulac and Leslie Colleaux and their spouses. We visited our friends, Willard and Mary Myrfield from Port Alberni and they knew of a two-bedroom trailer that was available in their park and we rented that. The trailer park had a nice club house with pool tables and entertainment so we were able to take advantage of that, plus visit my family a few blocks away, for happy hour, and ponder daily, "I wonder what the folks are doing back in Meadow Lake."

We took frequent trips to two border-towns in Mexico that were close by. It wasn't exciting, but it was interesting, shopping for Mexican blankets, leather goods, liquor, and haggling with the shopkeepers who were always happy, even if they were prepared to give a fifty percent discount, and were overjoyed if a tourist paid the full price on the ticket.

During the winter we had Annemarie and a boyfriend, and then Joy and Noel, stay with us and we took side trips to the Grand Canyon and the beautiful Sedona area with its picturesque buttes of red sand stone that are featured in many western/cowboy movies, and to San Diego.

We also visited Tucson and Tombstone. Tucson was beautiful, while Tombstone was interesting. Tombstone was the site of the very famous shootout, popularly known as the "Gunfight at the OK Corral", which pitted a gang of outlaws who called themselves "The Cowboys", comprised of Billy Claiborne, Ike and Billy Clanton, and Tom and Frank McLaury, versus the lawmen, Virgil, Morgan and Wyatt Earp, and Doc Holliday. The actual gunfight lasted thirty seconds and took place in a small vacant lot, six doors from the OK Corral. In the fight, Ike Clanton and Billy Claiborne ran and were unharmed, but Billy Clanton and both McLaury brothers were killed. Of the lawmen, Virgil, Morgan and Doc were wounded, and Wyatt was not hurt. Two months later, Virgil was wounded and two months after that, Morgan was killed, both in ambushes by the two remaining Cowboys. Wyatt went after them and avenged their shootings.

The other really interesting place in Tombstone was Boot Hill, the local cemetery, a piece of mainly dead scrub brush with graves scattered about, mostly mounds of gravel and dirt with crude crosses and the odd weathered head stone, usually showing the name and a terse comment, such as "Murdered", "Hanged", "Hanged By Mistake", "Lynched", etc. One large grave marker listed four or five names, and the notation "Taken From Jail and Lynched." Another, my favorite, read "Here Lies Les More, Shot by a Forty-four, No Les No More."

The Myrfield's had relatives from England visit and they brought another couple, the Rivers, with them. We offered to let the Rivers stay with us for a week and they proved to be very compatible; they also enjoyed our happy hours. They asked us to visit them at their farm at Carlyle, in northern England if we ever were in their area, and we did so in about 1998.

One of our short trips into the grubby little Mexican border town of St. Luis Rey was particularly interesting. We had been walking about among the shops and I suggested we go into a little hole-in-the-wall diner on a side street for lunch. Some tourists who came out assured us the food was okay. We entered and found the only table was already occupied, so we climbed up onto high stools at a counter. There was storage in the counter from the kitchen side, so where we sat there was no recess for our knees. Behind the far end of the counter, was a very large fridge and a small stove, with the cooking surface about two feet above the ground, and the very large Mexican cook was squatted at it as he prepared food for the table of tourists, and all the time he was talking to a friend beside him. The cook called to ask what we wanted to eat and we ordered, along with two cups of coffee. The cook got up and brought us two chipped mugs and spoons, and a pot of hot water. He filled the mugs with boiling water, Phyllis's almost right to the brim, and he walked back to his stove. I told him that we had ordered coffee, so he just pointed to the counter and a jar of Instant Sanka Coffee. We helped ourselves, and then Phyllis asked for creamers. The cook slowly got up, went to the fridge and brought over a four liter jug of milk, and filled Phyllis's mug right to the brim. Phyllis looked at me and asked "How am I supposed to drink that without spilling." I pointed to a glass containing a bunch of straws, so she took one and proceeded to sip at her coffee. Right in front of us at a sink was a boy of about fifteen who was busy washing their few plates for the cook to serve the people at the table. He almost fell into his tub of dishwater, laughing to himself, as he watched Phyllis sipping her coffee with a straw and made a comment to the cook in Spanish, about the "Loco Gringo". That remark in Spanish was fully understood and appreciated by both Phyllis and me, and we had many laughs over it.

When we returned to Vancouver, we just had a couple weeks before we took off in our camper for a tour of B.C. We visited the Kootenay's,

Okanagan, Prince George, Barkerville, and Fort St. John. We intended to drive north and tour The Yukon and Alaska, but when we were camped at Dawson Creek other tourists told us the AlCan Highway was in bad shape due to frost damage, and that our van was bound to be damaged by stones from trucks and buses that were on tight schedules and had to go faster than the road conditions warranted. In Fort St. John, we visited my cousin Pat, from Leask, who was living with a lady and looking in bad shape. After his wife was killed in a car accident, his life went downhill and he started drinking and lost his furniture store. Both of his beautiful children were grown up and had moved away. It was nice to see him, though, and we had a few laughs together.

We decided to take the car ferry from Prince Rupert to Port Hardy, and that proved to be a lovely experience, with gorgeous scenery on both sides of the ferry for much of the trip.

In October, we put the Westfalia Camper into storage and flew to Costa Rica. We had got the name and address of a pensione, or apartment hotel, in San Jose, from a guide book and sent a deposit. But when we arrived, we found the place had closed several years previously. We went to a hotel and the next morning, I bought a local English language newspaper and found a couple furnished apartments that were available. We took a taxi to one and found it to be unsuitable. The second one I called proved to be just what we hoped for. The owner picked us up and drove us to a gated fourplex, surrounded by a high, secure fence. The furnished apartment had two bedrooms and included cable TV, telephone, and daily maid service. It was located in a nice area, of San Jose about three miles north of the downtown center. About two blocks south was a nice shopping area with a bank, pharmacy, restaurants and grocers. The currency of Costa Rica is the colon, but most people earn and spend US dollars.

We enjoyed the maid who was named Layla, aged about forty. She had two good looking and well behaved teenagers and a husband that looked like a movie star and worked as a carpenter. Layla came in every day to clean, and washed whatever clothing that we had worn the day before, hung it to dry in the open patio at the back, and ironed the previous day's laundry. She even ironed my underwear. When I held them up for Phyllis to see, she actually snorted and made a rude comment. Layla didn't speak

English, so I would try to make myself understood with the aid of my English-Spanish dictionary. When Phyllis tried to tell Layla something that I had done in fun, I would stand behind Phyllis and signal that she was a loco gringo and was B..S..ing, which would cause Layla to crack up.

I went to a street market about two blocks away, every Saturday to shop. The mandarin oranges were 10c each, blood (red) oranges were 5c, large pineapples 75c, large (about 18" long) papayas 75c, little bananas that tasted as sweet as honey, were 5-10c, and large mixed bouquets of fresh, long stem flowers were 50-75c. There also were various types of vegetables as well as meats, fish, and eggs. I never bought meat or fish at that market, but I bought all the other foods for a week, two large shopping bags full, for about fifteen dollars. Phyllis would spend a couple hours making a huge bowl of fresh fruit salad and then would add more fruit later in the week. Once, when I was shopping, I bought a couple choyotes. Not knowing what they were, fruit or vegetable, they looked good, were green and about the size of a large apple and with one end puckered. When I got home, I asked Layla how to cook them. She tried for a minute to explain, then reached for a fry pan and proceeded to demonstrate. She cut the choyotes into cubes along with yellow onions and seasoned it, fried it, and served it to us. That established it as a cheap starchy vegetable of somewhat bland flavor but could be substituted for turnip or squash. Another tourist told us of planting a choyote seed in her back yard and the resulting vine grew about twenty feet long, up and along the fence into a tree, with tons of choyotes all along. She thought she would sell them, but people laughed at her, saying you can only get five cents for a big one and besides, everybody grows their own.

We often purchased a barbequed chicken from a little shop near our apartment, and they had the most unusual and delicious flavor, being barbequed over an open fire which used dead coffee bush branches as fuel.

We were impressed with the excellent health system. The doctors are trained in the finest colleges in Europe and America, and after their training is complete, they return to Costa Rica and serve their own people for a pittance. Phyllis went to a doctor for something like the flu and then to a dentist for a filling and both times the cost was twelve or fifteen dollars. She then went to a heart specialist who gave her an E.C.G. and spent three hours consulting with her and gave her a prescription, all for thirty dollars.

The funny part of that story was that when we went to the pharmacy with the prescription, the pharmacist told her to come into the storeroom at the back of the store so that he could give her the injection. She went into the storeroom and was directed to a kitchen chair near the far wall and noticed that there was a young man working among the cartons a few feet away. Phyllis was expecting to get a shot in the arm, but the pharmacist insisted it had to be done in her hip. She was directed to lift her skirt and lower her panties enough to allow him to give her the injection there. The young chap working nearby, politely turned his back, but couldn't conceal the grin on his face.

Several days each week, we took the bus (fare was ten cents) down town, and we would spend some time in the square looking over crafts that were offered for sale, and listening to various little groups of musicians under the trees. Some of the groups were quite good, at least the sound was happy and the songs were uplifting.

While downtown we bought fresh roasted coffee from a little factory that used locally grown coffee beans, and we were able to buy it still hot from the roasting process. It was delicious and we later brought home about ten pounds of it in our luggage. Lucky for us, when we arrived home, the customs agent didn't ask us to open our cases, because there was no way we could have explained that mouth-watering aroma of the fresh coffee beans.

We ate lunch at the MacDonald's restaurant downtown a few times and found the beef patties were tough but the chicken was tasty. It was unusual, though, to have a guard armed with a rifle, at the door, watching for possible trouble. Mind you, that didn't compare to visiting the bank when I wanted to draw some cash, and found at least four armed guards in the bank and two more outside the door.

There was an excellent museum in San Jose that displayed beautifully carved items and art work that dated from ancient empires in the area.

Annemarie came to visit for a week at Christmas and we spent a few days at a lovely resort on the northwestern coast in the Amarinda area. I recall that after we checked in and were on our way to our rooms, a voice greeted me with a Spanish accent, "Holla", and when I looked about I didn't see anyone. As I walked on, the voice was closer and more insistent, "Holla,

Holla", I stopped again and looked about and then noticed a beautiful parrot on a stand. Sheepishly, I replied, "Holla". The bird's wings had been clipped so it couldn't fly and it was dependent on people to lift it from its perch, but was otherwise capable of walking from table to table and managed to climb up onto a chair and then onto the table. It was pleasant, but it often became annoyed when someone in the bar refused to share their drink.

The bar and restaurant were open-air with just a roof overhead and cement floor, and most of the tables were under trees with just flagstones on the ground. A low, rough rock wall separated the eating and drinking area from the beach. In charge of the entire area, it seemed, was a bull iguana that had a harem of some six females and their young. The iguanas spent most of their time sunning themselves on the rock wall. In the periphery were about four bachelor iguanas that were constantly trying to steal one of the females. This necessitated that the old male maintain a constant vigil. As one of the bachelors got too near, the old male would throw himself into a chase, and there would be the loudest racket as they raced across the flagstones as their claws slipped and scratched as they tried to turn, back and forth across the yard. Diners just raised their feet as the iguanas scooted by.

When we returned from the coast, I rented a car for a few days and we went to visit a butterfly farm. The many varieties of butterflies were beautiful. We also visited a park that featured many varieties of orchids. Such beauty!!! We also drove to an area at the northern end of San Jose, where two volcanoes were erupting, although not violently, just a constant bubbling out of molten lava.

On January 15th, 1993, Holly gave birth to her little girl, Megan, in Surrey, BC.

On two Sundays, Francisco, our landlord, and his wife took us to their country club, about twenty miles north of San Jose, where we attended a church service followed by lunch and then a few hours of entertainment. From the grounds, it was possible to see both the Pacific Ocean and the Caribbean Sea. In the restaurant and bar was a small dance floor, and I went to watch the couples dancing. It was real Latin dancing, like you see in ballroom competitions, and I was very impressed with their graceful movements.

Just after Christmas, we attended a classical concert at the Louis Ferre Performing Arts Center, a state-of-the- art Opera House which seats about 1900 and has marvellous acoustics. The production is heavily subsidized by the government and the star (in this case it was Jessie Norman, a famous opera singer), charged only a small fraction of her normal fee. So, there we were, in the fourth row, just behind the President of Costa Rica and his party, and, when she moved to our end of the stage, Jessie stood no more than ten feet away. The concert was magnificent, and it only cost six dollars for each ticket.

In late January, our three months' visas expired and we were forced to leave the country for three days. I talked to Phyllis and we decided that the handiest would be a short trip to Panama. However, the travel agent talked me into going to a resort at Ila San Andreas, a tiny duty free island in the Caribbean, owned by the country of Columbia. It was a miracle that the pilot even found the island it was so small, about 22 square miles, including cays, outer cays, reefs, atolls and sand banks.

The resort was not bad considering the economic condition; tourism was their only income and the small island's population had to subsist on the crumbs from medium income people like us who were not that much better off. The meals were edible but not exotic, and the water through the pipes was salt water from the ocean, resulting in all of the plumbing fixtures being badly corroded. Swimming in the pool left your body coated with a salty crust, and having a salt water shower didn't much help. Many of the employees, from waitresses to maids to waiters in the lounge, asked us to sponsor their emigration to Canada, because they saw no future in San Andreas. Other than that, we found most of the people to be happy, the children were clean and well cared for and the small business community was doing a brisk trade in duty-free goods.

One afternoon, Phyllis and I were sitting in our room when she noticed two young men that were painting the outside wall of the third floor wing opposite our unit. One was standing on the railing to reach the top of the wall with his roller, while the other was sitting on the railing with his legs dangling over the outside. Neither was wearing a safety harness. Phyllis waved her arms to signal that he was in danger. The young painters took that as a signal to perform all sorts of stupid acts of daring, like standing on one foot on the railing and walking back and forth. We finally closed the drapes before one of them could kill himself.

The seventy two hours passed soon enough and we returned to San Jose. Before we left San Andreas, we noted that the waiting room of the airport now contained huge mounds of cartons containing TV's, microwaves and other items of electronics, appliances, etc., that had been purchased in the duty free shops and were destined for mainland Columbia. It amounted to several planeloads by itself. Phyllis had bought some perfume and I had picked up a lovely Pierre Cardin tee shirt.

Back in Costa Rica, we decided to visit the jungle on the Caribbean side and booked a three day stay at Tortuguero. We caught a small bus that took us down rough roads to a flat area where there was a pier on the river and a waiting flat bottom boat that had a sun screen over the top. It carried about twenty people. We took our seats for a slow ride of about an hour and a half. The river was a couple hundred yards wide and sparsely lined with trees at the start but gradually became jungle. High up in the trees we saw a couple sloths, doing what they usually do – nothing - but they do it in very slow motion. As we got further into the jungle, we were entertained by howler monkeys that made quite a racket.

The rough camp contained three or four small cabins and a small lodge. Among the seven or eight guests were four old buddies from university who now lived in various countries but got together every year for a stag holiday, as chosen by one of the group in turn. They were middle aged and had a ball, visiting exotic places, each man trying to pick a more interesting and exciting place.

One of our excursions into the jungle was on a small flat bottom boat carrying four passengers plus the guide and the boat operator. We slowly sailed through a narrow waterway, about fifteen feet wide, with trees, resembling mangroves, growing right to the shorelines. The tree roots exuded a black dye into the water, making it impossible to see below the surface. The guide cautioned us not to put our hands into the water, because if we did, we would soon find we had no flesh left on our hands due to the thousands of piranha fish in the river. As we slowly sailed along we were serenaded by several howler monkeys in the surrounding trees, annoyed at our invasion of their territory and were shaking the branches.

A Jesus Christ lizard dashed across the surface of the stream, so called because the 15-inch long reptile walks on water; actually it dashes across the surface with its webbed feet.

The most interesting display was when the boat stopped near a nest of caymans on the shore. The guide produced a bag of bread crumbs and tossed a handful into the water. The water resembled a boiling cauldron as thousands of piranhas all tried to get a bit of bread. We watched as the three or four caymans slithered into the water. The guide then tossed another handful of crumbs into the water with a repetition of the frenzied scramble by the fish, but this time there was also the sound of crunching as the caymans seized the preoccupied piranhas and had their own feast. Apparently, the piranhas can elude the caymans, except when they are distracted. Otherwise, while we were there, we saw several types of monkeys, sloths, snakes, birds and unusual vegetation.

Later on, we spent 10 days at a resort on the southern Pacific coast. We had a bit of good luck in that adventure. I had found a resort in the area of Puerto Quepos and we caught a privately operated bus to the little town. The two young Americans operating the relatively new bus service were very friendly and helpful and we were the only passengers. The one man asked us where we were staying and when we arrived, they drove us right to the motel. He said he didn't think we would be happy with the accommodation, so he walked into the place with us and when we entered our room, it was definitely not fit to stay in, so he said he knew of another, better place. We drove a couple miles on and stopped where a lady that he knew was renting a few suites in a large house. The lady lived in a separate house on the same property. Our friend from the bus spoke to the lady and arranged for us to move into a lovely one-bedroom suite on the following day. We climbed back onto the bus and drove on a mile or so to a resort, which we walked through to a neighboring house on the beach where the bus operator introduced us to an American engineer (who looked like he could be Sean Connery's identical twin) and who had several bedrooms that he allowed anyone to use – just clean up after yourself. The room was rent-free but we left him money for more beer and to wash the sheets. On the following day we moved into our rental suite for several days of tropical heaven. The suite was just off the beach, and we spent hours just relaxing on the sand with only a few dozen people nearby.

We shopped for a few items of food for breakfast and lunch and walked to a restaurant about eight blocks away for our dinners. The restaurant served excellent food and we enjoyed the "catch of the day" which was a salad and a fish, complete with the head and scales still attached, just gutted, usually a sea bass, which had been deep fried and was served fresh from the vat of boiling oil. The fish was about sixteen inches long and was arc shaped from the deep frying, and protruded over both ends of the dinner plate. To my surprise, it was delicious and it was easy to remove the skin and scales.

There was a nature park nearby which we visited, and, besides seeing beautiful orchids growing wild, as well as other exotic flowers and plants, we were fascinated by the many enormous blue butterflies, which measured at least six inches in wing span. The beach was the nesting place for a particular species of large turtles which came ashore at night to lay and bury their eggs, and I resisted the urge to observe the event, preferring to sleep rather than watch such a private matter (my joke).

I found a very amusing enterprise that took place on the beach. A man passed up and down the beach during the day with a cart, selling his version of "slushies". On his cart was a large block of ice, partially sheltered from the sun by a small canopy, and several bottles of flavored syrup. He had a small metal scraper with a serrated edge that he used to scrape ice off the block into a Styrofoam cup, and then sprinkled a bit of syrup over it, and sold it to people on the beach. I noticed as I walked past his cart that the cups had been used and had been washed (I think), because some were quite scarred and looked like they were being re-cycled, and not for just the first time.

Before we left the apartment in San Jose, we gave whatever items we had purchased for the apartment, mainly new pots and pans, to Layla. On our last evening, Layla invited us to come to her home for dinner, about five blocks away. Just as we arrived at her house, there was a sudden downpour and as we were introduced to Layla's husband and her mother, the two teenage children translated for us, and Layla made the comment that she hoped the rain would stop before it got late. I replied "Yes, because if it doesn't, I'll have to sleep with the Grandmother", to which the old lady just about fell on the floor in laughter. The evening went well and the meal was tasty, even though their custom was that guests were served and ate alone while the family stood by and watched us; the family had already eaten before we arrived.

We arrived home in the middle of April, just in time to file our income taxes.

Barbara met us at the airport and told us that my brother, Emile, had passed away on the previous day. We left the next day, with Margie, for Penticton and spent three days there. That gave us an opportunity to visit several members of the family, including my niece, Anita, who I hadn't seen for several years, as she was living in California.

Chapter 26

CANADA - US:
1993/94

We returned from Costa Rica in April, 1993, and after visiting the family on Vancouver Island and relaxing in our condo in the West End, we took off in July for another lengthy trip in our Volkswagen camper van, across Canada, south to Florida, and across to Texas, where we intended to spend the winter in Corpus Christie.

We stopped in the Okanagan to visit Mirelda and Frank and Julia and to attend a sales pitch for a timeshare at Winfield. The salespeople were very good at their job and we bought a time share for one week every second year at Labour Day, and received a gift of a free week at a resort in Freeport in the Bahamas in September. About two years later, the bottom fell out of the timeshare business and the value of our timeshare unit dropped by about sixty percent. The time share would expire in 2035.

Danny and Tami welcomed their new daughter, Jordyn, in June 1993.

We timed our trip to allow us to attend the 25th wedding anniversary in Saskatoon of Basil and Sally Ciepliski, (my niece), in July, and visit Lawrence and Doreen at Emma Lake in Saskatchewan. From there, we went into Manitoba where we camped for a couple days in Duck Mountain and Riding Mountain parks. We also stopped overnight at Dauphin, northwest of Winnipeg, and had dinner in a restaurant operated by a Ukrainian couple. We asked the lady to bring us a selection of their food, and she obliged by laying out a feast of various sausages and perogies, etc., followed by pastries. She then sat at our table and described their family history and brought out several photograph albums to show off their children in their costumes that they wore in various Ukrainian dance competitions, and their many awards and trophies. It was a very interesting evening, and the lady was so pleasant that we stayed much longer than was necessary and we gained more information than we needed or expected.

We took the Trans-Canada Highway through northern Ontario and stopped at a campground in Kenora, where we met a young Swiss couple that were travelling in a motorhome to Vancouver. We made suggestions of places they might enjoy visiting. As we left to return to our van, the man insisted that we accept a bottle of wine and a Swiss Army knife as a token of their appreciation.

We stopped for a few days in the Algonquin Park and then proceeded to Ottawa via North Bay. We visited the Parliament Buildings, including the Senate chambers where, as we expected, nothing was happening.

We stayed for a couple days at a campground on the outskirts of Montreal and had an opportunity to take a guided bus tour of the city as well as explore a good part of the downtown area and various tourist destinations, like the still-unfinished Olimpique Stadium.

We also visited the historic places in Quebec, but we took off after a few hours when we were not well received and even the gas station attendant was rude when we were unable to communicate in French.

We then proceeded along the south shore of the St. Lawrence and around the Gaspe Peninsula and we enjoyed the peaceful countryside and the easy life. Even sitting on a rocker swing on the bank above the St. Lawrence at a motel in the evening was very pleasant.

We then followed the coast through New Brunswick till we arrived at the ferry to Prince Edward Island, and spent a couple days on the Island. We were not terribly impressed with P.E.I., which didn't offer much besides a tour of Anne of Green Gables house, which we skipped.

Back on the mainland, we again drove the Cabot Trail, and enjoyed it, although it was too early for autumn colours. We continued to Sidney, and arrived at the Newfoundland Ferry terminal, at about five o'clock in the afternoon. We purchased our ferry tickets and then asked an attendant if there was a good restaurant nearby. He directed us back out of the terminal and to a seafood restaurant on the beach a couple blocks away and cautioned us to be back by 7:00 pm for the entertainment, a Ceilidh (pronounced kay-lee, and means party). We then had a fantastic dinner of fresh lobster and returned in time for the show in the terminal parking lot. The entertainers were a guitar playing singer/MC, a bass player/singer, a lady who sang and played accordion, and a girl of about fifteen who played fiddle while dancing jigs and other Scottish dances, while all the while she beamed the sweetest smile. The MC was a good entertainer and had hundreds of Newfie jokes which kept us in stitches.

We were able to use the washrooms and showers in the morning, after we were awakened by ferry worker and we boarded at about 7:00 am, for the 12-hour trip to the eastern end of Newfoundland. The dinner special we ordered was a "Jiggs Dinner", and consisted of beef, cabbage, turnips, and large pieces of carrots, all boiled together. It is a traditional Sunday dinner in Newfoundland, and reminded me of a favorite meal of mine that my Mom served on the farm. Some American tourists at the next table complained loudly about it, but I guess that not everyone has exotic tastes. We arrived in St. John's while it was still dusk and found a campsite in a city park in the downtown area.

We thoroughly enjoyed our stay in Newfoundland and visited Signal Hill, where Marconi received the first transatlantic wireless transmission from his station in Cornwall, England, on Dec. 12, 1901. Fortifications have been located on the hill at the mouth of the harbor since the 17th century, and the Americans manned cannons on the hill during World War Two, when Newfoundland was still not a province of Canada.

We travelled westward, mainly along the northern coast, and that allowed a visit to Bonavista, where we went to a church supper of fish and other local food. Unfortunately, we arrived toward the end and, after, paying for our meals and gradually moving along a line that started in the parking lot, we finally arrived at the counter to find that there were only two broken crab cakes and a couple bread rolls left, and we had to take them or go hungry. Just off shore, we could see icebergs.

We found the area around Gros Morne Park near the west coast of Newfoundland was very scenic and we drove north along that coast road for several miles before turning back to Port aux Basques and the ferry back to Sidney. Actually, Gros Morne reminded me a bit of Ayres Rock in Australia, in that it looks like a huge nearly bare rock placed in an otherwise mostly deserted wilderness.

When we arrived back in Sidney, we headed back to the Canso Causeway on Cape Breton, but a storm and darkness were both approaching and we pulled off the road into a clearing under the trees. That night we had difficulty sleeping as the storm was actually the fringe of a hurricane that had caused quite a lot of damage along the eastern coast of the United States. The wind bounced our van around quite a bit.

We then drove into New Brunswick, stopped to buy our medical insurance for the next several months, and headed south into the United States. We left the freeways, preferring to take more scenic and slower routes, so we headed for Bar Harbor and found it to be a beautiful area, including the nearby Acadia National Park. As our campsite was very high up with a view of the Atlantic Ocean, we stayed for a couple days, just relaxing and driving to the many interesting and scenic spots. On the hillside, just below our campsite was a big patch of ripe wild blueberries that we took full advantage of.

Back on the road, we headed south again and after a couple hours, we found that we were several miles from the shoreline, so I turned left on a good road and soon reached the shore. I was about to turn right, when Phyllis asked me why I was turning the wrong way, and I should go left. I asked her what the body of water in front of us was, and she replied it was the Atlantic. I asked her then, if she could visualize a map, what direction we must be facing. She was so confused that she still believed that I was going back to Canada, and I surely would be sorry that I didn't turn around. After driving around several corners and going in different directions, she finally decided that she was right and I was now going the correct direction.

We drove on secondary highways for the most part, enjoying the countryside. We contemplated going into New York City, and actually phoned Edith, our housekeeper in North Vancouver and Port Alberni. She was now working at a nursing home in Queens, and wouldn't be available, so we left a message and drove on into Pennsylvania.

We found the sweetest campground on Chocolate Avenue in Hershey and stayed for a couple days, touring the surrounding area. (No, I didn't go swimming in a pool of melted chocolate, although the thought intrigued me.)

We did take a trip to a town just to the south, called Intercourse. This was an Amish community which catered to tourists and they were doing a roaring business. The name "Intercourse" refers to the junction or uniting of two rivers in the town. The small factories were busy producing furniture, using all home made products such as wooden dowels instead of nails, and the workmanship was most impressive. The furniture would last a lifetime. The women were busy making patchwork quilts and other items like baking and canning. As you probably already know, they are a sect of the Mennonite Christian Religion and the people dress in an old style such as long dresses, black suits and hats, and travel by horse and buggy. They don't have such items as televisions and radios or other electrical appliances. They are anti-war and many don't even take part in the various benefits such as government pensions.

We went to an Amish restaurant in a farmhouse at the edge of town for an early dinner. We paid a flat rate of fifteen dollars and were shown to one of several long tables and they started bringing the food, home style, where you take as much as you want. After a delicious soup, we were brought a platter of various meats, and bowls of potatoes and vegetables, home-made bread and butter. It was delicious and we stuffed ourselves. They then offered us a choice of desserts. I ordered the home-made bread pudding and it tasted great. Phyllis ordered Shoo-Fly Pie which she had never tasted, but was intrigued by the name. When it came, she took one bite and almost gagged. As she passed it on to me she said, "Here, I'm sure you'll enjoy this." I found it to be only about three times as sweet as straight sugar. It was made with molasses and I couldn't distinguish any other ingredient. Even I couldn't eat it all.

Before leaving Pennsylvania, we visited the Civil War battlefield of Gettysburg and took a tour of the entire area. I believe that we rented sound equipment which recounted, as we drove along, the sequence of events throughout the battle. It was a very sobering experience for both of us.

We drove down through the Blue Ridge Mountains, and along a highway which followed the tops of the mountains. The mountains have a maximum elevation of about 2,000 meters, and are generally covered by forest. It was a pleasant drive and we looked down onto the Appalachian plain. We visited Monticello, Virginia, the home of Thomas Jefferson, now a museum. Thomas wrote the Declaration of Independence in 1776, served under George Washington, and then defeated John Adams to become the third president of the United States in 1800.

We then proceeded to Washington and toured the Arlington Cemetery, where we visited the grave of John F. Kennedy and row upon row of graves and observed the Pentagon nearby. From there we crossed the Potomac and spent a couple hours driving around the White House, Smithsonian Institute and various memorials, etc. Leaving town was a little scary for Phyllis. I made a wrong turn and ended up in what looked like a rough part of town. I was about to stop by some men who were sitting on their stoop drinking beer and ask for directions, when Phyllis screamed, "Don't you dare stop here, we'll both be killed." So I carried on down the street; I looked back and the men were laughing their heads off. I was able to retrace my route and found a highway sign directing us eastward out of town.

We camped in Delaware and on the following day drove across a seventeen mile bridge over Chesapeake Bay. The bridge was about eight or ten feet above the surface of the water and resembled a causeway. We spent an overnight in Virginia Beach and then, at Myrtle Beach, we found a nice campground and spent a couple nights there. We were on the coast line and as we walked on a path, next to the water, we could see alligators watching us. We took a side trip inland for a few hours and found it to be a most peaceful interlude, with tree lined country roads and pastures with beautiful horses and elegant homes.

In Georgia, we were driving down a mostly deserted highway through the bayous and I noticed a snake, about five feet long, crossing the road. It was too late to evade it and I ran over it. Looking back in the rear view mirror, I saw the snake almost stand on its tail before falling back onto the road. We stopped at a roadside café a few minutes later and we went in for a coffee. The only other customers in the place were a young black man with his little girl of about two years of age. She was beautifully dressed and the man asked if Phyllis would take his daughter to the washroom. While they were gone, I asked the man what kind of snake it might be and if I would have killed it. He laughed and said it was probably not a poisonous type and that I certainly would not have killed it. Later, Phyllis told me the little girl had held her hand going to the bathroom and had lifted her arms for Phyllis to lift her dress and pull down her panties, then again to pull them up and straighten her dress before taking Phyllis's hand and returning to her daddy, never saying a word, and without even for an instant losing eye contact with Phyllis, and with the same beautiful smile on her face. It was truly the face of an angel and Phyllis was moved almost to tears.

We arrived in Florida a few days before our cruise to the Bahamas, and stayed at a campground near a wildlife safari park. It was somewhat reminiscent of our visit to the Krueger Park in 1991, in that we could hear the animals during the night, but overall we were disappointed at the relatively close confines of the fences, and spent only about an hour in the park.

Our gift for buying the timeshare included a free two-day stay at the Hyatt Hotel in Fort Lauderdale and a one-day stay on our return, one-day cruises to and return from Freeport, as well as the one-week stay at a resort. It went well and the cruises amounted to about eight hours each way. It was a nice break to be able to stop somewhere for a whole week after being on the road for nearly two months.

On our return to Fort Lauderdale, while we were sitting in the lobby waiting for a sudden heavy shower to clear, we chatted to a group of three or four ladies who were just waiting for their bus to take them to their cruise liner, doing the same visit to Freeport that we had returned from the previous day. They asked what our plans were for the winter, and when we mentioned that we were expecting to spend it in Corpus Christie, they were horrified. One of the ladies, named Gladys, who could have been Marilyn Munroe's twin, gave me her card and said, "When you've seen Corpus Christie, give me a call and I'll fix you up with a nice place in a great trailer park in Desert Hot Springs in California."

With that we took off, not expecting to ever see them again.

We drove inland in Florida and stopped for a couple days at Disney World at Orlando, and the Epcot Center and other attractions. We also spent a lovely night at a little place that I believe was called Silver Springs, where a small lake was nestled in almost jungle growth, and the spring water was so clear and pure, that I still remember how it sparkled.

Leaving Orlando, we travelled westward and we suddenly passed through a swarm of love bugs, so called because, during their fertilization process, the pairs of bugs attach themselves to their mates and hover in mid-air in huge swarms. The bugs seem to be totally covered by a sticky coating. I got out of the van to see what it was and immediately I was covered with the bugs, so I quickly got back inside. Driving through one swarm seemed to pretty much coat the camper, including the windshield. Using the windshield washers only smeared it more, and by the time we passed through a dozen swarms, I felt like I was totally lost. What a mess we were in.

After a couple days we arrived in New Orleans, and checked into a motel for about three nights while we saw as much as we could of that wonderfully interesting city. We walked about the various streets that were the subjects of old jazz songs, like Rampart, Bourbon, and Basin Streets, the French Quarter, attended a concert at the Preservation Hall, which had already been active for over fifty years and has done so much to keep alive the music and culture of the jazz and blues era. We marvelled at the architecture of the French Quarter with its wrought iron balconies and hanging flower baskets. We ate gumbo and jambalaya, and crawfish in different dishes. We took a short ride on a paddle wheeler that took us a short distance up the Mississippi River and past the home of Anne Rice who was sitting in her yard and working on one her novels. We even drove around the local graveyard, where all of the coffins are above the ground because of the high water table, caused by the close proximity of Lake Pontchartrain.

From New Orleans, we drove west a few hours until we came to a small lake, about ten miles in diameter, with a museum type of old plantation house on the property. We checked into the campground and found that they also conducted an interesting boat tour, which we decided to attend. The flat bottom boat had a canopy to shelter us from the sun and carried about twenty tourists. What made this lake so interesting was that for many years a company had been mining salt and had hollowed out a vast labyrinth of tunnels under the lake before finally closing down. A few years before our visit, an oil company decided the lake was a likely spot to drill for oil. They had only drilled for a couple days when the drill punctured the roof of the mine and the resulting implosion caused the lake to disappear into the mine below, leaving no more than a few puddles on the surface. Not to worry, within minutes, the water backed up the little river from the Gulf of Mexico and re-filled the lake.

That wasn't the last of the interesting information we picked up that day. We sailed across the lake to the little river that connected the lake to the Gulf several miles away, and passed a little village with a few people on the levee and fishing. The guide explained that the fields were normally planted with rice or sugar cane, and under the ground there were millions of crawfish, somewhere in the process of eggs, hatching into babies and then growing through the season while feeding on the roots of the rice and sugar cane and laying more eggs for the next cycle. After the rice or cane was harvested, the land was flooded and the crawfish floated to the surface and were harvested themselves. Apparently that area, by itself, produced many tons of crawfish. Pretty smart, eh!!!

Back at the campground that evening, I learned that a few miles to the south was a huge factory that produced Tabasco sauces, and I could almost detect a red glow in the sky over the factory.

The drive to Corpus Christie was uneventful and uninteresting, as was our stay. We checked into a motel and took a drive around the town and contacted a couple places that offered rental accommodation. One, on the shore, looked like a possibility but we just couldn't get a good feeling about the place and so we phoned Gladys in Desert Hot Springs, who said she was expecting our call and our unit was ready. We said we'd be arriving in a week. Our accommodation for the winter now settled, we had a leisurely drive to California. The only place that we really were impressed with was San Antonio. The little river that flowed through town was lined with lovely little shops and restaurants and lovely walkways.

We arrived safely at the trailer park at Desert Hot Springs and found that our two bedroom trailer was in a fairly large park with a nice swimming pool and club house and a nine-hole golf course. Gladys acted as an agent for several absentee owners. Her remark to us was that she loved to rent to Canadians because the trailers were left cleaner than when they moved in; we were no exception because the previous occupants were accustomed to go barefoot indoors and the oil and dirt from their feet caused the carpets to be very grungy. I spent quite a few hours doing what I could to make them clean. Like I mentioned earlier, Gladys, could have been Marilyn Munro's twin and pictures of her in her younger years were identical, just beautiful, but she was now at the age of about sixty, and had put on quite a bit of weight.

Gladys drove a pink Cadillac convertible and in the park she tootled around in a pink golf cart. At about nine a.m., she would pull up at our door in her cart wearing a pretty, long, pink flannelette nightgown and pop in for a cup of coffee, and a short visit. Phyllis once asked Gladys if she was trying to seduce me by wearing her pj's, and Gladys answered in the sweetest drawl, "Honey, if I was trying to seduce your husband, I sure wouldn't be wearing flannelette and have pins in my hair". Gladys gave me a large Canadian flag to hang from the twenty foot flag pole in front of our trailer. After a week or so, the park association held an emergency meeting and passed a resolution demanding that I remove it, because I should recognize I was now in the sovereign land of The United States. Rather than cause an international incident, I complied with the demand and gave the flag back to Gladys. In the park were many little rabbits, road-runners, quail, and other little critters.

Our winter was quite lovely as Phyllis was able to join a ladies' keep fit class and worked out at the pool, while I was able to swim laps most days. We drove to Yucca Flats, just north of Desert Hot Springs to spend time in a national park that contained various species of cacti and yucca trees and other vegetation. We also found a warehouse store there, where they almost gave away stuff free. I bought a case of fine South African wine for two dollars per bottle. It was actually very good wine, and not to be confused with the "two-buck-chuck", that Joy and Noel had introduced us to in Portland.

We took in a few shows by old-time entertainers, like the Ink Spots of the 1950's, and took a couple side trips to visit my cousin, Leonard and

Margo in Lake Elsinore, some seventy miles away, and to San Diego and the Grand Canyon. We had a few visitors that came to stay for a week or so, like Annie and her boyfriend and Joy and Noel.

There was the odd dance in the club house as well as pot luck dinners, especially Christmas dinner.

Early in January, 1994, we learned that my niece, Mona Cruickshank passed away due to Cancer on January 4th, and her husband, Bob, died two weeks later.

We were ready to go home in April.

Chapter 27

BIGGER CONDO – SLOWER PACE

After being away for over nine months on our trip across Canada and through all of the eastern and outer eastern, southern and western states, we found ourselves back in our little condo of 560 sq ft. on the 25th floor in the West End of Vancouver. We tried to get back into some sort of a routine but just couldn't feel comfortable; and we were not looking forward to spending many years of being so restricted by space.

We resolved that we were finished with lengthy trips and must therefore find a larger home. Even the neighborhood no longer appealed to us as much due to the ever-increasing traffic and noise. Our daily walks on the seawall were no longer as pleasant because it seemed to be a mass of people confined to a 10 foot walkway that should be twenty feet wide. Compounding the problem was the large number of dogs on or off leashes, and kids on skate boards and bicycles darting in and out. During our last night in the West End, Phyllis counted being awakened ten times by sirens. (The month-end was a bad time for sirens because it was payday, and a larger number of drug users would over-dose.)

Good points were our lovely indoor swimming pool and our proximity to the Festival of Lights in English Bay, just about a block away. We would sit by the large windows of the viewing lounge on the 26th floor and watch the fireworks that were synchronized to the music on the radio. There would be usually six or so families there each night for the display. Another plus was the fantastic panoramic view from our apartment, extending from Lost Lagoon to Cypress Bowl, sweeping the North Shore Mountains and Burrard Inlet, and downtown as far South as the Vancouver City Hall. We had a clear view of the cruise liners that passed almost daily in and out of the harbor during the summer.

Barbara suggested we look at some new towers of condos that were being built near her in Coquitlam. We took a drive out and found a unit facing south on the eleventh floor with a view of Mount Baker and the Coastal Range and over Surrey, that would be ideal for us. We had a date to take possession and moved the day before we gave up our little condo. The little condo in the West End, besides being only half the size of the one in Coquitlam, was on a lease which now had only about 70 years to go. We applied for, and got a mortgage for the difference and went ahead with the purchase and moved in July, 1994. When we moved in, the carpets and some cupboards still had to be installed, but nevertheless we were in. Underground parking was another plus.

Our building had 114 units, and at the first meeting of the owners we elected a strata council which met monthly; I was elected and served for three or four years, in charge of finance. We had a management company to do most of the work and I only reviewed the statements and the relative accounts.

The ladies formed a loose group that met for tea and visiting. It wasn't long before Phyllis announced that she and three other ladies had decided to meet weekly for bridge. Then, a couple weeks later, she reported that the four ladies had decided to invite their husbands once a month for dinner. They would take turns hosting, and the host would provide the entrée and the others would each supply a different course – appetizer, dessert, and two bottles of wine. We found that we were compatible and became good friends, and the friendships continued until some of the members died or moved away.

One especially nice lady, Ella Somerfeld, got cancer and passed away in the next year, so that was the end of the bridge parties, but we continued to meet monthly for dinner. The first dinner after Ella's passing, the ladies told Ella's husband, Rein, that if he wanted to bring something, he could bring some bread rolls. He showed up with a pan of fresh buns that he had made from scratch and were hot out of the oven. From then on, Rein took a regular turn at hosting, and his dinners were equally delicious to the others. His comment was that Ella had left her cook books, and, if you can read, you can follow a recipe.

One especially bright spot was that we were directly across the street from Glen Elementary School, which Johanna attended. Joey was about twelve years old at the time. One day, early in September, we heard several girls in the school yard all yelling, "Grandma." We looked down and saw Joey there in the school yard with three of her friends, all looking up at our apartment. We went out onto the balcony and the little girls all shouted "Grandma, we love you." What a testimony, and Phyllis was overjoyed. The calls became a regular occurrence and often, after school, Johanna would come to our apartment with her friends, asking for a drink of water, knowing all the time they would get pop or milk with cookies from Grandma. Joey often embarrassed her friends by insisting that they feel my hair because it was already quite silver (silver sounds better than "gray".)

Holly gave birth to Trevor on June 20th, 1994.

Danny's wife, Tami, presented him with another son, Cole, in 1996. Danny had left the restaurant by now, and was working for an architect/ builder, named Peter. Danny's only training had been a year of Shop, in high school, but he was a good learner and became a master carpenter without even taking any apprenticeship training. He worked for Peter for several years, learning his trade, before going out on his own, building houses, and other items, and hiring his own crew.

Phyllis and I quite enjoyed our sixteen years in the condo, because we were so compatible with each other, and with all of the friends we made. In the first summer we put on the first of our annual residents barbecues. Pat Beecroft, son of Tony and Judy volunteered because he had worked at MacDonald's. After the first tray of burgers received complaints I was asked to take over and that became my regular job for the next 15 years. The Strata Council would supply the wine, burgers and buns, and the residents brought salads and desserts. Christmas parties were similar with the residents bringing meats and casseroles as well.

When we weren't travelling, we again started going regularly to church, first to the Fairfax Presbyterian Church just off Broadway on the West Side of Vancouver. When we told the minister that we were moving to Coquitlam, he said that we would really enjoy the church services and the minister at Coquitlam Presbyterian Church, Rev. Terry Hibbert. When we relocated, we went to that church and found it to be quite pleasant, both the services and the congregation. Terry visited us and asked if we would like to join one of the bible study groups, and suggested we would probably fit in best with a group led by Cliff Bablitz.

The group consisted of more than twenty members and were a mixture of ages, from university students to old timers and a large number of working people; several seniors, and included several Japanese, and Indonesians, plus Filipinos, Chinese, Koreans and couples from Guyana, Singapore, and England. Besides the Asians there were about eight or ten of us that were Canadian Caucasians. Over the years, we grew to be like family and really loved and supported each other. During our first year, the group met in the fireside room at the church for our studies, and then decided it would be better to be more like the early days of the church when the believers met in each other's homes. Thereafter, we took turns hosting the meetings, at least those that had homes that could accommodate that many people. One Japanese couple, Moto and Yoshiko Imanishi, regularly brought their toddler, Joy, to the meetings and laid out a four foot square of cloth for her to sit on and play silently with her toys. She never once said a word to me in about six years, but would accept candy from me, silently and with not a sign of pleasure.

It didn't take long for Phyllis and me to learn we were sadly lacking in our knowledge of the bible, and were soon caught up in the Good News that Christ had been brought to earth as a baby and, thirty two years later, had given his life so that we could be with him through eternity. During his short life on earth, Jesus taught us how to live and love and how to serve. We studied various books in the bible as well as subjects which drew information from various scriptures.

During our lives as Catholics, we had never been encouraged to study the bible, as the priests seemed to be the only ones considered capable of that, and they chose for us what few scriptures we should read. Now, we were encouraged to read and study all of it. Through the process, we were able to really commit to serving the Lord and to truly look forward to be together forever in Heaven.

One of the men in the group, Compton Singroy, was a particularly interesting person and we started meeting for lunch every Thursday at Tim Horton's. Soon after, I became friends with a retired minister, Ross Manthorpe, from our church, and I invited him to join us at lunch and we soon became best friends. I remarked once that I considered a man to be fortunate to have one best friend during his life, and since Bernie Martineau died in 1962, I hadn't had another until now, when at the same time, I found two best friends. Their wives, Pat and Agnes became close friends of both Phyllis and me.

Ross had been raised in the smoggy East End of London, which left him with damaged lungs; he joined the RAF at the outbreak of World War Two, trained in Nova Scotia, transferred to the Commandos, flew a glider into France on D-Day, landing behind the enemy lines and led his platoon in attacking fuel depots and blowing up bridges. After the war he returned to Nova Scotia and married Agnes who he had met when he was there for training. An unlikely pair, as she was a saintly girl, daughter of a minister, and Ross was a rough, tough, commando. Agnes never changed but Ross certainly did, and in fact he became an excellent minister and eventually he transferred to a church in Coquitlam and then he became the chaplain at the Oakalla Prison in Burnaby, where he could talk man to man to the convicts and made a huge difference in the lives of many of them. Ross died in 2012.

Compton was born and raised in Guyana, South America, where his family operated a sugar cane plantation. He received his engineering degree in Central America and moved with his family to Toronto. He met and married Pat and had two children while working for Bell Canada, eventually as a project manager. He was transferred to BC to work on a particular project and when that was completed, he retired. They moved back to Toronto in about 2011.

Other men from our church joined our group and we would number four to six for lunch. We called ourselves the Romeos, as in "Retired Old Men Eating Out".

I had worked as a volunteer at the Vancouver Food Bank whenever I was home. When we moved to Coquitlam, I offered my services again in the local Food Bank, but I was put to work in their Thrift Shop, making sure that donated items were clean and in working order, and making minor repairs. It was surprising how so many people dropped off their old junk with us instead of hauling it to the garbage dump, because probably half the items donated were not fit for resale.

I also volunteered for a group called Neighbor Link, and drove people that were disabled or had other problems, to doctor appointments and for treatment if they couldn't get there on their own. One of my passengers was named Ken, and he and his wife became my good friends. Ken had served in the merchant navy during World War Two and was required to stand watch on deck keeping an eye out for U-Boats and other enemy attackers such as the Luftwaffe. During the winter crossings of allied convoys in the North Atlantic, he would suffer freezing of his feet, come in after his watch period and thaw out his feet and then have to go for his next watch and end up with both feet frozen again. By the end of the war, Ken's feet were totally destroyed and the nerves so damaged that he was in constant pain. The doctors even tried to mitigate the pain by stripping the nerves out of his feet, but that made it only worse. Sores covered his feet and were open and weeping. All the time that Ken worked after the war as a mechanic, his wife, Doris, bathed and bandaged his feet before he went to work and again when he got home. Now, he was going to Vancouver General Hospital three times a week to spend two or three hours in a hyperbaric chamber for six months in an attempt to heal the sores. It was only minimally successful. Through all those years of suffering, Ken never complained about anything. That's my idea of a Hero!!

In 1998, Phyllis and I went to Ireland for a ten-day bus tour of the country and another two weeks on our own in a rented car touring England, Scotland and Wales. Getting there was less than pleasant as the BOAC flight, whose uninspired staff were surly for some reason, dinner was served at ten p.m., was cold, the beef was tough, and then it took a full hour to get our luggage off the carousel and another hour to get our Trafalgar Travel Agency transfer bus to the Holiday Inn at Victoria Station, and the hotel was terrible. The next day, we caught our Aerlingus plane to Shannon, but never got off the ground due to mechanical problems and had to wait for six hours in the lounge for another flight. It was the only bad couple days of travel we ever had. We missed the first day of the tour and joined it at Limerick, where we had a very nice dinner and finally went to bed happy.

The bus tour was the first time we had ever tried this method for such a long tour, ten days, and we enjoyed it thoroughly, and we were blessed with two very capable staff. The driver, Michael, was pleasant and very helpful and very patient with the group, especially with a lady from Kansas who always went shopping every time we stopped and we had to wait for her return so we could continue the journey. She was taking her daughter, who was a senior high school student, to learn of her "roots". This was the third daughter she had brought and had always taken the same bus tour and was always correcting the guide, Geraldine, about various items of information.

Geraldine had been a school teacher, and was extremely knowledgeable and articulate about her country. Each day as we drove along, she would give us a one hour lecture about a certain topic, such as the education system, economics, movie industry, national political system, arts, industry and business, etc. She had such a sweet Irish accent that I could listen to her for hours. She also had a great sense of humor, but her jokes were never coarse or lewd.

I won't list all the places that we visited, but the main ones were the Cliffs of Moher, where we saw thousands of sea birds nesting on the sheer cliffs which rose five or six hundred feet out of the water, Limerick, The Ring-of-Kerry (an extremely scenic circle route of quaint villages and countryside), the Black Mountains and Moll's Gap, Waterford (we visited the factory where they manufacture such beautiful and famous crystal), Dublin and Sligo.

One particularly interesting place that we visited for a few hours was the Irish National Stud Farm. Ireland has a lengthy history of breeding some of the top race horses in the world. This had to be a highlight for this farm boy from Meadow Lake. The stud farm was a very prosperous and well-kept place with several studs ready to do their jobs for the sheer pleasure of it, while the farm raked in millions in Euros. There were several mares visiting, including a couple from Kuwait and Saudi Arabia.

We stayed in B&B's, inns, hotels, and, once, in a castle that now served as a B&B. There was entertainment every evening. One evening, I and a New Zealand chap, named Colin, were called up to lead a sing-along; and on another evening I was volunteered to enter a competition, playing spoons with an Irish band (which I won). Amazing what I can do after I drink a glass of hot mead and several pints of Guiness.

The country was beautiful, with wild purple rhododendrons, considered a weed in Ireland, among the bright yellow gorse bushes and ferns, and a vivid green land everywhere. Many of the thatched cottages have been replaced by cement block houses with central heating. Ireland had recently joined the European Union and had been chosen to receive four years of funding to upgrade the country and its infrastructure.

We made friends with a few people on the tour, including Colleen and her sister-in-law, June, from South Africa. Colleen and her husband were planning to move to Australia, and they were removing their money as fast as they could. The removal of money was restricted to a certain amount per day, and so that's what the two ladies were doing, drawing money from their bank in South Africa and depositing it in an account in an Australian bank. Colleen and her husband were wealthy farmers, while June was quite poor and was happy just to have a free trip and tour in Ireland, while helping Colleen to move the money.

Another couple we met and enjoyed were Colin, a sheep auctioneer, and his wife, from New Zealand, and a couple from The Entrance, Australia. Before saying goodbye in Ireland, we exchanged addresses and offers to host visits by the other two couples in our homes. While having dinner of steamed mussels one night with Colin and his wife one evening, Colin boasted, "come and have dinner with us in New Zealand and I'll show you what real mussels look like." We were able to take him up on his invitation when we visited them a year later.

Phyllis and I then flew to London and rented a car to tour Eastern England, Scotland, a bit of Wales, and Western England before returning to London two weeks later to catch our plane back to Vancouver.

The highlights included a visit to the Lake District, including Lake Windermere and Hawkshead where I had visited with Pat and Chris in 1974; Carlyle on the Scottish border to spend a couple days with the

Rivers, John and Sheila, who had stayed with us in Yuma in 1992. The Rivers lived in a new brick home on their farm on which they raised prize cattle and sheep. Actually, their son was now operating the farm and lived in the old house/barn with his wife and little son and daughter, but John still helped out. The little four year old grandson was always there and was a really fun kid who always called his grandfather "Joe". Sheila made a roast lamb dinner for us that tasted delicious.

We drove up to Edinburgh and along the way we stopped to visit the sister of our good friend Ina Watson of Coquitlam. Again, we left after over eating. We drove around Edinburg and that night we stayed in a quaint inn just outside the city. On our way south, we went into Wales for a few hours and spent a night at a B&B at a sheep farm. The lady of the house was away, so the farmer made our breakfast and didn't have a clue what he was doing; we just wished he had given us each a bowl of corn flakes.

Back in England, we stopped to visit our good friends, Bill and Irene Brown and their really sweet daughters, Claire and Joy. The family had immigrated to Vancouver when the girls were very young, and the family had moved back to England just a couple years before our visit, and were living near Bath. Joy had studied landscape architecture and was working for a movie director on his big estate looking after the grounds. He and his wife had a flat in London and they only came to the estate on the weekends, when they entertained their friends. Irene was in charge of the house and supervised the maids and servants.

Bill and Irene took us to Lovick, a heritage village which was operated by the National Trust, which looked after the beautiful gardens and all of the buildings and rented them out to the public.

That summer, Phyllis and I took our final lengthy trip in our Volkswagen Camper, travelling across Canada again. We went to Prince Albert to see Lawrence and Doreen, and then we visited Sally and Basil in Saskatoon and attended the wedding of Dustin and Carla. It was a traditional Ukrainian reception (I think), and the wedding party and guests had a great time, doing Ukrainian dancing that many had trained for as kids. Phyllis and I just enjoyed being around all the relatives and meeting some for the first time, like Joanne O'Dell, Carol and Walter's daughter.

From there, we went south to the Qu'Appelle Valley, a beautiful area that I had always wanted to visit. We spent a few days there, among the lakes and rolling hills, before proceeding eastward. We camped near the Saskatchewan Forestry Tree Farm. The tree farm was developed many years earlier and provided free trees and bushes to any farmer in the province who wished to plant trees and hedges on their property for wind breaks and to trap snow and to prevent erosion and drifting of soil and snow. We were amazed, as we drove along the highway, at the many trees growing in the fields and around the farm houses, and the diversity of crops being grown, causing a patchwork of color that is so different to the sameness of wheat fields stretching for miles and miles when I was younger. The rest of the trip varied only slightly from previous journeys across the nation and we thoroughly enjoyed it.

When we got home, we sold the Volkswagen camper and bought a 1997 Chrysler New Yorker, a powerful beast that was very comfortable and had all the bells and whistles available at the time.

Matthew left the Co-Op in Ucluelet and joined his school chum, Calvin Millikin, in the meat department at the Quality Foods store in Port Alberni, in 1998, where he remained for about eight years. During that time, he bought a house in Port Alberni and rented one or two rooms to his friends, helping to cover his mortgage expense.

In April, 1999, we travelled to New Zealand and Australia for two months of sightseeing and visiting friends. It was a long flight so we had a couple days stopover at a resort in Rarotonga, in the Cook Islands. From there we flew on to Aukland, New Zealand, and rented a car which we used for our two weeks of touring the two islands. We drove around the perimeter of the north island, stopping to spend a weekend in Napier with Collin and his wife, who we had met during our tour of Ireland. We saw some Kiwis (birds native to N.Z.), and some unusual trees that resembled ferns, except they had trunks of about 15-inch diameter and stood about 10-12 feet tall with fernlike branches. We also spent an evening in a grove of trees in a park that had millions of glow worms that were creating beautiful scenes with their glowing paths as they moved about, resembling a laser light show. There were sheep everywhere, typical, being in New Zealand.

Highlights included an evening in Rotorua where we attended a hangi (feast), in which the food was cooked in geo-thermal chambers underground. Our table was next to the small stage, and, suddenly, a group of Maori warriors burst out of the wings and rushed towards us with their spears and their faces and bodies all tattooed, hair wild, and looking quite fierce. This dancing is called the Haka and is normally performed by men but occasionally by women. They proceeded to entertain us with several war dances and all the time sticking their tongues out and shouting loudly and stomping their feet. We were quite startled at the beginning, not knowing what to expect (like audience participation), but overall, we found it very unusual and entertaining.

The area around Rotorua has a large amount of geo thermal activity, with hot springs and mud and geysers, and steam coming out of the ground in many places. In fact, there was quite a large geo-thermal electric generation station nearby which ran on the steam from underground.

Our weekend with Colin and his wife was pleasant and we went for a nice dinner of large, tasty, mussels as he had promised.

We ended our trip around the north island in Wellington, where we caught a ferry with about a four hour ride to the south island. Among the highlights there were the beautiful scenery everywhere, Mount Cook, Christchurch, and Queenstown.

After our two weeks were finished, we flew to Brisbane and caught a taxi to the time-share that we had traded for at Surfer's Paradise on the east coast of Australia. The apartment was on the fourth floor, right on the shore in a little cove, with all of the amenities that we needed close at hand. We took a small bus tour of the area and it was a lovely spot. And no, I didn't go surfing!!

At the end of our week, we booked three days at Lady Eliot Island, a small coral island about 75 miles out in the Pacific, at the southern tip of The Great Barrier Reef. To get there, we flew from Brisbane to Bundaberg, about a hundred miles north and in the sugar cane part of the country, and then caught a little six passenger plane to Lady Eliot Island. During our three hour wait in Bundaberg, we saw members of the local sky diving club doing their thing, and I asked one of the divers about the area. When he learned that we were from Canada, he said that he spends his winters in Canada but was sure I wouldn't know the little place. After much prodding, he said he goes to Loon Lake to work at a fishing resort. Loon Lake is only about twenty miles from Meadow Lake and is where our family went for Sunday picnics when we lived on the farm.

Our visit to Lady Eliot Island was very interesting. The island had only small bushes and dwarf trees growing in the shallow soil and coral base. We went out daily in a glass-bottom boat to watch the beautiful marine life among the coral formations of the reef.

On our first night, we watched a bit of TV and read until the generator was turned off and the lights went out at about ten o'clock. We were lying in bed, still awake, when we heard the most eerie sound from outside, sort of a moaning or groaning, definitely sounded like ghosts. Phyllis was quite frightened when it began, and so I took my flashlight and went out to the porch to see if it was kids trying to scare us. I could see nothing, and Phyllis decided it was staff trying to scare us, and we went to sleep. In the morning, when we went into the lodge for breakfast, I asked what the spooky sounds were, and a staff person explained that it was the Mutton birds, and that there were lots of them on the island. The birds live in nests that they dig among the roots under the trees and stay out of sight in their nests during the day, and only come out at night. The birds had been discovered when Captain Cook stopped there during an exploratory trip. The crew caught some and cooked them, only to discover that they tasted like mutton and that's what he named them.

From there we flew back to Brisbane and rented a car for the next week until we reached Melbourne. We had a pleasant drive to Sidney, where we saw all of the usual tourist sights. The city of Sidney was preparing for the 2000 Olympics and so it was difficult to get around the streets due to all the construction of buildings and streets. We took a side trip to The Entrance, about 75 miles north and spent a couple days visiting another of the couples we had met on our tour of Ireland. They drove us all over the area and we were very impressed with the scenery.

By this time, we were hooked on Aussie meat pies and would make a point of stopping at a bakery at noon most days for fresh meat pies. I've tried them since we came home but even those guaranteed to be real Aussie pies, don't taste quite the same. I guess it's the same as when

I order jambalaya, and it's never the same as what I loved to eat in New Orleans.

We continued our journey south and arrived in Melbourne to spend some time with Maureen and Edwin's daughter, Veronica, and her husband, John. Veronica is such a sweet and kind lady, and we thoroughly enjoyed our stay with them. I returned the rental car and we then went with Veronica and John in their car on short trips.

One trip was eastward into the Dandenong Mountains where we toured in the beautiful area and stayed overnights at Marysville and Healesville. One memorable event was sighting, in a field, two huge kangaroos, called Big Reds, which can be quite dangerous.

Another longer and more impressive trip was westward, along the Great Ocean Road. What a lovely and interesting drive that was. We followed the shoreline and had to stop often, just to take in the beauty of various points, walking out to viewpoints that were often no farther than a few hundred yards from the last stop. There were many views of small areas where the shoreline line had eroded and were now left as little islets a few hundred yards off shore and their sheer sides were a few hundred feet high. One half-mile stretch of coast line alone had twelve such formations, and they were called the Twelve Apostles. Some had arches eroded in them from the centuries of wave action. Because of all the stops, we didn't travel more than a few hundred miles, and we stayed in lovely motels with awesome views.

We returned to Melbourne on an inland route and saw a good deal more of the wildlife in the countryside – koalas, and troops of kangaroos as well as large flocks of cockatoos. We stopped at a park/zoo and saw many more, including a Tasmanian Devil. What a viscous looking little animal that is; I would never want to meet one that was loose. I mean it looked really mean. There were several koalas there, babies to adults, and several people held the babies, but John cautioned me not to hold one, because they tend to pee on you if they are startled. There were also many kangaroos of various types.

We stopped for lunch one day during our return trip, at an Aboriginal Cultural Center, and stayed for their presentation. For my lunch, I ordered a kangaroo burger, which will never catch on as a specialty in restaurants in

Canada. After lunch, we watched a demonstration as a couple aborigines played the didgeridoo; what a pulsing, haunting sound that is, and the rhythmic beat seems to stay in your body long after. There was a demonstration of the boomerang being tossed and I passed on the opportunity to try, after I watched several other tourists chuck one into the ground five feet away. I bought a cane that showed it to be carved by the Allinjarra tribe, and the carving on it depicted the lengthy journey of someone who was doing a "walk-about."

Melbourne was a nice city and we went downtown several times, sightseeing and to the casino. We went up to the top of a skyscraper and were standing on the observation deck with a panoramic view of the city and ocean while Veronica was petrified and stood, shaking, just outside the door of the elevator.

We went to two Aussie Rules Footie games while we were there, and really enjoyed watching these bruisers, wearing no padding whatsoever, pound each other mercilessly. I had the feeling that their idea of "Aussie Rules" meant "no rules", or possibly the few rules just related to scoring, which the players tried to do, no matter what the cost was to themselves or to the other players. Hot Aussie meat pies were sold by vendors that circulated through the crowd and were delicious, and a great substitute for hot dogs and hamburgers that we get here. There were about ninety thousand fans at each of the games.

Veronica had a budgie in a cage in her kitchen and she and John were trying to teach it to speak words, like "hello", or "pretty bird". She was a bit upset when she caught me trying to teach her bird to say "quack". I think the bird was retarded or sick, and would never learn to speak. I usually referred to it as her duck.

Veronica has three sons who are all married and now have children in their teens. At the time we were there, only Allan, the middle boy, had a child and she was just a beautiful toddler, named Holly. All of Veronica's children were very nice, had good jobs, and were conscientious and treated each other and their mother and John well. They came to visit at Veronica's often.

We then went to stay for a few days with Noel Edwards sister, Olla, in the east end of Melbourne. Olla had come with Joy and Noel to visit us for a week in Port Alberni the year before I retired, and we found her to be a sweet lady, full of fun. Phyllis and I planned to drive to Adelaide and return along the Murray River, and so we asked Olla to come with us.

We again drove along the Great Ocean Road, not stopping at viewpoints but still enjoying the scenery, and on to Adelaide. Olla and Noel had lived in Adelaide as children and until Noel joined the armed forces during the War and so Olla knew her way around. While there, we took a bus tour of the wine region in the Barossa Valley and visited several wineries. On the tour were three young tourists from England. We would go into the tasting room of a winery and there would be a long counter with little glasses of various wines already poured waiting all along the counter. The three English boys would rush in and drink as many as they could and then make a second trip to re-taste as many more as possible. They never bought any wine, but they were all pretty smashed by the time we got back to town.

Australia is the source of a large portion of the world's opals and so we found a nice pair of earrings for Phyllis in a local jewellery store.

We then drove east, along the Murray River. It is referred to as "The Mighty Murray", but found it would be more accurate to compare it to the Coquitlam River than to our Mighty Fraser. Nevertheless it was a pleasant drive along the river, with many ibis and other birds nesting in the trees. The trees were all eucalyptus and the soil was a red color. I remarked that it was a pleasant drive in the countryside, to which Olla snorted, "I don't see anything pleasant, it's just red dirt and gum trees."

I was already aware of the term "gum trees", because, ever since we met, whenever Phyllis didn't agree with me, she always said to me, "Why don't you run up a gum tree and stick there."

We continued on to the east coast and visited Canberra, the capital of Australia. We also drove around the university and were impressed with the extensive government-supported sports training program that had already paid off with many more medals that usual in the Olympics and other competitions.

We returned to Melbourne and, a few days later, we caught our plane to come home. The trip was a killer - an afternoon flight of 17 hours to Los Angeles, three or four hours layover and then another four-hour flight to Vancouver and a one-hour taxi ride to Coquitlam – all without a wink of sleep for a total of about 38 hours.

Our funky purple and yellow hotel in Auckland, New Zealand

Giant silver ferns, New Zealand

Wairakei Geothermal Generating Plant

Lady Elliot Island, Great Barrier Reef, Australia

Elmer, Phyllis & niece Veronica at 12 Apostles, Great Ocean Road

Chapter 28

NEW MILLENIUM

After our trip to New Zealand and Australia in April to June, 1999, we took it easy for a few months. At Christmas, we went to Campbell River to spend the season with Monica and her family. David was working as a painter at Painter's Lodge, and he was able to arrange for us to stay at the lodge for a very modest price because it was closed for the winter.

We spent Christmas Eve at Monica's and returned to our room at about eleven p.m. A half hour later, while Phyllis was getting ready for bed, she felt chest pains and I called the ambulance, which took her to the local hospital, after they first called the hospital to tell them it was a heart patient. By the time we arrived, the heart specialist's assistant was there and the specialist himself arrived a few minutes later. He told me he had been working as specialist at a hospital in New York and wanted to administer a new drug, made from mouse protein, which would thin Phyllis's blood and clear the blockage. I agreed, he gave her the injection and, within a minute, Phyllis was dripping blood from her gums around her teeth. I guess the drug was as effective as hoped.

I notified the family and the Benoit kids soon arrived. We had Christmas dinner at Boston Pizza in Campbell River, probably the only place open. Arrangements were made for Phyllis to have triple by-pass surgery at Royal Columbian Hospital in New Westminster on about January 2nd or 3rd, because if she were to go home first, she would have to wait for months. After a few days, she was transported by ambulance to New Westminster for the surgery. I followed right behind the ambulance in my car and she was able to see me the entire way from the back of the ambulance. Welcome, New Millennium!!!

The surgery went well and after a few days she was transferred to Eagle Ridge Hospital in Coquitlam, not far from our condo and she came home about January 21, 2000. Stephen came to be with his mom for a few days at the time of her surgery along with the Benoit kids.

Our 25th Anniversary was on June 19, 2001. Quite certain that we wouldn't be around for our 50th, we decided to celebrate in a big way. We rented a hall and arranged for a catered meal with music, etc. and invited about fifty of our relatives and close friends. Pat Cruickshank and Basil Ceipliski shared the emcee duties and told many humorous lies about us. It was a fantastic and memorable evening. As we were packing up at the end, I mentioned to my two sons how proud of them I had always felt, and they seemed surprised to hear me say it. I assumed they always knew it, but apparently not. So, for anyone reading this book, remember that you can't take such an important thing for granted and tell them often.

I had triple by-pass surgery on my heart in 2002, and that was followed a year or two later with a diagnosis of chronic lymphocytic leukemia, which has been in remission ever since. The life expectancy from that condition is fourteen years, but when I asked my family doctor Ross, she laughed and said, "Don't worry, chances are, you'll die long before that from another stroke or heart attack." Actually, I did have two or three more strokes during the next few years but not serious; one was a facial stroke and only affected my speech in a major way for a week or so and a later one caused a lasting but not major deterioration.

We resumed our daily routines like reading the newspapers and doing crossword puzzles, and enjoyed life, entertained, and were entertained by, friends. We took occasional trips to the Island to visit family and old friends. We also went to our time share at Winfield for a week every second year, and followed that by a drive to Prince George to spend a few days with my niece, Marlene, and enjoyed barbeques with her and her sons, Trevor and Matthew, and their partners. From there, we would sometimes drive to Prince Rupert and take the ferry down the coast to Port Hardy and visit the family on Vancouver Island.

We were always happy to visit our sons and Holly and our grandchildren on Vancouver Island. Holly and Doug and their little ones moved to Port Alberni in 1995. They then moved to Airdrie, Alberta, in 1998. After Holly and Doug separated in 2000, they returned to BC and settled in Comox, on Vancouver Island. Holly started dating Terry a few years later.

We took one more trip across Canada, this time in the Chrysler, staying in motels and B&B's and eating in restaurants. We also included visits to family on the prairies and Steve and Aiyana in the BC Interior, and my cousin, Sylvia, in Winnipeg. The only touristy item of particular interest was my encounter with an eagle. Just past Thunder Bay, Ontario, we came around a curve, doing about 120kmh, with no other traffic in sight, and suddenly I saw an eagle on the roadway, feeding on some road kill about twenty yards ahead. I hit the brakes but it was too late, and as the eagle tried to take off, it hit my right headlight and glanced off the windshield right in front of Phyllis and then over the car. I looked in the rear view mirror and saw the bird wobble a few times and then straighten out and fly off into the trees. Phyllis had quite a fright. I pulled over onto the shoulder and got out of the car to check for damage, and, as I got out of the car, I saw the eagle fly back across the highway. I found the headlamp was not damaged but the bracket that held the whole headlight assembly was broken and, although it looked okay it was loose. Because we didn't intend to do any night driving, we didn't get it repaired until we got home. I believe the eagle was only badly bruised and had lost one wing feather which I found stuck between the fender and the hood. I recovered it and still keep it on my visor as a memento.

About 2004, Phyllis was diagnosed as suffering severe pulmonary fibrosis and the respirologist, Dr. Steve Blackie, the son of our good friends downstairs, began treating her. She was also found to have sleep apnea, which means she stopped breathing frequently for short periods while she was asleep, thus cutting off the flow of oxygen to the brain and killing brain cells. She was fitted for a CPAP machine and mask which blew air into her lungs all through the night. It was uncomfortable, but she was able to tolerate it. Phyllis was still as sharp as ever, and she was still able to do the entire New York Times crossword puzzle in the Saturday paper, something I could never do.

On April 30, 2005, Phyllis celebrated her 80th birthday. We arranged to hold a party in the large meeting room of our condo complex and all of the children and many other family members and friends came to honor her, including Monica's daughter, Angeline, who flew from her home in Los Angeles. Teena presented her grandma with a book of photographs from throughout her life. Many family and friends spoke of how she had touched their lives.

In 2006, Phyllis's condition deteriorated further, and she was given a year to live, so Dr. Blackie prescribed prednisone, a drug which can produce terrible side effects. Dr. Ross commented that the side effects of the drug can be worse than the condition you're treating. It was to be for a period of three months. After twelve weeks, Phyllis's body was very bloated and she was having a terrible time getting through the day and I had to rent a wheelchair for her. Then on September eleventh, she collapsed on the floor and I called the ambulance. At Eagle Ridge Hospital, they found that she had diverticulitis, leaking from the bowel into the abdominal cavity, and they began treatment with antibiotics. It was clearly understood by the doctors at Eagle Ridge Hospital that she did not want to have any further surgery, and that she was ready to die peacefully and be with our creator.

About noon on Thursday, September 21, her condition suddenly worsened and she was transferred to Royal Columbian Hospital, where they found that her bowel had ruptured and she had only hours to live. The doctors at Royal Columbian scheduled her for surgery, and when we complained that it had been agreed that Phyllis would not have surgery, the doctors said that that agreement only applied to Eagle Ridge Hospital and that she was definitely going to have the surgery. I called all seven of the children to come at once. Holly met Danny at the ferry and arrived at eleven p.m. that evening. The surgery was delayed for several hours because of another emergency, (a man had been shot in the head) but it proceeded at about ten o'clock. All afternoon and evening, Phyllis complained that she didn't want the surgery, but all the doctors would do was assure her that her chances of surviving the operation were slim at best. (What a weird reassurance!! Don't fret, you'll probably die anyways!!!) The surgery was to clean out her abdominal cavity and perform a colostomy. At two a.m., Holly, Danny and I were able to see her in the recovery room and were able to see that she had, in fact, survived, but her condition was critical. She was then transferred to the I.C.U. and we were able to stay with her, although she was not conscious. Danny then stayed in the waiting room, while Holly and I went home for a few hours of sleep.

When we returned to her bedside in the morning, Phyllis was still pretty much unaware of her surroundings, but she was definitely upset that she wasn't in heaven. She couldn't speak, so she just glared at me and pointed upwards with her thumb to let me know that was where she really wanted to be - in heaven. Later, when she could speak a few words, she just kept pointing upwards with her thumb and repeating, "You promised me", and all I could tell her was that we were overruled by the doctors. Actually, I thanked God for giving us more time together here on earth, although I did feel sorry for the pain that she was suffering. Stephen arrived from the Kootenays on Friday afternoon, and Matthew and Terry at noon on Saturday. Annemarie and Barbara came to see their mother on Sunday.

Phyllis continued to improve slowly and was finally transferred to a regular ward on Sunday, October 8th. Holly, Matthew and Danny came to see their mom every weekend for several weeks and then less often as Phyllis improved. Holly and Terry brought another large planter filled with various plants, including a ficus tree, similar to the one which they had given her in 2000, and which had grown so large that we gave it Teena and Jeremy. This one also grew quickly and became too big for our apartment and I gave it to the lady on the front desk of the Parkwood Manor when I moved to the Belvedere Residence in the following June. She had been very kind to us while we were at the Parkwood.

On Friday, December 1st, Phyllis stood for the first time in over two months with the help of parallel bars, and within a week she was able to walk three steps. On Saturday, December 9th, I was able to call a wheelchair taxi and take her to the Christmas pageant at our church. Everyone made a fuss over her and she enjoyed her evening.

In preparation for Phyllis's eventual return home, I arranged to have hardwood floors installed in our condo, to make it easier for her to get around in her wheelchair. Compton suggested that I buy the flooring at an auction and then he would help Roy Gibbons from our church to install it. Roy was a retired carpenter who still worked almost full time helping people with almost any chore, and he only charged friends like me, who could afford it, fifteen dollars per hour. It was free for those who couldn't pay much. Another friend from church, Walter, had a truck and he hauled the old carpet to the dump and gave what he charged me to charity.

The new floor was finished just before Christmas, and it was quite a surprise for Phyllis when I wheeled her in on Christmas morning to spend the day at home for the first time in over three months and she loved the hardwood floor. It was a lovely day for all of us. Getting her back to the hospital wasn't as easy as it had been getting her home that morning. In 2005, there were only a few taxis that were equipped to transport people in wheelchairs, so the arrangement I had made with the taxi in the morning to pick us up at eight p.m. stretched to after midnight. We didn't really mind the lengthy delay, because we just sat in the lobby talking and necking, the same as we would have done at the hospital.

On December 31st, Phyllis was transferred to Queen's Park Hospital for rehab and remained there for about three months. The staff tried to build up her strength so that she could get about with the aid of a walker. She did recover some of her strength, but was never able to walk again, and that necessitated buying a wheel chair for her.

While she was in hospital, some other damage was discovered. When the ambulance had come to our condo in September, she was lying on the floor in the bedroom. There was no room to bring the stretcher into the bedroom, so the medics dragged her to it in the hallway, pulling her by her hands. In the process, the tendons in her right shoulder/arm tore, and it couldn't be repaired because she certainly couldn't survive any more surgery. She also now suffered from carpal tunnel syndrome in her right wrist making her entire right arm and hand useless and in constant pain. Her medication for pain was ten milliliters of liquid morphine, morning and night, and six extra-strength Tylenol tablets per day. Over a period of time, I reduced and then discontinued the morphine as her need eased.

I should mention that during the entire seven months or more that Phyllis was in the three hospitals, our friend Ross Manthorpe came to visit her every week day and was a great comfort to her, and he was a prime reason for her not becoming bitter and depressed. Ross was always so cheerful and positive in his chats with her. He usually visited Phyllis before

I came and he stayed to talk to both of us for a short time before leaving us alone. Other friends came often, and the children came on weekends.

While Phyllis was in Queens Park Hospital, I daily drove past the cemetery where my parents were buried, and I made a habit of stopping at their graves to talk to them and pray. The first time I visited their graves, I was sad to see that their stone had moss growing on it and the letters were filled with dirt and grass clippings, etc., due to many years of neglect. I brought scrapers, brushes and other tools, as well as cleaning solutions and after several hours of work during the next couple weeks, it looked much better.

Phyllis was feeling much better and was able to return home in April, 2007, and she started getting out to the stores and restaurants in her wheelchair. Her days were boring and she spent hours reading. Often, she would put her book aside, and would face the picture window and watch for interestingly shaped clouds or just count cars passing by on the street. We talked to each other for hours.

We decided to go on a week-long cruise to Alaska in August with our friends, Marg and John Gayman. It was our first cruise of that length of time and we really enjoyed it. We had a "handicap" stateroom able to handle a wheelchair, with a balcony that was accessible by a little ramp. The weather was generally good and we spent our days either on the balcony or on the deck, reading. We had brought a couple bottles of wine and took turns with the Gaymans, hosting happy hour. The food was great and the entertainment was very enjoyable. Besides the beautiful scenery of the Inside Passage, we found the glaciers on the Alaska coast to be fascinating, with big chunks of ice breaking off every few minutes and falling into the ocean, called "calving".

Just a week after our cruise, we drove to Winfield for our week-long time share. We still did all the things we usually did there, and went to the same places as previous years, with me pushing Phyllis's wheel chair. From there, we again drove to Valemont for an overnight and then on to spend a few days with my niece, Marlene, and her husband, Stan Aksenchuk. Their home is on the river bank and has lovely grounds. A little red fox came by a couple times each day to receive his treats, raw eggs and pieces of meat. The fox would immediately take the egg to the river to wash, and then trot off to his home and family. We had a barbeque next to the river, with a big bon fire, with Marlene's sons and their partners, as well as Rita and her family.

After our return, we were invited and attended the annual Distinguished Members Luncheon of the Society of Management Accountants of BC. There, I was honored by receiving the title of "Fellow of the Certified Management Accountants of Canada". It was the highest honor that could be bestowed on a member. We attended the convocation for new graduating CMA's, and the banquet in the evening. We stayed on for the dance, but left after about an hour and went to our hotel room for the night. Altogether, it was a beautiful day for both of us, and we were treated royally.

In 2006, Matt was transferred to Nanaimo to a Quality Foods Store as the meat manager, to replace his friend Calvin who had just quit and was now the meat manager at the Co-Op store in Tofino. A few years later, Matt left his job at Quality Foods and went to work at the Co-Op in Tofino and was re-united with Calvin. After a couple years, Calvin was promoted to assistant store manager and Matt took over as Meat Department Manager and is doing just fine.

When Phyllis came home from the hospital in April, 2007, I started buying frozen meals from a catering service in Surrey. The meals were quite good and I ordered a one- or two-week supply that was delivered to the door. After nearly a year, we got tired of the twenty or so different entrees, and Phyllis suggested that she teach me to cook from scratch. I agreed, and so we went shopping for groceries. Phyllis would sit in her wheelchair in the kitchen doorway and give me instructions. After about a month, I told Phyllis to "Get out of my kitchen." From then on, I only asked her for advice when I needed it and mainly relied on her cook book "The Joy of Cooking", plus common sense. After a couple years, she commented that I was as good a cook as she ever was, but I'm sure, thinking back, that was just to encourage me.

Johanna and Teena, and Kyle and Jennifer came to see Phyllis and me as often as they could, and their visits were especially appreciated by Phyllis. We also saw Danny's and Holly's children often, when they came from the Island with their parents. They have continued to visit ever since, and I am so grateful for them.

I was still having lunch every Thursday at Tim Horton's with Ross, Compton, and other occasional members of our ROMEO group. At

Christmas, I mentioned that I craved and was going to barbeque a big turkey for dinner with all the trimmings and enough leftovers to last until my birthday three weeks later. Ross asked who all was I inviting and when I said it would be just Phyllis and me, he said that Agnes and he would be alone, so I invited them. They came and I cooked a big turkey on the barbeque, stuffed with just three lemons, over a pan of apple juice. It was the best turkey I had ever eaten, and everything else turned out nice.

Ross passed away on July 1, 2009, and I lost the "best friend" that I had ever had, for the second time in my lifetime.

Joy came to visit from Portland and stayed for over two weeks. I found it really tiring, even though we did go out to restaurants for dinner several times. I finally told her that she was going to be catching a plane back to Portland on Wednesday, either walking on or in a box.

In 2009, I arranged with Fraser Health Region to arrange for me to have a week of respite and Phyllis was placed in a Care Facility. I didn't do anything or go anywhere. A year later, it was arranged that I have another week of respite. During that week, I visited our friend Rein Somerfeld from the MacKenzie Tower and he was now living in an assisted living apartment building called the Parkwood Manor. I was very impressed with it and when I visited Phyllis, I described it. When she came home, we called a real estate agent that we knew from our church. The condo quickly sold and we moved into a one bedroom apartment at the Parkwood on December 15, 2010.

The meals were good at the start, but the place had just been bought by an Ontario company and they installed a management system totally centralized in their head office. The menu was decided in Toronto and the quality of the meals got really poor.

In about June, 2010 or 2011, we decided to take another trip that we had talked about for many years, to Utah, particularly the Bryce Canyon National Park. Actually, we picked a bad time because it was already unbearably hot during the days.

We drove first to Portland to visit our friend, Joy, in an assisted living residence, for two days and then proceeded to Utah. Just south of Salt Lake City, we turned southeast to Moab and soon began to see beautiful rock formations. We checked into a motel in Moab and then set out to explore the Arches National Park. What an interesting area, with tall rock formations with arches in many of them from erosion over eons.

We spent another day in Moab, exploring the Arches Park and taking many more pictures and seeing various interesting rock formations. Our intention was to drive southward on the following day for hours of spectacular views arriving finally at Bryce Canyon. From there, we planned to visit Zion National Park and then head for Las Vegas and, after breaking the bank, we would proceed home.

Unfortunately, when we awoke the heat got to Phyllis, and with the temperature already about 35 C, she said she would die if she didn't leave. She insisted that she was ready to die any time, but she was determined it not be anywhere but in Canada, and so I better get her back into her beloved B.C. I quickly loaded her and our luggage into the car and we left for home. I drove at about 125kph until we reached Salt Lake City and got into the HOV lane and was then able to make better time. As I drove along like a madman, I wondered what the reaction of any highway patrol officer might be if he stopped me, and my only explanation could be that my wife wanted to get back to Canada as fast as possible, because she didn't want to die in the United States. I mean, how insulted would he be. We stopped overnight in southern Idaho and on the following day we crossed the border at Kingsgate, near Cranbrook, at which time Phyllis was able to relax. On the following day, we were able to meet our granddaughter Aiyana for lunch in Castlegar, a great treat because we hadn't seen her for some time.

In 2011, I was found to have two cancer tumors on my bladder and had one tumor removed on November 29th. I arranged for a nursing service that worked in Parkwood Manor to care for Phyllis until I got home. The whole thing went fine and I returned home later that day.

I had the other tumor removed on January 30th, 2012, with the same care arranged for Phyllis, but due to a problem with my breathing, I was kept in the Eagle Ridge Hospital overnight. I was instructed to keep my mouth closed and just breathe oxygen through my nose. That night, every time that I dropped off to sleep, my mouth would open a bit and a student nurse standing next to me would wake me to tell me to close my mouth. I was so tired and became so frustrated over the following several hours, that, despite the sleeping pills I had taken, I finally had a minor stroke from the stress. The student was taken away and I got some sleep. In the morning they arranged for an echo cardiogram to assess my condition. They found that my carotid artery was 90% blocked and I would need to have it treated soon to prevent another serious stroke, but I could go home.

As I was leaving, I learned that Phyllis had just been admitted in the hospital, so I hurried to the emergency ward where I found Phyllis in bad shape, suffering from pneumonia. After a few hours of assessing her condition the medical team decided that she had only a slim chance of making it through another night, and I should call the family. By evening most of the kids were there, and all were able to take turns, two at a time, to visit with her. Steve was in Mexico for an extended vacation that winter. Holly and Terry were about to leave for a well-deserved holiday in Hawaii and they had to cancel it to be with Phyllis.

Phyllis again survived, but the pneumonia had stopped the flow of oxygen to her brain long enough to cause irreparable damage to her memory, and she needed to be on oxygen constantly, and would have to go to a care home.

I visited her three times per day, just going home for meals and to sleep until she got out of intensive care and went to a ward where she received frequent care and where she waited for the first bed to become available in a care home. We asked Fraser Health to arrange for her to eventually be moved to the Belvidere Care Center, so I could arrange for an assisted living place in their adjacent building. After a few more weeks, she was able to sit in her wheelchair and was able to take part in many of the activities with other patients in the ward.

Stephen arrived back from Mexico and arranged to stay with Barbara, in Vancouver, and he came to visit his mother every day at the hospital, until she was moved in late April to a Care Center on Foster Avenue in Coquitlam. He finally returned to the Nelson area in May, I think. I moved to the Belvidere Assisted Living residence in late May and Phyllis was transferred to the Care Center in the adjoining building on September 8th.

After Phyllis moved to the Care Center on Foster Ave., I continued to visit her at least every afternoon and often again in the evening. I would push her in her wheelchair into the garden if the weather was good, and otherwise, we would sit in the covered patio. We would reminisce about our lives together and often we would just sit facing each other, holding hands and looking at each other and repeating how much we loved each other. Some of the children came from Vancouver Island, as well as grandchildren, every weekend, and friends from church also dropped in to see her.

Terry had taken a job with a construction company in Kelowna as project supervisor and spent a good deal of time at various jobs in Yellowknife and northern B.C. and Alberta. In 2012, he was posted permanently to Kelowna and thereafter worked out of their head office. Holly moved to West Kelowna later that year and was transferred to the RCMP office so they could now be together. Soon after, Holly and Terry were married in December, that is, 12/12/12.

After Phyllis was transferred to the Belvidere in early September, 2012, her condition deteriorated quickly and after a few weeks, she was confined to her bed. Finally, she quit eating and soon after, she lapsed into a coma and passed away on November 1st. I had just come into her room and she was still breathing. I kissed her, had just turned to pull a chair closer, and when I looked at her again, she had died.

I made funeral arrangements and, with the help of our pastor, arranged for a memorial service. Danny and Tami came over and we rented a big house in Deep Cove with a beautiful view of Indian Arm for a few days over the period of Phyllis's memorial service, and we were able to accommodate all the family from out of town. We were also able to entertain all the nieces and nephews for meals. It was a marvellous tribute to Phyllis, and for all the love she had always lavished on every one. She was one classy lady!!!

The funeral for Phyllis was attended by about fifty or sixty people, relatives and friends, and a number of people got up to share their memories of her and of how deeply she had touched them through her cheery disposition, her smiles and her love and caring. Her photograph was displayed on a small table, framed by two lovely orchids.

After Phyllis's passing, I found myself with much lonely time on my hands. After all, I was getting all my meals and entertainment at the Belleville and had nothing to do anymore. I helped some of the old folks in the residence, but I still had hours to kill. My friend, Compton Singroy, had given me an old computer main frame and a keyboard to keep track of my investments, before they moved back to Toronto. When that computer broke down, I decided to take someone's advice and write my life story, so Holly and Terry came over and helped me to buy and install a new computer and printer. A couple months later, I found I still had too much time on my hands and was receiving more assistance and spending much more money than I needed to, so I decided to move into an apartment in Coquitlam. I mentioned it to Danny and he suggested that, since he and Tami, and Cole were planning to move to Nanaimo, I should rent a basement apartment in their house and move in with them. After a few months I decided to move back to Coquitlam and get an apartment on my own. Holly suggested that I move to Kelowna, and she picked me up in Nanaimo and drove me to Kelowna to find a suitable apartment. Over the next week, we must have looked at twenty units, from suites to apartments and condos to assisted living apartments. We finally found an ideal two bedroom unit in West Kelowna with a view of the lake and orchards and a pasture with horses, and room for guests.

During March, 2014, I took a trip with Matt to Freeport in the Bahamas. This was my week of time share from 2013, which I had deposited with Interval International because it had conflicted with my move to Nanaimo. We thoroughly enjoyed laying in the sun, hours of wandering about the International Market, even more hours in the outdoor bar, and with good food and live music.

In late July of 2014 I drove to Fort Macleod, Alberta, and attended the golden wedding celebration of Diane and Gene Koopman (Mirelda's third daughter) and spent a wonderful long weekend with family. Five generations of our family were there, and nieces and nephews by the dozens.

In the past years, since moving, I have enjoyed visits for various periods by Grandchildren Kyle and Jenny, Teena and her two little boys, Kaelen and Kai, Monica and David and Stephen, as well as my nieces Sally and Basil, and Carol and Walter. Both Matthew and Danny came by and Danny brought his family. I see Holly and Terry often for lunches or dinners at some good restaurants and wineries.

In the summer of 2014, I started to lose stamina and was having trouble walking even short distances. On Thanksgiving Day, Holly and

Terry drove me to the Kelowna hospital where I spent the following week having various tests done. It was found that I had a lung infection that was successfully treated with antibiotics. The respirologist, Dr. Sarbit, then diagnosed that I have chronic obstructive pulmonary disease along with heart disease, and pulmonary fibrosis, although the fibrosis is less severe than Phyllis had. He also found that I have a serious case of sleep apnea. The result is that while I'm asleep, I stop breathing 47 times per hour for ten seconds or more. Fortunately, I still had a CPAP machine that I bought new for Phyllis just before she passed away and only had to buy new masks.

While I was still in my apartment in the resort, I decided that I would soon likely need more security for getting around. I could still drive around safely for several hours, but I could only walk about 25 -50 yards, even using a cane, before I had to stop to rest. I checked the internet and bought a shower stool, folding walker with a seat on it, and a wheelchair. I haven't yet used the wheelchair, but I keep it in the trunk of the car in case we have to park some distance from a certain event, like a hockey game.

One of the places Holly and I looked in 2014 was an assisted living residence operated by the Baptist Church Housing and they put my name on their waiting list. Less than a year later, I found there were only four names ahead of me. Then they called and said they were about to open a new wing on their complex in West Kelowna just as my lease was to expire and I was able to rent a large one-bedroom unit there. It is close to my doctor, lab, drugstore, bank, and Holly and Carol. It is in the same residence that my brother-in-law, Francis Sader, spent his last several years. The staff members are very caring and kind. To date, I haven't seen a single incident where a staff person has even been short tempered with a resident. Certainly God is looking after me.

Danny is working for a company in Nanaimo that helps people to design their homes and then, if they wish, arrange for permits and hire contractors to build their houses. He mainly works from his office and no longer has to work in the cold and rain.

Matthew works long hours but he is in the store, warm and dry, and happy.

Holly has a good job with the RCMP, working in a warm office with a good home and husband to return to at the end of the day.

I can look back at my life with pride, having raised three wonderful children, and have provided them with a high school education so they don't have to work outside, and, according to my Dad, they can now do anything they want.

When Phyllis passed away I thought my life was over and I spent my hours wondering what possible use I could fulfill, and I still ponder that. I was soon unable to volunteer for anything. After much prayer and talking to friends, I accept that God has still some further plan for me and He will call me home when He is finished with me on this earth. Then I will be reunited with Phyllis forever and many years later, I hope, with my children and grandchildren.

During this last two or three years, I have spent my time recording my life story and I think this is a good time to end it – the story, that is.

Elmer & Phyllis - 25th Anniversary

Danny, Matthew & Holly – 2001

Barbara, Stephen, Annie & Monica

J. Elmer Benoit